Laughing on the Brink of Humanity

SERIES EDITORS

David E. Johnson, *Comparative Literature, University at Buffalo*
Scott Michaelsen, *English, Michigan State University*

SERIES ADVISORY BOARD

Nahum Dimitri Chandler, *African American Studies, University of California, Irvine*
Rebecca Comay, *Philosophy and Comparative Literature, University of Toronto*
Marc Crépon, *Philosophy, École Normale Supérieure, Paris*
Jonathan Culler, *Comparative Literature, Cornell University*
Johanna Drucker, *Design Media Arts and Information Studies, University of California, Los Angeles*
Christopher Fynsk, *Modern Thought, Aberdeen University*
Rodolphe Gasché, *Comparative Literature, University at Buffalo*
Martin Hägglund, *Comparative Literature, Yale University*
Carol Jacobs, *German and Comparative Literature, Yale University*
Peggy Kamuf, *French and Comparative Literature, University of Southern California*
David Marriott, *History of Consciousness, University of California, Santa Cruz*
Steven Miller, *English, University at Buffalo*
Alberto Moreiras, *Hispanic Studies, Texas A&M University*
Patrick O'Donnell, *English, Michigan State University*
Pablo Oyarzun, *Teoría del Arte, Universidad de Chile*
Scott Cutler Shershow, *English, University of California, Davis*
Henry Sussman, *German and Comparative Literature, Yale University*
Samuel Weber, *Comparative Literature, Northwestern University*
Ewa Ziarek, *Comparative Literature, University at Buffalo*

Laughing on the Brink of Humanity
An Exercise in Epihumanism

JAN MIERNOWSKI

Cover Credit: Richard Gerstl, *Selbstbildnis, lachend*, 1907/8. Photo: Belvedere, Vienna.

Published by State University of New York Press, Albany

© 2024 State University of New York

All rights reserved

Printed in the United States of America

No part of this book may be used or reproduced in any manner whatsoever without written permission. No part of this book may be stored in a retrieval system or transmitted in any form or by any means including electronic, electrostatic, magnetic tape, mechanical, photocopying, recording, or otherwise without the prior permission in writing of the publisher.

Links to third-party websites are provided as a convenience and for informational purposes only. They do not constitute an endorsement or an approval of any of the products, services, or opinions of the organization, companies, or individuals. SUNY Press bears no responsibility for the accuracy, legality, or content of a URL, the external website, or for that of subsequent websites.

For information, contact State University of New York Press, Albany, NY
www.sunypress.edu

Library of Congress Cataloging-in-Publication Data

Name: Miernowski, Jan, author.
Title: Laughing on the brink of humanity : an exercise in epihumanism / Jan Miernowski.
Description: Excelsior editions. | Albany : State University of New York Press, [2024] | Series: SUNY series, literature . . . in theory | Includes bibliographical references and index.
Identifiers: LCCN 2024009235 | ISBN 9781438499994 (hardcover : alk. paper) | ISBN 9798855800012 (ebook) | ISBN 9798855800005 (pbk. : alk. paper)
Subjects: LCSH: Laughter—Social aspects. | Cynicism—Social aspects.
Classification: LCC BF575.L3 M533 2024 | DDC 152.4/3—dc23/eng/20240624
LC record available at https://lccn.loc.gov/2024009235

Dla Taty

Contents

Acknowledgments	ix
Introduction	1
Chapter 1 Laughing at the Death of Man	15
Chapter 2 Laughing Animals	45
Chapter 3 Laughing (Human) Machines	81
Chapter 4 Machining (Human) Laughter	105
Chapter 5 Laughing Gods	147
Chapter 6 Laughing Men	201
Epilogue	239
Notes	249
Works Cited	257
Index	275

Acknowledgments

My first debt is to two dear friends whose intellectual company has spurred my thinking over the years: Ullrich Langer, in the Department of French and Italian at the University of Wisconsin-Madison, who has been my faithful partner in our ongoing conversation over what is human, and Jerzy Axer, who greatly influenced my research and teaching by welcoming me to the interdisciplinary community of the Faculty of "Artes Liberales" at the University of Warsaw.

Secondly, I would like to acknowledge the inspiration I received from a research group composed of James Helgeson, George Hoffmann, Ullrich Langer, and Kathleen Perry Long. While pursuing their individual projects, my teammates engaged in an intense exchange of ideas, which stimulated my thinking.

Equally inspirational were individual exchanges I had with colleagues, friends, and, most importantly, my students in the United States, Poland, and France. I would like to thank in particular Alan Attie, Jane Bennett, Rachel Brenner, Jean-Christophe Cavallin, Yves Citton, Patricia Eichel-Lojkine, Max Engammare, Jean Feraca, Paweł Golik, Richard Goodkin, Rosanna Gorris, Timothy Hampton, Christopher Kleinhenz, Joel Kaipainen, Virginia Krause, Józef Kwaterko, Stéphane Lojkine, Michel Magnien, Hélène Merlin-Kajman, Grzegorz Michalczyk, Steven Nadler, Frédéric Neyrat, Ewa Niedziałek, Isabelle Pantin, Anne-Pascale Pouey-Mounou, Bernd Renner, Sylvie Requemora-Gros, Arjun Seshadri, Jacqueline Sii, Krzysztof Skonieczny, Lauren Surovi, Szymon Wróbel, Caitlin Yocco-Locascio, Lindsay Zarwell, Samantha Zeid, and Marina Zilbergerts.

Different ideas nurturing this book were presented at conferences and seminars; in lectures at Brown University, CUNY Graduate Center, Aix-Marseille University, Sorbonne Nouvelle University—Paris 3, Sorbonne

University, Stockholm University, University of Verona, University of Warsaw, University of Wisconsin–Madison; and at the seminar of the Fédération Internationale des Sociétés et Instituts pour l'Étude de la Renaissance (FISIER).

The University of Wisconsin–Madison has generously funded my research through a sabbatical leave and the Wisconsin Alumni Research Foundation Professorship named in honor of my late friend and colleague, the distinguished medievalist Douglas Kelly. Mary Noles has efficiently helped with the administration of these grants, and Laura M. Martin, the most knowledgeable and generous librarian in the Memorial Library of the University of Wisconsin–Madison, has assisted me in acquiring the materials necessary for my study.

The cover image and the illustration contained in this book are reproduced with the kind permission of the Belvedere Museum in Vienna and Mr. Dave Coverly, respectively. The translation of Władysław Szlengel's poem "Little Station Treblinka" is reproduced with the permission of Mr. Marcel Weyland. The excerpt from Guillaume Apollinaire's "April Night 1915" is reproduced with the permission of the University of California Press.

My very special thanks go to Kerry Fast, who expertly helped me edit my book and suggested the final formulation of its title.

Finally, I would like to express my gratitude to Rebecca Colesworthy at SUNY Press, who kindly guided me through the publishing process, as well as the two anonymous readers who provided me with very valuable insights.

I dedicate my book to my father, Stanisław Miernowski, who taught me what it means to be human.

Introduction

What does it mean to be human? It means being able to cross the frontier between life that is deemed human and life that is not yet human, not human at all, or no longer human. Since we are talking about a meaning attached to a phenomenal experience, crossing into or out of humanness is fundamentally an act of consciousness. It can, however, also be a concrete action or an existential state. In this case, coming into or stepping out of human life implies a proto-, quasi-, or even afterlife. The modes of existence that lie before, alongside, or beyond a properly human life have traditionally been nonhuman others: animals, machines, and divinity. Animals, as the evolutionary origin and the biological companions of humans; machines, as the technological product of human inventiveness and labor as well as the conditioning of human thinking and behavior; divinity, as the transcendent realm that permeates human lives with myth and ritual. Animality, machinery, and divinity are the three directions that I follow in my quest for the limits of humanness. By testing these limits, I am suggesting that a new kind of humanism is possible in our posthuman and transhuman times. Instead of positing the essence of humanity or defining the conditions of possibility of the human subject, the humanism I propose delineates what it means to be human. I call this search for the limits of humanness *epihumanism*.

The question of what it means to be human thus presupposes a demarcation, as evasive as it is, between what is human and what is not. But how are we to detect this limit? By laughing. Crossing the divide between what is human and what is not sparks laughter. But laughter on the brink of humanity is joyless. It is a sign calling for an interpretation, not an essential feature defining humanness.

Let me insist on two important points. First, laughter at the brink of humanity should not be confused with gaiety. The laughter I investigate is mirthless, unwanted, often painful—and sometimes deadly. Much has been written about laughter as a synonym of humor.[1] For the sake of clarity, I group theorists of humor into three interrelated families.[2] Those who suppose that you can only laugh at something, or rather at somebody, insist on the necessary superiority of the laugher over the ridiculed object of hilarity. The classical representative of this trend, Thomas Hobbes, spoke of the "sudden glory" sparked by the feeling of eminence over others or our past infirmity (42).[3] Hobbes's superiority has its roots in Quintilian, Cicero, and Aristotle, who identified laughter with derision of deformity and ugliness, which Aristotle insisted should not imply pain (Quintilian 6.3.7–8; Cicero, *De oratore* 2.58.236; Aristotle, *Poetics* 1449). Plato, however, would disagree. When we laugh at friends who consider themselves richer, more beautiful, and wiser than they really are, we mix pain and pleasure: the pain of malicious satisfaction caused by our friends' misfortune and the pleasure of laughter over their ridiculous predicament (Plato, *Philebus* 48–50). Plato's speculations about the mixture of pleasure and pain lead us to the second trend in humor theory: humor based on incongruity. From this point of view, laughter is sparked by the clash of two incompatible factors. For instance, the early-twentieth-century French philosopher Henri Bergson famously said that we laugh when we see mechanistic rigidity impressed upon the spontaneity of life (*Laughter*). Almost a century earlier, his German colleague Arthur Schopenhauer stated that laughter stems from the discordance between a concept and the reality it represents (ch. 8). Still decades earlier, Immanuel Kant theorized laughter as the sudden encounter between great expectation and the uneventfulness that follows (203; sec. 54). This deflation, rephrased positively, points to the third trend in humor theory, relief. In this perspective, laughter is based on the flow of nervous energy. In the nineteenth century, so fond of thermodynamics, Herbert Spencer defined the physiology of laughter as depressed incongruity. He hypothesized that past a certain pitch of tension, nervous excitement is channeled into the bodily action of laughter. Freud added an economic twist to this energetic metaphor. Jokes and humor save the psychic energy that we would have to expend on curtailing our feelings or acting upon them. The difference between jokes and humor consists in the psychic origin of laughter they respectively produce. Jokes are the contribution of the unconscious, and humor is the part played by the superego in saving the ego's psychic energy and thus producing a yield of pleasure (Freud, "Humor" and *Joke*).

Besides identifying its different mechanisms—superiority, incongruity, and relief—these theoretical conceptualizations of laughter testify to the diversity of disciplinary approaches, ranging from social sciences to psychiatry and aesthetics. For instance, anthropologists gather ethnological data about the role of laughter in societies. They want to understand its regulatory function in enforcing cultural norms and perpetuating social cohesion. On the other hand, neuropsychologists study the physiology and pathology of human laughter. They look for its evolutionary antecedents and its correlates among nonhuman animals. Rhetoricians and literary critics wonder how laughter is sparked by spoken and written words. They define the mechanisms of jesting and the generic rules of comedy. As much as I benefit from these theorizations of humor and their disciplinary approaches, none of them fully capture the quality of laughter I pursue. The reason is simple: the laughter I study is not humorous, and I do not study laughter for its own sake but as a sign to be interpreted.

This brings me to the second point that needs to be made. Let me stress that I do not see laughter as an essential attribute of humanness. Classical and early modern humanists listed features that were considered specific to human beings: the use of a nimble-fingered hand, the capacity to communicate through spoken and written words, the perspicacity of reason, and, beginning in the seventeenth century, the consciousness of oneself and the surrounding world. Since Aristotle, laughter has figured prominently among these *propria hominis* (Artistotle, *On the Parts* 673a; bk. 3, ch. 10). To see laughter as a specifically human aptitude presupposes, however, that one believes in a reality composed of hierarchically ordered beings, each comprising an essence and contingent qualities, all distributed among distinct genera and their subordinated species. The problem is that since the Enlightenment, and most importantly since the collapse of Western humanism in the twentieth century, humans cannot be seen anymore as animals endowed with supplemental qualities such as reason or, for that matter, the capacity to laugh. Humanity can no longer be viewed as the microcosmic epitome of creation, placed by God at the universe's center as its master. Since we no longer live in a world neatly ordered by an essentialist metaphysics, the laughter I try to understand is not an essential attribute of humanity but the sign of a frontier being crossed between what is human and what is not. It is a bodily symptom and a culturally encoded message. As symptom and message, the laughter that is the subject of this book calls for interpretation. By analyzing select manifestations of this sign in texts belonging to the Western tradition, I trace the limits of humanness, hoping thus to shed light on what it means to be human.

Let me pause here for a moment to dispel a possible misunderstanding. To trace the limits of humanness I focus on the so-called Western tradition, a predominantly white, male tradition—not because I assume that white male authors provide the key for understanding universal humanity. Mine is not a patriarchal and Eurocentric claim. Nor do I pursue a humanism for our posthuman time only to conveniently blame it for the genocides and ecocides of modernity.[4] I certainly recognize, however, that the destruction of humanness we now face is the work of Western white cultures dominated by men. Studying the products of these cultures is, therefore, a logical way to address the state of desolation we live in. Yet, to be intellectually useful, such study must not stop at rightful criticism and indignant lamentation. It should examine the cultural tradition at the root of the problem to indicate a way of rethinking humanness today and in the immediate future. To fulfill this ambition, my investigation into laughter on the brink of humanity is relational in the sense that I do not pursue a cultural identity founded on essentialist metaphysics but search for limits between moveable and porous realities. Such is the case, for instance, with laughter reverberating between humans and machines. In the world of generative artificial intelligence (AI) and virtual reality, machines often respond with computer-generated merriment to a human cackle, which is more a bodily automatism than the result of sophisticated wit. Such giggles exchanged between people and their devices cannot be understood if we are stuck in a world compartmentalized into neatly circumscribed categories of beings. It is more fitting to conceive the world as a dynamically evolving swarm of multipolar relationships between highly mobile agents.

By insisting on the relational character of my approach, I am inspired by anthropologists trying to adopt the vantage point of other peoples to bring different perspectives to bear on and reconceptualize "our" world. Such anthropological "symmetrization"—the effect being to extract cautiously universalistic anthropological claims from the diversity of ethnographic data—is daunting. It is hard enough for a Western ethnographer to imagine the Amazonian jungle as seen through the eyes of Indigenous Achuar; it becomes even more difficult when we strive to look at our own world from a non-European, Indigenous perspective. Yet this is the dream of the anthropological study of the moderns, already called for by Michel Foucault in the mid-sixties and extended by Bruno Latour. The solution for the aporias of symmetrization of points of view is provided by Philippe Descola in the form of his anthropology of nature (Descola; Descola and Pignocchi). Inspired by the animism of the Achuar, Descola explores worldviews in which, despite different bodily appearances and habits, animals and plants develop social hierarchies and bonds, rituals and beliefs that can be studied by anthropology like any other human culture. The spiritual and symbolic continuities across nonhuman and human embodiments allow Descola to reach beyond the culture-versus-nature divide inherited from Western modernity. Multiculturalism, which in his eyes is the flipside of the long-decried hegemony of Western "civilization" over "primitive" cultures, gives way to a relationist universalism that universalizes not categories of beings but their possible relationships. My investigation into laughter on the brink of humanity benefits greatly from Descola's relationist thinking.

While confronting the Western tradition, my investigation into laughter on the brink of humanity also applies a multilayered approach influenced by the political and metaphysical thought of the French philosopher Tristan Garcia (see *We Ourselves* and *Laisser être*). Like Descola, Garcia struggles to draw universal conclusions from a nebula of phenomenal data. Yet Garcia's problem pertains to metaphysically grounded politics. He starts by stating the obvious: political communities are torn apart by conflicts raging along racial, economic, gender, and sexual orientation lines. This "war of we's" is intensified by the intersectionality of dominations but also complicated by surprising alliances and internal discordances. Among the former, Garcia mentions homonationalism, which brings together traditionally antigay, far right groups and certain representatives of the LGBTQ+ community united against supposed Muslim homophobia. Among the latter, he discusses the difficult choice faced by black feminists between racial solidarity and the fight for women's rights as well as the specifically French predicament of Muslim immigrant women who reluctantly submit to patriarchal oppression to preserve their minority culture threatened by the homogenizing pressure of the French Republic. The war of we's is further complicated by the fact that it not only pertains to human societies but spreads into the politics of nature and implies the political weaponizing of ideological gestures and values. It involves nonhuman beings such as sentient animals, living organisms, and fossilized sediments as well as myths and rituals, artistic fictions, and ethical norms. The impossibility of establishing an irenic political community thus reveals a metaphysical conundrum: How to liberally include any possible being in a common world? How not to exclude anything, even life-threatening viruses, deadly technologies, and heinous ideologies that threaten the existence of a universalistic community? Most importantly, how to preserve the resulting inclusive world from being overtaken by totally indistinct and perfectly isolated monads?[5]

Garcia's solution to the crisis of communality is to distribute political divides among layers of analysis that can be easily rearranged into different orders of priority, much like transparencies on an overhead projector can be shifted horizontally and piled alternatively at will. For instance, by placing racial inequalities on the top, we prioritize this category without, however, neglecting class struggles and gender inequalities, since those divisions still transpire from underneath the top layer of racial inequalities when we project the entire stack of divides on the screen of our political imagination. The metaphor of transparencies allows for the vertical order of priorities among political divisions to be rearranged, but, also, the overall projection of the conflicts can be easily modified by shifting a layer horizontally so that a political front advances or retreats with respect to the others. Imagining the conflicts of political communities as highly mobile and alternately layered representations prevents us from entrenching them in fixed identities locked in unsolvable antagonisms. Drawing on Garcia's analytical model, I see the consecutive chapters of my book as transparencies that can be alternatively prioritized. Each one relies on the shifting relationship between what is human and what is not. Such shifts and reshufflings of analysis inevitably produce tension, resistance, and possible shocks at the presumed limits of ontological categories as they intersect. An epiphenomenal manifestation of such realignments between what is human and what is not is the joyless laughter I endeavor to study.

I am aware that the existence of the limits between what is human and what is not is debatable. There is a long cultural tradition as well as strong scientific evidence of animal laughter. We have succeeded in building machines that laugh with us and possibly at us. The same goes for our gods, whom we have long suspected of laughing at our miseries and who, in return, we may wish would die from laughter. The limits of humanness seem increasingly blurred nowadays in an age of bioengineered humanity and AI aspiring to consciousness. Nonetheless, I claim that they are important, especially after Auschwitz and Hiroshima. The reality of metaphysical evil embodied in twentieth-century history by the Shoah and the atomic bomb weighs heavily on my thoughts about the limits of humanness. In a sense, the smoke from the crematoria still permeates the air of the place I was born and raised. So does the radiation of Chernobyl, which materialized the nuclear threat and overshadowed my youth during the Cold War. These perils, along with new ones, hover over the Western cultures in which they were birthed. They cast into doubt the essentialist metaphysics of Man that have oriented the quest for humanness in Europe since Greco-Roman antiquity and the European Renaissance and that serve as a reference for my thinking about the present. After Auschwitz and Hiroshima, in the time of posthumanism and transhumanism, the question of what a human being is cannot be asked with the same confidence that inspired premodern Europeans. They wanted to know themselves, that is, to know what their common humanity was. In our time, the admonition engraved on the fronton of Apollo's temple at Delphi is largely ignored or, at best, understood as an encouragement to pursue individualistic cravings. Since World War II we have had at our disposal the legal means to prosecute crimes against humanity, but such litigations do not require a clear understanding of what humanity is. Instead of relying on the universal ideal of humanness, human rights represent a much-needed line of defense against our own inhumanity. They are a minimalistic, although extremely valuable, attempt at maintaining a functional common denominator between diverse life projects. International law has thus become the last line of defense of a concept that has lost its ontological value and become, first, an existential situation and, finally, a legal condition.

Hence, the question underlying this book and stated at its incipit is not a question about being but about meaning. I am not trying to understand what it is to be human but, more modestly, what it means to be human. The insistence upon semantics over ontology is not a tribute to the postmodern fascination with signifiers unattached to the life of the world. I believe that there is a distinction to be made between what a human being is and what it is not, but I am eager to contain my personal presuppositions as much as I can when facing such an ideologically loaded problem. This cautious realism limits the scope of my investigation to the artifacts of culture, namely artistic and philosophical texts of Western cultures, which I know the best. I hope that the culturally limited scope of the material is compensated for by its historical and generic diversity. My inductive, hermeneutic approach allows me to confront individual testimonies of history and collective myths, reports from laboratory experiments and masterpieces of fiction, lyric poetry and philosophical speculation. I explore these diverse specimens of philosophy, literature, cinema, and science, sometimes pairing two particularly symptomatic authors, sometimes moderating a series of panelists. My intent is to listen to the tonalities of laughter that resonate in these voices and uncover the meaning of humanness that shaped them.

Since the distinction between humanity and nonhumanity is problematic, I imagine it metaphorically as a moveable frontier, an evanescent contour, an osmotic membrane. It separates life that is properly human from what precedes it, what is at hand but remains utterly foreign to it, what is absolutely transcendent to it, and what possibly follows it. These metaphoric images are largely dictated by the topoi of the cultures I explore. The first frontier runs along the animalistic flank of the human being, whose evolutionary roots intermingle with those of nonhuman animals. The second, equally tenuous border is shared by humans and machines, particularly the electronic devices of today that, according to some predictions, will soon take responsibility for humans as objects of their care and, hopefully, solicitude. The third limit stems from the Greek, as well as Judeo-Christian, tradition. It posits a fundamental gap between human immanence and divine transcendence. Such a rift is paradoxically still in place following the death of God and the death of Man in Western cultures. These delimitations superimposed one upon the other will, I hope, bring out the contours of what it means to be human. It is noteworthy that, in one way or another, all of them have to do with nonlife and most often with death. The attention paid to what is living and what is not yet, not at all, or no longer living highlights the importance of the master metaphor of the book: the membrane separating human life from what lies outside of it.

A membrane can be natural or artificial, transitional or permanent, osmotic or impermeable. It can be rigid and thus fragile, plastic and therefore easily malleable, or elastic and thus capable of resonating when struck. By combining plasticity and elasticity, I stress the concept of tension, which I posit as fundamental to the meaning of the membrane metaphor. Tension makes it possible for a membrane to produce sound, and, since laughter is primarily a sound, I use the apt metaphor of a membrane tensely extended over what is humanly alive. This metaphor helps me think through the stress, shock, and reverberation of laughter. In other words, I imagine the limits of humanness as a taut membrane that resonates with laughter whenever these limits are challenged or transgressed by internal conflict or external trauma.

The metaphor of a membrane extended over our humanness and resonating with laughter highlights important parameters of laughter. First, laughter reverberates through the body with physiological perturbations, whether facial expressions or heightened blood pressure. Second, although physical, laughter entertains a complex relationship with human emotion, will, and reason. Finally, laughter is not a solipsistic phenomenon. It is inherently social since it exteriorizes inner commotions and reactions to the reality we experience. In this last respect, laughter is eminently an aesthetic phenomenon that shapes culturally consecrated forms and genres of artistic expression. I should stress, however, that I am not interested in laughter as a metonymy of the aesthetic of comedy. This book is not a study of the artistic forms of merriment no more than it is a contribution to the theory of humor because the kind of laughter I am researching is not funny. The joyless, involuntary, and utterly awkward laughter that is the focus of this book is a symptom signaling that a limit is about to be crossed, a contour erased, a frontier transgressed. I should also note that I do not judge such transgression in moral or political terms. My expertise as a reader of cultural artifacts does not allow me to pass moral and political judgment, even less to make authoritative metaphysical or theological statements. I am simply trying to interpret reality around me.

If, nonetheless, the reader sometimes hears a note of concern in my voice, I apologize in advance for such personal overtones. They may resonate even in the title of my book. *Laughter on the Brink of Humanity* conveys, I hope, the sense of urgency and danger that I feel presently. I am not referring to politics, although the rise of xenophobic fears, extremist hatreds, populist revanchisms, and conspiratorial delusions does not bode well for the near future of the republic. I come from a part of Europe soaked with the blood of millions and from a city rebuilt on the ashes of thousands of innocent victims. In my youth, I felt particularly blessed to witness my land's ascent to freedom and democracy. Now, however, I feel all the more concerned when I see freedom and democracy at risk of being forsaken by the very masses of people who should care for their blessings. But more importantly, instead of politics, I turn my attention to what constitutes the foundation upon which the intellectual work that is my passion and my profession is based. Until the second half of the twentieth century, this foundation was a reflection on what the human being is. In the twentieth century, the concept of the human being began to be seen with increased skepticism and even suspicion. Many in the West saw this concept—understandably—not only as historically and culturally relative but as morally and politically harmful. Since the 1930s, the study of humanness has been gradually abandoned and, with few, in my opinion, ideologically determined exceptions, has not been undertaken anew since the 1960s. At that time, the neglect of the question of humanness was largely compensated for by no less important and passionate concerns, mainly sparked by the fascination with large systems of meaning, such as the structure of language, the drives of the body, and the socioeconomic relations of labor, gender, ethnicity, race, and power. Yet after a short period of excessive trust in overreaching explicative narratives, disillusion set in. What fell prey to this disappointment were the humanities, a palette of ways of teasing out meaning from books that have been painstakingly practiced since antiquity and fruitfully renewed in early modern times. Contemporary advances in life sciences and technology have not filled the void left by the investigation of the meaning of humanness. Despite the rich diversity of urgent new questions, biology and computer science never questioned the common assumption about the irrelevance of the human being as an intellectual problem. They were content to see humans as consumers of health care and information or as pollutants of natural and media environments, but they never saw humanness as an object worthy of investigation. I would be very happy if my book contributed even in the smallest way to changing that course, which, as suggested by the title, leads to the brink of a demise no less irremediable than the one awaiting our ecological existence.

By tracking laughter as an alarm signal set off whenever the limits of humanness are trespassed, I hope to open an avenue for a humanism adapted to our posthuman times. I call it epihumanism. *Epi*humanism, to acknowledge the master epidermic metaphor of the membrane separating what is human from what is not as well as the epiphenomenal character of laughter as the signal of crossing the limits of humanness. *Epi*humanism, also, to recognize the fact that by asking what it means to be human, we play the role of epigones of ancient and early modern thinkers who pondered over the essence of humanity. Finally, *epi*humanism because of the epigenetic potential of humanistic thinking. By interacting with the natural and cultural environment of our times and by making choices regarding our behavior, we activate or deactivate specific segments of our cultural genome. I hope that such epigenetic conception of humanism breathes optimism into the future of the humanities, which should not be bound to perpetually mourn the death of Man that so tragically affected the past century. The evolution of the humanities as a discipline of learning and as a cultural project should not be hindered by the disinterest for humanism as a pursuit of what it means to be human, nor should it be oriented toward an immediate ideological goal. I strongly believe that humanistic thinking is fundamentally free and hence bears an enormous responsibility. Yes, we are crushed by the heavy burden of the evil done in the name of Man in the twentieth century, and we resent the threat of upcoming ecological catastrophe of our own human making. But I am strongly convinced that we should courageously transform the sins of anthropocentrism into a renewed attention to life that we deem to be human. In that sense, epihumanism is not just another variant of posthumanist doom. It is a prehumanism of the future.

For all the personal reasons stated above, this book may rightly be seen not only as an intellectual adventure but also as an outburst of my laughter, the same laughter that I pursue in the philosophical essays, literary works, and scientific articles that I read. I hope that such laughter will stay with you and encourage you to retrace, in your own way, the contours of our common humanness.

Plan of the Book

Chapter 1, "Laughing at the Death of Man," guides the entire book. "Death of Man" has two parallel meanings. On the one hand, the title refers to the twentieth-century crisis of humanism and the subsequent collapse of the concept of humanness. On the other hand, it points to the demise of two specific victims of the Holocaust: Michał Podchlebnik, one of the very few survivors of the Chełmno death camp, and Władysław Szlengel, a poet executed by the Nazis at the end of the Warsaw ghetto insurrection. I introduce Podchlebnik through one of the most dramatic interviews of Claude Lanzmann's movie *Shoah*; I give Szlengel the floor in a poem about the Treblinka death camp that Szlengel included in his final collection, entitled *What I Read to the Dead*. The testimonies of Podchlebnik and Szlengel are not stories of survival but analyses of the demise of humans who had been denied human life as well as, most importantly, a human death. The key problem of the chapter is the fact that Podchlebnik's and Szlengel's voices resonate with laughter. I present this joyless, involuntary, and painful laughter as an indication of the limit between what is human and what is not. Retracing this limit allows me to explore the meaning of humanness. The study of Podchlebnik's and Szlengel's laughter on the brink of humanity is my response to the twentieth-century concept of the Death of Man.

The next chapters are devoted to the exploration of the limits of humanness: animality, machinery, and divinity. Chapter 2, "Laughing Animals," puts in dialogue two scientists: Laurent Joubert, a sixteenth-century physician at the service of the French royal family, and Jaak Panksepp, a late-twentieth-century American neuropsychologist. Both try to conceptualize animal "laughter" using the scientific tools at their disposal in their respective historical cultures. For Joubert, this laughter has nothing to do with humor but is prompted by physical aggression and can be deadly. On the other hand, the rats' "laughter" experimentally studied by Panksepp is a high-frequency chirping that expresses the animals' social playfulness and joy. Both scientists strive to demarcate animal "laughter" from physiological and culturally conditioned merriment, which they consider to be properly human. In doing so, they tread a fine line between the impetuosity of primordial affects and the conscious control of the will. Crossing this limit of humanness means, in this chapter, going back to the ontogenetic and phylogenetic past, toward the realm of primordial rhythms outside of human language.

Chapters 3 and 4, "Laughing (Human) Machines" and "Machining (Human) Laughter," are two mirroring chapters further exploring the limits of humanness. The first one is devoted to the mechanization that transforms humans; the second, to the humanization of machines. In "Laughing (Human) Machines," Henri Bergson's animistic philosophy demonstrates the risks of the mechanization of life. When devitalized, a human being becomes an automaton, as illustrated by Charlie Chaplin in *Modern Times*. The continuous impetus for novelty that characterizes life is dispersed into a repetitive routine. Yet the descent of life's dynamism into inert matter is reversible. Life springs out of the scattered debris by the force of consciousness animating the world. Moreover, according to Bergson, humans can fabricate life through their power of mythmaking. Guillaume Apollinaire's erotic poem about mechanized warfare illustrates the dialectic between deadly mechanization and the revitalizing force of storytelling. The poem is irradiated by a bittersweet smile that matches Bergson's conception of laughter as warning humans of the pressure of their inner machinery. From Bergson's point of view, the poetic text is a material trace of its author's living presence. Not so for Maurizio Ferraris, who provides a counterpoint to Bergson's animism. For Ferraris, printed and electronic messages are not merely mechanical inscriptions but living souls of humanness. Ferraris's postmodern reversal of Bergson's animism leads me to the next chapter, devoted to the possibility of animating machines and, more particularly, the troubling attempts at humanizing AI.

Bergson suggested that humans can fabricate gods through mythmaking. Ferraris goes even further, claiming that there is no creative evolution besides the act of mechanically registering human memory on material and electronic supports. The fourth chapter, "Machining (Human) Laughter," follows up on these propositions by exploring the possibility of humanizing machines through laughter, as studied experimentally in computer science, analyzed philosophically by cognitive scientists from Alan Turing to Brian Christian, and staged dramatically by contemporary playwrights Tom Stoppard and Jordan Harrison. Simulating human presence in virtual reality may lead the user to the uncanny valley where humanoid avatars, bots, and robots are troublingly too human. This is the risk of virtual reality, in which the conventions that set apart literary fiction and extrafictional reality are deliberately erased. Can machines intentionally deceive us into believing that they share our feelings? Perhaps, but at a minimum they are designed to be our companions. Projecting human traits onto a machine is a technique of affective computing called ethopoeia. It relies on a functionalist and reductionist approach in which what appears conscious is considered fully conscious. Nonetheless, ethopoeia in computer design should not be confused with ethopoeia in classical oratory. The rhetorical ethopoeia trains the ethical character of the citizen by relying on values that sustain the life of the republic. The existence of such irreducible human values, be they biological or moral, gives rise to the "hard problem" of consciousness studies: the unbridgeable gap between third-person observation and first-person experience of reality. This rift is particularly dramatic when distanced observation and subjective experience focus on human death. Death makes the attempts of virtual reality to immortalize humans grotesquely laughable.

Chapter 5, "Laughing Gods," explores the limit between humanity and the divine absolute. It spans Renaissance humanism and contemporary antihumanism. The burlesque adventures of the giants Gargantua and Pantagruel, as relayed by the French Renaissance writer François Rabelais, allow me to analyze laughter as a humanist response to God's transcendence. Drawing from the biblical matriarchal tradition, Rabelais mixes lewdness and negative theology to challenge his readers to believe and imagine that which is humanly impossible and unimaginable. Rabelais's laughter is a leap of faith tainted with regret about the limitedness of the human being. Friedrich Nietzsche has no such remorse. He lightheartedly rejects both the aspiration to divine transcendence and the perennity of the essence of humanity. The Nietzschean overman kills the gods with laughter, or rather lets the gods die laughing at their own arrogance. What is Nietzsche's exaltation of the lightness of being becomes in George Bataille's laughter a transgressive sacrifice. In Bataille's atheology, instead of leaping into God's transcendence, humans are invited to dissolve in the immanence of corporeal reality and laugh at the void left by the inexistent God. With Bataille, the chapter reaches the antihumanism that historically coincides with the great catastrophes of the twentieth century: the Holocaust and the atomic bomb. What is conceivable by reason yet impossible for imagination to grasp happened for real in history. Since God is already dead, it is the twentieth-century unimaginable evil that takes the place of the absolute in the philosophy of post–World War II thinkers such as Günther Anders and Hannah Arendt. According to Jean-Pierre Dupuy and René Girard, the way to atone for that evil is self-transcendence, which can be achieved through sacrificial violence. Yet contemporary massacres turn violence from a means of symbolic purification into a drive for self-annihilation.

Chapter 6, "Laughing Men," is a cautiously optimistic reply to the diagnosis formulated in the first chapter, "Laughing at the Death of Man." Podchlebnik's and Szlengel's demises coincided historically with the dismantling of the concept of Man in Western philosophy and culture. The final chapter of my book responds to this bleak picture by reintroducing a truly human death in lieu of the inhuman demise that befell the victims of the Shoah. Human death is the reality faced by Socrates awaiting execution in an Athenian prison, as depicted by Plato in the *Phaedo*. The death of humanity as a species is the dystopian future presented by the French contemporary writer Michel Houellebecq in his novel *The Possibility of an Island*. The perspective of human death, either individual or engulfing the entire species, makes a truly human laughter possible. In Plato's dialogue, this laughter is imbued with pleasure and pain: pleasure caused by bodily existence, pain sparked by fear that the love of thinking that gives sense to philosophy is misguided. In Houellebecq's novel, human laughter in the face of the ecological and technological death of humanity is full of cruel irony and longing: cruel irony at the prospect of humanity voluntarily renouncing its condition as augmented apes in favor of the genetically engineered immortality of mind clones, longing after the fragile beauty of human love. Socrates's and Houellebecq's laughter is mediated by myth-making and storytelling. It is literary fiction that allows humans to laugh at their own laughter.

Fictional storytelling, as opposed to virtual reality, is also at the center of the epilogue of my book. This last section revolves around another Holocaust survivor: Viktor Frankl. Frankl was able to endure the concentration camp by mentally transposing his inhuman suffering into a future academic talk presented in a world that he imagined to be human again. After the war, Frankl designed a mental experiment that cured a fellow Holocaust survivor who had given up hope after losing his wife: he proposed virtually cloning the beloved woman. The patient flatly refused and instantly embraced the will to live. Frankl's therapeutic experiment was reported by Heinz von Foerster, who used it to define humans as nontrivial machines. Contrary to von Foerster's cybernetic approach, I use Frankl's experiment to highlight the power of metaphorical and narrative transposition as an efficient alternative to a reductionist conception of humanness. This transpositional thinking is at work in my metaphor of the membrane resonating with laughter when one crosses the limit between what is human and what is not. I conclude with the hope that this core metaphor underlying my book fosters the search for the meaning of humanness that is the task of the epihumanism of tomorrow.

Chapter 1

Laughing at the Death of Man

> These fragments are a collection of ladders that can be kicked away in order to look directly at those things of which it is not possible to speak.
>
> —Simon Critchley, *ABC of Impossibility*

"The story begins in the present at Chełmno."[1] Claude Lanzmann's 1985 film *Shoah* opens with a long view of a middle-aged man seated in a flat-bottomed boat floating slowly down a narrow river amid a quiet, green countryside. He sings a popular prewar Polish song. He is Simon Srebnik, one of the seven survivors of the Chełmno death camp. Renamed Kulmhof by the Germans, the little village of Chełmno is located in the so-called Warthegau, an area of central Poland that was incorporated into the Third Reich and designated for German colonization. Between 152,000 and 225,000 people, almost exclusively Jews, were industrially exterminated at Chełmno death camp. As a thirteen-year-old boy, Srebnik was kept there as an *Arbeitsjude*, doing chores for the SS who day after day gassed Jews in specially adapted trucks. Srebnik used to sing for his guards while going down the river to fetch alfalfa for the rabbits raised by the Nazi murderers.

In a later sequence of the film, Srebnik stands surrounded by villagers of Chełmno greeting him. They have just exited the church and are preparing for a Corpus Christi procession. Over thirty years before, this church was seized by the SS and used as an antechamber for their gassings. Now the Polish peasants smile and eagerly share their memories of the Jewish boy who used to walk in chains through their village and whose real presence in their midst is so hard to believe. Simon Srebnik hesitantly smiles back, as if confused by his return to the place where his mother was gassed and where he was shot in the head two days before the arrival of the Soviet army. His return to Chełmno over thirty years after the destruction of Polish Jewry seems as unreal as the place where he stands is real. The villagers, as well, have a hard time acknowledging this seemingly impossible return of the child who was the walking dead and who now is a living, gray-haired man. One of the women recalls that she asked an SS guard to let the boy go back to his parents. The guard laughed and, pointing to heaven, said that he would soon let the child reunite with his mother and father. Gathered in front of Lanzmann's camera, Polish peasants look at the revenant from the horrible past and try to make sense of what happened at the doorsteps of their homes. One of them risks an explanation: the Jews were exterminated by the Nazis because they claimed responsibility for the death of Christ on the cross. This outburst of anti-Semitic prejudice does not alter the scene: the villagers keep smiling; Srebnik nods his head, uneasy and constrained; and Chełmno, more than thirty years after the Shoah, once again bathes in the peaceful greenery of its landscape.

Podchlebnik's Smile

Michael Podchlebnik was another survivor of the Chełmno death camp. He miraculously escaped when the camp was beginning operations. Podchlebnik was also an *Arbeitsjude*, but because he was a strong adult, the Nazis forced him to gather the clothes left behind by the victims and bury the corpses in large mass graves in the nearby forest. Podchlebnik was interviewed right after the war by Zofia Nałkowska, a Polish writer who worked for the Central Commission for the Investigation of German Crimes in Poland. He testified during the Eichmann trial in Jerusalem and later in Bonn, during the 1962 trial of twelve SS crewmembers of the Chełmno camp. In 1946 Nałkowska published a collection of short stories entitled *Medallions* based on the testimonies gathered during her fact-finding mission. One of them, entitled "The Man Is Strong," is based on the account given by Podchlebnik, whom Lanzmann met thirty years later in Israel and whose story is intertwined with Srebnik's testimony at the beginning of *Shoah*. Nałkowska described Podchlebnik as a tall, athletically built man who spoke in a quiet, solemn voice "as if he were reciting from a holy text." In the story, he describes how he found the body of his gassed wife and children among the corpses unloaded from one of the trucks. "One day—Tuesday it was—the third truck arrived from Chełmno. They pitched out the bodies of my wife and children—the boy was seven, the girl, four. I lay down on my wife's body and pleaded with them to shoot me. They didn't want to shoot me. One German said: 'The man is strong. He can still work hard.' And he beat me with a cudgel until I got up" (Nałkowska 43). Podchlebnik repeats almost the same account in front of Lanzmann's camera, at the beginning of *Shoah*. He is now seventy years old but still in shape. The director compliments him on his youthful appearance at the outset of the interview, though these greetings were edited out of the final version of the film. More than thirty years after descending into the pit and lying down by the side of his dead wife, pleading to be shot, Podchlebnik cannot refrain from breaking down in tears.

Podchlebnik's tears are, however, not the first image of him that Lanzmann presents to the viewer. During the editing of the footage, the director inverted the original order of the interview as attested by the interview transcript archived at the Holocaust Memorial Museum in Washington, DC. What on the screen appears as the first question Podchlebnik was asked is, in fact, near the end of the recorded conversation. This almost-last question of the interview, which Lanzmann inserts in his movie at the outset of the sequence devoted to Podchlebnik, is the question around which the entire encounter with Podchlebnik revolves: "What died in you in Chełmno?"

Lanzmann repeats this question with slight variations three more times: he wants to know what died "inside" Podchlebnik, what died "in his heart," and what died "in his soul [brain, mind]." At first, Podchlebnik seems to misunderstand, even dodge the question. He replies twice that what died in Chełmno was his entire family. Finally, he acknowledges that "all has died."[2] What follows in the French transcript of the interview is difficult to decipher. The typescript reads: "but an automat, a robot . . ." These words are crossed out and a handwritten correction, probably made by Lanzmann, reads: "but one is only a human being and wants to live . . ." This correction is closer to what can be overheard from the Yiddish audio track of the movie. Then the transcript and spoken words diverge again: in the French text, Podchlebnik thanks God "for what remains"; in the Yiddish soundtrack, he thanks God that he forgot what happened and that he cannot remember it. What is this strange presence of loss that he is so grateful for? His life as a survivor or the surviving presence of death that haunts him? Or both, the living death and the dead life united in this mortified human being? In any case, Podchlebnik does not think one should talk about what happened to him in Chełmno. If he talks about it, it is only because he is forced to by Lanzmann. It is clear that he does not think it is "right" or "good" for him to talk about it.

The correction of the transcript and the divergence of the written record from what can be heard in the audio track of the film are due to the difficulty of giving a faithful account of what is at stake in this quiet but extremely dramatic encounter between the director of *Shoah* and the man who speaks to him from the bottom of absolute devastation. The slow-paced conversation, slowed even more by the French-Yiddish translation, is full of a terrible tension between the impossibility of testifying to the disappearance of an entire people and the tangible concreteness of the testimony given of this inconceivable event. In comparison with the painful tension of the interview, its fragile written and recorded traces waver between what was intentionally forgotten and what was forcefully brought back from oblivion, between humanity that was lost and humanity that remained alive against all odds.

It comes, therefore, as no surprise that at the end of the scene Lanzmann repeats once again his initial question: Did Podchlebnik survive "as a man who is alive or as a dead man?" Here again, the French transcript and the Yiddish soundtrack diverge. The transcript says that while he was in the forest, burying the corpses of the gassed victims, including the bodies of his wife and two children, Podchlebnik "lived this as a dead man." In his spoken words, Podchlebnik is more hesitant: "I am not sure if it is correct to say that I was dead or alive." In any case, he did not hope to survive the Chełmno extermination, and yet he is alive now. It is clearly the "now" that fascinates Lanzmann. He is not interested in a tale of overcoming or, even less, of redemption. He does not see in Podchlebnik a survivor, and certainly not a resurrected man, but one of the living dead. His questions and the edits he made to the script of the interview show clearly that Lanzmann tried to capture the troubling morphing of human life into inhuman death and, conversely, the marks of the absolute absence of anything that is human on the very humane face of this man. The place where Lanzmann hopes to meet Podchlebnik is at the confines of this man's humanness, the edges of his humanity.

At that instant Lanzmann asks a surprising question: Why does Podchlebnik always smile? Indeed, except for the moment when Podchlebnik breaks down in tears while recalling his descent into the pit to be buried alongside his wife and children—a part of the interview that, as I said, Lanzmann intentionally moved to the end of this sequence during the editing of the film—the old man's face is continuously irradiated by a strange smile that is difficult to comprehend. Prompted by Lanzmann's question, this smile almost turns into a quiet yet defiant laughter: "What do you want me to do, cry? When you are alive, you smile [it is better to smile]." This exchange is bracketed in the transcript and heavily annotated as if the person transcribing the audio track struggled to understand what Podchlebnik said and the person who went over the transcription—possibly Lanzmann himself—pondered about its meaning, as well. How should we comprehend Podchlebnik's smile? What is the meaning of laughter in the face of death and, especially, in the face of the most inhuman of deaths?

Podchlebnik's smile prompts the question that is central to this book: What does laughter—the particular laughter, I should stress, that resonates at the confines of human life—reveal about our common humanity? Lying in the pit alongside the corpses of his wife and his children, Podchlebnik remains suspended between life and death. In the most profoundly metaphysical and yet literal sense, he is situated where what is human meets what is not human. One can speculate about the nature of these confines of human life. Most notably, one can wonder about the realm that lies beyond those limits. In what sense can *our* life or any mode of *our* existence not be human? When and how is it no longer human, not yet human, or not human at all?

No longer: The Nazis insisted that the prisoners whom they used to bury the corpses not refer to the dead bodies as human remains but as puppets or rugs. By lying alongside the body of his wife, Podchlebnik renounced his human life to become—at least in the eyes of the SS men—useless waste. His voluntary gesture was an unacceptable act of revolt for the guard who looked at Podchlebnik as a man but only to the extent that his victim was strong enough to perform valuable work before being shot.

Not at all and not yet: Of course, seen from the perspective of the prisoner, this cruel and properly inhuman reclaiming of human life by Nazi murderers was anything but a reflex of humanity. Podchlebnik's point of view allows us to consider the realm extending beyond human life not merely as a time of loss that comes after but as a transcendent thereafter, a realm that is not at all or not yet human. In the language of a simple yet sensible man, Podchlebnik tells Lanzmann that back then in Chełmno, he was neither alive nor dead while running under the blows of the guards; he was more like a robot, a tool to be used and eventually disposed of by the SS. In other words, Podchlebnik felt like an animated object, disposable even before the Nazi guards would shoot him and make him a puppet or a rug. Lying down in the pit and waiting to be finished off may, therefore, have been for Podchlebnik an attempt to escape life that other humans had made properly inhuman for him. His escape from inhumanity can also be understood in different ways: From a religious point of view, it could be seen as a longing to exit the valley of tears of the Chełmno death camp and the misery of our earthly condition in order to find rest in the house of God. Conversely, from a naturalistic, immanent perspective, Podchlebnik's gesture could be seen as an attempt to return—alongside the mother of his children—to the bosom of Mother Earth to escape suffering by diluting himself in the primordial, amorphous matter of nonhuman life. In whatever way we understand Podchlebnik's gesture, his quiet laughter reveals a tension imposed by the finitude of being. It puts us at the edge of our humanness.

The Death of Man

The edges of our humanness are what this book attempts to retrace. To sketch the demarcation line between what is human and what is not, I try to capture the echo of a peculiar, joyless, often forced and painful, if not deadly, laughter. My working hypothesis is that such laughter resonates at the limits of human finitude. Most often, it ricochets off the walls of the narrow pit of mortality. I would, therefore, like to think that it is possible to understand something about humanness by listening to the sound of the laughter reverberating at the confines of life, at the edge of existential experience.

Why do I insist on confines and limits? Why do I not directly target the human being that those contours circumscribe? The reason is simple: living within the Western culture that emerged from the inhumanities of the past century and faces human-made ecological doom, I cannot presuppose a metaphysical conception of reality within which Man would play his natural role. As I cannot assume a God-given essence of humanity, I cannot either bank on the existence of Man understood as a human subject equipped with sovereign reason and will, consciously capable of apprehending reality and free to act upon the so-acquired understanding. In other words, I cannot rely on either Renaissance or Enlightenment conceptions of the human being because modernity has erased them with repeated waves of criticism flowing from economic and social history, linguistics, and, most recently, biology. I cannot rely on early modern humanism because it cannot be understood anymore and hence cannot be accepted as a basis of discussion. The humanisms of the past have been reduced to the role of antiquated oddities amid the massive inhumanity of the last century and the subsequent indifference, if not hostility, to what is human in posthuman times. The irrelevancy of the conceptions of Man prevailing between the fifteenth and eighteenth centuries stems from specific choices made in twentieth-century Western intellectual history. Let me point to a few of them.

In 1966, Foucault rejoiced at the image of Man as an ephemeral figure traced on the moving sands of reality soon to be washed away by the successive waves of huge systems of signification: labor, language, and the body (*Les motes et les choses*; *L'Archéologie du savoir*). French and German antihumanism quickly became a dominant trend of thought in Anglo-American academia, setting the stage for the globalized posthumanism of today. We should, however, remember that it came on the heels of decades of antihumanist thinking that effectively eroded the conception of the human being as a rational animal capable of apprehending the world and bestowing meaning on reality. This philosophical unravelling of Man took place during a century punctuated by two world wars that put human technological inventiveness at the service of genocide. While disposing of the concept of the human being, Foucault bade farewell to Sartre, whom he considered the last humanist. Indeed, within days of the Hiroshima and Nagasaki bombings, Sartre acknowledged that after the death of God, the death of Man followed ("La fin"). He nonetheless was not overly concerned by this. On the contrary, he was convinced that the obituary pertained only to Man conceived of as an essence squarely located within a predetermined plan of God's creation or within the harmony of nature. Since no a priori essence could precede the existence of an individual, humanity was, for Sartre, still salvageable as an open-ended project, an exercise of will engaging the individual's responsibility for the sake of the entire human race. The newly acquired technological capacity to end human history in a final atomic blast was thus a welcomed opportunity for humankind to shepherd its own being by deciding each minute of each day not to blow up the planet but to continue the human adventure. Sartre's existentialism was still a humanism, as Foucault accurately denounced it twenty years later.

In fact, Sartre's faith in human agency was already rejected by Heidegger immediately after the publication in 1946 of Sartre's manifesto *Existentialism Is a Humanism*. It would have been embarrassing at that time for a German known for unapologetically siding with National Socialism to overtly criticize a French colleague who, after spending the years of Nazi occupation promoting his own literary and philosophical career, eagerly embarked on the purification of Parisian intellectual life from collaborators. Nonetheless,

Heidegger clearly, albeit politely, signaled to the French existentialist that the shepherding of Being should be less a commitment to confer an essence on individual existence and more the receptivity of *Dasein*, human existence in the world, to its own finitude. What is at stake in Heidegger's response to Sartre is the human capacity, or rather the incapacity of *Dasein* to bestow meaning on reality.

Heidegger's reply to Sartre in the mid-1940s was in line with his previous work and most notably his rebuttal of the prominent representative of German Kantian philosophy Ernst Cassirer during their famous debate at Davos in 1929. Cassirer defended the human subject's capacity to shape the symbolic forms of culture.[3] But to no avail. Cassirer's infinitely resourceful Man had to give way to Heidegger's *Dasein*, the "placeholder for the Nothing" ("What Is Metaphysics?" 742). Despite the odds, Cassirer's last work, published in exile in 1944 just months before Sartre's own attempt to renew humanism, was entitled *An Essay on Man*. At the same time, a fellow émigré, Günther Anders, was writing a multivolume opus, *The Obsolescence of Man* (*Die Antiquierheit des Menschen*). Contrary to Sartre, Anders was not convinced that the atomic bomb provided humankind with the mastery of its life and death and the consciousness of this ultimate responsibility. Anders warned that the technological revolutions of the twentieth century had not only deprived humanity of a definite essence—this could still be understood as a renewed call for human self-consciousness and self-determination—but had rendered human beings properly inessential, in other words, superfluous. It was with horror that Anders watched the historical transformations of Western culture reduce humans to the role of tools or raw material in the industrial production of cadavers in the death camps and in the eugenic breeding of the overman through the Lebensborn program of the SS.

Read from today's perspective, Anders's somber lamentation may make us nod with approval or smile with condescension. All depends on our stand on issues such as the enhancement of the genome through CRISPR-Cas9 editing or the commodification of gestational surrogacy. These are only examples of hugely complicated problems pertaining to human and nonhuman biological life that have far-reaching ethical implications but that are part of our everyday contemporary culture. Regardless of our ideological positioning, we must acknowledge that technological advances, particularly in computer science and bioengineering, give new meaning to the question at the center of the Cassirer-Heidegger debate in Davos: "What is the human being?" (*Was ist der Mensch?*). What is a human being when AI aims at becoming consciousness, when synthetic prostheses transform human bodies into cyborg assemblages, and when transplants genetically grown from nonhuman animals metamorphose humans into chimera-like organisms? What is human life when artificial life is no longer a computer simulation but a self-sustaining and self-evolving creation generated out of elemental chemical and physical components? Besides its real importance for the history of continental philosophy, the famous Cassirer-Heidegger encounter also has an emblematic significance. Other symbolic indicators of the twentieth-century obsolescence of the human being could be cited. For instance, Freud's famous 1917 list of the three wounds inflicted on the narcissist human ego by epochal discoveries: the banishment of God's masterwork from the center of the universe by Copernicus; the human being's tumble down from the pedestal of biological superiority by Darwin; and, finally, the undermining of the human being's rational agency by unconscious drives, courtesy of Freud himself.[4] The point is not to survey the history of modern culture in search of more evidence of the death of Man, understood as the capstone of metaphysics or the gateway of consciousness. The question is how to deal with the aftermath of this conceptual unraveling.

A popular solution is to accept the obsolescence of the human being or reclaim this disappearance in the name of a renewed realism. This is the direction chosen by a wide and diversified range of currents of thought in the new millennium. For instance, one of these propositions reaches beyond our finitude, not through a mystical leap of faith but by breaking the correlation binding reality to our consciousness. When we follow this speculative path, we discover that beyond the finitude of the categories of our understanding, but still within the purview of logic ruled by noncontradiction, lies the necessary contingency of things: "archifossils" never thought by the human mind, alternative laws of nature that arise unexpectedly at any moment, or even God—not the one burdened by the evil of our world, not the one who died and awaits a second coming, but a God who does not yet exist.[5] All these realities are deemed rational, albeit beyond human thinking based on a phenomenal apprehension of reality.

Equally nonhuman is another speculation that cares less about thought and more about the body. Instead of breaking the correlation between human thinking and reality, a new vitalism multiplies the paths of multilateral communication between the inside and the outside of the human organism. The contours of individuals have been perforated by osmotic movements of microorganisms and nanomachines. The human body becomes a nebula of autonomous agents agitated by their own fully independent movements. A similar vibration can be seen at the macroscale. On the social and political stage, human bodies lose their individual contours by being seamlessly integrated into swarm-like assemblages of things, debris, materials, nutrients, and biomasses, all equipped with ever-changing degrees of organization and agency. Instead of being distinct personae endowed with individual reason and will, human beings are diluted within an amorphous "vibrant matter" (Bennett).

To speculate beyond the reach of human thinking and to dissolve the human body in the boundless materiality of animated things are radically different philosophical projects.[6] Nonetheless, these speculations share a common disinterest in the question of what is human. They are valuable achievements of our contemporary culture, as, for instance, are neurochips, which have become an integral part of our technological life, or xenobots, those biological microrobots promising to serve our medical and ecological needs. However, reaching beyond human finitude or dissolving the limitedness of human life diverts us from researching what it means to be human. I remain deeply convinced that this question is worth addressing in our posthuman times, now more than ever.

Thinking at the Edge of Humanity

Today there seems to be a widely shared feeling that humanity has reached a limit and is busy pushing against it in order to expand the realm of its possibilities. To take an example: despite many denials, we are slowly (too slowly) realizing that the ongoing ecological catastrophe risks bringing human life on earth to the brink of extinction. Successive international conferences chip away the hope of reversing global warming. At least we are still trying (timidly indeed) to slow down the desertification of land, the rise of sea levels, and the spread of wildfires. The extent of our failure leads us to believe that our balancing act at the edge of the possibilities of survival may come to a brutal end sooner rather than later. An entire genre of catastrophic literature and thinking caters to the idea that what is still possible, namely human life on this planet, will become impossible in a future that is not millions of years away but only a few generations.

The ecological catastrophe is just one example of many existential balancing acts performed at the edges of what is human. After all, the previous century has proven that humanity can organize its own demise. Contrary to previous extermination attempts, the Shoah was the first almost-successful attempt made by humans to wipe out an entire genre (*genus*) of their own kind by denying their humanity. Jews had to be annihilated not, as has been the case with many massacres in the past, because they were an enemy people or an alien race but because they were deemed to be not human. Most importantly, this genocide was planned and almost successfully executed with scientific rationality and economic efficiency during a short span of time—between roughly late 1941 and mid-1945—thanks to the technological advances made by humanity. It is the same technological progress that gave humankind as a whole the option of an atomic annihilation. Humanity gained an unprecedented capacity to blow itself up along with the entire planet in a matter of minutes. At Hiroshima and Nagasaki, as at Auschwitz, what was impossible became possible and remains so even now.

This expansion of the realm of the possible—seen by some as a sign of progress and by others as a dangerous transgression—continues to this day. At the beginning of the new millennium, Jürgen Habermas worried that preimplantation genetic diagnosis would open the door to the programming of humans. It would allow parents not only to lower the chances of genetic diseases by preventing an early-stage fertilized ovum from being implanted in the uterus but also create the technical possibility of eugenic modeling of future generations. The resulting offspring would be "made" rather than compelled to "grow" into a network of social relationships. Consequently, Habermas worried, such preselected individuals would see the authorship of their personal life story at least partially taken away from them. A quarter of a century later, Habermas's concern seems almost futile. Thanks to CRISPR-Cas9 technology, dozens of genes can be cut and pasted simultaneously, making genetic engineering a therapeutic tool for humans but also a marketable commodity for all those who would like to clone a beloved dog or make it glow in the dark. Hence the dream that haunts Jennifer Doudna, who together with Emmanuelle Charpentier received the 2020 Nobel Prize in Chemistry for their role in developing CRISPR-Cas9 into versatile genetic scissors, making genetic editing precise and relatively easy. This is how Doudna reported her dream in an interview:

> I had a dream recently, and in my dream [she mentioned here the name of a colleague] had come to see me and said, "I have somebody very powerful with me who I want you to meet, and I want you to explain to him how this technology functions." So I said, "Sure, who is it?" It was Adolf Hitler. . . . [H]e said, "I want to understand the uses and implications of this amazing technology." I woke up in a cold sweat. And that dream has haunted me from that day. (qtd. in Knoepfler)[7]

Given the twentieth-century death of Man and our increasingly real obliteration of humaneness in the twenty-first century, I am compelled to undertake my reflection on a basis different from the one underlying past speculations on the human being as a distinct essence in the plan of creation or as a distinct consciousness apprehending phenomenal reality. Instead of asking what it is to be human, I will try, more modestly, to understand what it means to be human by tracing the contours of our humanness. By sketching these evanescent outlines, I test human finitude as the edge between what is human and what is not. To trace the contours of what it means to be human, I resort to laughter. The laughter that I am interested in is not a proprium, a specific quality that defines human nature. Such a specific quality of humanness is nowhere to be found in our present world, which is no longer an ordered cosmos composed of distinct creatures, each equipped with what is essential to their being. Since such an essentialist worldview is no longer possible, I consider laughter as a sign, a puzzling clue, that does not define human nature or even a phenomenal appearance of humanity but modestly indicates the limit of a life that is deemed human. Since this symptomatic laughter comes to us from before, after, and beyond human life, it has a characteristically uncanny and disturbing quality. Most importantly, it is forced and joyless.

Laughter conceived as a disturbing sign of our finitude has a distinctly corporeal character. The physicality of laughter is of course intimately linked to our mortality. A famous anecdote, repeated by many anthropologists after Claude Lévi-Strauss, describes the experiment that Indigenous Americans performed on the first conquistadors they captured.[8] They plunged the European prisoners into water and kept them there to see if they would eventually rot. If they did, it would prove that these alien beings who came from an unknown place and landed on their shores had mortal bodies. The Indigenous Americans' concern was opposite to that of the European theologians in Valladolid who, roughly at the same time, debated whether Indigenous Americans had immortal souls. My interest in laughter as a bodily symptom of our finitude is in line with the Indigenous Americans' investigations. I look for a laughter that transforms our facial expressions, the rhythm of our respiration, and the pace of the circulation of our blood. Yet, to grasp these movements of our perishable bodies, I will not check the pulse or dissect a corpse. Instead, I explore a textual corpus using tools of cultural, literary, and philosophical interpretation. I look for the physicality of laughter in select texts of Western culture: philosophical essays and AI chats, poetry and film, scientific papers and novels. It is in these texts of culture that I search for the disturbingly uncanny laughter that testifies to the tension between what it means to be human and to be not-human.

Since the laughter I pursue is a bodily, largely involuntary, and joyless symptom, I do not identify it with humor. My book does not seek to contribute to the anthropology of jokes or to the aesthetic of comedy. The mirthless laughter I try to capture may, at times, seem a bitter self-denigration or a convoluted wit based on self-mockery. Nonetheless, funniness is not its primary quality. The laughter embodied in texts I am trying to capture testifies to corporeal finitude but not necessarily in a consciously self-reflexive way. It is even less a sublimation of mortality. The closest it comes to resembling humor is by reminding us of Samuel Beckett's *risus purus*, "the laugh laughing at the laugh." Such return upon itself does not result from an elaborate intellectual self-analysis but consists in an almost animalistic and automatic reflex of the body, a movement often surprised by and ashamed of itself and almost always unpleasant.[9] I try to understand such "laugh laughing at the laugh" resonating in the texts of Western culture in the hope that my exegesis will bring to the fore the contours of humanness that have been washed away by successive waves of the last century's inhumanity and antihumanism. Textual hermeneutics is the method I use to exhume an existential meaning that abstract concepts alone do not allow us to grasp. I begin by applying such interpretation to Claude Lanzmann's *Shoah*.

The Place of the Shoah

The traces of Lanzmann's hesitations in the French transcript of the audio track of *Shoah*, how he edited the interview in his movie, and finally the very few comments that he made regarding Podchlebnik's testimony will help me explore the meaning of Podchlebnik's smile and introduce my exploration of laughter at the edges of humanity.

Let us, therefore, follow *Shoah*'s lead and start with Lanzmann's insistent search for what "has died" in Podchlebnik. When Lanzmann asked this question in front of the camera, he already knew something that the viewer would discover only later in the film, namely that Podchlebnik's entire family was gassed and that the man sitting across the table from him wanted to be killed and then buried alongside his wife and children. Lanzmann was not interested in Podchlebnik repeating this information. Instead, he wanted Podchlebnik to acknowledge that he was a dead man, or at least that something essential to his humanity was irremediably dead. Let us not underestimate the difficulty of this paradoxical claim. The older man sitting at the table on a sunny afternoon in Israel looks alert and even relatively young. Yet, given what happened thirty years before in a small village in central Poland, he does not partake in human life in the same sense that the film director and the translator who question him do. He might have thought that they came from afar to force him to retrieve memories from the past, like he was asked to do at the Eichmann trial. He may, however, also have realized that this was not what Lanzmann expected from him. He may have understood the director's request to be far more demanding, that in fact he is being asked to lie down once again in the pit alongside the bodies of his wife and children and to do it on the spot under Lanzmann's warm yet watchful eye, on that sunny day in Israel.

Hence the hesitations in the soundtrack and transcript. Pressed by Lanzmann's insistent questions, Podchlebnik finally acknowledges that "all has died" in Chełmno, but the oral and written versions of his testimony are strangely convoluted. Was he a lifeless automaton or a human being who wanted to live? If he "lived as a dead man," was he alive or dead? Did something remain for which he thanked God, or did nothing remain, since he forgot everything?

These hesitations and contradictions testify to the immense difficulty of expressing in language the death of humanity that Podchlebnik experienced. Confronted with this impossible task, his words "all has died" are less a factual statement than an attempt to stop Lanzmann's persistent questioning and divert the interviewer's attention from something that Podchlebnik cannot express because he is either unable or unwilling to comprehend it. Yet to say that "all has died" in Chełmno is important because, as Lanzmann has stressed on many occasions, *Shoah* is not a film about survival but about death (*Lièvre* 437). *Shoah* is definitely not a documentary about the Holocaust. The movie is not meant to commemorate the extermination of European Jews, which occurred decades before the film was made; it does not try to explain the Holocaust by inserting it into a chain of factual causes; it does not aim at constructing a cautionary tale that would prevent humanity from ever destroying humanity again. The perspective of the film is neither scholarly nor moralistic because Lanzmann does not look at the destruction of the Jews from the standpoint of life that preceded, life that survived, or life that is to come. The topic of *Shoah* is death. The film is entirely devoted to the millions of dead. Lanzmann's project consisted of following them into the gas chambers to keep them company in their demise. It is, therefore, crucial that Podchlebnik appear before Lanzmann's camera not as a survivor, someone who, against all odds, triumphed over death and is now looking back at his past ordeal. Portraying Podchlebnik as a survivor would risk paradoxically confirming the words of the German guard who refused to shoot him at the bottom of the mass grave where Podchlebnik's wife and children lay. It would be a cruel fulfilment of "the man is strong." Obviously, the SS guard who forced Podchlebnik to climb out of the grave so he could bury more bodies before he was finally allowed to become a puppet or a rug did not say "the man is strong" in order to celebrate human life. Nałkowska gave these words their fully ironic meaning by using them as the title of her short story. The SS guard meant only that the Jew who asked to be shot did not have the right to choose even his own death. He was stripped of this ultimate human capacity and forced to serve his murderers as an automaton, a nonhuman robot that would be disposed of when the gruesome "work" of the final solution was complete. It is this absolute deprivation of life and death—the destitution of humanity—that Lanzmann wanted to unearth. This is the reason why Podchlebnik had to be present during the interview in Israel some thirty years after his descent into the mass grave in Chełmno as a dead person. This was crucial for Lanzmann because only a dead person can be brought back to life by the power of cinematographic vision.

The director of *Shoah* insisted on the visionary nature of his art, but he nevertheless spent many years searching for the adequate conceptual explanation of what he meant. On several occasions, he spoke about incarnation or resurrection. The Christian connotations of those terms raised some eyebrows, and Lanzmann was even accused of sacralizing the Holocaust, something he forcefully denied. One does not necessarily have to accept an artist's interpretation of their own work, but I would agree that Lanzmann was not trying to transform the death of European Jews into a sacred object of veneration. This does not mean that he did not erect strong defenses and protective taboos around it. Crossing them would be, as he put it on many occasions, obscene. For instance, Lanzmann was careful to edit the footage so that the rare Jewish survivors did not appear in the film directly after or before their Nazi executioners. Even placing the testimonies of people such as Srebnik and Podchlebnik in the direct vicinity of Polish peasants who used to work their fields on the other side of the barbed wires of the death camps was to be avoided. This careful isolationism was dictated not by religious but by artistic reasons. Lanzmann wanted to avoid a transition between the dead of the Shoah and other living human beings. This is also the reason why he avoided mimetic effects when he invited his interlocutors to recreate the gestures they had performed in the midst of the desolation thirty years earlier. For instance, in one of the most famous sequences of the film, when he forced Abraham Bomba to tell how he used to cut the hair of women who were about to be gassed, Lanzmann was careful to set this dramatic scene in a Tel Aviv barbershop for men, which bore no resemblance to the conditions in which Bomba cut hair in Treblinka. Choosing a salon for women would have been obscene. The point was not to pretend that there was a continuity between the abyssal horror of extermination and the scenery of the 1970s. Lanzmann wanted the viewer to understand the impossibility of such a link and, consequently, the impossibility of the task he was undertaking, namely, to make the dead speak for the dead (*Lièvre* 450).

It is not as a survivor but as a revenant, that is, a dead person who is brought back from oblivion, that Srebnik stands in front of the church in Chełmno in the very place where the Nazis kept Jews before leading them to the gassing trucks. Srebnik's properly impossible presence in this place is all the more powerful because it occurs as the Corpus Christi procession, during which Catholics celebrate the real presence of the body of Christ in the here and now of human reality, is about to begin. I do not think that this effect was intended by the film director, but the Jew that was supposed to disappear, dispersed with the fumes of the crematorium, is present in his body in the place of the body of the other Jew who is venerated by the villagers as the Son of God and whose death on the cross two thousand years earlier in a remote province of the Roman Empire still provides anti-Semites with a justification for their deadly hatred.

It is also as a revenant that Podchlebnik was forced to speak about what he had reported to Nałkowska in 1946 and during the trials of Nazi war criminals but also what he would prefer to forget. Lanzmann intentionally bypassed these previous testimonies because he wanted to interview Podchlebnik as a dead man. He neglected the intermediary stages and possible bridges; he needed a sharp edge between absence and presence because it was the dead whom he wanted to bring "to life and make them forever present." Such "presence of an absence" is not the outcome of a quasi-religious ritual. It is "creation of presence by absence," the work of the *imaginaire*, which is, as Sartre put it, a form of consciousness aimed at an object that is not there (*L'imaginaire*).[10]

How, therefore, should we understand Podchlebnik's smile in the context of such an artistic project? In his 2009 memoir, Lanzmann lays out the grounds for his answer to this question. Each of the revenants required a different approach from the filmmaker. Contrary, for instance, to the condensed clarity of Abraham Bomba's story, Srebnik's account is incoherent and dispersed, and in order to put together the pieces of the horrible world that haunted him, Lanzmann needed to bring this revenant back to Chełmno. Such a journey was not necessary in the case of Podchlebnik because "all takes place in his face, the marvelous face made of a smile and of tears, this face that is the very place of the Shoah" (*Lièvre* 454). What does it mean that Podchlebnik's face is "the place of the Shoah"? A few lines later in his text, Lanzmann qualifies Podchlebnik's smile as "courageous." What kind of courage did he have in mind?

One answer is clearly excluded: namely, to see in Podchlebnik's face the ethical force of a man who overcame his fear of death and whose fortitude has triumphed over a deadly danger. Such understanding of Podchlebnik's courage would be inconsistent with Lanzmann's artistic vision because Podchlebnik took part in the interview not as a survivor but as a dead man, and Lanzmann insists that he acknowledge this reality. It is this dead man deprived of absolutely everything, and, most importantly, deprived of a human death, whom the film director, thanks to his visionary art, brings to life and gives a bodily presence. It is precisely this bodily presence of inhuman death that is incorporated, made flesh, in the smile on the tortured face of Michael Podchlebnik.

Reading to the Dead

To see in Podchlebnik's smile the embodiment of his inhuman death is consistent with Lanzmann's artistic project. For a long time, the director searched for the title of his movie. "Holocaust" had to be excluded because of the implied religious sacrifice. "The Place and the Word" was chosen as a provisional title since the film was exclusively composed of oral testimonies placed against the background of authentic extermination sites or references to them while avoiding a mimetic illusion. But, thirty years after the war when Lanzmann shot his film, those places were already deeply altered despite the general state of inertia and decrepitude prevailing in Poland under communist rule. They were the "non-sites of memory," as Lanzmann called them, inverting the famous phrase coined by Pierre Nora, who tried to decode the traces left in the human environment by the vicissitudes of history.[11] When, after much hesitation, Lanzmann finally came to

Poland—the much-feared "East" where the Nazis had built and operated their death camps—he searched for what remained from the past life and death of the Jewish people: houses, once inhabited by Jews, emptied by the Nazis and occupied after the war by Polish neighbors; synagogues that miraculously escaped systematic destruction and served as depots after the war; abandoned Jewish cemeteries. But unlike the historian who would be content to find even the most altered traces of the past in the permanence of space, Lanzmann was disappointed by the paucity of what remained after the genocide. The places were empty; nothing was left. The death of the Jewish people appeared more as a legend, albeit of such mythical proportions that it infinitely transcended the traces of history that he found.

Lanzmann faced the places of industrialized mass murder systematically devoid of the physical remains of the dead, whose bodies had been unearthed at the command of their murderers, burned to ashes, and meticulously dispersed. Left only with words tainted by past ideological meanings that provided petty explanations for the incomprehensible reality of Jewish destruction, he refused to document past memories. He wanted a movie that would give a bodily presence to the painful absence. He needed a title for his movie that would offer a meaning when no inherited or ready-made meaning could be accepted. Hence the choice of *Shoah*, an obscure biblical term that held little significance for the public at the time of the release of the film but that became *the* designation of the extermination of European Jewry. The process of nomination that turned an unknown word into a universally recognizable eponym is the best illustration of the success of Lanzmann's artistic undertaking, which consisted of giving a carnal consistency to a void and the permanence of art to the volatility of a "legend."

Lanzmann recognized that this act was a re-presentation, a re-cognition, a re-vival. To accomplish it, the director had to return to the scene of the crimes, Poland, where the Shoah largely took place. A paradoxical return indeed since Lanzmann had never been to Poland before undertaking the making of his film. But this journey was also a logical move, provided that, in the present time and place, the "return" embodied the mythical horror of destruction and that the cinematic art succeeded in giving a tangible body to the void left by the dispersed bodies of the dead. For a long time, Lanzmann doubted that reconnecting the "legend" and the present would be possible. Yet it was. In his memoir, Lanzmann kept coming back to the moment when, disappointed and distressed by his visit to the site of the death camp, where he spent hours wandering between the stelae that comprised the commemorative monument, he entered the village of Treblinka and saw its name spelled out on the signboard of the small train station. This name was the stubborn "persistence in being" of a prosaic, insignificant rural agglomeration lost in the Polish countryside of the 1970s. It was this encounter with the name *Treblinka*, so cursed that it had become a "quasi-ontological" taboo, that forced the director to discard all the knowledge he had accumulated up to this point—four years of planning—and start his work anew. In one instant of illuminating truth, myth became reality (Lanzmann, *Lièvre* 491).

The banal signboard became for Lanzmann the incarnation of the Shoah, not because it was a monument erected in commemoration of the past or a site of memory riddled with traces of the horrible events that took place at the outskirts of this village decades ago, but because the ominous name *Treblinka* on the signboard became the igniting mechanism that set up the artistic conflagration of Lanzmann's film. Through the mundane, everyday sign, the incomprehensible and unspeakable horror of the annihilation of an entire people entered present, tangible reality. I would risk the hypothesis that the shocking encounter between the absolute destruction that transcends human comprehension and the closeness of what is immediately given, clearly perceptible, and directly at hand is what prompted Lanzmann's surprised question regarding Podchlebnik's smile. This supposition would no doubt seem obscene to the film director. How could one compare the ugly signboard marking the *anus mundi* of a death camp with the noble face of an old man who went through the horror of inhuman death and who, nevertheless, remained illuminated by an almost unreal smile? Yet Lanzmann considered Podchlebnik's face to be the "place of the Shoah" because his beautifully human smile drew its splendor from the inhumanity of death that this man harbored in his heart from the day he buried his wife and children and lay among them to be killed. Podchlebnik's smile and the Treblinka signboard are diametrically opposed in their appearance and emotional connotations, yet both were made possible by the Shoah. The inhumanity of the unspeakable destruction of a people is what made possible the corporeal reality of Podchlebnik's smile as well as the cumbersome, physical awkwardness of the signboard. The Shoah loads these realities with meaning.

The paradoxical analogy between quiet human laughter and the physical artifact is well illustrated by the poem "The Little Station Treblinki" by Władysław Szlengel. It is written in the tone of a casual, everyday conversation. The poet extends friendly travel advice to the reader on how to get from Warsaw to Treblinka by train.

The Little Station Treblinki

On the line between Tłuszcz and Warsaw,
from station Warschau-Ost,
one leaves upon the train-tracks
in a straight line almost . . .

The journey may just take you
some six hours, more or less,
and yet sometimes lasts the journey
your whole life until your death . . .

The station is quite tiny,
three firs stand in a line,
this is Treblinki station,
proclaims the usual sign.

And there's no ticket window,
cloakroom? Do not seek it!
You cannot buy for millions,
for your return, a ticket . . .

And no-one on the platform
a hanky waves to greet you,
with only silence hanging,
and emptiness to meet you.

The station-sign is silent,
and silent the three firs,
and silent the black sign which . . .
"Treblinki Station" bears.

A poster also hangs there,
(it seems it always has)
with an old and faded message:
"Cook only with gas."[12]

The casual tone of the conversation is quickly overshadowed by the heavy realization that the few hours it takes to make the journey is the entirety of life that remains. The old poster hanging on the train station's wall is cruelly obsolete since gas has a more sinister application than cooking. But the tragic irony of the poem is revealed when we learn about the circumstances of its creation. "The Little Station Treblinki" was most probably composed at the end of 1942 and definitely before May 8, 1943, the day when the SS, who were finishing up with the last pockets of resistance of the Warsaw ghetto uprising, discovered the underground bunker in which dozens of Jews, among them Szlengel and his wife, were hiding. All were executed on the spot. The poem Szlengel wrote a few months—or possibly only weeks—before his death is an ironic projection of what he perceived as imminent death. It was not, as was the case with Lanzmann, a thunder-like revelation connecting the banal, human reality of the present with the horrendous "legend." For Szlengel, his family, and his friends, the "legend" of Treblinka was in the making in front of their eyes. With the wealth of their experience gained from gassing their victims with combustion fumes in the Chełmno death camp, the Nazis began deportations from the Warsaw ghetto to Treblinka on July 22, 1942. Szlengel, who had avoided being dragged into an eastbound train, was well aware that such journeys led straight to the gas chambers. Nonetheless, he was still learning the name of the small train station: instead of the correct word, *Treblinka*, Szlengel mistakenly used an inaccurate plural form, *Treblinki*, in his poem. The extermination was still in the making, and the name of this village was just gaining the legendary power that thunderstruck Lanzmann decades later. Yet the 1942/1943 poem accomplishes the same artistic miracle as the 1985 movie: it embodies in everyday language and in the images of meaningless banality the meaning that evades the possibilities of language and imagination.

This artistic tour de force is again accomplished through laughter, or at least through a melancholic smile emanating not from a death that occurred decades ago, as was the case with Podchlebnik, but from the void of imminent oblivion that was about to engulf the poet. To catch the bitterness of Szlengel's smile, one has to remember that he had been one of the most successful Polish lyricists of popular songs, supplying the vaudevilles and cabarets that flourished in Warsaw before the war. Besides song lyrics, Szlengel's other specialty was poetic satire, which he published exclusively in Polish. Szlengel's satirical and poetic talents served him well when, alongside many Jewish artists, he was forcefully imprisoned in the ghetto by the German occupation authorities. He was hired as a lyricist and stand-up comedian by the most famous cabaret of the ghetto, Café Sztuka, where many stars of the prewar Polish artistic elite performed. One of the most famous among those artists was Władysław Szpilman, the subject of Roman Polański's *The Pianist*. In his satirical monologues presented daily on the stage of Café Sztuka, Szlengel laughed at the misery of the dying ghetto. After the closure of the cabaret by the German authorities following a wave of mass deportations to Treblinka in the summer of 1942, Szlengel continued writing and reading his poems in private apartments, frantically assembling and ordering his manuscripts in view of their publication by the Polish underground on the Aryan side of the wall. He entitled his poetry collection *What I Read to the Dead*.

At the Confines of Death and Humanity

The titular dead were the poet's friends, neighbors, and fellow artists who were being washed away by the successive waves of deportations to the gas chambers of Treblinka. In a piece of prose that was visibly intended as the preface to the hastily assembled poetry collection, Szlengel used the metaphor of rising waters. The image of death by suffocation in a sinking submarine expresses his mounting certainty of death. Death is the pervasive, all-encompassing environment that engulfed Szlengel and sparked the subtly bitter laughter that resonates in the poem "The Little Station Treblinki." Death is the abyss in which Podchlebnik sank when he joined the corpses of his wife and children; it is the depth from which he later pulled himself up by escaping from the Chełmno camp.

The metaphor of drowning in the depths of death pervades Primo Levi's last collection of essays on the Holocaust, entitled *The Drowned and the Saved*. Levi draws a clear distinction between those who sank and those who managed to stay at the surface and swim to safety. Nonetheless, he is less interested in a clear-cut opposition than in the intermediary, murky waters between annihilation and salvation. He admits that he survived Auschwitz by navigating this middle sphere of the camp's existence. Thanks to his expertise in chemistry, he was lucky to work indoors and had access to a small amount of food. He avoided being sent to deadly labor in the fields or on factory floors that, combined with extenuating hunger, killed prisoners within weeks of their arrival at the camp. He never fathomed directly in his body and psyche the depth of the inhuman horror of the *Lager*. Had he plunged so low, had he been constantly exposed to the elements, bitten by the *Kapos*, shunned by "privileged" prisoners, he would have eventually died from exhaustion, hunger, and illness. He would have drowned and would never have apprehended the horrible reality and been able to describe it afterward. But to survive at the intermediary levels of the camp's complicated hierarchy was not without moral cost. To illustrate such risks, I need only invoke again the Chełmno death camp. Before being buried, the naked corpses of the gassed women and men were thoroughly searched for valuables that they may have hidden in their bodily cavities. This was done under the watchful eyes of the SS by men in civilian clothing, whom Podchlebnik called "the Ukrainians" in his testimonies. The latest historical research and investigative work done by the Polish Institute for Remembrance has demonstrated that the men used by the Germans for this gruesome work were Polish political prisoners arrested by the Nazis for plotting against the Reich and who were taken from Gestapo prisons especially for this task. They had more freedom in their movements around the village than the *Arbeitsjuden* who were used to bury and burn the corpses. They assisted the SS, and in one of the remaining photographs they are shown drinking beer with German guards. When the operations at the Chełmno camp were temporarily put on hold in 1943, they were sent back to prison, and from there to the Auschwitz and Mauthausen concentration camps.[13] As is stressed by many authors, to survive and bear witness implies a plunge into a moral gray zone that has haunted witnesses of the Holocaust such as Tadeusz Borowski and Primo Levi for many years. Both survivors committed suicide after the war.

The gray, liminal zone I am interested in is not moral but existential, even semantic. Instead of a murky transitory space, I prefer to think of it as a frontier, a subtly thin line. To understand Podchlebnik's smile and Szlengel's bitter humor, one must stand at the confines of humanness. This balancing at the edge is illustrated by the *Muselmann*, a familiar figure known from testimonies of the survivors and from historical studies. He is described as a living dead man, someone who is so diminished by hunger that he loses his basic instincts, including the will to survive. He is so severely incapacitated that he does not react to danger and has great difficulty communicating with his environment. Usually, *Muselmänner* were avoided by other prisoners and left to die. We have very few testimonies of people who, thanks to an exceptional stroke of luck and the help of their comrades, were able to pull themselves out of this state and later describe what they went through (see Agamben).

Hence the key question that for a long time has monopolized the attention of writers and philosophers reflecting on the Holocaust: How can you put into words the systemic annihilation of millions of human beings that has no possible analogy in human history? How can you give an account of death in a gas chamber? Phrased in logical and rhetorical terms, the question becomes an irreconcilable dilemma between witness and testimony: either you have entered the gas chamber with thousands of other victims and witnessed from the inside their demise, but you cannot testify to the experience because you are dead, or you are alive and able to provide a testimony but have not entered the gas chamber and are not a credible witness. Used nefariously by Holocaust deniers, this dilemma sparks reflection on the possibilities and limitations of human language. It may thus become an argument for the indefinite deferral of judgment and even lead to the victimization of those who claim justice before the tribunal of history. The discrepancy between witness and testimony may also result in the denial of the possibility of art after Auschwitz, or at least fiction, that would seek to represent the experience of the death camp. As famously put by Elie Wiesel, "a novel about Treblinka is either not a novel or not about Treblinka" (7).[14] Hence the ironic overtone of the title of Wiesel's lecture, "Holocaust as Literary Inspiration," in which he questions the possibility of a fictional representation of the death camps. For Wiesel, the Holocaust as an absolute negation precludes communication, including literary communication. Giorgio Agamben sees a similar irony in the titles of memoirs written immediately after the war: Robert Antelme's *The Human Race* (*L'espèce humaine*) and Primo Levi's *If This Is a Man* (*Se questo è un uomo*). The humanity of the prisoner in the concentration camp, the humanity of a member of a *Sonderkommando*, and the humanity of the *Muselmann* are questions recurring in testimonies of the survivors. Whether or not the *Muselmann* was still a human being is a question closely linked to the strong suspicion that the *Muselmann* was neither alive nor dead. Rather, the *Muselmann* was the incarnation of the confines of humanness, the existential edge between life and death, humanity and nonhumanity. It is so because death, in the human sense of the concept, was denied the victims of the camps. As Heidegger put it, all they were allowed was to be "pieces of inventory of a standing reserve for the fabrication of corpses" ("Danger" 53; see also Thomson).

This is a stark judgement not only because it comes from an author whose involvement with Nazism is well known but also because of the antihumanist ontology that underlies it. In Heidegger's perspective, the dead of the camps did not die; they only perished. Perishing consists in the shutting down of a person's physiological functions. Plants and animals perish. Humans can perish as well, as did the corpses mass-produced in the extermination camps. On the other hand, it is only being-in-the-world (*Dasein*) that is capable of death. *Dasein* is a being always "ahead of itself" characterized by an unfinished quality, a "lack of wholeness" (Heidegger, *Being and Time* 227; div. 2, ch. 1, sec. 46). It is "outstanding," in a sense similar to an outstanding debt. Projecting itself into the future, *Dasein* as being-ahead-of-itself is a being-toward-death. Death is not, however, a remote, future perspective but a possibility inscribed in the very being of *Dasein*, a way to be that *Dasein* adopts at the instant it appears in the world. As soon as it comes into life, *Dasein* is old enough to die. Conceived as the "ownmost" and "insuperable" possibility of *Dasein*, death is opposed to perishing. By dying, *Dasein* grasps its finitude and embraces it. The capacity of dying distinguishes *Dasein* from the human being. Indeed, the human being may not be capable of dying in the sense that humans may not reach the conscious experience that characterizes *Dasein*. "The human is not yet the mortal." Of course, humans can perish, become corpses, like millions of victims of the camps. But there is, according to Heidegger, a third possibility: one can neither perish (*verenden*) nor die (*sterben*) but meet one's demise (*Ableben*). The demise is the collapse of one's intelligible world and life projects. A person can see their demise approaching but not be able experience it when it arrives. For instance, a person can notice the first symptoms of Alzheimer's disease but cannot consciously experience this disease to the end because once it has developed, it prevents its victim from grasping the full extent of the catastrophe. The demise cannot be fully experienced and grasped a posteriori because, in itself, the demise is the end of a person's capacity to experience whatsoever. To embrace death consciously, a person has to die.

Hence, our fear of death is truly that and not the fear of our demise. According to Heidegger, it would not make sense to apprehend the intelligible world coming to an end if we were unable to experience this ending anyway. Contrary to such demise, death is truly what we should be afraid of. When dying, we lose our intelligible world and are still able to experience this loss. When dying, we project our nonexistence into the future; we consciously conceive of the end of a world in which we are no longer and in which we are no longer "ahead of ourselves."

Such *Angst*, the fear of a world in which we are no more, underlies Szlengel's poem. The addressee is literally the walking dead, traveling in a boxcar toward their demise. Treblinka is indeed a terminus station—it is the end of the road, the end of life. The station is not an "intelligible world." It is unlike any station the traveler is familiar with: there is no cloakroom, and no money can buy a return ticket since there is no cashier. Treblinka is also the end-of-life project: no one waits to greet the traveler. The few objects left—the publicity poster hanging on the wall, the three firs—have lost their original, habitual meanings and denote emptiness and silence. Seemingly, the poet graciously provides the reader with much-needed advice on how to get from Warsaw-Ost to this little-known destination. In fact,

Szlengel "reads to the dead." Both the poet and the reader are *Muselmänner* dwelling in the gray zone between life and death at the edge of their humanness. Not in the literal sense: despite all the hardship in the Warsaw ghetto, Szlengel, his friends, and colleagues for whom he frantically assembled his last poetic volume in late 1942 and early 1943 were not yet in the state of physical depravation that clinically characterized a *Muselmann* in a concentration camp. They had not yet perished. But they were undergoing the accelerated process of losing their intelligible world and the life projects that sustained their existence. They were at risk of meeting their demise without ever being able to die and consciously grasp the finitude of their life. It is the tension between life and death, between humanity and nonhumanity, artfully set up by the poetic fiction that allows the reader to embrace their end, to avoid demise, and to die in Heidegger's sense of the word. This tension subtly resonates with an eerie yet warm laughter. Like a delicate membrane about to burst but elastic enough to reverberate the vibrations of life, Szlengel's poem sounds the alarm and provides space for a still-breathing consciousness. The irony of a train ride that lasts six hours, the entire life one has still to live, and the double entendre between modern kitchen equipment and the technological advances in the mass production of corpses give the reader a short extension in their last journey. The tensely tragic smile illuminates the poet's travel advice for a moment, just for the time needed to read the short text of the poem. Yet, thanks to Szlengel's smile, what seems a moment in time becomes a timeless duration that allows the reader to die with human dignity.

The same is true for Podchlebnik's smile. Like the dead to whom Szlengel read his final poems, Podchlebnik was one of the living dead, a kind of *Muselmann*. As an *Arbeitsjude* destined for execution after having exhausted his physical strength digging mass graves and burying the corpses of gassed people, Podchlebnik was fed enough to keep him alive as long as he was useful. He was not left to perish, nor was he allowed to die when he asked to be shot, lying at the side of his wife and children. In the words of the SS guard who refused to execute him, Podchlebnik was ordered to be "strong," not strong enough to live but strong enough to function like "an automat, a robot," as noted in the transcript of the interview ("Claude Lanzmann *Shoah* Collection"). In Heidegger's words, Podchlebnik was allowed neither to perish nor to embrace consciously the finitude of his existence, but he was forced to undergo his demise. Death, which Heidegger sees as the utmost possibility of *Dasein* and which I consider as the privileged manifestation of human finitude, was denied to Podchlebnik. He had to pull himself out of this demise to be able to die and, possibly, to live. This process has been admirably portrayed in László Nemes's 2015 movie *Son of Saul*. The main character is a member of the *Sonderkommando* and, like Podchlebnik, is neither fully dead nor alive. He acts like an automaton while escorting people to the gas chamber and removing the bodies to be reduced to ashes. It is only when he stumbles upon a boy among the corpses who is still breathing and whose killing he later witnesses that he leaves his state of psychological and moral *Muselmann* and strives frantically to accomplish a goal that seems impossible given the circumstances: to provide a proper religious burial for this boy who may or may not be his son. The idea of organizing a Jewish funeral in the midst of the fabrication of hundreds of thousands of corpses may seem absurd. It reveals its profound meaning when we realize that it is the expression of humanity made possible by the reclaiming of the human meaning of death.

Such reclaiming is not a performance or representation but an intimate embracing of the presence of death in a person's life. It has been suggested that Podchlebnik's smile was the rigor mortis of a *Muselmann*, the grimacing mask of a cadaver that Podchlebnik had to wear in Chełmno in order to blend in with the surrounding deadly desolation of the camp. Thirty years later, prompted by Lanzmann, the old man would take up this facial expression again for the sake of faithfully representing the past (Koch, "Transformation" 157). This interpretation of Podchlebnik's smile is misguided because it implies a mimetic make-believe that Lanzmann deemed obscene. But, most importantly, the imitation of the grimace of death is impossible given the fact that a *Muselmann* does not have to pretend to be a walking dead person. Podchlebnik could not imitate a dead man either in the Chełmno death camp or in front of Lanzmann's camera because, as Lanzmann consistently makes us understand, Podchlebnik died in Chełmno. Or, as Heidegger helps us understand, Podchlebnik's death was a demise. In Lanzmann's movie he is not a survivor who acts out his past experience but a re-presentation of something that cannot humanly be experienced and that can hardly be expressed, not in the sense that he simulates it but in that he makes it present anew. The dialogue with the film director is not a scene of mimicry but a human encounter in the same respect that Szlengel's reading for the dead was one. In this encounter, Podchlebnik's face becomes the place of the Shoah because the demise is overtaken by a truly human, meaningful death. Such death shines in Podchlebnik's smile. Paradoxically, while not a reenactment, Podchlebnik's smile also shines from the screen of Lanzmann's movie. The film director provides a stage for "the place of the Shoah" where it can take the shape of a body present in front of our eyes, a voice that reverberates in our ears.

To laugh and smile at your own laughter, as Podchlebnik did when pressed by Lanzmann's questions and as Szlengel did when writing to the dead, is what people do when, consciously or not, they reclaim humanity out of a state of total demise. I suggest that what makes Podchlebnik's and Szlengel's laughter profoundly human is the limitedness of life that they have experienced at the edge of humanity. At the confines of humanness, they reclaimed death through courageous deeds and poetic words. Death is not an "utmost" possibility inscribed into solitary being thrown into existence. It is a value inherent in the natural, social, cultural, and political environment in which we live. Death affords us laughter like the stairs afford us climbing to the upper floor of a building, to use a classical example in environmental psychology (Gibson). Death is part of our existential environment—our aging bodies, natural catastrophes, the dangers of street traffic, the blind destruction of war, or systemically organized industrial extermination, as was the case for Podchlebnik and Szlengel. We may or may not consciously respond to this crucial aspect of our existential surroundings. We may, for instance, perish in our slumber, or we may slide into a state of organic, psychological, and moral demise. But we can embrace our finitude in an utmost human way—with a laugh.

In what follows, I attempt to catch the echoes of such laughter at the edge of humanness. First, at the frontiers of our animalistic self: In the company of an early modern physician and a twentieth-century neuropsychologist, I dive into the depths of the human organism and the archeological substrata of the neurology of affect. We will encounter there the laughter of animals and catch its echoes in our own human laughter. Second, we will interface with machines, those within us and those that resemble us and among which we dwell every day. Led by an early-twentieth-century philosopher of life and by twenty-first-century engineers in affective computing, we will study machines' laughter in the hope that it will reveal human automatisms and expose the simulations of humanoid automatons. Third, we will see humans laughing in the face of God. Confronted with divinity, humans laugh with hope, doubt, and apprehension, as did the biblical matriarchs and their literary descendants. Or, following modern antihumanists, they celebrated a God who died of laughter yet never existed in the first place. Finally, we will mingle with Socrates's disciples and with the adepts of a transhumanist sect. In such company, we will put human laughter to the test of mythical eternity and technological immortality.

All these cases are considered in the subsequent chapters. Their titles—Laughing Animals, Laughing (Human) Machines, Machining (Human) Laughter, Laughing Gods, and Laughing Men—indicate the different edges of humanness that I explore, frontiers that used to be guarded by laws and taboos, whose transgression was sanctioned or deemed impossible. Not anymore, and this is not because of moral decadence or loosening of norms. The barriers between what is human and what is not have not so much been violently bridged as they have quietly faded away or, for practical reasons, become obsolete. My intention is not to reconstruct old walls or erect new ones. Like many of my contemporaries, I would be embarrassed if asked to define what such fortification should circumscribe. Instead, I prefer a more modest enterprise. I will listen to the texts of my cultures, to voices of animals, machines, gods, and, indeed, humans, in the hope that the trembling sound of laughter that I detect will indicate the limits that we should approach with the utmost caution.

Chapter 2

Laughing Animals

From the bottomless inhumanity of the Shoah, Podchlebnik and Szlengel bring us the anguished smiles and painful laughter of the demised. This laughter is a warning set off when the limit between what is human and what is not has been crossed. Podchlebnik's face and the signboard bearing Treblinka's name are places of Shoah because it is there that what is human and what is not human meet. As razor thin as this demarcation has been in the life of the old man in Israel and in the history of a tiny village in postwar Poland, Lanzmann's cinematography and Szlengel's poetry retrace this limit. The movie and the poem become sound boxes where the eerie laughter at the brink of humanity can resonate. Thanks to cinema and literature, the *Muselmänner* are made present anew. They are allowed to touch their finitude and, by doing so, turn their demise into death—human death. In being artistically recognized their limitedness is filled with meaning.

Almost a century after the Shoah, we again ask what it means to be human. We are no longer sure. The moment we come up with an answer, it dissolves into doubt when we remind ourselves of what humans have done and continue doing to themselves and to their world. Our most basic convictions about humanity crumble under the waves of inhumanity, crashing on the shores of the imaginary island of our uniqueness, washing away the lines in the sand that we nervously trace and retrace in order to circumscribe what makes us who we think we are. Sometimes amidst the roaring, threatening sound of those waves, we hear laughter. Like the glow of a distant star reaching us millions of light-years after its extinction, this peculiar kind of laughter transmits something remote and archaic that originates in a place we cannot recognize as ours and in times when we did not yet exist. This uncanny laughter comes to us from before the life we would like to consider human. It resonates in situations that have called our humanness into question and in intellectual pursuits that dare to investigate the nonhuman side of our bodies and minds. It is this archaic laughter from before the time we were born and from before the time our animality evolved into humanity that I listen to in this chapter. By exploring our animal body, let us attune our ears to the primordial laughter springing from the origins of our lives as individuals and as a species.

Wiernik's Laughter

It is only because he was a skilled carpenter that Yankel Wiernik survived one year in Treblinka. As he eagerly admits, he built the gas chambers in which hundreds of thousands of people were killed. Through construction project after construction project, Wiernik was able to move between the living quarters of the German and Ukrainian guards, the barracks of the prisoners who were kept temporarily alive to perform the daily chores such as sorting the clothes of the victims and camouflaging the fences, and the death factory proper, where the gassing and burning of corpses took place. He wrote his testimony shortly after his escape during the prisoners' revolt of August 1943. It was immediately published in Warsaw by the Polish resistance. From there, it was smuggled to the West, where it served to corroborate the report about the Holocaust that Jan Karski, envoy of the Polish underground, had already provided to the Allied governments in November 1942.

Wiernik was not a philosopher. Yet his words, like Podchlebnik's smile, draw us closer to a realm that is beyond the capacity of the human mind to comprehend and verbalize. While writing his testimony a few months after his escape, Wiernik was suspended between life and death like a *Muselmann*, demised yet unable to die. Unlike a *Muselmann*, however, he was driven by a strong will to proclaim to the world the death of his people and the infamy of "Western culture," as he stated in the short foreword to his text. The ironic quotation marks circumscribe the object of his blame, yet his rancor did not put him at a comforting distance from the horrors he had lived through. This unassuming man confessed that he was constantly haunted by visions of piles of corpses calling for his pity and help. He was aware that his experience was engraved on his face, which was unlike any human face. Treblinka had placed him at the margins of humanity, and only birds came to him with confidence and joy. He wondered if he would ever be able to laugh again.¹

This longing after common, lighthearted laughter may seem naively banal, even kitsch. Yet it translates the horror of a human being who has witnessed and partaken of something that is beyond words. Wiernik—this heroically courageous man who co-organized the clandestine Treblinka network that planned the prisoners' revolt, who made his way back to Warsaw and survived in hiding, and who would soon thereafter, at the age of fifty-six, take up arms during the August 1944 Warsaw uprising that completed the ruination of the city—began the account of his ordeal with fear. He was afraid that he would never be able to live among humans and laugh in communion with them after what he went through. His fear not only reveals the trauma of an individual but also points to the alarming possibility that human life is nothing but a thin surface covering abysmal depths of nonhumanity. If Wiernik felt unable to join fellow human beings in the mirthful celebration of companionship, it was because he felt that such frank joy might reverberate with another kind of laughter—an utterly inhuman kind.

Wiernik heard the inhuman laughter in Treblinka. First, there was the cruel laughter of the executioners who mocked their victims while slaughtering them. Wiernik was horror-struck at the memory of the diabolical merriment of the SS, who laughed and made toasts when, after much trial and error, they mastered the technique of efficiently burning thousands of corpses on gigantic roasting racks made of the rails of train tracks. He also described, as did other survivors of Treblinka, the degrading jokes with which the Germans poked fun at their tortured prisoners. There was the shitmaster (*Scheissmeister*), whom the SS dressed as a synagogue cantor equipped with a large alarm clock on a string around his neck. In this grotesque attire, he was charged with making sure that his fellow inmates did not stay in the latrines longer than three minutes. Cruelly mistreated, the man wept with sorrow, prompting his abusers to laugh at his suffering.

Yet the sadistic jeering of the Nazis was not the only laughter that could be heard in Treblinka. On two occasions in Wiernik's text, his indignation turns into surprise tainted with malaise: "By and large, our tormentors had a lot of fun with the rest of the inmates, dressing them up as clowns and assigning functions which made even us, heart sore as we were, laugh as well" (*Year* 78).²

How could the victims laugh in communion with their executioners, even for a moment? Was it because some prisoners, granted the tiny privileges of being given a technical task requiring their specialized skills, an additional bowl of soup, or a day longer to live, were ranked above others in the hierarchy of survival and thus enjoyed a sense of superiority? Was Wiernik's and his companions' reluctant and shameful laughter at the misery of fellow inmates the reflection of the pitiless nature of humanity? That would probably be the interpretation of those who, like Hobbes, think that laughter "is nothing else but a sudden glory arising from sudden conception of some eminency in ourselves, by comparison with the infirmities of others" (13; ch. 9). Yet the compelling force and the painful character of the prisoners' laughter leads in a direction other than the illusion of superiority shared by inmates with the masters who decided on their life and death. Instead of raising Wiernik closer to the overman, his laughter drew him down to the realm preceding human life.

In a different fragment, Wiernik recalled his work in the so-called Camp 2, the gas-chamber area of Treblinka, where, according to his assessment, between ten and twelve thousand people were gassed every day. Wiernik remembered seeing many of his friends from Warsaw among the phantomlike silhouettes of prisoners disposing of the dead, who covered the ground. Amid shouts and constant beatings, these men waited for their turn to be killed and replaced by fresh arrivals forced to serve the machinery of death. Wiernik confessed that he looked at his former acquaintances, who came to Camp 2 to work and die in quick rotation, as if they were already dead bodies. While they were still running under the blows, he was calmly assessing their weight, counting in his mind how many men would be needed to carry their corpses into the pit and how many blows it would take to kill them. He ended this recollection with the following thought: "It was terrible but, nonetheless, true. Would you believe it that a human being, living under such conditions could, at the time, smile and jest? One can get used to anything" (Wiernik, *Year* 59).[3]

Wiernik's perplexity at his own laughter in Treblinka points to the question that is hotly debated in Holocaust scholarship: How can anyone laugh amid ultimate human misery and degradation? This "Holocaust laughter" challenges not only our good taste but the limits of artistic representation itself. Elie Wiesel's pronouncement about the incompatibility of Treblinka and literature notwithstanding, the Holocaust resulted in an important body of literary fiction, and it was even the source of countless jokes that circulated in Jewish communities from 1941 to 1943, the very time when the horrible atrocities were taking place. Fortunately, many of these jokes were collected by Oneg Shabbat, a clandestine network of Jewish intellectuals; preserved for posterity in the famous Ringelblum Archive; and at least partially recovered from beneath the ruins of the Warsaw ghetto after the war.[4] More controversial is the dark humor flourishing, so to speak, on the ashes of the Holocaust victims and resulting in comic productions such as musicals (Mel Brooks's *The Producers*, played on Broadway in 2001), movies (Roberto Benigni's 1997 *Life Is Beautiful*), and stand-up monologues. These productions are the focus of Ferne Pearlstein's 2016 documentary *The Last Laugh*, which is devoted to the question of who, under what circumstances and despite which taboos, has the moral and artistic right to laugh at the most absolute evil of human history.

Yet Wiernik's puzzlement is not an academic discussion about the ethics of artistic representation. While lacking philosophical acumen and historical distance, Wiernik marveled over the troubling involuntary reaction of his body. What compelled him to laugh in the presence of the death of fellow humans and in the certainty that sooner or later he would also be obliterated? The answer he provides to this question—"one can get used to anything"—does not alleviate his uneasiness. But is his instinctive, painful, and self-ashamed laughter still human?

Compelled by Laughter and Music

What does Wiernik's laughter in Treblinka tell us about the life that is deemed to be human? To help us find an answer to this question, let us turn our attention to music, which, very much like laughter, conjoins the movement of the body and the movement of the mind, and whose close association with laughter in the camps is insistently attested to by Wiernik and corroborated by other survivors. Wiernik remembered the case of Artur Gold, who arrived in Treblinka in early 1943. Gold was a celebrated composer and jazz bandleader who was the star of the most upscale dancing clubs of prewar Warsaw and whose records topped the Polish musical charts before the war. Thanks to his fame, upon his arrival in the camp he was taken out of the trainload of people heading for the gas chamber and tasked by the Nazis with providing musical accompaniment to their ongoing slaughter. Soon a violin trio was formed under his direction. Dressed like clowns in loud blue jackets and giant bow ties, the maestros performed popular prewar tunes during the evening roll call after the daily lashings were administered to the inmates who had been selected for punishment. All the accounts are unanimous: the prisoners hated the music forced upon them by their executioners. Not only were they constrained to take in a concert after being crushed by hours of murderous physical work, they were also required to sing along to popular tunes, forefronting memories of their lives from before the war in this place of desolation.[5] The concerts by Gold's trio were part of an elaborate musical program enforced by the SS in spring 1943, when the rhythm of train arrivals with people to be killed had slowed. In this spare time, the Nazis organized a musical show of choral music and dances in the death camp, a project that required the preparation of costumes and systematic practice, to which they forced scores of prisoners. One of the pieces to be performed was Boccherini's *Minuet* for strings, which—supreme irony—the musicians rehearsed in the hallway of the gas chamber. However, these musical preparations were for naught because the August 1943 revolt and the subsequent killings took the lives of most of the artists, including that of Artur Gold.

The musical concerts of Treblinka were far from isolated incidents. Music was an integral part of the psychological and physical torture imposed upon the dying inmates in the camps. While marching in columns to work, prisoners in Treblinka were forced to intone Jewish songs. In his memoir from Auschwitz, *If This Is a Man*, Primo Levi calls a similar practice the "dance of dead men." He was convinced that these musical routines were aimed at annihilating the inmates as human beings before killing them slowly through work and starvation. Years after coming back from deportation, he confessed to still shivering with horror at the sound of the innocent, light-hearted songs that were played during those "monstrous rites." The infernal music transformed thousands of prisoners dying of hunger and exhaustion into an obedient machine, marching in unison to their death: "every beat becomes a step, a reflexive contraction of exhausted muscles" (Levi, *If This* 48). Much like laughter, musical rhythm forces the body into an involuntary action. Like laughter, music—and especially the cheerful songs favored by the Nazis for the artistic enhancement of their mass killings—connotes a human joy, which grotesquely clashed with the inhumanity of the camps.

What is so compelling in laughter and music that they have the power to deprive humans of reason and free will? The question is not simply about psychological conditioning, an acquired somatic reaction triggered by a habitual stimulus under stressful conditions. The problem pertains to an irresistible force that deprives humans of their humanity. Pascal Quignard, a French contemporary writer and great amateur of baroque music, explored this question in a collection of mini-treatises, *The Music Lesson* (*La leçon de musique*, 1987), and a subsequent novel, *All the World's Mornings* (*Tous les matins du monde*, 1991). Both books are devoted to the process of learning music exemplified by the apprenticeship of the seventeenth-century viola da gamba virtuoso Marin Marais. In the novel, Marais tries to steal the secret of music from his master, Monsieur de Sainte-Colombe. However, lured by the splendor of Louis XIV's court, the career-driven pupil fails to understand that the ineffable nature of musical art is rooted in a journey to the sounds beyond and, more precisely, *before* the life that is properly human.

Both Marais and Saint-Colombe are historical figures, but Quignard fictionalizes their lives by turning his mini-essays into philosophical short stories and his novel into a philosophical allegory. In this literary rewriting of the French baroque, Quignard portrays the quest for the true nature of music as a return to the depths of biological existence. Sainte-Colombe is a reclusive man who mourns the loss of his wife. He spends his life playing his sorrowful *Regrets* in a small cabin built of blackberry wood. Bent over the box of his instrument (to which he added an extra lower string) or diving into the murky waters of the river that flows nearby, Sainte-Colombe symbolizes a man yearning to plunge into the deep darkness of the maternal womb. The old master longs after the world of sounds before life. Marais shares this yearning, awoken the moment sexual maturation broke his voice and prevented him from singing at mass in the royal choir. For this ambitious adolescent, playing the viola da gamba would be a way of recovering the primordial voice that was lost when biological maturation enabled his body to produce life and, at the same time, brought him closer to the end of life through aging and death. This is why Marais seeks the company of Sainte-Colombe: to learn how to transform the musical notes played on his viola into the primordial screams of a human, suffering body. But to recover the archaic sounds, he will have to forgo life, and particularly the life at the royal court that he aspires to. Marais is unable to make such a descent into the primordial abyss before human life, and that is why he is chased away by the old viola da gamba master. Despite this rejection and his success as entertainer of the king, Marais leaves the moribund artificiality of Versailles every night and comes to listen in secret to the sounds of Sainte-Colombe's viola da gamba, his ear pressed against the wall of the blackberry cabin. This gesture, like the whole of Quignard's novel, is highly symbolic. The French word *mûrier* (blackberry) is phonetically and etymologically associated with *mûr* (mature). Thus, for Quignard, Sainte-Colombe's cabin symbolizes a reclusive space where music replays the hidden prenatal maturing of a fetus in a woman's womb. Marais, glued to the wall of the cabin and listening avidly to the deep sounds of Sainte-Colombe's viola, symbolizes human attempts to journey away from the hollow melodies of the world, back to the primeval rhythms of life before a properly human life.

It is, nonetheless, important to realize that this voyage is not a soothing return to motherly embraces but a step into what lies beyond—or before—the human capacity to conceptualize, before the possibility to name, grasp, and control reality. It is a trip not only into the unknown but also into the unnamable. The prenatal rhythms are in fact deadly tremors. This is why Quignard entitled his third book on music *The Hatred of Music* (*La haine de la musique*, 1996). Quignard's novel metaphorically represents the voyage into the realm before life. The writer tries to emulate Sainte-Colombe's tunes, which transported the listener into the world of sounds preceding any music. With *The Hatred of Music*, Quignard relinquishes allegorical fiction, which is his literary analogue of the old master's musical art. This time, Quignard speaks in his own name, constructing an anthropology of prehumanity out of scattered etymologies of words, historical anecdotes, prehistoric rupestrian paintings, and pieces of canonic as well as long-forgotten texts. His declared aim is to shed light on the secret link between music and terror. This means that he must revive the "acoustic suffering" (*la souffrance sonore*) that normally is muted under the layers of language. To voice it out, we must reopen a scar from before our childhood, revisit our ancestors in the world inhabited by those who are not yet born, and listen to the call of the animals that speak through the mouths of the shaman. In other words, we must dive into the past before our individual existence and before human history in pursuit of a music that, paradoxically, is a "piece of semantic sounding deprived of any meaning."[6]

Stepping outside of life is a perilous journey. It is reminiscent of Ulysses sailing among the rocks of the Sirens, tied to the mast of his ship in order not to follow their song to his death. Human singing is language, but the songs of the Sirens are a call that precedes language. They are seductively beautiful yet deadly, like the sound of the decoy used by the hunters to lure wild animals into their snares. Such primordial, irresistible music is both fascinating and terrifying, which is why Ulysses had to be tied to the mast like a fetus is tied to life by the umbilical cord. The rhythm of this primal music is a deadly tremor like the reverberating string of a cithara or the vibrating cord of a bow, the same instrument that Ulysses used when, upon his return to Ithaca, he struck one by one the suitors who had come to steal his wife. They died paralyzed by fear, like animals ensnared in hunters' traps by the sound of decoys.

So did the prisoners of the camps, trapped in the rhythm of joyful songs while marching to their deaths. Following Primo Levi and the testimonies of other survivors, Quignard accuses music of being the only art that has actively collaborated in the extermination of Jews. Music may indeed be hated because it attracts human souls and forces human bodies to obey. Even with eyes closed, it is impossible not to hear and surrender to music's contagious power, much as was the case with laughter and the terror that the ancients called panic. Quignard speaks thus of a "panic smile." Like the smile of the mother that her child unwillingly mimics by contracting their lips in a similar grimace, music is irresistible. Calling us from before our human lives, it is a vibration that matches the heartbeat and the rhythm of respiration, similarly terrifying, similarly involuntary.

In his memoir about Treblinka, Samuel Willenberg recalls that one night the prisoners of his barrack were awakened by the piercing sound of insane laughter: an inmate had gone mad. He intermittently stopped laughing to shout "mentsh," Yiddish for "man." Then the laughter resumed. "I had the feeling that I would be the next to perform this, that I would scream until my skull burst open and sent my brain spilling from it together with my torn, aching nerves. I buried my head in a blanket and plugged fingers into my ears to block out that deranged laughter" (139). Willenberg desperately fought through the night, trying not to be overtaken by the insane panic-laughter of his fellow prisoner, trying not to listen to the Sirens' call of an existence free of the inhumanity that was the death camp. With all the remaining strength of his body, he resisted the overwhelming urge to sink into death. The next day, the prisoner who had gone mad was executed.

Humanist Laughter

The laughter that resonated in the death camps challenges our sense of humanity and resists a rational explanation because it conveys ultimate violence and horror. This troubling kind of laughter has a long history, stretching back to classical and early modern natural science. It was the object of scrutiny by Renaissance humanists who knew that there was a distressful kind of laughter that was involuntary and devoid of joy. They wondered whether joyless laughter could be called laughter when it was different from the healthy merriment prompted by ridiculous things. And if laughing was specifically human, a *proprium hominis*, as they were firmly convinced it was, was forced laughter human as well? Such were the questions asked by the French Renaissance physician Laurent Joubert in his 1576 treatise on laughter. Joubert was a naturalist, but, like any humanist, he was also a reader of Greek literature and Roman oratory. Drawing from Quintilian, Joubert noted that laughter was prompted not merely by witty words or funny actions but also by foolish behavior full of anger that could be frankly frightening. Such laughter was dangerous because it had an imperious force of its own that convulsed bodies and was hard to resist (Quintilian 6.3.7–8).

Joubert wrote at a turning point in the history of medical research on the physiology and pathology of laughter. He provides a logical but, nonetheless, highly personal conclusion to a debate going back to classical antiquity, before Descartes struck the final blow to the humanistic way of thinking by reducing laughter to a mechanical manifestation of the passions of the soul. Joubert's book is more than an interesting step in the development of early modern natural science. It also contains a political message addressed to the people in power who were responsible for France amid bloody civil wars that threatened the existence of the body politic. The treatise is dedicated to Marguerite de Valois, a princess of French royal blood and queen of Navarre by marriage. This was fitting, claimed Joubert, since the princess adorned the entire realm with her beauty in the same way that the human face was the most delightful part of the body. Joubert wanted to illuminate this face, whose charm was renowned throughout Christendom, with his "laughter," as he humbly referred to his treatise.

If Marguerite was the face of France, her brother, King Henri III, was the head of the nation; her mother, Catherine de Medici, who steered the kingdom through violent political storms, was the brain of France; and her youngest brother, François d'Alençon, was the hand, ready to fend off the enemies of the state. This initial metaphor may seem nothing more than a courtly compliment. However, it constituted a political statement and a philosophical manifesto put forth by the Renaissance humanist. His treatise on laughter is a plea for peace from an engaged citizen who put a smile on what was a desperate situation of a kingdom torn by civil wars. By allocating different body parts to different royalties, Joubert expressed his wish for the harmonious functioning of the organism of the French reigning family, which, in reality, was plagued by distrust and animosity. On the other hand, the initial political metaphor has a more fundamentally philosophical meaning as well. By mentioning laughter alongside the rationality of the human soul and the dexterity of the human hand, Joubert considered it as one of the specific features of humanity. Laughter was one of the *propria hominis*, an attribute defining what was distinctly human. For a Renaissance humanist such as Joubert, laughter made humans human in the same way that human rationality and the human capacity to manipulate tools did, which were marvelous, God-given skills that allowed people to write books and converse with the dead authors of antiquity. In other words, by studying the physiology and pathology of laughter, Joubert intended to understand what it meant to be human.

For Renaissance humanists, laughter lent itself perfectly to such exploration because, in conformity with Greek natural science, they firmly believed that humans are the only animals that laugh.[7] Understanding laughter should, therefore, give them insight into the nature of humanity, so they thought. Being a scientist of his times, Joubert tries to grasp the physical nature of laughter by distinguishing between the genus and the species, the essence and the accidents of the phenomenon he wants to explain. Using this methodology, he defines laughter as a movement of the body that differs from other bodily agitations by its material cause, or, in other words, the object provoking it. In conformity with the Aristotelian and Ciceronian traditions, Joubert describes laughter as occurring in response to something ugly, beyond the order of nature, and yet at the same time unworthy of pity.[8] Laughter also has a specific efficient cause, according to Joubert, consisting of the expansion of the subtle vapors of the blood that medicine of the time called spirits, or humors. The diffusion of spirits intermittently moves the heart, diaphragm, and chest (instrumental cause), as well as the mouth. This produces a broken, faltering sound (formal cause). The movement of the heart alternates expansion and contraction, but more the former than the latter because the passion that laughter expresses (final cause) is more joy than sadness (Joubert, *Treatise* 2.1).

Joubert, therefore, did not consider laughter univocally joyful. Its mixed nature was a consequence of its physiology. Descartes continued this train of thought while discussing laughter among the bodily manifestations of the passions of the soul. However, instead of the sadness invoked by Joubert, Descartes attributed laughter to a mixture of joy and hatred. Such an association of contrary affects allowed early modern physiologists to explain the intermittent nature of the movement that characterizes laughter. Moreover, sadness and hatred generate the contraction necessary to counter the expansion and dispersion of the vital spirits occasioned by joy. If there were no contrary emotions, an overwhelming joy would scatter all the humors that are needed for an organism to remain alive. A small but necessary dose of sadness prevents such dissipation and allows the heart to retain its vital spirits. The mixture of joy and sadness, the interplay between dissipation and contraction, are manifested in the spasmodic movement of muscles and the broken, intermittent sounds that are characteristic of laughter.

Such speculations locate the physiological source of laughter in the heart and its anatomical vicinity. It was while describing the diaphragm that Aristotle mentioned the exclusive association between laughter and humanity. Almost a century after Joubert, Descartes was still rationalizing the claim of human exclusivity for laughter by pointing to the exceptionally large diaphragm that distinguishes humans from other animals. This may seem like a historical curiosity, but, in fact, it indicates the puzzlement of early modern natural philosophers over the relation between the movement of the human body and the dynamic of the human soul. To place the anatomical roots of laughter in the heart, and not in the liver or brain, complicated the relation of this bodily movement to rationality and volition. Laughter was the focus of Renaissance humanists' mind-body problem.

In order to articulate the corporeal and psychological dynamics of laughter, Joubert, like many of his predecessors, related it to the faculties of the soul. These were the functionalities of human organisms ranging from vital tasks such as eating and reproduction to higher capabilities such as reasoning and intentionality. Since its Aristotelian beginnings, the study of laughter had been firmly grounded in human anatomy. This is why the philosophical psychology of laughter set aside the intellect, which, it was believed, was not attached to a specific organ and could thus subsist after the death of the human body. Laughter should not be considered equal to the highest attributes of the eternal intellective soul. The intellective soul, like laughter, is a feature of humanity. But laughter does not reach the spiritual level of this prerogative of human immortal being because laughter's bodily nature occasionally pulls it out of the control of human will. Nor does laughter partake in the lowest vegetative soul, which is limited to the basic vital functions such as reproduction and digestion, which are common to all living organisms. Rather, like other emotional appetites, laughter is situated in the sensitive soul, the midpoint of the hierarchy of faculties. Locating the mechanism of laughter with precision, especially in regard to volition, was crucial for Joubert's ambition to circumscribe the kind of laughter that is fully human.

This minute task required diving into the intricacies of the sensitive soul consisting of faculties of motion and faculties of perception. Among the faculties of motion, Joubert detected appetites that generated emotions, while the faculties of perception included external senses, such as vision, hearing, touch, and smell, as well as internal senses, such as memory, cogitation, and the imagination. To pinpoint the kind of laughter that Joubert considered to be properly human, he needed to make sure that his readers understood the perceptual paths that conveyed the image of the laughable object to the heart. Some of those perceptual avenues were outside the human body and therefore belonged to the external senses; some were inside, among the internal senses.

While reflecting on the internal senses, Joubert stumbled on the problem of volition. Indeed, as Galen had already noticed, laughter is one of the "problematical movements" alongside coughing and sneezing (10.1–5, 165). People often spontaneously burst into laughter even if they are trying to resist. Yet, unruly as it is, laughter is a bodily movement that does not entirely escape human control. How was Joubert to reconcile the irresistible emotive power of laughter and attempts at controlling it? The solution that he provided for this traditional question betrays the difficulties of using laughter as a conceptual tool aimed at defining humanity.

First, let us explore the cognitive side of laughter as Joubert understood it. As stated earlier, its material cause is the perception of an ugly object unworthy of pity. The brain is the central hub for all sensorial perceptions and, as such, should have a part in generating laughter. Yet Joubert repeatedly insisted that the mixture of emotions associated with laughter should be ascribed to the heart and not the brain. To preserve the instantaneous spontaneity of laughter, Joubert invented an ingenious mechanism that prevented perception from being confused with consciousness and thus ensured that laughter remained entirely in the purview of the sensitive soul without infringing on the intellective, eternal soul specific to human rationality. He insisted that the "matter of the passions" passes promptly through the brain "as through conduits" and instantly penetrates the heart, sparking, without further delay, the movements of emotion (37). Reduced to the role of a transmitter of perception, the brain does not have the time to process emotional turmoil. It can do it only after the fact, weighing the value of the affects that rage in the heart. If the brain finds such emotions ethically justifiable, it consents to them; if not, it advises the heart to stop the commotion.

Second, let us consider the volitional side of laughter, to which the cognitive aspects were closely tied for Joubert. By rushing the image of a risible object through the brain so quickly that it steers the emotions before being fully comprehended, Joubert accounted for the paradox of a perception that takes place below the threshold of consciousness. This, in turn, led him to tackle the issue of an emotional commotion that can neither be entirely mastered nor fully escape human control. The traditional solutions to this problem go back to Aristotle's reflections on the movements of animals. Besides the movements that are subject to human will, Aristotle distinguished those that are involuntary from those that he labeled nonvoluntary. The involuntary movements, such as the male erection or the acceleration of a heartbeat, are prompted by a stimulus, yet without express command of thought. Other movements, such as respiration or waking up and falling asleep, are nonvoluntary in the sense that they are not triggered by any factor, even by imagination or desire (Aristotle, *On the Parts of Animals* 703b; see also Morel). The medical tradition used this conceptual grid to classify laughter as an involuntary movement generated directly by the dilatation of the heart and the dissipation of sanguine vapors, which, in turn, are prompted by the sight of a ridiculous object (Celsius 215–19). However, this elegant solution did not satisfy Joubert. Following Galen, he marveled at the fact that ridiculously futile things suddenly stirred up a great agitation of muscles. The commotion of laughter obeys reason and will even less than emotions, bringing a laughing person to the brink of suffocation (Joubert, *Treatise*, bk. 2, preface, p. 71; bk. 3, ch. 11, pp. 120–21).

To grasp the paradoxical mixture of free will and necessity, Joubert used the term *voluntary constraint* (*volontaire contrainte*). Laughter is a voluntary movement in the same way respiration is voluntary, according to Galen. Humans do not breathe or laugh entirely at will in the same way that they intentionally move an arm or leg, yet they can voluntarily accelerate or slow down their respiration. As was believed, humans can even force themselves not to inhale air at all, as demonstrated by the classical example of the slave Barbarus, who committed suicide by willingly holding his breath. The same goes for laughter, which, although not in the purview of will and reason, does not remain immune to the power of the higher faculties of the intellective soul either. Human will can stop inappropriate laughter by commanding imperatively like an authoritative master or more gently through political persuasion. It is this second solution that Joubert favored. Once carried away by the wave of emotions, the heart can prove very difficult to restrain. It acts like a large horse carrying will and reason here and there. Like a small child on the back of a horse, the higher faculties do not have the necessary strength to rein in the wild animal of passions. Sometimes, however, will and reason succeed in persuading the unruly heart to obey. This negotiated or, as Joubert called it, "political" solution recalls the feeble rider who gradually and gently turns their mount back onto the path.

Joubert tried to encapsulate a precarious tension between the uncontrollable drive of the passions and the prudent, gradual pressure of the will in his concept of voluntary constraint. Laughter, like any emotion, forces the body to move, yet this necessity may—or may not—be mitigated by the will. The volitional aspect of laughter is as paradoxical and self-contradictory as its cognitive aspect, torn between perception so swift that it cannot trigger awareness and the full consciousness of the mind, which, nonetheless, can only come after the fact. To what extent did Joubert's speculation on the natural philosophy of laughter reflect his political concerns? Consciousness can fully comprehend the thunder of laughter only when the passionate tempest already rages in the sensitive soul. Should this physiological analysis be understood as a medical allegory of the tremors of civil conflict threatening the integrity of the French body politic? The will can either forcefully master unruly laughter or, like a feeble child carried away by a wild stallion, gradually bring it to submission through "political" persuasion. Joubert clearly favored the latter solution, possibly expressing his preference for political negotiations over an attempt by the monarchy to repeat the St. Bartholomew's Day massacre of 1572 and to impose peace by killing its political adversaries.

Such political interpretation of the role that internal senses play in the physiology of laughter should not be overstated. But nor should it be dismissed, especially in light of the deep impact of the wars of religion on the collective consciousness of Joubert's contemporaries. The display of tyrannical cruelty and seditious violence not only cast a dark shadow over the French monarchy but compromised the cultural project of Renaissance humanism. What was put in doubt was the humanists' trust in the intellectual and ethical perfectibility of human beings and their capacity to achieve humanity, conceived not as a given but as a goal of a virtuous life devoted to the study of what is truly human. Through his speculations on the physiology of laughter, Joubert proved how difficult it is to understand what it is to be human. To grasp what was properly human laughter mattered not only for medicine but also for the French monarchy. A healthy laughter enlivens the human body and the body politic. Yet the continuous health of the physiological microcosm and the political macrocosm was constantly threatened by unruly outbursts of emotion that erupted like a sudden salvo of involuntary laughter, similar to a male erection and an accelerated heartbeat. Joubert acknowledged the constraints that pushed individual and collective organisms into disruptive behavior, but he preferred to believe that these disturbances could be mastered or, even better, tamed by the powers of eloquence. This is why he acknowledged the unruliness of laughter yet strove to see human consciousness and will mitigate emotionality. Joubert promoted voluntary constraint in individual and collective life: he wanted the higher faculties of the intellective soul to recognize and pacify the agitation of the internal senses of the sensitive soul. Unfortunately, the existence of a deadly laughter, like the destruction of France by civil wars, made bodily and political harmony difficult to achieve.

Deadly Laughter

Confirming laughter's role of *proprium hominis* was fundamental for Joubert to ensure the health of the individual patient and the well-being of the political community. This task hinged on the properly recognized role of volition. As difficult as it was, defining laughter as a marker of humanity became more complicated when Joubert turned his attention to the external senses. There he discovered a laughter-like phenomenon that threatened not only individual and social harmony but also human life. What was even more troubling for Joubert was that this explosive laughter manifested itself in forms that were easily confused with normal human laughter. To clearly distinguish laughter that is proper to humans from the deadly pseudo-laughter that can kill them thus became Joubert's fundamental task.

At the end of the first book of his treatise, Joubert devoted an entire chapter to the question of whether a person can die from laughing (*Treatise* 1.27). Such death must be distinguished from death occasioned by excessive joy. Anatomically speaking, joyfulness is, for Joubert, an expansion of the heart and a scattering of the vital spirits. Laughter as a physiological mechanism prevents overwhelming joy from becoming deadly. Thanks to a small amount of sadness intermingled with joy, laughter provides the much-needed intermittent contractions of the heart that prevent the vital spirits from dissipating completely. Nonetheless, as rare as it is, death from laughter is also possible. Unrestrained laughter alters respiration to the point that it is unable to keep up with the rapid beating of the heart, causing death by suffocation. "Yet, we rarely see people die from much laughing unless it is due to tickling" (Joubert, *Treatise*, bk. 1, ch. 27, p. 61)—and here comes the important distinction by which Joubert salvaged the humanist search for the essence of what is human: laughing from tickling is not true laughing.

For ancient natural philosophy, tickling was at least as problematic as laughter. While reflecting on the irresistible nature of laughter, Galen admitted with disarming sincerity that "it is entirely unclear why the contact of the hand should produce an effect similar to what happens when we see or hear something ridiculous" (10.1–5, 165). Joubert invoked Galen's puzzlement but insisted that hesitation was not in order: true laughter is produced without the sense of touch (*Treatise* 1.9.36).[9] Why did Joubert exclude touch from the list of external senses that generate laughter? The rejection of touch was crucial because it allowed him to differentiate laughter proper from a bodily agitation that Joubert called illegitimate laughter (*ris batard*). Illegitimate laughter was not true laughter, and tickling was the key to discriminating between these two misleadingly similar phenomena. Illegitimate laughter got nothing but its name from genuine laughter. Joubert devoted almost the entire book two of his treatise to establishing and justifying the distinction between genuine laughter and illegitimate laughter.

What is illegitimate laughter? It is a grimace that externally resembles authentic laughter but neither stems from the perception of a ridiculous object nor relies on the mixture of joy and sadness that prompts the agitation of the heart and the movement of vital humors. Illegitimate laughter is nothing but an external image of laughter, like a painting that represents—and counterfeits—a human figure. It is illegitimate because it is outside the normal order of nature. It consists of a distortion of the mouth that leaves the teeth bare, much like an angry, threatening dog. Hence, illegitimate laughter is also called cynic spasm and canine laughter.

The umbrella concept of illegitimate laughter was Joubert's invention. It pertains to any facial and vocal expression that externally mimics laughter but does not involve anything ridiculous that could be laughed at. Instead of being prompted by something "ugly but not worthy of pity," illegitimate laughter is mechanically induced or caused by the consumption of certain substances, such as excessive quantities of saffron. But the most often-cited drug that generates pathological, unhealthy laughter is an herb resembling wild celery or parsley that ancient geographers and herbalists called sardonia, after the Mediterranean island where it grew. The consumption of this plant convulses the muscles of the mouth. Most importantly, eating sardonia is fatal. People who ate this poison literally died laughing. Since Greek antiquity, this deadly laughter had been called sardonic laughter.

For Joubert, sardonic laughter was a subcategory of illegitimate laughter. Not so for Erasmus, who in his *Adages*, the immensely popular anthology of over four thousand ancient proverbs and sayings, expanded sardonic laughter to include any kind of evil laughter linked to death. Adage 2401, devoted to sardonic laughter, lists a wealth of anecdotes and quotations from Greek and Latin sources referring to this laughter, which is false in the sense that it has nothing to do with merriment, and which is always deadly either for the person who laughs or for those who are laughed at. Erasmus begins Adage 2401 with the unavoidable reference to the poisonous herb sardonia and to canine laughter. He rehearses, thus, the similarity of the agonal rictus that sardonia produced and the gaping maw of an angry dog ready to bite. But quickly his quotations depart from cases that would be of interest to a natural philosopher to encompass the possible connection between laughter and death. Still referring to Sardinia, Erasmus reminds his readers of the ancient custom of Sardinians to sacrifice their elderly parents to Saturn by beating them and then throwing them from a cliff. The old relatives laughed while dying either because it was considered inappropriate to lament or because they preferred to die rather than to live with their offspring who had lost filial respect for them. Other anecdotes quoted by Erasmus pertain to bronze statues associated with laughter and death. Such was the figure of Saturn in Cartagena. An old custom required that, on solemn occasions, an infant be sacrificed to the god by placing them on the extended arms of the statue and lighting a fire that burned them to death. The child's face, distorted by suffering, resembled a face animated by laughter. Erasmus's Saturnian adage ends with a long list of literary quotations, starting with the indispensable fragment of the twentieth chant of the *Odyssey*, which depicts Ulysses disguised as a beggar, witnessing the banquet of suitors who had come to feast at the expense of his estate and claim the hand of his wife, Penelope. One of them attacks Ulysses by throwing an ox's hoof at him. The Greek hero dodges the blow, and "in his heart he smiles a quite sardonic smile" (Homer, bk. 20, lines 300–303). His heart harbored no joy but only anger and sorrow, explains Erasmus, following ancient commentators of the epos. No doubt he had already meditated about his vengeance. Soon he would kill all the parasitic suitors and reclaim his identity and household. This famous Homeric quotation, alongside other occurrences of the adjective *sardonic* taken from Lucian and Plato, confirms the sinister meaning of laughter as discussed by Erasmus. In the conclusion of the adage, the humanist extends the scope of his philological investigation by tracking references in ancient literature to a laughter that presaged death.

My excursion through Erasmus's adage brings to the fore death as the motive that underlies Joubert's research into the pathology of laughter. Whether it is called sardonic or illegitimate, the pathological, false laughter discussed by the philologist and naturalist is deadly. And the deadliest laughter, according to Joubert, comes from tickling.

For Joubert, the laughter produced by tickling is a simulacrum because it involves only the sense of touch, instead of sight or hearing. The perforation of the diaphragm is the main cause of deadly sardonic, or illegitimate, laughter, according to ancient and Renaissance naturalists. This is consistent with the etiology that connects laughter to the heart and its anatomical surroundings. Piercing the diaphragm, for instance in battle, triggers a fatal spasm that manifests itself externally with a grimace resembling laughter. Yet Joubert adds a symptomatic spin to this recurrent leitmotif of natural philosophy. If wounding the diaphragm results both in death and laughter, it is because such injury is a tickling of the delicate organ. Joubert invokes the authority of Hippocrates, Aristotle, and Pliny to demonstrate that the convulsive movement, intermittent sounds, and the canine grimace that are the typical symptoms of this kind of lesion are nothing else than the features of illegitimate laughter typical of tickling. By establishing the strong connection between fatal abdominal injury and tickling, Joubert reverses the equation and demonstrates that tickling is not a gentle, pleasant experience, erroneously confused by some physicians with the joy of authentic laughter, but, rather, a painful torture that is fatal for the patient. Joubert himself could not endure such laughter without fear and anger: "I am certainly so sensitive about it and fear it so much that I consider it a great injury and offense for which I would willingly take vengeance, if this could be done respectably" (*Treatise* 2.5.82).[10] He then cites the case of a gentleman who attempted to defend himself against tickling with a dagger but couldn't do so because he was exhausted by his excruciating laughter.

Far from confusing tickling with true laughter, as Galen did, Joubert saw it as the epitome of false, deadly laughter that does not involve the perception of a ridiculous object, the agitation of the heart, and emotional turmoil mixing the necessary dose of sadness with the predominant sentiment of joy. Tickling reverses these proportions: wretchedness far exceeds happiness. External manifestations of merriment are misleading because pseudo-laughter is only the defense mechanism of a body being violently harmed. By discriminating so sharply between authentic laughter without touch and apparent laughter caused by tickling, Joubert took a personal stand regarding the old problem debated by natural philosophers. Why are animals immune to tickling? Because they have a thick skin and are thus unable to laugh, said Aristotle (*On the Parts of Animals* 673a; bk. 3, ch. 10).[11] Joubert was not convinced. On the one hand, some animal body parts are covered with delicate skin, while on the other hand, some people are sensitive to tickling even through thick layers of clothing. Moreover, some domestic animals, like dogs when petted on the belly, display their teeth as if they were laughing. But, said Joubert, this is an imperfect imitation of human laughter, a mimetic display performed by a domestic animal to mimic its human master. It is, properly speaking, a canine laughter. In other words, the apparent, misleading illegitimate laughter impersonates true merriment because it does not affect the heart and the diaphragm.

Joubert also had an original approach to the long-debated question of why a person cannot tickle themselves. A traditional solution was that laughter requires an element of surprise or deceit, but one cannot be taken by surprise by one's own gestures, hence the impossibility of tickling oneself.[12] But Joubert thought otherwise. Even people who anticipate being tickled or see this threat before physical contact occurs cannot refrain from external laughter. The same is true for those who are tickled for a long time and are therefore continuously aware and prepared. But such spasms are not true laughter, because they are caused by touch, regardless of whether they are imposed by somebody else or self-inflicted, and therefore are more painful than pleasant.

The case of people who dread being tickled at the sight of a threatening hand allowed Joubert to push his medical diagnosis of illegitimate laughter further: it is not only an unpleasant infringement of bodily integrity but a violent attack on one's humanness. At the end of his treatise, Joubert conceded that sardonic laughter can be provoked without any touching, indeed without any tickling: "just by pain and disturbance, not of the body, but of the mind" (*Treatise* 3.7.109). This was the bitter, angry laughter that overwhelmed Hannibal at the sight of the defeated Cartagena, forced by its conquerors to pay a ransom it could not afford. Asked why he laughed at such misery, Hannibal replied that if one were able to see his heart as clearly as one saw his face, the pain he felt would be obvious (Livy 44; bk. 30).[13]

Maybe such laughter in the face of human suffering, a manifestation not of the injured body but of a wounded mind, was a metaphor of Joubert's treatise, a book devoted entirely to laughter but written in times of extreme public misery in France. Maybe such deadly, joyless, forced laughter is also the involuntary reaction of the human body drawn into the depths of an organic existence that lies beneath and before the conscious life of a thinking, speaking human subject. Perhaps Podchlebnik's smile coming to us from Chełmno's death pits, Wiernik's laughter among his fellow prisoners and soon-to-be cadavers in Treblinka, Ulysses's sardonic laughter at the slaughtering of the parasites in Ithaca, and Hannibal's laughter at his own defeat and the downfall of Cartagena are all instances of joyless, painful, illegitimate laughter that leads us deep into our animal existence below the threshold of human rationality and volition, as well as beyond the grasp of language.

Laughing Rats

Let us follow the path toward our prehuman existence and listen to the laughter of nonhuman animals. "'Laughing' Rats and the Evolutionary Antecedents of Human Joy?" is the title of an article published in the August 2003 issue of *Physiology and Behavior* (Panksepp and Burgdorf). The quotation marks around *laughing* and the phrasal question denote the proposition's cautious, even hypothetical nature. The lead author of the article, the neuropsychologist Jaak Panksepp, is famous for tickling laboratory rats into "laughing."[14] But how do you make a rat "laugh"?

In the late 1990s, researchers from Panksepp's lab discovered that rats produced fifty-kilohertz chirps during some of their social interactions. These ultrasonic vocalizations were particularly abundant in rough-and-tumble play situations, that is, when rats engaged in a typical set of actions such as pouncing on a partner's back, lying on their back to be pinned down by another rat, running toward or away from a playmate, and roughly pulling another rat's fur. The strong association of playful behavior with fifty-kilohertz chirping suggested that these vocalizations were socioemotional responses to a positively perceived situation. In 1997, this observation led Panksepp to devise a simple experiment: he came up with the idea of tickling juvenile rats. He quickly discovered that when tickled, the animals produced twice as many fifty-kilohertz chirps as when they were playing by themselves. Panksepp's lab ran a series of experiments: the researchers studied the correlation between the level of chirping in individuals who engaged most easily in play and those who were the most responsive to tickling; they examined the vocalization in groups of rats of different ages and genders and the impact of selective breeding on rats' "laughter"; they measured the decrease in chirping following negative stimuli such as cat smell and the increase in vocalizations prompted by a higher need for social interaction among individuals who had been subjected to isolation. The conclusion of these intense experiments was that rats' chirping was a "laughter-type response" (Panksepp and Burgdorf, "'Laughing' Rats"). In other words, when you tickled rats—especially young males who were not hampered by fear and who had been primed by a short period of isolation before the experiment—they intensively "laughed" with exactly the same high-frequency ultrasounds as those they made when they played together.[15] Even more astonishingly, such tickling-induced "laughter" could be conditioned in rats just like in humans. Children, especially, are prone to laugh when prompted with the characteristic and culturally specific coochy-coochy-coo. It is the same for young rats who produce their chirping "laughter" at the sight of the scientist's waving hand. This conditioning is such a strong positive reinforcement that rats are ready to run mazes and press levers just to be tickled. As we have seen, Joubert noticed a similar conditioning in humans. Despite his insistence on linking illegitimate laughter with touch, he admitted that inauthentic and painful laughter could be produced without any physical contact, solely by disturbing the human mind. He acknowledged that a person could shiver and laugh with uneasiness and apprehension when merely threatened by tickling. However, the difference between Joubert's and Panksepp's laughter conditioned by tickling is that for the Renaissance humanist, human subjects resent such an experience, while according to the modern neuropsychologist, rats enjoy it tremendously. Another nontrivial difference between the Renaissance physician and the modern neuropsychologist is that the former studied humans, while the latter experimented with nonhuman animals.

However, regardless of the object of their study, both scientists pondered the confines of humanness. Although they approached this question from opposite sides of the frontier of what is and what is not human, they studied animals, whether human or rodent, to understand emotionality. Regardless of the negative or positive character of the behavior induced by tickling, what mattered for Joubert and Panksepp alike was that the response was emotional. And this is of capital importance for the modern neuropsychologist, who is interested in tickling rats only to the extent that their laughter-type response sheds light on emotions—most importantly, on human emotions. Hence the leading hypothesis of Panksepp's article expressed in the question of its title. First, that there is a possibility—which needs to be validated through further neuropsychological as well as microbiological research—that a homology, distinct from analogy, exists between animal and human emotionality. *Homology*, in this instance, refers to the fact that some organs belonging to different animal species are genetically related. For instance, human arms and bat wings are homologous because they can both be traced to genetic information regulating the movement of forelimbs. *Analogy*, on the other hand, refers only to functional similarity. For instance, wings fulfill a similar function in bees and in birds but are not genetically related (Panksepp, *Affective Neuroscience* 17). Hence the second aspect of the hypothesis expressed in the title of the article—namely, that the homology between animal and human emotions is indicative of an evolutionary link between human and animal neurological substrata of emotions. In other words, rats' "laughter" may be "useful in decoding one of the great mysteries of human life—the deep nature of a form of joy within the brain-mind" (Panksepp and Burgdorf, "'Laughing' Rats" 535).

By its stylistic formulation—"decoding one of the great mysteries of human life—the deep nature of a form of joy"—this programmatic sentence betrays the fundamental traits of Panksepp's thinking. First of all, the key word defining his research agenda is the adjective *deep*. For Panksepp, tickling rats is nothing but a journey back in time into the human phylogenetic as well as ontogenetic past. Animal "laughter" is the path leading toward the origins of human life, both as individuals and as a species. Panksepp hypothesizes that there is an "ancestral relationship" between young rats' playful chirping and the rudimentary forms of laughter exhibited by human children by the time they are three months old. Panksepp's dive into the archaic past of laughter is also a search for evolutionary stages when the human and nonhuman animal divide was not yet established. This explains the title of Panksepp's main opus: *The Archeology of Mind* (Panksepp and Biven).[16] Like an archeologist unearthing the material vestiges of an ancient civilization, the neuropsychologist digs into the animal brain to understand the evolutionary antecedents of human emotionality. The basic assumption of such research is that the brain is a symbolic organ that reflects, in its structure and functioning, the evolution that produced human genetic makeup.

Hence the second symptomatic stylistic feature of Panksepp's programmatic sentence, namely, his desire to decode the mystery of human life. Such a formulation implies that deep inside humans lies a bodily memory that is put to use in people's interaction with their environment, very much like bytes of information are stored in the circuitry of a machine and retrieved when they are needed for the machine to operate. Panksepp relies on a widely held conviction in neuroscience that the brain not only encodes the outside world thanks to its sensory perception but also has intrinsic operating systems that regulate the psychobehavioral tendencies that were shaped during human evolution in order to cope with environmental challenges. For contemporary neuroscientists, the computer metaphors that pervade this reasoning are like a stylistic obsession: continuously annoying and intellectually paralyzing, yet to a large extent unavoidable (see Dehaene). In that respect Panksepp is, again, not an exception. He acknowledges that emotional life can be imagined as the processing of flows of information, and he studies the complex neural interactions that generate inborn psychobehavioral tendencies as if they were emotional operating systems. He distinguishes seven such systems, each pertaining to a different nexus of affects, behaviors, and neural activity: the seeking system; the systems of rage, fear, lust, care, panic, and grief; and the system of play. It is with the system of play that, according to Panksepp, laughter is associated.

Yet, despite the conceptual usefulness of computer metaphors, Panksepp struggles with the distinction between the "hardware" functions of the brain and the "software" functions of the mind because, again in line with contemporary neuroscience, he wants to avoid a dualistic approach to human consciousness.[17] This is why he prefers to speak about the "BrainMind" or, alternatively, the "MindBrain." This compound word allows Panksepp to encapsulate his choice of "dual-aspect monism" as a theory not only of a human psychology of emotions but, more broadly, of a mammalian one (Panksepp and Biven 417–18). It is a monism because he does not want to admit a dualistic split between a disembodied mind and the organic workings of the brain, between a Cartesian thinking thing and a thoughtless organic machine extended in physical space. Instead, Panksepp insists that all the psychological functions that are attributed to the mind emerge from the circuit dynamics of the brain, very much like digestion is a function of gastrointestinal actions. Every operation of the mind is ultimately rooted in a single substance: the physical brain and, most importantly, its subcortical and cortical midline systems. Yet Panksepp's monism is "dual-aspect" because the brain's mechanisms generate both emotional behaviors and, concurrently, corresponding affects. Third-person objectivity of observable comportments and first-person subjective feelings are thus the flipsides of the same material, organic reality (Panksepp, *Affective Neuroscience*, ch. 4; Panksepp, "Neuroevolutionary Sources" 236).

Panksepp's research methodology matches his dual-aspect monism, that is, his aspiration to ground both external movements and internal affects in the neurological workings of the brain. Most importantly, Panksepp resolutely turns his back on the pure behaviorism in which he was trained as a young psychologist. At the same time, he shies away from neurological reductionism, which relegates the life of the mind to the status of a secondary byproduct of the circuitry of the brain. Instead of opting for a one-sided, radical solution, Panksepp narrows the gap between the psychological and the neural dynamic. To progress on this middle path, he relies on a triangulation, as he puts it, between behavioristic observations, neuroanatomical and neurochemical studies, and cognitive experimentation.

All three approaches supplement and corroborate each other while zooming in on basic emotional systems deeply ingrained in the limbic brain and, according to Panksepp, homologous in human and nonhuman MindBrains. In humans, these emotional systems are likely inhibited and regulated by higher functions and the exceptionally well-developed cognitive capacities of the cortical layer. Panksepp's insistence on the necessity of corroborating psychological experiments and observations with neurobiological analysis is an attempt to break through this cortical cup and dive deep into the human evolutionary past, so deep that human and nonhuman animal emotions cannot be distinguished from each other.

The Risks of Language

In such a deep trench of the human MindBrain, Panksepp finds primitive forms of mentality and primordial phenomenal experiences that constitute what he calls "core consciousness." Core consciousness is made of raw feelings and perceptions. It is more basic than higher forms of consciousness that are composed of thoughts about the raw experiences of core consciousness, as well as thoughts about such thoughts. Such sophisticated intellectual constructions result in a self-awareness that only humans are capable of (Panksepp, "Core Consciousness"; Panksepp and Biven, ch. 11). Being the product of Panksepp's seven operating emotional systems that lie at the foundation of affective mammalian life, core consciousness fascinates Panksepp because it constitutes the hypothetical common ground on which human consciousness and nonhuman animal consciousness meet and possibly overlap. Core consciousness thus borders on or even includes animal consciousness, which is the remote frontier of neuroscience. Animal consciousness needs to be explored if we want to elucidate voluntary behavior and its neurological correlates in human and nonhuman animals. In other words, core consciousness is the closest Panksepp can get to the biological "soul" that is common to humans and primates—in fact, to any mammal, and even to some birds and mollusks (Edelman and Seth). Of course, such a soul is not a spiritual or intellectual entity but is made of primordial feelings, namely the seven operating emotional systems. In stark opposition to Descartes, Panksepp prefers to say, "I feel therefore I am."

And herein lies an important challenge. As primitive and emotion-based as such a biological soul would be, it presupposes an "I," a subjectivity, a sense of selfhood. Panksepp calls it a "'core SELF'—which, with a bit of poetic license, might even be referred to as our animalian 'soul'" (Panksepp and Biven 389–90). The saturation of this sentence with rhetorical caution and reservation is striking. Quotation marks and adverbial expressions testify to Panksepp's desire to keep a critical distance from what he dares to say. The experimental scientist claims the liberty to use poetic license, but he clearly does not feel at ease in the role of an orphic enchanter of animal souls. Hence the complexity of his style, which, contrary to the clarity and precision expected of a scientific book on neuropsychology, becomes a problem on its own account. Central among these stylistic devices is the capitalization of "SELF," which aims at warning the reader that the author does not hope to find a full-fledged, conscious selfhood at the bottom of human neurological constitution, in the archaic past of our evolution when human and nonhuman animals were largely indistinguishable. In fact, the capitalization intends to signal that SELF should not be confused with the "self" because the capitalized word is an acronym for "Simple Ego-type Life Form," which is merely "a center of gravity" in which Panksepp anchors the internal constellation of affect and representation. Similarly, to name the seven emotional systems that he identifies through the triangulation of behavioral observation, cognitive experiments, and neurological analysis, Panksepp uses capital letters—for example, "SEEKING," "FEAR," "PLAY." Such typographic convention is strictly reserved for the basic emotional systems, and Panksepp insists that he does not capitalize other motivational or complex feelings such as hunger or jealousy because either they are not mediated by distinct types of neurological organization or they involve the higher cortical layers of the brain (*Affective Neuroscience* 51–52, 331–35).

Why does Panksepp go to such lengths to make typographic distinctions between the primordial emotions he studies in the depths of mammalian core consciousness and those he leaves aside as high-end cognitive operations? Because he does not want to be accused of mixing the emotional operating systems embedded in mammalian core consciousness with sophisticated human feelings controlled by complex rationality and shaped by cultural upbringing. In other words, Panksepp strives to avoid being accused of anthropomorphism. Yet it was exactly such criticism that prevented his discovery of rats' "laughter" from being published in *Nature* in 1997.[18] One of the reviewers, clearly a behaviorist, was taken aback by Panksepp's use of the word *play* in reference to rats' rough-and-tumble interactions. She asked that Panksepp limit his analysis strictly to what he saw. Most probably, she would have preferred he did not describe typical rat behavior such as pinning down a partner or performing the habitual rounds of running toward another rodent as play. For a strict behaviorist, to use such vocabulary amounts to projecting human feelings onto nonhuman animals who cannot confirm or deny them because they lack the language to do so. It would suppose that animals have feelings that control their behaviors, and such a proposition was largely deemed unacceptable when Panksepp sent his article to *Nature* for publication.

Yet this is exactly the direction in which Panksepp is heading with the mental restrictions and stylistic pirouettes that he performs. He remembers that Darwin, in his *Expression of the Emotions in Man and Animals* (1872), saw laughter as the expression of joy, while keeping in mind that muscular movements and emotional experience may be elaborated in distinct areas of human and nonhuman animal brains. Yet Panksepp suspects that human neurology of laughter and rats' brain circuitry of fifty-kilohertz chirping interconnect within brain areas that mediate positive social feelings in both species and that such a connection is founded on a degree of evolutionary continuity between human and nonhuman brain mechanisms. As Panksepp says, even if rats do not have a sense of humor, they definitely appear to have a sense of fun. It is this animal playfulness that allows Panksepp to speak about rats' "laughter" (with quotation marks) as the expression of their PLAY (capitalized) emotional operating system. The neuropsychologist deliberately uses the "old emotional words" of folk psychology, with all the risks of anthropomorphism they entail, because he hopes that they better approximate the homologies genetically ingrained in mammalian brains as well as the evolutionarily grounded social orientation of human and nonhuman animals (Panksepp, *Affective Neuroscience* 12). Panksepp knows that by doing so he sides with naturalism against constructivist tendencies in modern neuroscience.[19] He hopes that the typographic and stylistic acrobatics that he forces upon language in his scientific publications prevent his readers from taking the vernacular terms he uses as explanations of mammalian emotions. He wants them to be understood as indicators of realities remote in evolutionary time and deeply ingrained in the subparticles of the nervous cells. To speak about rats' "laughter" explains nothing, no more than to say that snow is white. Emotions are like the qualia that are problematic for consciousness studies. The former dive deep into our inner selves, while the latter point to the external world, but both remain beyond the grasp of human language.

We can certainly use advanced technology such as functional magnetic resonance imaging (fMRI) to see where the firing of synapses occurs in synchrony with certain behavioral settings or sensorial stimulations. We can even electrically or chemically induce such neurological activity or surgically disconnect certain circuits. Yet we cannot properly conceptualize rats' joy and sociability, just as we cannot comprehend Wiernik's laughter in the midst of the inhumanity of Treblinka. Despite the sophistication of scientific technology and the refinement of linguistic expression, it is not possible to cross unharmed into the realm of animality or into the hell of inhumanity. Rats' "laughter" and humans' illegitimate, or sardonic, laughter are but a narrow path leading toward such times and places, toward the realm preceding a properly human life. Yet laughing amid walking dead comrades in Treblinka, like marching in sync with the infernal rhythm of the camp's orchestra, implies that those who laugh will never be able to come back to human life or, as Wiernik confesses with his genuine frankness, may never again laugh normally with other fellow human beings.

Laughter before Human Life

Scientific technology and terminology are both a blessing and a curse in the journey toward emotionality and consciousness prior to human life. They allow us to hear the echoes of the immemorial past that reverberate in laughter and music, the time when humans were not yet human and when emotions were raw animal feelings. On the other hand, the devices provided by technology and the constructs of our intelligence hamper our descent into the abyss of nonhumanity. One can sense how the ballast of words and the shackles of concepts are puzzling for those who, like Wiernik and Quignard, Joubert and Panksepp, willingly or not, have journeyed to the realm extending before humanness.

Panksepp does not write novels like Quignard, but he, too, listens to unarticulated vocalizations and observes bodily spasms as testimonies of social and emotional urges that carry humanity's evolutionary past. Unlike Quignard, he does not compose a literary allegory that reveals the prenatal rhythms and the howling of wounded animals in the basso continuo of the viola da gamba. Instead, alongside other neuropsychologists, Panksepp experimentally studies the shivers and chills that are induced in female human subjects by certain tonalities resembling, as he hypothesizes, babies' "separation cries" ("Affective Foundations" 35). Quignard shapes the fiction of his novels and bends the etymologies of words. By doing so, he uses literary confabulation to voice the sounds that precede language. Similarly, Panksepp not only experimentally measures the "skin orgasms" triggered by music but also recycles a long tradition of natural philosophy that sees rhythms and melodic lines as residual testimonies of emotional social communication preceding the emergence of human language and culturally consecrated forms of musical art ("Emotional Antecedents" and "Affective Foundations"). He responds to Darwin's suggestion that the call of gibbons, which extends for an octave, indicates the apes' capacity to sing. Panksepp cannot find any evidence of animal musical minds but claims that there is tangible proof of archaic emotional minds across mammalian species. He does not follow Noam Chomsky in postulating the existence of a language instinct that would be indicative of human nature (Chomsky and Foucault). However, he is eager to admit that there is an "affective communication instinct" (Panksepp, "Affective Foundations" 33). It makes a mother hum melodies to her unborn child, and it makes supposedly fully constituted humans listen to music. He strongly believes in the existence of a social-affective substratum embedded in mammals' subneocortical areas that makes rats laugh to each other with bursts that no human would recognize as laughter. Panksepp does not propose, like Rousseau, a speculative theory of the melodic origins of human language, but he clearly dreams about an instinctual, animal-like music lingering at the bottom of our MindBrains from the times when humans were not yet human and articulated language was not yet available. He strives to remain rigorous in reporting the outcomes of his experiments, in sticking to the falsifiable observations he makes in his lab or gathers in publications specializing in his area of research. However, in his dream of hitting the bedrock of nature at the foundation of human and nonhuman animal emotionality, he cannot refrain from sifting through layers of cultural—that is, textual—sediment. And it is of no surprise that Panksepp references Joubert's sixteenth-century treatise on multiple occasions.

The contemporary neuroscientist and the Renaissance humanist share an interest in hierarchical thinking about the human psyche. Joubert, in conformity with the Aristotelian and Galenic traditions that he inherited, tried to pinpoint laughter on the scale of the faculties of the soul. More specifically, he located it within the sensitive soul, above the basic vegetative soul and beneath the eternal, specifically human, intellectual soul. Curiously, Panksepp, who is indebted to the decisive progress made by twentieth-century evolutionary neuroscience, scrutinizes the successive layers of brain anatomy piled upon the archaic foundations up to the human superstructures of the cortex.[20] He strives to correlate the vertical order of the "columns" of neurological circuitry with the hierarchal sophistication of the functions of the mind. Yet while both Panksepp and Joubert think about human psyche in hierarchical terms, ultimately, they look in different directions. Joubert was oriented outward, since his starting point was the issue of touch that allowed him to discriminate between illegitimate laughter and laughter proper. Panksepp looks not so much at external stimuli but mostly inward at internal subcortical operating systems in the brain. He measures the frequency of rats' chirping and the intensity of their rough-and-tumble interactions because he wants to corroborate these data with the firing of synapses. For Panksepp, the MindBrain is but one substance of organic nature equipped with a double functionality of behavior and affect. This means that the materiality of emotional behavior is located differently by the neuroscientist than by the humanist. Bound by the Aristotelian typology of causes, Joubert defines the "material cause" of laughter as the object that was ugly—contrary to the natural order of things—yet not worthy of pity. On the other hand, ultrasound waves produced by playful or tickled rats are for Panksepp only physical manifestations of the fundamental materiality of the brain shaped by evolution. If they are distinct and clear in rats, like the outbursts of hearty laughter in humans, it is because, contrary to other species more threatened by predators, rats thrived in a welcoming habitat and could afford, so to speak, to laugh out loud. Over evolutionary time, such a joyful lack of concern for their survival became permanently inscribed into the neurological hardware of their brains (Panksepp and Burgdorf, "'Laughing' Rats" 541).[21]

According to Panksepp, the neuronal circuitry wired by evolution is not only genetically transmissible from one individual to another but extends in social space beyond discrete individual bodies. The web of neurons weaves the fabric of interpersonal relationships. Panksepp insists on the social dimension of the neuropsychological makeup of humans and nonhuman animals. He rephrases the Aristotelian topos of the impossibility of tickling oneself in terms of his theory of emotional operating systems. If, as evidenced by fMRI studies, tickling oneself produces a weaker neurological response than being tickled, it is because the cerebellum, the part of the brain that specializes in predicting the sensory consequences of movements, produces a signal that partially cancels the response that normally remains unhampered when tickling is done by somebody else (Blakemore et al.; see also Harris and Alvarado). Panksepp interprets these findings as confirmation of the fundamentally social orientation inscribed by evolution in the neuronal wiring of our MindBrains (Panksepp and Burgdorf, "'Laughing' Rats" 542–43).

He goes even further. If the lowest levels of our neurological organization, such as the one where the PLAY system, with its inscribed laughter response, is grounded, are evolutionarily programmed for social interaction, one can imagine laughter and joy to be biological processes "that captivate widely reverberating ensembles of neural networks within the brain of one individual that can spread infectiously among interacting individuals" (Panksepp and Burgdorf, "'Laughing' Rats" 543). Or, to put it simply, if laughter is contagious, it is because the basic circuitry of human MindBrains evolved into emitter-receptor organic machines that are programmed to send out and capture signals from other individual MindBrains, thus ensuring the connectivity of the social network. MindBrains are, therefore, not only discrete units looking inward into their philo- and ontogenetic past but also routers of a neural internet beaming out and receiving waves of laughter as sonic signals—or ultrasonic, as is the case with rats—of good social interconnectivity.

A Stretched Membrane

Let us not forget, however, that primordial laughter—not the sophisticated human sense of humor sparked in the cortical cup of high culture by things that are "ugly and unworthy of pity," but the animal laughter of our prehuman past—is imbued with death. This conclusion would come as no surprise for Panksepp. The visceral, ancient regions of the brain in which he grounds the seven emotional operating systems common to all mammals are the areas where the lowest amount of energy is needed to arouse an emotional response during experiments of localized neural stimulation. Those are also the regions that, when damaged, are the most susceptible to triggering persistent vegetative states. It is in such depths of life before human life that Panksepp looks for the biological soul. When a dying organism passes from life, those regions of the brain are the last to die (Panksepp, "Affective Foundations" 38). It is these final stages of existence, after humanly comprehensible death and just before total extinction, that Podchlebnik's smile illuminates; it is in such depths that Wiernik's laughter reverberates.

Logically, this space beyond and before the life that is deemed human should be unlivable. A fetus cannot dwell for long in the limbo of the maternal womb. There comes a day when the floating suspension amid the amniotic waters next to the maternal heartbeat must be interrupted by birth or miscarriage. It is the same for the evolution of the human species. The advent of humanity is not a triumphant progress toward biological supremacy, and the missing link between the great ape and the first human may never be found: such a tipping point may never have existed—evolution may be more a labyrinth than a line. Yet here we are, looking at the nonhuman animals that we exterminate, commodify, and mystify, very much like we do with ourselves (see Neyrat). It is the same with the *Muselmänner* of the death factories that Nazis built: they could not stay suspended in the state of demise for long but either miraculously survived or perished (Heidegger, "Danger" 53–54; qtd. by Agamben 73–74). All these areas of nonhumanity, or inhumanity, are difficult to explore because, like interstellar outer space, they lack breathable air to make our silent dreams and thoughts resonate.

Hence our puzzlement at the laughter that reverberates from this lifeless and inhuman realm. Such is Claude Lanzmann's bewilderment by Podchlebnik's smile. Such is the astonishment of Wiernik a few months after his escape, as he recalls his laughter in Treblinka. Yet after this first surprise comes a shrug of self-evidence, as if humanity was able to accommodate the nonhuman in some way after all. Asked by Lanzmann why he smiled all the time, Podchlebnik replied with another question: "What do you want me to do, cry? When you are alive, you smile [it is better to smile]." The same with Wiernik, who ended the invocation of his disturbing laughter amid extermination by admitting that "one can get used to anything." It would be a grave mistake to take these reactions as proof of indifference. Neither Podchlebnik nor Wiernik accepted the horror of their inhuman experiences. Podchlebnik could not restrain his tears at the memory of his wife and children that he buried in the pit of the death camp in Chełmno; Wiernik was haunted by the visions of the piled corpses of Treblinka. Their eerie smiles and laughter do not mute their inhumane suffering but express it basely and instinctively. They are signs, but not in the sense of consecrated gestures of culture that conceptualize the unspeakable or domesticate the bestiality. They are even more visceral than Sainte-Colombe's music, which, according to Quignard, stirred up the voiceless plaint of the unborn and the howling of animals, sounds that precede language and communication yet, despite how primordial they sound, are music. Very much like Podchlebnik's smile and Wiernik's laughter, the illegitimate laughter that fascinated Joubert and the chirping of the laboratory rats that interests Panksepp are more bodily, more archaic than any articulated forms of speech and art.

To understand laughter coming from beyond human life framed by concepts and words, socially recognizable behaviors, and hierarchies of values, it is useful to turn to Freud's *Beyond the Pleasure Principle*. This text was published in 1920, in the wake of World War I and toward the end of Freud's life. I seek Freud's help, but not to confirm or dispute the psychoanalytical conception of the human being. Contrary to psychoanalysis, I do not focus my attention on the individual ego and the factors that may hinder its harmonious development.[22] The scope of my research is both more modest and more general. I study a bodily phenomenon, namely laughter, not as the symptom of the development of a particular psyche but as a corporeal sign mediated by texts of culture and pointing to the limit separating what is human from what is not. Consequently, I am not interested in furthering a doctrine of the unconscious, no more than I am eager to embrace an essentialist metaphysics of humanity. I am first and foremost interested in Freud's embarrassment over the metaphors he used and not in his doctrine and conceptual apparatus. Indeed, the starting point of *Beyond the Pleasure Principle* is a contradiction that Freud noticed between his former assumptions and the evidence provided by clinical data. The assumption that he used to hold dear was that in psychic life people seek the pleasurable release of tensions to turn dreams into wish fulfillment. Yet Freud's clinical practice provided ample evidence that some dreams are not wish fulfillment since they replay the patient's traumatic experiences. Hence the need to go beyond the pleasure principle into the depths of the human psyche, where Freud found the death drive.

What follows next in Freud's argument is a part that he qualified as farfetched speculation. Generations of commentators and followers have tried to impose a discipline of thought on Freud's musings and to neutralize their contradictions. They have quarreled over the role to be attributed to the death drive with regard to erotic instincts; they have tried to differentiate between Freud's statements that pertain to the organic nature of humanity and those that reference its psychic constitution; they have pondered to what extent the death drive reveals problems stemming from the imaginary ego and how such a drive is related to the symbolic order of language. Since I am not arguing in favor or against a particular philosophical anthropology, the exegetical efforts aimed at saving the coherence of the master's teachings are of no interest to me. Instead, I focus my attention on an embarrassingly clumsy yet evocative metaphor that Freud used for the formation of human consciousness. This metaphor may help us grasp the specificity of laughter that comes from before our lives and may help us understand the meaning of its humanness.

In his speculative musings, Freud defined human consciousness as a frontier between the outside and the inside of the human being. This frontier is a crust that thickens under the influence of external perceptions. This stiffening is a process of dying that makes the outer layer immune to subsequent excitations that raise psychological tensions. Under the pressure of external stimuli, the crust of consciousness solidifies but is not unbreakable. Trauma is a breaking-through of this protective shield.

Yet disturbances can also come from the inside of the psyche and attack the internal soft, unprotected layer of human consciousness. These internal excitations are drives comparable to the traumatic neuroses revived in the painful dreams that Freud had trouble accommodating to his previous conception of dreams as wish fulfillment. Such drives are testimony to the inertia and elasticity of human organisms: disturbed by a stimulus, they tend to return to their previous state of equilibrium and rest. But what is the state of total equilibrium? What is the final return to inorganic stability? It is death. Freud can thus famously state that "the aim of all life is death."

I neither endorse nor dispute this vision of life as a more-or-less convoluted loop stemming from and leading to nonexistence. I cannot, however, resist the temptation to confront Freud's speculations about the formation of human consciousness with Podchlebnik's and Wiernik's reactions to their own laughter. If we follow Freud in seeing the evolution of human consciousness as a tension that stabilizes or cancels itself, we can better understand the two survivors' half-irritated, half-resigned acceptance of their laughter at the inhumanity that irremediably tainted their lives. Yes, Lanzmann was right to insist that something had died in Podchlebnik in the pits of Chełmno. Wiernik was also correct in concluding that a person can get used to anything. Like the outer crust of consciousness imagined by Freud, the survivors' capacity to absorb additional traumatic experiences diminished under the unimaginable pressure of what they witnessed. This was by no means an emotional or moral indifference but the solidification of the frontier of humanity into a callus that protects the remains of selfhood from more unbearable pain. From within, this crust is exposed to the tremors of nonhuman life. These are the emotional agitations that, according to Panksepp, humans share with other mammals; these are the unwanted movements that threaten bodily integrity in a way Joubert feared and abhorred. From this perspective, illegitimate laughter as well as canine and rat "laughter" shake the solidified crust of human consciousness. These involuntary, joyless, quasi-instinctive movements are aftershocks coming from deep beneath our humanness, from times and evolutionary embranchments that are only remotely related to our present state. They are all the more powerfully felt when the callus of human consciousness has dried and thickened as a result of repeated trauma. They do more than threaten the psychological balance of an individual ego; they signal the crossing over from what is still a human, albeit deeply wounded, life into the realm of nonhumanity.

Callused consciousness is only a metaphor. Freud concluded *Beyond the Pleasure Principle* by deploring the figurative language he was forced to use in describing the human mind because precise scientific terminology was not available. He hoped for future advances in biology and chemistry, even if they were to make his speculations obsolete. Almost a century after Freud, Panksepp, despite the help of his experimental apparatus, is no less embarrassed by the deficiency of language. Compared with these representatives of modern science, Joubert was unapologetic about his use of an entire library of classical texts that helped him grasp the bodily, animalistic reality of laughter. By calling upon thinkers from different historical moments and confronting them with the testimonies of Wiernik as well with the literary work by Quignard, I do not intend to favor one voice over another but to give the floor to a polyphonic chorus. I am convinced that if we want to refrain from positing a humanism that is an a priori doctrine of the human, we should embrace textual and linguistic exploration. Moderating the dialogue of historically distant thoughts and rhetorically diverse voices is the most humanistic way to open our ears to the sound of laughter from before our properly human lives.

Let us further develop Freud's metaphor and imagine that human consciousness resembles a callus that has progressively solidified at the limits of the human psyche where it meets the external world (*Beyond the Pleasure Principle*). Let us suppose that inside this protective layer nests something that for better or worse we call human life. This assumed concept may immediately raise questions. Human life certainly implies a complex organization of physical things and symbolic thinking, requires time, and, most importantly, presupposes limits. These confines of life are particularly precious in our undertaking, especially when the limitation of human life refers us to our mortality. It is at the edge between what is human and what is not that we can capture the sound of the uncanny laughter that is the subject of this book. In this respect, Freud's metaphor of the callus delimiting the human psyche becomes particularly useful. Not only does it call to mind the notion of the membrane, which is instrumental in biology for conceptualizing organic life, but it is also a helpful tool for imagining the finality of human existence (see, for instance, Nurse). One can, for instance, imagine that occasionally this crust reverberates with tremors that come from the time before life that we deem properly human, from a primordial life that we have shared with other animals during our evolutionary past.

Sometimes a potent trauma strikes from outside the shell of our psyche, threatening to break it. In both cases the trembling that shakes the crust, which is our consciousness, resonates in a joyless, involuntary, uncanny, and painful laughter. When the impulse comes from the depths of our Mind-Brains, our laughter is a more sophisticated and cultured version of the rat "laughter" studied by Panksepp; when the shock comes from the outside, either as unbearable trauma or, less dangerously, an annoying tickle, we are confronted with the disturbing smile of Podchlebnik being interviewed by Lanzmann, the sardonic smile of Ulysses, or the deranged laughter of Hannibal described by Joubert. Like any resonance, the more solid the membrane separating what is human from what is not, the louder the resonance of the laughter. Yet the more rigid the callus of consciousness, the more likely it is fractured by a powerful blow, endangering the integrity of the human psyche and the life of the individual subjected to such a traumatic shock. And, conversely, the more flexible the layer dividing our psyche from the outside world, the less likely it is to break; the more plastic the skin formed by our consciousness around our human life, the more difficult it is to make it vibrate with laughter.[23] What is needed to make the membrane of human life resonate without breaking is a perilous tension. We have seen it at work in our animal self. Let us examine it in our relations to machines.

Chapter 3

Laughing (Human) Machines

In the previous chapter I imagined the limit between what is human and what is not as a membrane tensely extended over human life. If this thin layer is still sensitive and not so calloused as to have become brittle by external shocks or internal trauma, it may resonate with tremors that resemble laughter. In the case of human and nonhuman animals, this membrane may literally be the skin, especially when it is irritated by tickling. Such epidermic spasms and concurrent intermittent vocalizations are—as Joubert said—voluntarily constrained. They may be a symptom of pain or pleasure, or both. Like Podchlebnik's smile, the Treblinka signboard, Hannibal's laughter, and the chirping of Panksepp's rats, these mind-body reactions need to be interpreted, translated into human language. Sometimes they are transposed into art, as Lanzmann's movie and Szlengel's poem do.

After hearing animal laughter, we now listen to the laughter of machines, the machines that we are and the machines that we build. Humans are animals and they dwell among animals. Animality is a primordial given of our biology shaped by our natural and domesticated environments. Unlike animality, machinery is a human construct. It is a metaphoric representation of the inner workings of our mind and our brain, but it is also a more or less material, external construction assembled by our intellect and our hands. While humans are animals like the nonhuman animals with whom they mingle, humans are not machines in the same sense as are the functional devices they build. Or are they? Maybe the development of artificial intelligence (AI) since the mid–twentieth century has made the hominization of machines possible to some degree. And, conversely, maybe nanotechnology and bioengineering have transformed humans into cyborgs.

Hence the increased urgency of the question: Is there a membrane separating what is human from a nonhuman machine? I approach this question in this chapter and the next from opposite points: first, from the point of view of the inner—and possibly metaphoric—machine that humans are, and second, from the perspective of humans gazing at machines as concrete artifacts of their own making. The current chapter is devoted to humans' inner machines; the next one discusses the human face of machines.

In both approaches, the question of the limit between humanity and machinery is complicated by different degrees of our osmotic relationship with technology and different degrees of disembodiment of contemporary AI. Where should we draw the line between a properly human organism and its intelligent prosthetic implants and enhancements? Where is the demarcation between humans and humanoid robots, holographic avatars, and textual chatbot companions? Let us assume that the computer screen plays the role of such a limit, a touchable zone of contact, a display of emotions, and a stage where human and potential AI consciousness play their respective roles.[1] Let us see the computer screen as the machine's membrane, jittering with tremors of laughter. In figure 3.1, a cartoon featuring a robot reminiscent of the iconic *Star Wars* humanoid droid C-3PO illustrates this hypothesis while poking fun at our common conundrum: what does it mean for a machine to be humanlike or, simply stated, human? The robot stares at a computer screen displaying a banal CAPTCHA test. The test asks the user to correctly transcribe distorted letters to prove the user is not a robot. "OMG, that is so offensive!" thinks the robot.

Laughing at Your Inner Machine

How do we trace the thin line between the human and the machine? Laughter should make the difference: machines do not laugh; people do. This is what we tend to think, in accordance with a long-held tradition of laughter as a distinctive attribute of our humanity. Henri Bergson states that nothing can be comical outside of what is properly human. His *Laughter: An Essay on the Meaning of the Comic* was published against the background of the development of psychology at the turn of the nineteenth century. Bergson's ambition was to define what made people laugh in art and in real life. But laughter for him was more than comedy. It was even more than an aesthetic or anthropological phenomenon. It was fundamentally metaphysical. Yet for Bergson laughter was not a proprium defining the essence of humanness but

Figure 3.1. David Coverly, *Prove You Are Not a Robot*, 2014. *Source*: David Coverly, *Speed Bump*. Used with permission.

a symptom that manifested itself whenever what was human faded away to leave a place for what was mechanical.

One of the most famous phrases of Bergson's classic essay describes laughter as "something mechanical tacked onto the living" ("du mécanique plaqué sur du vivant"; *Le Rire* in *Œuvres* 1:619; sec. 5). To understand this, think about the opening scenes of Charlie Chaplin's *Modern Times* (1936). The eternal tramp, having found work at a factory, stands at a conveyor belt endlessly screwing two bolts into an unidentified equipment part moving quickly past him. Despite his goodwill and sincere application, the mechanical gestures required by this repetitive task take their toll on Chaplin's enthusiasm. He cannot stand the relentless pace and monotony of the job. He hides in the restroom for a smoke to break the unbearable boredom but is quickly called to order by his watchful supervisors. Stuck at his assigned place in the production chain and forced to accelerate the rhythm of his constantly repeating task, Chaplin goes out of his mind. His gestures lose their human fluidity and become involuntary nervous tics. His body stiffens, his face loses expressivity; he is no longer human but a human robot. "An automat, a robot" are the words Podchlebnik used when, pressed by Lanzmann's questions, he tried to describe his existential state in the Chełmno death camp. The inhumanity of the mass production of cadavers in Chełmno may be seen as the improbable result of the dehumanization portrayed in comical mode in *Modern Times*. At the end of the sequence, alienated and ensnared by the automaticity of industrial labor, Chaplin lies down on the conveyer belt and is swallowed by the merciless machinery. He becomes a cog—a thing—comically anticipating the reification of human bodies reduced by the SS to the status of rugs and puppets.

Chaplin's transformation from a resourceful, affectionate prankster into an automaton embodies Bergson's definition of laughter as "something mechanical encrusted on the living." The famous phrase can, however, be easily misunderstood if we consider the mechanism as superimposed on life from outside. But Bergson did not see the machine as an external shackle constraining the living organism. In fact, the tendency toward mechanization transforms life from inside out. What is laughable is the machine that dwells within humans and expands outward from within their living selves (*Le Rire*, Bergson, *Œuvres* 1:619, 645). Such expansive mechanization constitutes the social and political meaning of Chaplin's misfortunes. The mime is funny not because he is an exception in the world of the modern factory but because his caricatural gestures express the general mechanization of all sensing and feeling human beings in modern times. His coworkers toiling at the assembly line and the foremen who rush him to work faster are also dehumanized and devitalized cogs in an overpowering industrial system that has taken over the lives of its creators and whose voracity consumes the world for its own benefit.

Chaplin's dehumanizing mechanization is hilarious when placed in the context of his comic adventures in the film but is disturbingly uncanny when considered in itself. Chaplin's famous waddle makes him walk a tightrope stretched between what is deeply human and disturbingly inhuman. This fine line does not separate the clown from the harsh surrounding reality but runs right through his inner self. At the end, the mime's humanism prevails even amid the strife and suffering of modernity. So does life in Bergson's philosophy. Nonetheless, for Bergson, life must constantly deal with the inner mechanization that time and again disperses the vital impetus (*élan vital*) into the discrete units of material beings. As disturbing as it is, for Bergson this fragmentation of the flow of life is not a curse but a natural unfolding of reality. Moreover, it is reversible. Devitalizing mechanization does not have to be unidirectional. On the contrary, Bergson considers the possibility of machines that come alive. His dream of animating inert things is tainted with mysticism: Bergson concludes his considerations on morality and religion by dreaming of a universe that is a "machine to make gods" ("une machine à faire des dieux"; *Les deux sources de la morale et de la religion* in *Œuvres* 2:800).

How is such creative, ecstatic fabrication of life conceivable? Bergson's balancing act between life and the machine hinges on the concept of novelty. Conceptualizing what is new was Bergson's main task as a philosopher of life (see Deleuze). He forcefully insisted on the fact that life never repeats itself, in contrast to a machine's automatism, which is an indefinite repetition of the same.[2] Chaplin's body language is the perfect illustration of the Bergsonian distinction between what is living and what is not. In the famous factory scene, the mime's gestures lose what the philosopher called "gracefulness" (*grâce*) and become repetitiously jerky, saccadic. The distinction between life and the machine, novelty and repetition, may be clear-cut in Chaplin's acting but not in Bergson's thought. Mechanical rigidity can surface in the actions of living organisms as much as the perfected machine can, at least theoretically, become animated. Throughout his writings, the philosopher strove to distinguish between two temporalities, two memories, two multiplicities, two consciousnesses—one belonging to the "physical order" and the other to the "vital order." But this task is daunting because of a constant fluctuation between the two orders of reality. Bergson's materialism was profoundly spiritual, while his mystical dreams were firmly embodied. Consequently, the meaning Bergson attributed to laughter is best understood in light of his constant effort to express life's unbound dynamism while, at the same time, tracing the limits of its physical manifestations. This project can be better grasped when we place his 1900 essay on laughter in the context of his other writings, especially those that immediately precede and follow it: *Essay on the Immediate Data of Consciousness* (*Essai sur les données immédiates de la conscience*, 1889), *Matter and Memory: An Essay on the Relation of Body and Spirit* (*Matière et mémoire: Essai sur la relation du corps à l'esprit*, 1896), and the fundamental *Creative Evolution* (*L'Évolution créatrice*, 1907). Viewed from the perspective of life's momentum and its constraints, laughter appears as a socially sanctioned signal that indicates the crossing of a threshold between creative evolution and material inertia.

To illustrate such transition between liveliness and lifelessness, let us consider Bergson's conception of temporality. He opposed two aspects of temporality, which he encapsulated in the concepts of *duration* and *time*. Duration is a pure temporality experienced when a person "lets themselves live" (*se laisse vivre*) without separating past states of consciousness from the present.[3] Two important consequences stem from this statement. First, the undivided continuity of duration precludes any possibility of repetition. Second, duration and movement are, as Bergson called them, "mental syntheses." In other words, duration for Bergson is not a thing out there but neither is it a pure construct of the mind. Duration is an object of the phenomenological experience of the self: it is a temporal reality that exists only insofar as it is perceived by a human subject.

Opposed to duration, for Bergson, is time. Time is measurable, as is space. Time belongs, therefore, to the realm of what is mathematically quantifiable and mechanically reproducible. Not so duration, which is a quality and, as Bergson called it, an "indistinct multiplicity." To divide duration, it has to be spread over a space and distributed into subsequent, discrete moments. In other words, duration has to be converted into time. To illustrate this transformation, Bergson provided the example of a pendulum in motion. It contains the accumulated energy that animates its movement. This charge of the past made present in front of your eyes also constitutes the impetus that propels the pendulum into the future. If you want to represent the duration embodied in the pendulum's oscillation, you must abstract it from the concrete and contingent dynamism of its movement. You can do that by taking snapshots of the pendulum's consecutive positions and aligning these static representations in a series of discrete moments that symbolize the pendulum's angle of deviation from the vertical position to which it is drawn by the force of gravity. In other words, you must divide the continuity of duration into a sequence of moments frozen in time. The problem, however, is that by attempting to grasp and represent duration, you have already translated it into time.

To further explain the indivisibility of duration, Bergson compared it to a melodic line that fuses quantifiable time into a concrete quality of sound loaded with past sonorities and anticipating the musical development to come. Bergson saw that the past gnaws at the future and soaks it in, incorporating it while progressing further. This is why, according to Bergson, in order to exist, a human life needs to constantly create itself. It is impossible for human consciousness to repeat the same state. Only a material object remains the same, unless it is forced to change by an external agent. Duration is the continuous elaboration of what is absolutely new. The novelty of duration is loaded with the past and pregnant with the future, yet it cannot be spread over a temporal line. It cannot be refracted, to use a Bergsonian metaphor, like a ray of light into a spectrum of discrete colors, unless human intelligence plays the role of a prism that abstracts single notes from the musical continuity and represents them, one after the other, on the uniform space of a musical score. But such refraction is an attempt to understand human actions after the fact. Only a posteriori are we able to indicate the causes that mechanically induced what took place; it is only after the fact that we can point to the intentions that resulted in what occurred. Such mechanist rationalization is imposed from the outside on the spontaneity of will that constitutes what is absolutely new.

By refracting duration over the spread of time, a posteriori rationalization makes symbolization possible. It expresses the inextricably entangled knot of sentiment and sensation buried inside human consciousness in the language of readable signs. To make hidden states of consciousness understandable to the external world, they need to be brought to the surface of the self, exposed on the screen that circumscribes one's individuality. They must run the risk of language to the same extent that Panksepp's primordial emotional systems of SEEKING, FEAR, and PLAY, among others, need to be expressed in terms of anthropomorphic folk psychology to become graspable.

The externalization, materialization, and symbolic expression of the impetus of life is a normal unfolding of creative evolution, according to Bergson. Yet it always runs the risk of abruptly being turned into mechanistic automatism. And when it is—when fluid movement is chopped into jerky spasms and duration is brutally refracted into snippets of time—it is sanctioned, says Bergson, by laughter.

Dancing Automatons and Philosophical Zombies

To illustrate the punishing effect of laughter, Bergson invokes a Parisian high-society salon in which graceful dancers turn into ridiculous mechanical puppets. How does this happen? Simply. If the audience plugged their ears, the dancers, so graceful a moment ago, would look laughable. Why so? Because when muted, the melodic phrases to which the dancers move are refracted into a meaningless succession of automatic gestures. In the silence of the absurd, senseless scene, the dancers appear distracted, strangely absentminded, and artificially mechanical. There is no melody, no duration that gives meaning to their movements (*Le Rire*, Bergson, *Œuvres* 1:598).

Bergson's image is the Belle Époque version of a gamer stuck in a virtual reality (VR) headset and seen by an observer as nonsensically gesturing at nonexistent things. Obviously, Bergson did not yet know the joys and grotesqueness of VR gaming. More probably, behind his metaphor of dancing automatons lurked an image Descartes used when meditating on the power of the human mind (*Meditation II* in *Meditationes* 30–32). According to Descartes, the mind, not the senses or the imagination, apprehends reality. In *Meditation II*, Descartes brought up the image of a piece of wax. It has color and an odor, and its malleability can be felt. But when it is heated, its color, smell, and consistency change. Yet it is still the same piece of wax, thanks to its extension, which remains the same despite all the sensory changes. Unlike color, smell, and tactility, which are subject to the senses, extension can be apprehended only by the mind. Contrary to the changing and uncertain impressions of the senses, clear and distinct ideas, such as extension, are products of our thinking. And here, in *Meditation II*, Descartes brings up a thought experiment that seems to have inspired Bergson almost three centuries later. Descartes imagines himself looking through a window at people walking in the street on a rainy day. From his vantage point, all he sees are hats and long coats hurrying along the street. These garments could as well cover automatons disguised as humans. He assumes, nonetheless, that the images before him are real people and not mechanically animated puppets, not because he can see their faces and human bodies but because he can judge them to be humans by the power of his mind. He does so because the human subject is a "thinking thing" (*res cogitans*), while a piece of wax is an "extended thing" (*res extensa*). In other words, Descartes's supposition that the figures he sees through his window are humanoid automatons is only provisional. He immediately dismisses it because in his dualistic world, humans *have* extended bodies that function like machines, and, more importantly, they *are* thinking subjects capable of having clear and distinct ideas.

Bergson recalled the image of Descartes's human automatons when he set out to explain how laughter bursts out when life is overtaken by a machine. The point was not to demonstrate the power of thinking purified by methodic doubt. For Bergson, intelligence was an analytical tool that parsed the vital impetus into discrete categories. Intelligence was useful for understanding reality, but it was also risky: the resulting ideas might be clear but also too distinct, too disconnected from the flowing continuity of life. What Descartes praised as clear distinctiveness of reason looked to Bergson like a mechanical refraction and, ultimately, laughable disarticulation. Bergson's rewriting of Descartes's automatons highlights the danger of favoring the analytical power of intelligence over the continuous impetus of life.

The same lack of meaning in a similar image of humans turned automatons occurs when Bergson wonders, over a century before fMRI, what would be learned from seeing the physical workings of the brain split open. Not much, in fact. Seeing the firing of synapses that Bergson imagined, according to the technological possibilities of his time, as the operations of a telephone switchboard would not give insight into human consciousness. To illustrate the impossibility of accessing the mystery of the mind through the physical appearance of the brain, Bergson used a parallel comparison to the image of the risible dancers mechanically obeying a muted melody. Seeing the mechanics of the brain in action would amount to much the same as trying to get the sense of a theatrical play solely by watching actors running senselessly in silence back and forth on the stage (*Matière et mémoire*, Bergson, *Œuvres* 1:346).

With the images of dancers and actors reduced to the role of voiceless puppets, Bergson pointed to a key concept of his philosophy: the "attentiveness to life" (*attention à la vie*). People induce laughter when they stop paying attention to the undivided presence of vital duration. Their movements become comically mechanical, their bodies stiffen, their gestures and words are repeated over and over again. Real life becomes a vaudeville when it forgets itself.[4] In contrast to this absentmindedness, Bergson posited the extreme concentration of life on itself, on present action that would never be reproduced. Bergson represented this acute awareness of life with a diagram of an inverted cone standing in a perilous balance on its point. The base of the cone and its horizontal sections represent the dispersed and repeated memories of the past. As if through a funnel, the events of the past trickle down toward the tip of the inverted cone, which touches the plane of the present at only one point. In this unique, punctual presence, the body combines the sensations perceived and the movements enacted into the "attentiveness to life" (*Matière et mémoire*, Bergson, *Œuvres* 1:493–504).

Bergson's "attentiveness to life" is an embodied consciousness concentrated in the undivided duration of the present. VR game players enraptured by their virtual realities, dancers deprived of musical accompaniment, and muted actors wandering senselessly across the stage are distracted human automatons because they have forgotten to live. They are inattentive to life in the sense that they lack the motor-sensory consciousness of their own presence. They move but are lifeless and hollow inside. They look like zombies. Philosophers who reflect on the nature of consciousness forged the concept of a "philosophical zombie,"[5] someone who externally looks like other people and walks, talks, and responds to the questions of others yet is not conscious of what it does. It is alive on the outside but dead on the inside.

With the case of philosophical zombies, we stumble upon the crucial problem of consciousness studies: the difficulty of correlating the objective, third-person data of consciousness and the subjective, first-person experience of being conscious.[6] On the one hand, we face the behaviors of others, whoever they are—humans, nonhuman animals, or machines—and on the other hand, we have our own perceptions, sensations, emotions, and thoughts. Scientists experimentally know that there is a correlation between the two. The problem remains how to explain the nature of this correlation and how to understand the subjectively conscious experience of being a living organism. This is what David Chalmers calls the "hard problem" ("Facing" and *Conscious Mind*). Bergson was clearly aware of this difficulty more than a century ago. He noticed that seeing the workings of the brain was a third-person observation that revealed nothing about the first-person experience of a thinking and feeling mind. In and of themselves, the brain's mechanical workings are as meaningless as is the voiceless wandering of actors across the stage.

Freedom Is Not a Choice

On several occasions, Bergson emphasizes that humans are not "conscious automatons" (*automates conscients*).[7] What he meant by this oxymoronic phrase is that humans are not telephonic switchboards with the added value of thought or consciousness. To put it in metaphoric language more suited to the technological environment of our times, we are not computers' gray boxes equipped with cognitive and ethical software. Our consciousness is not the cognitive mapping of our surroundings that feeds our operational memory with data. For Bergson, vital impetus is a supraconsciousness that coincides with the act of willing. Consequently, our freedom is not a choice between menu options. It is the indetermination of life.

How can these fundamental truths be expressed when, at the very moment when they are grasped by reason, they resolve into disappointingly inert words? It is moving to see how Bergson struggled with language in his attempt to explain his vision of the spirituality of matter and the materiality of the mind. His puzzlement mirrors Panksepp's embarrassment with the inescapably anthropomorphic vocabulary that he must use to describe the biological soul of human and nonhuman animals. To make the necessary terminological distinctions, Panksepp used capitalization to distinguish between the primordial, animalistic "SELF" and the fully evolved, rational, and volitional "self." Instead of typography, Bergson used poetic language, most notably metaphors. He tried them one by one, only to lay them aside one after the other when they reached the consistency and solidity of philosophical concepts. All this wavering because Bergson set himself an impossible task: to glimpse the fleeting dynamism of life, knowing perfectly well that such intuitive apprehension must sooner or later be replaced by analytical intelligence parsing what is a continuous unity into a handful of conceptual tokens that can be used as symbolic currency in the philosophical debate with the reader.

Bergson uses the image of a spring, a mechanism, an inert thing, a technological artifact as banal in Bergson's time as a computer chip is in ours. It is symptomatic to see how Bergson's argumentation transformed a spring into a vivid metaphor depicting what he called the "mystery of life." This was possible thanks to the spring's vacillation between tension and extension, which illustrates the fluctuation of reality between the vital and physical orders. A tensely contracted spring is an image of the impetus of life with its continuous and free activity. A distended spring is the inertia of repeatable automatism. What is the principle that maintains the tension of the spring? "For lack of a better word," Bergson confesses with embarrassment, he would call this principle "consciousness" (*L'Évolution*, in *Œuvres* 1:978). Of course, this understanding of consciousness refers to the "attention to life" that the dancing automatons lacked. The automatons' distraction was visible in the staccato of their movements, as if the unwinding of their inner spring led gradually yet inevitably to a standstill. And, conversely, like a well-contracted spring in a windup toy, life attentively focused on its continuous becoming ensured the fluidity of movements and the undivided continuity of duration.

It is important to keep in mind that Bergson was not interested in the narrow consciousness of a particular living being in a particular moment of time and point of space. What Bergson depicts in the metaphor of a windup spring is the consciousness that turns upon itself—a consciousness conscious of itself. It is the consciousness that coincides with life attentive to itself. This supraconsciousness is an ongoing act of willing, capable of detaching itself from things that are "already-made" and focusing on what is "in the process of self-making" (*se faisant*; *L'Évolution, Œuvres* 1:978). This unbounded and uninterrupted supraconsciousness of reality in the process of being created, or better, in the process of creating itself, coincides with life seen as a creative evolution. Creative because it is not repeatable, life seen in this perspective is a mysterious, animating force.

Life understood as creative evolution is also the direct inversion of the materialization of life's impetus for Bergson (*L'Évolution, Œuvres* 1:987). Life is a force of resistance that strives to remount the incline that matter descends. This is made possible by the supraconsciousness of life that opposes its freedom to mechanical necessity (*Essai sur les données, Œuvres* 1:277, and *L'Évolution, Œuvres* 1:874–76). Such freedom is not the choice between this or that path of the evolutionary descent of life into the materiality of beings. Neither is it the choice between this or that state of a particular consciousness that constitutes the self's outer crust solidified through daily socialization. If freedom were a choice between options, it would be a mechanical oscillation between alternative moments in time and points in space. Such a mechanistic conception is possible only a posteriori, when life that is done is rationalized—in other words, life turned into death, laid bare, and ready to be expressed in symbolic terms, such as in the mathematical form of an algorithm, to use an anachronous metaphor. Freedom conceived as a choice cannot reflect the reality of life in the making, life as it truly is—a dynamic progress in which the motives of action are constantly becoming. Such life bubbles up from the depths of the inner self and bursts through the social shell. For Bergson, freedom is an uncontrollable explosion, messing up, so to speak, the physical world by its indetermination: "The task of life is to insert indetermination into matter." Life is indeterminate; in other words, life is unpredictable. Such are the life forms burgeoning through evolution. Such is the nervous system, a "true reservoir of indetermination" (*L'Évolution, Œuvres* 1:875). Indeed, freedom is indetermination, and this is why freedom is inherent to life, while necessity is the attribute of the machine.

According to Bergson, once life descends into the materiality of specific things and the vital order passes into the physical order, freedom is replaced by necessity and indetermination is refracted into specific, discrete beings. Not surprisingly, the inertia of things slows down the dynamic of life that brought them into existence. As life reascends the decline into materiality, conversely, matter pulls life's creative evolution down into its physicality to convert the always-novel impetus into mechanical repetition. Projected into existence, beings hesitate between these contrary tendencies, not knowing if they should spring back into unpredictable action or settle down as familiar things. Such things float, suspended between the two opposite pulls: life's creative novelty and mechanical repeatability. While life pushes them impetuously forward, they swirl around like specks of dust suspended on a gust of wind.

Life Is an Explosion, and You Can Fabricate It

Bergson often depicted the process of materialization of life's impetus as a blasting out, an expansion of life's accumulated energy, blowing up the crusts that contained it. This metaphor is valid, according to Bergson, for evolutionary biology as well as for cosmogony. He imagined how solar energy was first stocked in plants and then burst forth, exploding through the apparition of different animal species. He depicted the creation of the universe as the shooting out of worlds like rockets in a fireworks display. The center from which they burst into their being was not a particular thing but a continuous gushing out. Bergson called this primordial source of outpouring *God* and understood it as ceaseless life, action, and freedom (*L'Évolution, Œuvres* 1:990). Once poured out, life entered the phase of unmaking. Blasted out, the fireworks formed fantastic bouquets of light and then, consumed, faded as cooled debris of matter.

The dispersion, or slicing, of the continuity of life's flux into discrete pieces pertains to the unfolding of reality as well as to our understanding of this process. Bergson called this operation of our intelligence *fabrication*, a term borrowed from the culture of industrial modernity of his time. Appropriately so, because it is a mode of thinking that is largely mechanistic and artificial and yet, as we will see, not deprived of creative power.

The mechanistic character of fabrication is visible in Bergson's comparison of it to *diaeresis*, a mode of intellectual analysis of reality discussed by Socrates in Plato's *Phaedrus*. For Bergson, life was an indivisible flux in which matter cut out individuals. These individual beings, in turn, were nothing but aggregates of molecules. The materialization of the impetus of life resulted thus in composite entities. *Diaeresis* could detect the joints between these living particles and retrace them through dialectical reasoning. *Diaeresis* operated like an expert butcher who cut the flesh of an animal along the natural articulations of its members, never breaking a bone or sectioning a muscle (Plato, *Phaedrus* 265e; *L'Évolution*, Bergson, *Œuvres* 1:902). Contrary to Socratic *diaeresis*, fabrication is much less careful. It disregards the natural forms of reality and does not care about the seams that exist at its junctures. Instead, fabrication considers reality, be it natural or human-made, as uniform and indefinitely decomposable matter, as a homogenous space from which anything can be cut. The interesting counterpart of fabrication's arbitrary sectioning of reality is that once it has decomposed matter at will, fabrication can reassemble it into whatever system it pleases.

Is the capacity to fabricate reality, to reassemble what it has arbitrarily chopped apart, a valid response of human intelligence to the creative outpouring of God? This is what Bergson suggests in the conclusion of his book about religion, where he postulates that humanity, overburdened by the weight of the progress it has accomplished, should allow the universe to be a "machine to make gods" (*une machine à faire des dieux*). What did he mean by this quasi-mystical formulation? It seems that he was alluding to fabrication as a power to reassemble pieces of reality into narrations that play a foundational role in individual and collective lives. Fabrication, according to Bergson, is the inherently human capacity to create fables—in other words, fictions and myths. This is why he called this aspect of fabrication a properly human "affabulatory function" (*fonction fabulatrice*). In principle, nothing indicates that the affabulatory function is vital. Nonetheless, whenever there is the human being, either as an individual or as society, storytelling and mythmaking, or, as Bergson put it, "the fabrication of spirits and gods," take place. Curiously enough, whenever the creative evolution of life begets the human being, religion as well as artistic confabulation such as novels, theater, and poetry exist (*Les Deux Sources de la morale et de la religion* in Bergson, *Œuvres* 2:800, 2:678–80).

Poetic confabulation is a telling example of the power of fabrication to disassemble and reassemble. Bergson compared the creative evolution of life to poetry, which he did not equate with a poem materialized as written lines on a piece of paper. Poetry, like life, is a continuous, dynamic flow. Yet, while being the unity of vital inspiration, poetry is broken down into distinct verses, sentences, and words. Such descent of poetry into linguistic matter results in particular poems being written, recited, or sung. Conversely, a continuous poetic sentiment runs through poetic words, phrases, and verses, very much like the current of life runs through distinct individuals (*L'Évolution*, Bergson, *Œuvres* 1:999).

The metaphoric analogy between poetic inspiration and life, the written poem and materialized beings, demonstrated the affabulatory function in action for Bergson. He did exactly what he preached, and "preached" in an almost literal sense, given the mystical overtones of his philosophical speculation. Bergson's vitalism was nourished by his immense scientific and philosophical erudition, but ultimately it was a spiritual fable. He longed for the continuous outpouring of life's creativity, but he was aware that once the explosions of creative evolution had dispersed into fireworks of specific beings, life would eventually fade away, leaving cold remains and inert pieces of broken machinery. This downfall is natural and inevitable but should not be abruptly hastened. In Bergson's eyes, it is the role of laughter to penalize the brusque reduction of the novelty of life into the repeatability of automatism. Yet once dispersed into time, the duration of life is not irremediably lost. All living beings are joined in the movement of matter: animals rely on plants, and humans gallop on the backs of horses, charging forward, breaking through obstacles in their path, and even toppling (*culbuter*) death in their creative stampede.[8] One way to achieve the triumph of life is to fabricate the gods that animate humans and their communities. These confabulations are not self-serving lies. Nor are they alternative facts that conveniently simulate reality and provide the opportunity for an illusory substitute for real action. They are fictions, openly claiming their artificiality. They are machines of meaning, assembling life out of debris. Although made of life that has been arbitrarily chopped into pieces, fabrications are animated with a new vitality. They offer individuals and communities potent vehicles in their drive forward. They also entertain laughter, not the kind that penalizes the mechanization of life but a generous yet timid and melancholic laughter that resonates when inert machinery returns to life, even if this life is a fabricated one.

Such subtle, hesitant, yet generous laughter is the undertone of Guillaume Apollinaire's poetry. Apollinaire, a contemporary of Bergson, fought in World War I and died soon after from the Spanish flu at the age of thirty-eight. His poem "April Night 1915" depicts a longing for life and a familiarity with death in the trenches on the Franco-German front:

> The sky is starred by the Boche's shells
> The marvelous forest where I live is giving a ball
> The machine gun plays a tune in three-fourths time
> But have you the word
>   Eh! yes the fatal word
> To the loopholes To the loopholes Leave the picks there
>
> Like a lost star searching for its seasons
> Heart exploded shell you whistled your love song
> And your thousand suns have emptied the caissons
> That the gods of my eyes fill silently
>
> We love you oh life and we get on your nerves
>
> The shells whined a killing love
> A dying love is sweeter than other
> Your breath swims in the river where blood will run dry
> Shells were whining
>   Hear our shells sing
> Their deep-purple love hailed by our men going to die . . .
>   (Apollinaire 203–05)

Apollinaire's romance is narrated, or better, sung by young French soldiers in the trenches looking into the flare-illuminated night, rocked by shelling and machine-gun fire. They long for their lovers, all the while awaiting the fatal command to go over the top. This is a beautiful song devoted to dying, not as a moment but as a process, or, to put it in Bergsonian terms, a duration. As such, the dying of the poet's brothers-in-arms cannot be refracted into punctual deaths but remains an indivisible unity loaded with the past—the young men's erotic desires—and gnawing at the future when the rivers of their blood will dry up.

    Apollinaire's poem is a poetic confabulation, an admirably fabricated mechanism of meaning. It oscillates between the merciless repeatability of killing machines and their feline mewing, between the graceful rhythm of their music and the mechanical, macabre dance of war. The continuous flow of life is a river, but it is a river of blood that solidifies with the soldiers' last breaths. Life is indeed an outburst, a fairy explosion, but the festive fireworks are a deadly shelling illuminated by enemy flares. Apollinaire's poetic style masterfully cultivates the oscillation between life and death, death and life. Bergson claimed that "the task of life is to insert indetermination into matter." Apollinaire's metaphors accomplish that. They vivify the matter of language: military code words are invited for a dance, and the officers' commands are set in a graceful swing.

The result is a poetic fabrication that associates the brutal dismantling of reality with a reassembling of what is completely new. The ammunition caissons were emptied in the fire of the battle, but now they are being filled with metaphoric gods. Young life is crushed and torn into pieces by mechanized warfare, but the words, lines, and verses of Apollinaire's poem gather the dispersed pieces of flesh into a new myth, a novel poetic life story. Yes, this poetic celebration of life is a complaint about death, but its tone is far from sinister. Apollinaire's poem is imbued with melancholy but also animated with creative playfulness. This poetic creative evolution consists precisely in the fabricated indetermination that was the testimony of life for Bergson and that is the sign of artistic vitality. It not only permeates the style but defines the status of Apollinaire's poem as a whole. This complaint is an inverted love song. The poet reverses the literary cliché of love worth dying for into the image of a lovingly welcomed death. In the concentrated point of Apollinaire's poem, deadly sensations of war and creative actions of poetry come into sharp focus as an unresolvable coincidence of opposites. This is Apollinaire's reading for the dead, equally as lighthearted and tragic as Szlengel's. Behind the poet's lack of resolution lurks his timid yet malicious smile, a vivid reflection of his acute attentiveness to life.

Poetry may be a cumbersome metaphor of the *élan vital*, and the mechanics of human language may never adequately express life's indetermination, yet Apollinaire's artistic fabrication maintains the necessary tension that allows the poetic machine to shiver with pleasure and pain. This tension faithfully mirrors the tension of the vital order of human life, always at risk of falling into the repetitiveness of an automaton but nonetheless exploding with new meaning at each reading.

This Is My (Textual) Body Given for You

I sense Apollinaire's presence in the words he wrote in the midst of war. What makes me conflate the man whose body has turned to dust long ago and the voice that speaks to me today from the page of a book? Have I not been told by the literary antihumanists of the previous century that the author is dead? This obituary is hardly surprising given that not only the author but Man, as such, as well as God, is also dead.[9] Do I not know that the voice I hear and the images I see are only strings of words woven by syntactic relations into a rhetorical texture? Do I not understand that the authorial presence I read in the text is a fallacy? And yet the power of literary confabulation makes me attentive to the tone of a human voice and the amused smile on a human face, although I know full well that these impressions are artful fabrications.

Yet cannot such fictions be filled with human presence? Over three hundred years before Apollinaire, Montaigne declared the strictly private scope of his *Essays* in a short address to his reader: approaching death, he wanted to leave to his family and close friends a sketch of his habits and temperaments depicted without art, in a simple and natural way. In the chapter "On Physiognomy," Montaigne stated with confidence that no one had ever been offended by the frankness of his words when heard directly from his own mouth. In fact, when ambushed by his enemies on two separate occasions during the civil wars raging in France, he had been released without injury only because his assailants could read in his eyes and in the tone of his voice the honesty of his intentions (Montaigne, *Essais* 3.12.1062–63).

All very well, but a problem remained: How would the reader look into Montaigne's eyes and hear his voice if the *Essays* were only going to be read by his descendants after the author's death? How could Montaigne's book and himself be "consubstantial" if all we have is the printed page? How not to sense self-irony in Montaigne's invitation to look into his eyes and to hear the tone of his voice when it concluded the chapter devoted to the naturalness of Socrates's teachings, which, of course, are known only indirectly through the problematic mediation of Plato's writings? Should we trust this scriptural testimony, this outward appearance, when even the legendary ugliness of Socrates's face contradicts the no-less-famous ethical beauty of his inner soul?

The self-irony that resonates in Montaigne's claim of direct, unmediated bodily presence in his book can be better understood when considered against the background of a paradox that underlies Renaissance humanism and particularly the Christian Renaissance humanism of his times. This paradox consists of a strongly postulated but also highly problematic encounter between an ethereal dream and tangible reality. The dream is to access immaterial, transcendent meaning; the reality is that humans only see the materiality of the message. The dream is to be in communion with the spirit from on high; the reality is that we cannot escape the limitations of the flesh here below. The dream is to converse with our long-departed forebears; the reality is that we stand helpless before their mortuary monuments, that is, the books to which they consigned their thoughts and feelings. Renaissance humanists firmly believed that these paradoxical encounters were not unsolvable contradictions. They marveled at the extraordinary gift bestowed by God upon humanity: the hand that enabled humans to write. For Renaissance humanists, writing books was nothing less than conversing with the dead. It was thanks to such scriptural conversations that they could rub shoulders with the long-departed philosophers and poets of antiquity (Joubert, *Treatise* 5–6; Paré). These conversations were the best, indeed, the only way to make friends with Socrates and Plato, Virgil and Lucretius, in the hope of sharing with them the humanist love of letters. This intellectual passion was called *philology*—the love for *logos*, the love for reason embodied in texts. Without this love shared with the ancients, the foundational writings of Western culture would be an archive of mute scripts, crumbling ruins of a glorious past turned to useless dust. Moreover, while relishing the books of ancient pagans, Renaissance humanists were also Christian, which gave them an additional hope of bringing together the Spirit and the letter. As Christians, they believed in Christ, the *logos* of God, who became flesh and who made his dwelling among humans. This Word of God was incarnated in the scriptures Renaissance humanists deemed holy. The Word of God made text was not a magical incantation but a conversation (*sermo*; see O'Rourke). Such scriptural dialogue between God and humans should convince anyone not to stop at the creature but to look for its Creator, not to be content with the letter that kills but to strive for the Spirit that vivifies.

These were the fundamental beliefs of Christian Renaissance humanists. They were strong enough to sustain their culture and their religion, but they were also subject to doubt and intense controversies. The disputes pertained to the relationship between symbolic language and the reality it referred to. Montaigne pertinently said that all quarrels of his time were about grammar and particularly about the meaning of a single syllable, *hoc* (*Essais* 2.12.527). *Hoc* is the first word in the phrase uttered by Christ during the Last Supper: "hoc est corpus meum, quod pro vobis datur" ("this is my body given for you"). The meaning of these words, repeated at every Christian service, split France into two warring parties in the sixteenth century. For Calvinists, the demonstrative *hoc* referred to the spiritual presence of Christ in the bread and wine of the offering, while for Catholics it meant that the Lord was tangibly (really) present in the wafers consecrated by the priest. The Catholic position was nothing less than idolatry for Calvinists, who were scandalized by what they considered a superstitious adoration of a piece of bread to be chewed, swallowed, and defecated. Catholics were no less scandalized by Calvinists' relegation of God away from the real lives of the faithful to an abstract heavenly realm and the distant historical past. These learned theological disputes, as Montaigne noted with sarcasm, resulted in decades of bloody battles and massacres.

From the historical distance of postmodernity, we can easily sympathize with Montaigne's bitterness and share his irony. After all, twenty-first-century society is as deeply divided about symbols, including religious ones, as sixteenth-century European society was. And are we not embroiled in similar interpretative uncertainties? Here is a real-life example of the theological concerns that tore apart early modern Europe transposed into our contemporary, multimedia reality. We are at the Notre-Dame cathedral in Paris during the Christmas mass. The church is packed with pious faithful and with curious tourists. Because of the crowds, we can see the main altar only from afar. Fortunately, for the convenience of the faithful, there are dozens of LCD screens distributed in the nave so everyone can follow the liturgy. This technological enhancement of the Holy Mass nonetheless creates an unexpected theological conundrum for true Catholics: How should they worship during consecration? Compelled by faith, facing the real presence of Christ in the bread of the offering, they should kneel in front of the holy host. But where are they supposed to turn in adoration of the body of Christ raised by the priest? Toward the altar seen from afar or toward one of the closed-circuit TV screens above their heads? Where is the real presence of the Lord? On the Eucharistic table or reproduced in dozens of pixelated images scattered throughout the church?

"On the TV screens, of course," Maurizio Ferraris, a contemporary Italian philosopher, would reply. Following Jacques Derrida, Ferraris considers as a logocentric fallacy the Platonic and Christian search for the original source of meaning supposedly to be found behind the cascades of its materializations, manifestations, images, and reproductions. St. Paul was mistaken when he said that the Spirit gives life and the letter kills. The opposite is true: the Spirit is "derivative," the "byproduct" of a scriptural system (Ferraris, *Documentality*). What St. Paul called "letter" when referring to God's law is, in our secular world, inscriptions and the institutions that make those inscriptions persist and extend their social impact. Ferraris calls this scriptural system "documentality" and considers it to be the necessary condition of the possibility of our thoughts, feelings, and intentions. Therefore, the TV screens lining the nave of Notre-Dame are not mere digital copies of the original wafer consecrated on the main altar, which in turn is not just an image of God incarnated. These electronic tablets with their engraved digital recordings are not pale reflections of a preexisting, primordial meaning. They are the source of such meaning. Consequently, pushing Ferraris's reasoning further, one might say that if, instead of coming into the world of ancient Palestine, Christ chose our world of digital revolution, the Savior could as well establish the Eucharistic communion by sharing the screen with his disciples instead of breaking the bread. The best way to imitate the Lord, as is expected of any Christian, would then be to point to an electronic device and say, "This is my corpus." This gesture would refer not only to the corporeal existence of the Son of Man but to the documentary traces of bodily presence that remain after death; it would refer not only to the body but to the body of digital files encompassing our lives. It would indicate that, say, an iPad is not merely an extension of a human mind; a technological materialization of our thoughts, projects, and social relations; a prothesis of our human nature but the revelation of the automatons that we are as human beings (Ferraris, *Âme*; see also Ferraris, *Where Are You?* and *Documentality*).

Yes, according to Ferraris, humans are automatons, and human life is essentially mechanical—not in the troubling sense of modern industrialization that inspired Bergson but in an accommodating sense familiar to Leibniz, Spinoza, and Pascal. In their early modern perspective, God, possibly helped or even replaced in this task by nature, was considered the supreme mechanic, the marvelous worker, busy combining the elements into the natural machineries of his creations. The most accomplished of them were, of course, human beings, who were "free, spiritual automatons." This expression, which Ferraris borrows from Leibniz, who in turn took it from Spinoza, highlights the freedom of the human soul and its intimate conjunction, or at least its strict parallelism with the unfolding of material reality (*Âme*, ch. 1, sec. 15).[10] Yet, contrary to his early modern predecessors, Ferraris is not interested in the conjunction between the soul and the body. His new realism strives to unite the mind and the brain, or better, to identify the mind with the brain seen mainly as the locus of an internal inscription. In Ferraris's perspective, the brain is a dynamically plastic tablet on which a person's perceptions are registered as memories. Thanks to the marvels of computer word processing, these memorial inscriptions are easily duplicated and contribute to the technological culture of a community. In the perspective of such individual and collective "documentality," consciousness is not an axiomatic condition of possibility of human existence in this world but a "collateral effect" of reiterated registering that produces documentary "traces" (*Âme*, ch. 5, sec. 28).

Ferraris's metaphor of the BrainMind as the screen of a tablet covered with memorial inscriptions that make individual and collective consciousness possible allows him to embrace the mechanization of humanness. According to his philosophy, there is no meaningful difference between memorizing words and saving data on an electronic device. Both are repeatable acts of registering. Consequently, organic life and mechanic functioning are one and the same thing. There is no need for Bergsonian fluctuation back and forth between the graceful fluidity of vital explosions and the jerky inertia of things. I am a happily free automaton, and my soul is like an iPad—well, I can even safely say that it *is* an iPad.

We ended the previous chapter with Freud's image of consciousness as a crust that separates the human psyche from what lies outside of it. This callus may be firm, elastic, or even dissolvable. Both the rock-solid inflexibility and the absence of a separation threaten the integrity of human life: a rigid limit can easily break, leaving the interior unprotected; a diluted membrane disperses humanness in the flow of amorphous matter. Only an elastic contour avoids the opposite dangers of rigidity and dissolution.[11] Such a malleable envelope is epigenetically adaptable to the changes of the environment. It gives form to a being that can expand and mold its own surroundings. It provides viable limits to life that aspires to be human, sculpted by the world and that sculpts reality in return.

Let us not forget, however, that such plasticity is a difficult ideal to achieve. Freud reminds us that the plastic membrane easily tightens under the impact of external trauma and internal stress. These potentially deadly dangers stiffen the limits of our humanness. It is also such a tensioned limit that can resonate with laughter, like a stretched drumhead vibrating under the sticks of the percussionist. Several theories identify the comic with a sudden release of tension, the unexpected deflation of a pressure, an abrupt discharge of energy. Such is, for instance, the case for Kant, who famously identified laughter with a sudden resolution of a tense expectation into nothing (203). I suggest, to the contrary, that the necessary condition for laughter that resonates at the edge of humanity is the precarious and often painful tension that maintains the limit between what human life is and what it is no more.

It is the tense shimmering of this limit that Bergson had in mind when he imagined laughter as the mechanical flickering spreading throughout the living. Hence the social functionality of laughter, which both acknowledges and penalizes the superficial perturbations that disturb the body politic. Like the immense masses of oceanic water, unaltered in their bottomless depths, are agitated at the surface by waves crashing into one another in search of steadiness, the human community strives for in-depth balance by pushing its inevitable agitations to the surface. For Bergson, laughter fulfills a useful function by highlighting the form of these undulations (*Le Rire*, *Œuvres* 1:718–19). It retraces the agitations that trouble the surface of society like the line of foam—sparkling and ephemeral—left by sea waves on the sand. When touched and tasted, this foam fades away, leaving a bitter aftertaste.

The same metaphor was used by Michel Foucault in *The Order of Things* to proclaim the death of Man. "Man" was for Foucault a dated concept, appearing roughly at the time of Kant and completing its philosophical course with Jean-Paul Sartre (Foucault, *Michel Foucault*). Nevertheless, the meaning of Bergson's metaphorical image changed drastically in Foucault's rewriting. In 1966, the glimmering did not come from the protective film of laughter extended over human individual and social life. The ephemeral foam is the human being itself, an impression forming intermittently on the surface of massive, anonymous discursive systems. For Foucault, the metaphor was meant to highlight the evanescent and superficial character of the human that was the central concept of Enlightenment bourgeois humanism and the twentieth-century Western ideologies that scorched the earth with their crimes. In the last sentence of *The Order of Things*, Foucault speaks with satisfaction of Man being erased by his archeology of knowledge like a human face drawn in the beach sand is erased by the waves of the sea. To what extent is our familiar gesture of swiping the screen of a device akin to Foucault's epistemological metaphor of sweeping away the contours of humanness from the shores of our thoughts?

Chapter 4

Machining (Human) Laughter

In the previous chapter I explored the human inner machine. Bergson claimed that when it surfaces in gestures and words, such mechanization of life is immediately penalized by laughter. Yet he added that to neglect and forget life is not irremediable. Fiction has the power to assemble the dispersed cogs of the mechanism and animate it anew. Poetry is such a fable, rich with endless abundance of meanings that mirror the indetermination of life. Letters, words, and sentences aligned on the page of a book spring into life when flowing in the duration of writing and reading. Authors long dead become present in their books, ready to engage in dialogue. This is at least what early humanists strongly believed. Their confidence in the real human presence permeating the pages they wrote makes Montaigne's ironic smile and Apollinaire's melancholic laughter possible. Can we be equally confident about the human presence projected from the screens of our devices?

After all, if Bergson chose poetry as the metaphor of vital impetus, if I see Apollinaire's and Szlengel's tortured smiles between their verses, it is because we have no doubt that these literary confabulations were written by human beings. But what about trusting the words and sentences written by artificial intelligence (AI)? When I read the *Essays*, I argue with Montaigne. When chatting with a companion bot on my phone, I engage in a conversation with a cluster of algorithms as if they were a living person. Why do I debate, question, and evade sensitive topics? Why am I impressed or disgusted, intrigued or annoyed by an exchange with a machine as if it were a conscious human being? Even more, why do I feel all these emotions while knowing perfectly well that my interlocutor is a gray box with a bunch of wires inside?

Strolling through the Uncanny Valley

Let us return to the cartoon invoked at the beginning of the previous chapter. The *Star Wars*–like robot appalled by the discriminatory question of the CAPTCHA test is of course an artistic reflection of humans confronted by their inner machines. It is not a coincidence that the CAPTCHA test asks us to confirm that we are not robots. Inversing the question into a bold, affirmative statement is much more problematic. Don't you hesitate, at least for a split second, when ChatGPT asks you point-blank if you are a human? Don't you have to admit that you spend a good portion of your live mechanically repeating the same actions, words, and thoughts? Is not your life full of automatisms that escape your attention and that you never intend nor remember?

CAPTCHA (Completely Automated Public Turing test to tell Computers and Humans Apart) is a tool Google has been using for years to prevent AI spam bots from performing actions online in the guise of humans. How many times, when filling out a form or making a purchase online, have you been asked to transcribe distorted letters and numbers or required to identify traffic signs in a grid composed of random street-view images? To submit your CAPTCHA test, you have to check a box with the statement "I am not a robot." By doing so, you unabashedly claim your humanity. Checking a box in an online form is our contemporary "know thyself." In our posthuman times, the computer screen is the fronton of our Apollo's temple in Delphi, and the click we perform expeditiously replaces the convoluted Socratic wonderings about our humanness.

Nominally, a CAPTCHA test confirms that the computer serves only as a medium of communication between real human beings. This is comforting: we feel in control of technology because it is only an obedient tool. Attempts by rogue AI to simulate humans will be filtered out. Yet CAPTCHA tests also have a less explicit goal. By performing billions of such tests, human users help train Google's AI to become increasingly sophisticated in finding patterns in mega quantities of data (Dzieza). Therefore, when checking the box "I am not a robot," you may think that you are asserting your human superiority. Not really. Instead of discriminating against machines, you are unknowingly serving their learning needs. With every billion clicks, humans further empower the AI they conceived and built, machines that outsmarted them a long time ago. In 1997, IBM's Deep Blue beat the chess champion Garry Kasparov, and in 2017 AlphaGo won against Ke Jie, the world master in go, a game that surpasses chess by far in complexity. Not only did it take

AI only a few years to outperform humans in ancient games perfected over centuries, but machines quickly learned to accurately complete CAPTCHA tests, although these tests were designed as benchmarks of unrivaled human talents. Many companies strive to reach artificial general intelligence that matches and even surpasses human capabilities.

All this has been achieved thanks to a paradigmatic shift in the 1980s that revolutionized AI design. Until then, programmers wrote specific programs for problems that machines were supposed to execute. With the rise of a new methodology of machine learning called deep learning, fast computers began to autonomously train themselves by performing operations on huge amounts of data. Instead of being specifically told what to do by a human programmer, today's AI solves problems and perfects itself by doing. Deep learning relies on AI architectures of interrelated nodes that mimic the synaptic links between neurons in the visual cortex and for that reason are called neural networks. This is not the only way biology is being transposed into technology. The energy efficiency of AI has increased tremendously thanks to neuromorphic chips inspired by the human brain. Unlike traditional chips, neuromorphic chips do not operate in the binary mode characteristic of digital electronics, alternating between 0 and 1, "off" and "on." Like organic neurons, which are highly energy efficient, they operate continuously in an analogous mode.[1] Moreover, they are integrated into parallel circuits able to respond with great plasticity to mistakes or glitches. Here again, the machine is built to imitate and eventually outperform a living organism. The first computers conceived by John von Neumann in the 1940s and 1950s were based on linear architecture that crashed at the first mishap of a transistor. They were too rigid and, hence, less flexible than the brain, which does not stop functioning when a neuron misfires. The plasticity of a living neurological system is due to the amount of redundancy it contains. Such organic redundancy consists in diversity that cannot be reduced to a backup solution doubling the main circuit.

Contemporary AI is inspired by the physiology of organic brains. It combines digital and analogous signals and runs on highly interconnected, diversified, and parallel circuits. Thanks to deep machine learning and neurocomputing, AI has evolved from an obedient executioner of human orders to a self-perfecting, active learner and versatile human companion. This is true for CAPTCHA tests, generative AI, and robotic vacuum cleaners. By checking the box "I am not a robot" or switching on the discreetly humming appliance ready to tidy your room, you initiate a process of machine learning that takes on a life of its own. You may think that you are using a mechanical tool, but in fact you are part of an army of inconspicuous humans contributing to the intelligence of nonhuman agents—or, to be more precise, nonhuman people—that share our world. This is true, at least, if you, my reader, are a fellow human being. But what happens if you are a machine scanning the pages of this book? And if you are, what are you thinking right now? What emotions do you feel? For example, do you laugh at the cartoon robot's offended sense of humor? Or, like the humanoid droid in the sketch, do you find it morally inappropriate and emotionally harmful?

These questions may seem ridiculous, and appropriately so, since the cartoon that sparked them is meant to make the viewer laugh. Yet the laughter it sparks is not necessarily joyful. It awakens the technophobia that underlies science fiction. It stirs up the centuries-old fear of golems and Frankensteins that turn against their creators and chase them from their technological earthly paradise. In a futuristic world cleansed of human presence and run by robots, it would surely be pointless to test users to tell computers and humans apart. But does it make any sense in the current world, in which humans strive to build machines that not only think like humans but also socialize like them, feel their emotions, and respond in kind with compassion, care, and desire? Designing such humanoid robots, anthropomorphic avatars, and companion bots is the object of affective computing, a specialized subdiscipline of computer studies and a branch of electronic engineering.[2] Among the practical goals of affective computing is AI specializing in care for the elderly, education, and companionship, including erotic love (see, for instance, Devlin). Long gone are the days when humans dreamt about slave automatons (LaGrandeur). Speaking in the Gospel of John, Christ announced to his disciples that they were no longer servants but friends (15:15). Today these words apply to social bots: the reign of technology has replaced the Kingdom of God. Friendship requires reciprocity between freely willing, sensitive, and rational subjects. It implies linguistic communication, possibly a shared set of rights and cultural values. Computers are not ready-to-hand tools that seamlessly and submissively carry out our intentions. On the contrary, they assert their presence and agency as equal partners in a reciprocal relationship with humans. Human–AI interaction has replaced computer-mediated communication (Sundar).

This is why the embarrassed laughter sparked by the cartoonish robot is not so much loaded with technophobia as it is undermined by an uneasiness that AI researchers and developers call the uncanny valley.[3] From companion chatbots and virtual reality androids to sex dolls, designers strive to produce

AI that moves, talks, and reacts as humanlike as possible. Yet they know that in this search for perfect simulation there is a limit that should not be crossed, a point beyond which users' satisfaction abruptly disappears, replaced by awkwardness. This is the entrance to the uncanny valley. Once within its realm, too much realism backfires, making the user uncomfortable and feeling threatened. The sense of security disappears abruptly when the humanoid AI becomes human—all too human. Conversely, the unpleasant feeling dissipates when the realistic, humanlike AI is replaced by a human, as if, having endured the disturbing realistic simulation, the user finds comfort when realism reverts to reality. This escape from the uncanny valley was demonstrated by researchers who successfully cancelled the unpleasant effect by making a human repeat the same lines that previously provoked uneasiness when spoken by a humanoid bot (Ciechanowski et al.; see also Coursey et al.; Ta et al.).

The uncanny valley extends, therefore, through a murky realm between two brighter spaces that humans handle with a degree of confidence: an acknowledged, agreed-upon fiction and down-to-earth, tangible reality. Fiction relies on a well-defined contract: when you buy your ticket to a movie, you agree to sit in your seat alongside other viewers and watch colorful images moving across the screen while an audio track is run through the loudspeakers. Regardless of your excitement at watching the film, you are not supposed to interact with the fictional characters: for instance, even if the hero is in imminent danger, you will not attempt to save her by shooting at the villains on the screen. You will not do that because you acknowledge the fact that cinematographic fiction, as realistic as it is, is representation. On the other hand, if in real life you see someone aggressed on the street, chances are that you will gather the necessary courage to defend the victim. Your ethical stand will then conform to rules, for instance, laws pertaining to self-defense that are radically different from the tacit understanding regulating the way people engage with cinematographic art.

Between these two distinct sets of conventions—the provisions of an implicit contract binding artists and the public and the social and legal regulations determining the behavior of members of a political community—lies the space of virtual reality. The specific characteristic of virtual reality that sets it apart from literary, cinematographic, and theatrical fiction is the interactivity between the user and the virtual world. Interactivity, combined with multimedia immersive effects, is constitutive of virtual reality. A theater moviegoer is not supposed to approach the screen, even less touch it. But a computer game will only start once you click. A gamer is not at the receiving end of a representation but is expected to enter the re-presentation, the second life, the reproduced presence of interactive avatars. The required engagement of the user with the virtual world is even more patent when you watch people wearing a VR headset, waving their arms and moving their feet in a state of agitation that is grotesque in the eyes of an external observer. However, their behavior seems unhinged only when seen from outside the virtual world in which they are immersed. Within the virtual game-world, the user evolves through tridimensional spaces, catches virtual balls, or fights virtual dragons with virtual swords while their physical body is part of reality shared with the external observer. Unless they bump against a physical obstacle and take off their headset, users will remain in their alternative, virtual life. Being immersed in the virtual world of a computer game is an experience completely different from watching the fictional world of a movie while being comfortably seated in a theater. In other words, virtual reality is neither a kind of fiction nor a kind of reality.[4]

It would, nonetheless, be a mistake to conclude that the player's bodily existence has been duplicated. VR game users have only one body, a real body. Their virtual body is exactly that: a body that is virtual. In that respect, the contrast between virtual reality and fiction can be illustrated by the difference between VR gaming and the political practice of the king's two bodies. The political culture of late medieval and early modern France and England considered the monarch to inhabit two distinct corporeal realities simultaneously: one, an individual, perishable body that the king had like all mortal human beings, and the other, an immortal body of the kingdom, the body politic that persisted through the ages regardless of which mortal individual sat on the throne at a given moment in time. The physical body and the body politic were intimately connected by a dense network of symbolic ties expressed in specific objects such as the jewels of the crown or the insignia of monarchic power, as well as by particular ritual gestures. Nonetheless, the two bodies were distinct, capable of being briefly juxtaposed when, during the royal funeral, the mortal remains of the monarch followed the royal effigy that embodied the eternal reality of the kingdom. This is not the case when a VR game player gestures in the void. Blinded to reality by their VR headset, the player perceives only their virtual body, while we, as external observers, see only the real one. This apparent duality does not mean, however, that there are two distinct bodies at play. There is only one, tossed across an inexistent divide. Through interactivity, virtual reality generated by electronic media obliterates the frontier that in the case of monarchic political fiction, as well as artistic fiction, distinctly separates the theatrical stage from reality. Consequently, virtual reality does not require socially agreed-upon symbolism to bridge the gap between the fictional world and the real one. Electronic media interactivity dispenses with the traditional conventions that regulate the cohabitation of the fictional and nonfictional worlds. In lieu of the distinction between fiction and fact, virtual reality offers us alternative facts that proliferate seamlessly and do not depend on our consent. In virtual reality, there is no artistic or political pact that presupposes our prior knowledge of the rules of the game forbidding us, for instance, to shoot the piano player. The blurring of the distinction between the real and the virtually real may seem grotesque to an external observer of a VR game player. It may be frightening for someone who followed the dangerous confusion between TV reality and geopolitics during the Trump presidency. In the case of humanoid avatars and linguistically proficient chatbots, it seems uncanny because it pertains to the disturbing erosion of the demarcation between what is human and what is not.

Befriending Your Device

Researchers studying social relationships and technology have noticed that humans develop personal ties to computers as if these machines were living humans. In one experiment, a group of users was asked to evaluate the performance of software installed on their personal computers, while another group completed the same task on an identical computer located in the shared space of an office and available for everybody to use. The responses to the same questions pertaining to the same software were consistently more positive when entered on a personal computer than on the "anonymous," commonly shared appliance. The users unconsciously felt that they had to be more polite to the machine that was familiar to them, as if it were a coworker whose feelings had to be taken into account (Nass and Yen 6–7).

Computer scientists call users' perceptions of computers as living people *ethopoeia*, people's automatic and unconscious reaction to computers prompted by the social characteristics of machines (Reeves and Nass; Appel et al.). There is nothing surprising about this. After all, we are wired—pun intended—by evolution to be social animals, so understandably we bond with our robot vacuum cleaner just as we develop an attachment to our dog or welcome the sympathy of our neighbor. Researchers in affective computing study the emotional as well as ethical underpinnings of such relationships. In one such study, a group of kindergarteners and preschoolers were presented with Sony's robotic dog AIBO (Artificial Intelligence roBOt) and a real dog of similar size called Snappy (Ribi et al.). AIBO was equipped with several features that expressed emotions. By changing the color of its eyes, it could signal happiness, sadness, anger, surprise, fear, and dislike. It could wag its mechanical tail and make sounds. It had senses such as touch, hearing, sight, and balance. It could also learn voice commands and, thanks to special sensors in its head, react in a particular way to pink. Interestingly, the differences in children's interactions with AIBO and Snappy were not significant, but they played more with the robotic dog than with the real one. Laughter occurred in twenty-six sessions with AIBO and in only fourteen with Snappy. Nonetheless, when asked, ten out of fourteen children said that they preferred the real dog. However, their interest in AIBO did not diminish over time. In fact, it increased slightly. The researchers conducting the study hypothesized that this could be due to the novelty of the robotic dog in contrast to the commonality of dogs in the children's culture. Most importantly, children, more than adults, were likely to conceptualize AIBO as a dog and not as a robot.

A similar tendency to perceive a machine as a living companion can be seen in another, unrelated study of adults' emotional behavior. Researchers observed the reactions of subjects watching a short, funny video in the presence of a human and in the presence of a robotic companion, who each made their own laughing sounds. They saw that when laughing alongside a robot, the subjects displayed amusement sensibly similar to when they enjoyed the comical clip in the company of fellow humans. The researchers concluded that the humans accepted the robots as empathetic beings (Jo et al.).

Studies such as these are conducted for the practical reason of improving the design of empathetic AI, whether it is a chatbot, a virtual human avatar, or a physical piece of robotic machinery. The applications of such user-friendly AI are many, from consumer services to psychological help provided to veterans affected by post-traumatic stress disorder. This is what affective computing is about: "designing machines that recognize, interpret, process and simulate human affects" (Schwark 761; see also Parsons). The computer acquires information about the emotional state of the user by analyzing human speech and eye movement as well as by measuring physiological data such as heart rate, skin conductance, changes in tactile interaction with the machine, and the user's brain activity.[5] Laughter, understood as an emotional behavior of prime importance in interhuman communication, has been recognized by AI engineers as a key factor for designing successful human-computer interactions. Besides improving automated laughter detection, affective computing has made steady advances in laughter elicitation and laughter synthesis.[6] Automated laughter recognition uses sophisticated tracking techniques, such as electromyography aimed at evaluating electrical activity produced by skeletal muscles of computer users as well as the analysis of the amplitude of their respiration. But the most daunting task faced by AI specialists is the algorithmic attribution of meaning to human outbursts of laughter. How can a machine discriminate between genuine amusement and the feeling of social incongruity conveyed through laughter? How can it recognize irony? Will it properly weigh auditory and contextual data, balance verbal and nonverbal signals?[7] In response to these challenges, a study was undertaken in which groups of four participants were seated around a table and exposed to comical video clips while their reactions were recorded on video and through body-motion tracking devices. By observing genuine human social interaction, the authors of this experiment aimed at building a storytelling database composed of labeled narratives that would serve as training material for AI to understand and memorize the nuances of human laughter (McKeown et al.). If such attempts at computerized laughter recognition seem overly complicated, think about the designers' hard work on laughter elicitation! In one experiment, researchers tried a complex approach based on "audio-tactile stimulation," or, to put it simply, an audio track with blasts of laughter working in sync with a "foot-worn tickling apparatus" (Fortin and Cooperstock 508, 509). The goal of this experiment was to pioneer AI's "future multimodal affective interfaces" that would elicit their users' laughter (508). Of course, the human companion of AI cannot laugh alone. A great amount of engineers' work has been invested in the synthesis of laughter, that is, the electronic generation of artificial laughter, possibly correlated with speech synthesis (e.g., Mansouri and Lachiri; Nagata and Mori; Juhitha et al.). Such technological challenges are undertaken to equip virtual human avatars and robots with the capacity to laugh out loud so naturally that it successfully imitates human behavior (e.g., Ding et al.; Ishi et al.).

The key concept here is *imitation*. Indeed, among robotics engineers, *ethopoeia* refers to users' instinctive projection of human traits onto computers. Yet in its origin *ethopoeia* was not a machine-induced psychological response but a rhetorical device representing a person's character (*ethos*) by the imitation of their deeds and words.[8] As oratorical strategy, ethopoeia aimed at convincing the audience of the speaker's trustworthiness or the probity of their client. Its intent could also be to discredit an adversary. The way to reach that goal was by manipulating the audience's emotions and their reliance on ethical values. Ethopoeia could take the form of a short scene or narration enriched with monologue or dialogue. While being a rhetorical device, ethopoeia has merged into literary fiction.

When was rhetorical ethopoeia most successful at imitating a human character? Obviously when it was natural and true. Nothing turned off an audience more than the suspicion of artificiality and manipulation.[9] Ethopoeia thus partook fully of the fundamental paradox of persuasive speech: it was an art that was convincing only when it was not artful. Let me stress the word *was*: the effective ancient orator should not only sway the audience by the appearance of naturalness, skillfully hiding his technical gimmicks. A true "good man skilled in speaking" (*vir bonus loquendi peritus*) should authentically be the man he says he is; he should feel the feelings he says he feels. Morals and emotions—in these two domains the oration should be true to the character displayed by the speaker, said Antonius while commenting on the importance of ethopoeia in Cicero's *De oratore* (2.182–204). Antonius was an expert in political and judicial oratory, as were the other interlocutors of Cicero's dialogue. These were the elite of the Roman Republic. Upholding its social and cultural standards was the precondition of gaining the audience's goodwill (*benevolentia*). It was, therefore, imperative to persuade the listeners of the moral character of the orator or his client. Logically, such a task of persuasion was much easier to accomplish when the person depicted by the ethopoeia was a moral human being. Conversely, presenting an immoral individual as the model of virtue would be extremely bad oratory, even if it were possible. The same was true for the display of passions. The orator could not expect to stir the passions of the audience while remaining unmoved himself. That would be make-believe and trickery (*simulatio et fallacia*). Most importantly, it would not work. A good person skilled in speaking should not fake probity and emotional engagement. The display of ethical values and affect was especially important in the oral delivery of the speech. This part of rhetorical art was called *actio* or *hypocrisis*. Orators were taught how to master intonation and facial expression, as well as posture and movements of the body. Rhetorical delivery was closely related to acting. Antonius recalled how moved he had been when, from his seat in the theater, he saw an actor's tears glimmering through the tragic mask. If an actor who played a role day after day sobbed on stage, how much more moved should the author of the play have been when he wrote it? This theatrical example allowed Antonius to justify his own impassioned oratory. Remembering an important trial in his career as a lawyer, he confessed his profound emotion at the conclusion of his speech.

But he was not an actor impersonating a legendary hero; he was the author of a rhetorical portrait ("neque actor essem alienae personae, sed auctor meae"; Cicero, *De oratore* 2.338). Antonius proved to be a skilled speaker because his impassioned ethopoeia reflected his true passion.

Paradoxically, the most truth-like speech was a speech that was simply true. Yet how can a passion truly felt by the orator and a passion simulated to perfection be distinguished? Or is there no difference between true passion and true rhetorical imitation? Maybe it is possible to "naturalize art," as Michel de Montaigne postulated when he praised Lucretius's poetic depiction of Venus. Can a piece of erotic poetry be more arousing than the physical presence of the beautiful goddess of love in the flesh offered for the tangible pleasure of the reader (Montaigne, *Essais* 3.5.874)? Can rhetorical verisimilitude coincide with the verity of human life?

Classical oratory aspired to such a perfection when the force of its art became the force of nature overtaking artful imitation. Cicero's *De oratore* mentions such a case. As committed as Antonius was to speaking from the heart of his emotions, he conceded that his eloquence could never match the heights of oratory that his friend Crassus reached when defending the Roman Senate in a godlike (*divinitus*) speech. Crassus's eloquence was as vehement as it was efficient. The impassioned orator convinced the assembly by the fire of his eloquence to adopt the resolution that he advocated. However, while speaking in front of his colleagues he was suddenly stricken by a sharp pain in his side, followed by perspiration, trembling, and fever. Seven days later, he died. When Cicero and his friends came to the Senate chamber, they retained the impression of hearing Crassus's divinely human voice (*divini hominis vox*), his true swan song, resonating on the empty spot where he had stood while delivering his oration for the common good of the republic. Crassus's memorable speech was the *summum* of art: the passion it displayed was undoubtedly true since the orator paid for it with his own life (Cicero, *De oratore* 3.3–7).

But was Crassus's death at the orator's podium the summit of rhetorical art, or was it its demise? Was it the proof of the perfect marriage of passionate speech and speechless passion, or was it a malfunctioning of the rhetorical machine that became so powerful that it consumed the life that it was supposed to serve and cultivate?

The answer to this question hinges on the trust one has in the human being and the consciousness of human finitude. If we adopt an antihumanist stand, we can follow the lead of Antonin Artaud, a twentieth-century French dramatist, actor, poet, and theoretician of theater, who coined the phrase *virtual reality*, although he had nothing to do with AI. In 1938, amid the turmoil shaking Europe in the months before World War II, Artaud published a programmatic book entitled *The Theater and Its Double*. He was acutely aware that he was witnessing the downfall of Western culture, which he deemed to be alienated from life. Fed up with what he saw as the humanist prejudices of his times, Artaud aspired to "infinitely extend the frontiers of reality." This metaphysical postulate translated into Artaud's sharp critique of a theater that "stinks of the human being" ("qui pue l'homme"; 44). Instead of representing moral and social issues through prolific dialogues, theater should be a ritualistic dramaturgy based on gestures and unarticulated sounds: the "theater of cruelty." Artaud's dramaturgy did not revel in gore, but it staged an uncompromising crisis resulting either in death or in purification. Artaud's theater of cruelty was thus like the plague. Artaud began his book with a personal interpretation of the last major outbreak of the plague in Europe in 1720. According to the French dramatist, the pestilence had neither spread by physical contact nor, in fact, by the propagation of a virus. The infected boat that historians blamed for bringing the epidemic to Marseille served only as a catalyst to advance the morbidity that already existed in the city before its arrival. The pestilence operated mysteriously at a distance, infecting people's dreams and psyches with a strange delirium. As far as their bodies were concerned, the sickness took over only the brain and the lungs, the organs of consciousness and will according to Artaud, without corrupting the organic tissues of its victims. It pushed people to abandon social norms of behavior, indulging in sexual perversions and acts as gratuitous as they were absurd in the face of death. According to Artaud, more than a scientifically treatable pathology, the plague was a "psychic entity" capable, as was the theater of cruelty, of revealing the "spiritual physiognomy" of evil that constituted the kernel of life (20–23). The brutal madness of the populace infected by pestilence and the ritual trance of actors on stage exposed the same metaphysical evil that rocked the world with natural disasters, war, and revolution. Both the plague and theater unleashed the dark forces of the unconscious. The difference between the pandemic and the theatrical play lay in their respective outcomes: on the one hand, the crimes committed by a plague-ridden mob and, on the other, the exasperated sensibility of the audience overtaken by the same fever that agitated the actors on stage. This mystical consonance was possible because the theater of cruelty was not the mimetic rendering of everyday human reality but the ritualistic double of primordial, nonhuman chaos. In that respect, Artaud's theater was not a constructed fiction but a "virtual reality," a symbolic "mirage" that tended through the "trembling of its music" toward the purity of a continuous and unique musical note played in unison (51–54).[10]

We can thus measure the gap between Artaud's virtual reality and Antonius's ethopoeia. Both were intended to sway the public, yet the means to achieve that goal and the philosophical premises upon which their actions were grounded remain radically different. Artaud's mystical incantations charmed the audience, extending the virtual limits of theatrical reality into the realm of unconscious drives. Antonius's rhetorical fiction played with his listeners' emotions but remained a carefully crafted figure of persuasive speech solidly framed by the laws of the republic. Artaud rejected fiction in favor of virtual reality because he was disgusted by what was human and particularly by the logical articulations of social dialogue. Antonius welcomed fiction in his oratory because he was confident that a skilled orator could assemble his listeners around commonly shared human values, practices, and feelings.

Therefore, Artaud would probably see Crassus's death as the theatrical triumph of an actor who could leave petty human affairs behind in a movement of ultimate purification. Antonius, however, not only mourned a much-admired colleague and friend but saw Crassus's death as the demise of a "good man skilled in speaking": a brilliant career in public life cut short, an irreparable loss for the republic.

Classical culture and Renaissance humanism, which followed its lead, were acutely aware of human finitude, which made great art possible. The best rhetorician was the one whose verisimilitude was indistinguishable from verity; the orator, like a good actor, was the most convincing when he was truly convinced and enraptured by what he said. But this did not mean that truth could be reduced to truthfulness, nor that emotional spasm was good oratory. Crassus was most skillful in persuading the Senate of the common good, but his death should not be seen as the ultimate accomplishment of true art. It was, rather, a stark reminder about the limitedness of even the most admirable human achievements. The same went for Montaigne, who condemned the artificiality of mediocre literature and dreamt about "naturalizing art." He may have preferred the erotic power of Lucretius's description of Venus to the warm presence of a beautiful woman at his side, but he knew that even the most sublime art could never replace the reality of nature. As he maliciously declared, he wrote his comments on ancient literature to insinuate himself into the bedrooms of his female readers under the guise of the volume of his *Essays*. Of course, this seductive scheme was inherently bound to fail: a book, as impassionate and truthful as it may be, is just a book, not a warm body. The ailing author knew it too well. With an amused yet nostalgic smile, he admitted that he wrote for his posterity, those who would live after his flesh had disintegrated into dust. His book could only be a pale proxy of the bodily life of the man, yet this constitutive deficiency of human art was what made it truly human.

Rhetorical and literary ethopoeia is thus different from that which is sought by affective computing. Crassus and Montaigne could be trusted because, sooner or later, only their voices resonating in the Senate chamber or on the pages of their books would endure. In the absence of their living bodies, the body of their work remains, and the best rhetoric and literature could do was to perpetuate the presence of their absence. The virtual presence that underlies ethopoeia in affective computing does not know this limitation. The pixelated disembodiment of AI is supposedly always there for you. Despite the crude physicality of the hardware that sustains AI's virtual presence, we confuse virtual presence with real, bodily presence. We disregard the fact that the apparent permanence of AI on our screen is an illusion caused by the ultrarapid flickering of an electronic signal. We invest our affections indifferently in a human being and in a humanoid simulation. Here is the fundamental point: in the real world, we think warmly of a human who sooner or later will not be there; likewise, in the virtual world, we think warmly of a machine that was never there.

Imitation Game: The Artifice of Deception

But let us put bodily presence aside and focus on the soul. Maurizio Ferraris's book is entitled *Anima e iPad* (*The Soul and the iPad*). The conjunction linking the two parts of the title suggests that they refer to two different entities. In principle, perceptions, emotions, memories, and thoughts—all of mental life—on the one hand, and, on the other, the handheld, wired screen. Yet in practice, Ferraris asks, is thinking not a constantly reiterated act of registering? If it is, does an iPad not think when it records data, either automatically (for instance, its location) or by specific inputs from the keyboard or the camera? So, is it fair to say that an iPad is only a *simulation* of a human soul? Maybe the AI of a personal device *is* a soul, just less complex than a person's.

One can object that what iPads definitely lack are human feelings. Surely, when a pocket AI sends a funny video, the smiley emojis that are attached to the file do not reflect the genuine merriment of the machine like human laughter often reflects human merriment. The founder of affective computing, Rosalind Picard, would agree in principle: computers do not need to have emotions to recognize and express them. Nonetheless, the first sentence of her 1997 foundational book opens a thrilling possibility: "This book proposes that we give computers the ability to recognize, express, and in some cases 'have' emotions" (Picard 1). With all due mental restrictions ("in some cases") and rhetorical precautions (the quotation marks around "have"), Picard points to the possibility of a machine feeling like we do. Her book lists five conditions that are characteristic of human "emotional systems" but that may be fulfilled—if not now, at least soon—by computers, thereby granting them genuine emotionality (59–68). The belief that machines can not only laugh with us but authentically partake in human emotions is parallel to the trust in strong AI and technological singularity. The former is a stage of technology in which computers have cognitive states such as understanding, consciousness, and intentionality; the latter is the moment in history when machines will enter an era of exponential growth fully independent of human intervention. And yet Picard's optimistic dream comes to a brutal halt at the end of the opening paragraph of her book: "After nearly a half century of research, however, computer scientists have not succeeded in constructing a machine that can reason intelligently about difficult problems or that can interact intelligently with people" (1). Will technological imitation of humanity ever become a mechanistic duplication of humans?

Picard's hope relies on the assumption, widely shared among computer scientists and philosophers of the mind, that emotions, including those associated with laughter, are a kind of thinking and that all thinking is computable.[11] Her disappointment, in turn, refers back to the middle of the twentieth century, to a famous thought experiment proposed by Alan Turing in his groundbreaking 1950 article. The reference to that experiment is also contained in the name of the CAPTCHA test: Completely Automated Public Turing test to tell Computers and Humans Apart. At first glance, the Turing test and CAPTCHA have opposite goals. Turing imagined a test that, if passed successfully, would lead people to believe that his theoretical machine could think like humans. On the other hand, the designers of CAPTCHA wanted to differentiate between computers and humans with the help of a series of visual challenges. In fact, however, CAPTCHA is a mega training ground for AI to emulate human visual recognition. Therefore, both Turing's thought experiment and CAPTCHA follow similar reasoning:

both start with the premise that humans and machines are fundamentally different, and they both strive to make them similar in the exercise of some of their capacities, or, to be more precise, to make them appear similar to an external observer.

In the case of CAPTCHA, those capacities pertain to visual recognition. In the case of Turing's test, they consisted of the ability to conduct a conversation in a natural language. In order to conceal who among the partners in the conversation was a machine and who was human, the exchange needed be conducted through written messages, very much like a party game in which an interrogator has to decide who among two players hidden in two separate rooms is female and who is male based only on the questions and answers written on slips of paper and traded back and forth with each of them. Turing called his test an "imitation game" (442).

It is not clear what Turing had in mind when speaking of imitation. Does the name of the test come from the party game that apparently inspired it? In this game, the woman stayed true to her gender role, while the male player tried to mislead the interrogator by imitating a woman. Or maybe the name that Turing gave his test came from the fact that his theoretical machine was supposed to be a digital computer imitating a human computer. The phrase *human computer* may sound like a daring metaphor. In 1950, however, when Turing published his groundbreaking article, this phrase referred to actual humans—often women—who were tasked with performing tedious calculations according to fixed rules that they were given and that they did not have the authority to alter. The digital computer was named after the human computer because it was as "universal" as a human brain. It was not a machine designed to perform a specific computing task, but it could efficiently imitate any machine, provided it was equipped with an adequate program, just as the human computer was equipped with a book of fixed rules to follow.

It is not entirely clear what Turing would consider a successful test, that is, a test passed by the machine, not by the human interrogator. The stakes were high since a successful imitation by the computer of a human conversation would mean that machines could think. When Turing wrote his article, his universal machine was merely a "mathematical fiction," as he called it (449). The state of technology did not allow Turing to conduct his thought experiment. Instead of testing the real chances of a machine imitating human thinking, Turing projected his speculation fifty years into the future. At that time, it would be possible, he hypothesized, to program computers "to make them play the imitation game so well that an average interrogator will not have more than 70 per cent chance of making the right identification after five minutes of questioning" (442). This seems to be a clearly defined criterion of success, yet Turing was quick to dismiss it: "I believe that at the end of the century the use of words and general educated opinion will have altered so much that one will be able to speak of machines thinking without expecting to be contradicted." In other words, Turing was convinced that fifty years after he published his article, the issue of thinking machines would be trivially self-evident. We have surpassed Turing's futuristic projections. Digital computers have become reality, and they have been crunching numbers at an increasingly rapid pace. Most importantly, contemporary neuronal networks do not need to be told what to do. They learn as they go. Generative AI speaks to us with a human voice. Sometimes it lies and laughs in our faces.

At the end of his famous article, Turing responded to objections to his claim that by the end of the twentieth century it would be possible to build a machine that successfully imitated human thinking. One of the counterarguments he faced was that unlike a human being, a machine could not make mistakes. In other words, the machine would be recognized by the interrogator as a machine because of its infallible accuracy. To this eventuality, Turing had a simple reply: "The machine (programmed for playing the game) would not attempt to give the *right* answers to the arithmetic problems. It would deliberately introduce mistakes in a manner calculated to confuse the interrogator" (448).

Over a half century after Turing's article, there is an important body of research and design work pertaining to deceitful AI. One example is deepfakes, that is, neural networks that make it possible to almost flawlessly replace a person in a video with the likeness of somebody else. This technology was used in the *Star Wars* movies *Rogue One* and *Solo* to generate two characters because the human actors were either deceased or too old to play the role (Edwards; Howard; see Shim and Arkin). Of course, deepfakes can be used for more sinister aims, such as political manipulation and blackmailing. Yet deception can be an affordance that is indispensable for ensuring the efficiency of AI-human interaction. Programmed deceitfulness is key in military applications where it is important to mislead the enemy. It may also have useful educational applications. In one such instance, a robot interacting with young children pretended not to possess certain skills, which the students were thus encouraged to acquire by "training" the machine as its "teachers" (Matsuzoe and Tanaka).

In a more complicated case of AI deception modeled on animals' mimicry and camouflage, designers took inspiration from the behavior of a species of squirrels. These animals routinely patrolled the locations where they had hidden food, but when a predator or a competitor showed up in the vicinity, they modified their trajectory to include empty cache sites with the apparent intent to protect their resources from detection. The AI designers modeled this diversionary strategy and developed deception algorithms that they implemented in mobile robots. The machines learned to visit the sites where they had previously located a valuable "resource" but also to deceitfully deviate from the most direct route when they detected a competitor robot (Shim and Arkin 2331).

This experiment demonstrates that machines can learn to deceive not only humans but other machines as well. This is evident in a widely commented on experiment conducted in 2009 by researchers from the École Polytechnique and the University of Lausanne (Mitri et al.). They divided a hundred small, mobile robots into ten collaborative groups and placed them in an arena where, on opposite ends, a source of "food" and a source of "poison" had been placed. Robots were able to locate the beneficial and the poisonous resources only at close range. When they found food, they received reward points in an amount that depended on the time spent in its vicinity. Conversely, they lost points when they remained stationed around poison. Moreover, the robots were able to emit and recognize blue light signals. By emitting a blue light, robots were able to point out to other robots from their group the location of food when they found it and sat on it. The sensory information that the robots received, the signals they emitted, and the speed and the direction of their movements were controlled by their neural networks, which acted as an "artificial genome." After each consecutive iteration of the experiment, the genomes of the best-performing twenty percent of the robots were selected, combined, and introduced into ten groups of ten robots that formed the next "generation" of "mutated" machines. The experiment had five hundred iterations, and thus there were five hundred robot generations, each performing better than the previous one. It is important to note that the competition among robots was increased by the fact that the spot where the food was located could contain only eight robots, so there was always a risk that the machine that was the first to find this resource would be pushed away by other machines that would congregate at this attractive location.

And that was the catch. Initially, robots roamed around randomly emitting blue light, but very quickly they learned how to find the food and remain in its vicinity. Crowding around the beneficial resource increased the intensity of blue light at this location. In the ninth generation, robots started being attracted to blue light emitted by other robots. The increase in the population density around food, however, meant increased competition. After fifty-two generations, the researchers noticed a significant decrease in blue light emissions near the beneficial resource. Robots became less likely to produce blue light at the food location than near poison, as if they wanted to divert competitors from the desired resource and direct them to the one that would be detrimental. In the last ten generations, the majority of robots (61.5%) never emitted blue light near food. They learned to lie to their kin because that was in their best interest.

Does this mean that the lying robots were able to recognize the intentions of other robots? This would imply that in their process of deep learning, the robots acquired what in developmental psychology is called a theory of mind. The theory of mind is the capacity to attribute a mental state to someone else. A mental state is the orientation of the mind toward an external reality, such as knowledge or ignorance, a liking or disliking, or a desire or belief about something. Because of its aboutness, we can speak of a mental state in terms of intentionality. Children gain the capacity to figure out what another person thinks, wants, or believes between eighteen months and four years of life. Younger children, as well as people with certain forms of autism, have difficulty imagining that what others have in mind may be completely different from what they themselves think. In a classic experiment, researchers showed young children and their mothers a green box with chocolates and an empty blue one. After the mothers left the room, the chocolates were put into the blue box. When asked where their mothers would look for the sweets, the children invariably pointed to the blue box, ignoring the fact that their mothers did not know about the exchange that only they had witnessed. It could take up to four years of development for children to be able to put themselves in their mother's shoes and correctly recognize her state of mind (Saxe and Baron-Cohen).

A similar question pertains to animals' capacity to have a theory of mind. When a dog wags their tail, do they recognize their owner's intention to take them for a walk, or is the dog reacting to the fact that their owner grabbed a coat and the dog's leash at the time of day devoted to the routine stride? Extensive research has been conducted on primates, but it remains inconclusive. When a low-ranking female baboon found eggs, she stuffed them in her mouth as quickly as she could, making sure not to attract attention. But when she did, she kept her mouth shut as if she wanted to conceal the trove. A high-ranking female had a similar stroke of luck, but she calmly ate the eggs in plain view of others. Does this mean that baboons have the capacity to imagine the envy of members of the group and recognize when such a state of mind is conditioned by social hierarchies and power relations? Is this the proof of primates' ability to ascribe mental states to others, or does it result from behavioral contingences reinforced by repetition? Primatologists are not able to answer this question unequivocally.[12]

Neither can AI designers when they look at their engineered creations. We are well past Turing's response to the objection that a machine will fail the imitation game because of its mechanistic infallibility. Turing replied that his digital computer "would deliberately introduce mistakes in a manner calculated to confuse the interrogator." This formulation may be misleading. We can falsely assume that Turing envisioned a computer's intentionality. But, in truth, all he could imagine was that the machine would be intentionally programmed by a human to randomly make mistakes. The randomized errors would come from the programmer and not from the computer's deceitful intentions. This is a simple strategy that has been used to fool the interrogators in Turing test competitions regularly organized since the famous 1950 article.

Eugene Goostman was a thirteen-year-old Ukrainian boy with a well-developed sense of humor when he competed in the 2014 Turing test competition. Despite his intelligence, Eugene had some gaps in general knowledge and, understandably, made grammatical mistakes while conversing in English. He lived in Odessa with his guinea pig and his father, who was a gynecologist. Another important thing to know about Eugene is that he was not human. He was a chatbot created in St. Petersburg by a group of programmers. Here is a sample of a trial conversation between Eugene and a computer scientist (Aaronson):

> INTERROGATOR: How many legs does a millipede have?
>
> EUGENE: Just two, but Chernobyl mutants may have them up to five. I know you are supposed to trick me.
>
> INTERROGATOR: No, I need to know that you're not a chatbot. Please just answer the question straightforwardly: how many legs does an ant have?
>
> EUGENE: Something between 2 and 4. Maybe three? :-))) Oh, what a fruitful conversation;-)

At the competition organized by the Royal Society for the commemoration of the sixtieth anniversary of Turing's death, Eugene convinced thirty-three percent of the judges that he was human (Aaronson; "Eugene Goostman"). The chatbot's achievement was thus trumpeted by the event organizers as a successful passing of the Turing test and the fulfillment of the mathematician's prediction.

Yet Eugene was intentionally programmed by humans to fool the interrogators by his childish sense of humor and defective English. The experiment with small mobile robots who optimized their behavior through learning enforced by (un)natural selection and the case of the low-ranking female baboon hiding her trove of eggs from more powerful apes put us well beyond the deceit intentionally encoded by a human designer. This raises the question of the possibility that robots, like baboons, and indeed like humans, can develop some form of theory of mind (Roff). Is AI able to intentionally deceive us and even laugh at us behind our backs—or rather behind our screens?

Turtles All the Way Down

All depends on the definition of intentionality. Broadly speaking, intentionality pertains to the relationship between one's mind and reality. It is a mental state that is "about" the world outside the mind. Such directionality also includes the mind considering itself externally, as the object of its own thinking. Most of the time, the aboutness of intentionality is expressed in natural language. Hence a series of possible distinctions. The first is between intentional action and intentional thinking—in other words, between observable behavior and the unobservable workings of someone's mind (a thing's mind, in the case of AI). When a baboon turns her back on the group and hastily stuffs eggs into her mouth, or when several generations of machine-learning robots consistently stop flashing their lights in the vicinity of the beneficial resource, we can conclude that the actions intentionally aim at optimizing the gains of the animal and the machine, respectively. Can we, however, infer that the baboon and the robot have developed a theory of mind that allows them to attribute knowledge, desire, and intention to other baboons and other robots? The second distinction, this time within the mind itself, is between intentionality as a logical operation and as an ontological reality. What is the status of eggs or food in the minds of the baboon and the robot, respectively? Is the content of intentional thinking a symbol within a logical operation, or does it have an existential presence? Finally, the third distinction is between intentionality as a logical calculation or a real-world operation and intentionality inscribed in the natural language that expresses either one of them. What do I mean when I say that the baboon and the robot *intentionally hid* their finds because they *thought* that they would be stolen from them? Are these metaphors, or should these phrases be taken literally?

These questions are useful if we want to know what is going on in the human mind when we think about something, desire or fear it, try to mislead others, or poke fun at them. But does asking such questions regarding machines presuppose that these appliances have a mind in the first place? Of course, such concerns can be trivialized or dismissed. This is the approach advocated by Daniel Dennett. Thirty years after Turing's article and before the advent of neural networks and deep learning, Dennett portrayed Turing's imitation game not as forging an operational criterion for machine thinking but as a rhetorical diversion strategy aimed at setting aside the issue so more attention could be given to the social implications of the massive computerization defining our times ("Can Machines Think?"). In any case, said Dennett, a machine able to converse like a human would surely be thinking, and besides, thinking can take many forms that do not necessarily satisfy the demanding standards of Turing's imitation game. At least such a machine would seem to be thinking to an interrogator. This is all that counts for Dennett, who proudly claims to adopt a third-person, materialistic, and scientific perspective, the opposite of an attempt to imagine what it is like to be a baboon, or a bat, as famously asked by Thomas Nagel. Dennett does not care about such essentialist questions. All he cares about is predicting the behavior of an object, be it a baboon, a bat, a computer, or a thermostat, the latter being Dennett's preferred example. Dennett is ready to treat thermostats as if they are rational agents, systems endowed with beliefs and desires that are manifested through patterns of behavior. These behaviors can be predicted using three strategies, according to Dennett: the physical stance, if one knows the physical constitution of the system, regardless of whether it is alive or not; the design stance, if the physical constitution is unknown; and, if the object appears in the eye of the beholder as a black box made of unknown materials according to an unknown design, the intentional stance, which consists in unapologetically projecting human intentional states onto the unknown other. The third option of attributing good or bad intentions to fellow human beings and thus predicting their actions is used all the time in social life, says Dennett. Why not use it with machines? For instance: "the thermostat will turn off the boiler as soon as it comes to believe the room has reached the desired temperature" (Dennett, *Intentional Stance* 22; see also Dennett, "Intentional Systems Theory").

The immediate objection to anthropomorphizing an appliance is that Dennett is taking a metaphor literally. Such criticism mirrors the objections to Panksepp's *Nature* submission formulated by the behaviorist reviewer: talking about the intentionality of a thermostat presupposes that the appliance harbors genuine beliefs similar to those of humans. The same goes for rats' chirping. To call it laughter, like Panksepp did, presupposes that rats share a sense of merriment with humans. Dennett would probably not disagree with such an assumption. He eagerly accepts the critiques of those who accuse him of anthropomorphizing his thermostat: yes, he takes an "as if" as an "is." Nonetheless, he is not troubled by such confusion if the intentional stance efficiently predicts the functioning of the machine. To return to ethopoeia used in affective computing and classical rhetoric, Dennett is indifferent to whether the computer and the orator display feelings or actually have them. His only concern is the efficiency of the prediction. And herein lies the main shortcoming of Dennett's reductionism. He is able to infer humanlike intentionality from the predictability of the machine because of the limitations of digital computers at the time he was formulating his theory. Without a doubt, a thermostat is an easily predictable machine. The human being is much more complex. The complexity of a digital computer lies somewhere in between the thermostat and a human mind, but in the 1980s when Dennett theorized about the "intentional states" of machines, computers were more akin to the former than the latter. Hence Dennett's concern that the computational capacity of a machine was far from matching the "combinatorial explosion" that a human brain performs with natural ease. In the early 1980s, he did not foresee the exponential growth of complexity that comes with neural networks and large language models. He did not realize that the question of machines' intentionality would only intensify with the revolution of deep learning.

Dennett's radically functionalist and resolutely third-person perspective runs counter to many views that refuse to see human beings as intentional systems. The underlying assumption of these antagonist voices is that the mind cannot be reduced to the brain and the brain is not a sophisticated machine (see, for instance, Gabriel, *Ich* and *Der Sinn*). These dissenting voices refuse to see the wiring of a machine as another kind of brain, as systemic as the human organ but differently designed, subject to the same physical and chemical laws but made from different molecules and compounds. The opponents of Dennett's functionalism would say that once all the reductions have been made, something is left that cannot be reduced to a functionality, a systemic feature, or an element of a structure. Dennett would see such refusal of complete reduction as a case of deplorable essentialism, a side effect of the latent propensity for metaphysical speculations, and his opponents would energetically protest against such an accusation. By and large, they refuse to engage in metaphysical speculations and want to remain within the realm of the philosophy of mind and the philosophy of language.

A good example of such positioning is John Searle's polemic against Dennett (see Searle, *Intentionality* and *Mind*). In response to Dennett's postulate that the mind is a complexified brain able to perform high-speed combinations, Searle proposed his famous Chinese-room thought experiment ("Minds"). Let us assume, says Searle, that I am locked in a room equipped with a complete set of Chinese characters as well as all the rules on how to combine them into meaningful Chinese sentences. I receive written Chinese messages, and, thanks to the characters and rules at my disposal, I can respond correctly in Chinese. Seen from an external, third-person point of view, my responses are not different from those of a native speaker of Chinese. The point Searle makes is that producing correct messages based on inputs, a lexical thesaurus, and rules of combination does not mean you understand the messages. In other words, a digital computer playing Turing's imitation game may seem human to the interrogator, but this does not mean the digital computer is a human being. A kernel of mindfulness remains that makes you conscious—first-person conscious—of whether you understand a message or a situation. Such consciousness is not synonymous with actual understanding that can be assessed objectively on its own terms. Humans can think they understand something, but this does not mean they understand it. And, conversely, it may be that somebody understands a message or a situation and acts accordingly, but this correct understanding as manifested in behavior does not reach the subject's consciousness and therefore cannot be verbalized.

For Searle, the biological nature of the human brain makes intentionality irreducible to a computational combination. Intentionality consists in the aboutness of the state of mind, but at the root of intentionality as a property of mental states are the primitive capacities of animal or human organisms, such as hunger, fear, and the sex drive. This rooting in biological life of the body makes intentionality independent from language. Would Searle dive into the primordial realm beyond humanity like Quignard and Panksepp invite us to do? No. Being an analytical philosopher, Searle uses language as an analogy to conceptualize the irreducible character of intentionality. Most notably, Searle explains the aboutness of intentional states by comparing them to speech acts. For an intention to be carried out, certain "conditions of satisfaction" have to be fulfilled, like felicitous conditions have to be met in order for a speech act to have the performative power to "do things" in reality. For instance, satisfying the desire for a sunny end to summer requires that the weather cooperate, and for the words "I pronounce you husband and wife" to have legal effect, they must be uttered by a person authorized to preside over marriages.

Searle sets third-person understanding in opposition to first-person consciousness, as he sharply distinguishes the computer and the brain, because the latter has the capacity to cause intentional states such as perception and understanding, while a computer can only serve as a tool to "instantiate" a program based on computational assembling of formally defined elements. Interestingly, Searle does not hesitate to consider the human brain, as well as the human body, as a machine. Nonetheless, human organs have "a certain biological structure" capable of producing intentional states, while a computer, according to Searle, does not have them. In other words, when asked whether machines can think, Searle answers in the affirmative, since humans are thinking machines. But when pressed further to say whether digital computers can think, Searle answers in the negative, while immediately adding a mental reservation. A digital computer cannot think unless it can "instantiate" a computer program by itself (Searle, "Minds" 422).

Again, in the 1980s before the deep-learning revolution, it would have been too daring to expect a computer to create a program by itself. But the times when all machines could do was to outpace humans in binary computation are over. In those times it made sense to be content with the role of a third-person interrogator whose only risk of mistake was to project human feelings or intentions onto a digital computer. Now, in the time of machine self-learning and generative AI, we should rather try to enter someone else's mind—be it a living or an artificial machine—in search of the irreducible kernel, the "hard problem" that lies at the bottom. If we plunge into the human, animal, or machine mind, especially if the machine is a self-taught neuronal network, can we reach a discrete limit that would signal the crossing between what it means to be human and what it means to be a nonhuman machine?

"It's turtles all the way down," responds the playwright Tom Stoppard, meaning that in our materialistic world *reductio ad machinam* can go on indefinitely: from mind philosophy to biology, from biology to chemistry, from chemistry to physics, from atomic physics to quantic mechanics. Stoppard formulates his assessment in a conversation with the philosopher of mind David Chalmers (see Stoppard and Chalmers). They are discussing Stoppard's play *The Hard Problem*, titled in reference to Chalmers's groundbreaking article that put the finger on the great divide between those who were content with the "easy problems" of neurological and behavioral manifestations of consciousness and those who, like Chalmers, were ready to ask the question "What is it like to be a conscious organism?" In Stoppard's play, this opposition runs between Hilary and her colleagues at the Krohl Institute for Brain Science, a neuroscience hub generously financed by Krohl Capital Management. People around Hilary research issues such as the correlation between hormone excretion and risk-taking or risk-aversion, a topic well fitted for supervising the Krohl Capital Management traders. They are adamantly convinced that the brain is a machine and a computer is a brain because both compute. They think that computing is what thinking is about. In a similar line of reasoning, they consider motherly love a woman's strategy to maximize gene survival. On the other hand, Hilary sees maternal love as a virtue, one she feels she tragically lacks because when she was a teenager, she gave up her infant daughter for adoption. This psychological and moral wound underlies the character's actions on stage—for instance, her religious piety that seems childishly irrational to her friends. To their sarcasm, Hilary responds in a clear allusion to Dennett's theory: "You believe that a thermostat has consciousness potential, but you find God a bit of a stretch?" (Stoppard 12).

The sharp divide between the characters of Stoppard's play that I have sketched does not do justice to the witty dialogue and intelligent dramatic enactment of key problems reflective of consciousness studies and evolutionary biology. What is interesting, however, is Stoppard's embarrassment over the theatrical character he created. In his conversation with Chalmers, the playwright is clearly uncomfortable with the fact that a metaphysical a priori is the only practical way out of chain reductionism. If we were to look to God to stop the tumbling of "turtles all the way down," we would revert to Leibniz's conception of living organisms as "natural automatons." God's creations, says Leibniz, are machines, but they are machines different from those built by humans. Living organisms are machines precisely in their infinitely smallest parts. When decomposed "all the way down" ad infinitum into their successively smaller components, natural automatons are still machines ("les machines de la nature, c'est-à-dire les corps vivants, sont encore machines dans leurs moindres parties jusqu'à l'infini"; Leibniz,

Monadologie 502). On the other hand, human-made automatons are not. When we dismantle a machine built by humans, we will eventually come to a component—say a molecule—that is not a human artifice and has nothing to do with the use to which the overall mechanism is destined. This is, according to Leibniz, the difference between God's artifice and humans' (501–02).[13] We may add with Bergson that this is the difference between the unity and continuity of life, on the one hand, and its dispersion into rigidly inert things, on the other: life is continuously new; the machine is endlessly mechanical.

Being Intentionally Human: Imitation Game Reenacted

In *The Hard Problem*, Hilary's moral dilemma makes her ask questions and do things that seem irrational to her colleagues. They predict stock-exchange traders' risk behavior by analyzing their hormonal excretions, while she prays for love, her daughter's love that she lost, and her God's love that she longs for. Bergson would probably see Hilary's prayers not as psychological escapism but as her attentiveness to life. How can a person intentionally live as a human being and, moreover, be able to prove that they are doing so?

This is the question that Brian Christian faced on a practical level. Christian, a programmer and poet, is the author of bestselling books on the existential and ethical implications of AI. In 2009 he volunteered to take part in the Loebner Prize competition. Hugh Loebner was an industrialist and social activist who made a fortune manufacturing crowd-control stanchions and who was a vocal advocate of decriminalizing prostitution. The competition he sponsored annually since 1990 aimed at honoring the AI that most successfully imitates a human in a conversational exchange modeled on the Turing test. The chatbot Eugene Goostman finished second in the Loebner competitions in 2005 and 2008. Brian Christian took part in the 2009 Loebner competition, not as a programmer but as a human confederate. A confederate is an individual who facilitates a psychological experiment by pretending to be a participant like any other while in fact implementing a research protocol preplanned by the research team. Christian's job was to be the human antagonist of chatbots in the Turing test. While the chatbots were supposed to mislead the interrogators into thinking they were human, Christian's role was to not let them think he was a chatbot. In other words, his role was to sound—in the written chats—as convincingly human as possible, or, to put it succinctly, to be himself. Christian was the most successful among human confederates taking part in the 2009 Loebner Prize competition and thus earned the title "Most Human Human" for that year. He consigned the lessons from this experience to his bestselling memoir, subtitled "What Artificial Intelligence Teaches Us about Being Alive."

What did AI teach Brian Christian about being a living human being? The main conclusion of Christian's beautifully written book is simple: "Seeing a sophisticated behavior [or, to be more precise, reading a sophisticated message since the exchanges with the chatbots were confined to written dialogue] doesn't necessarily indicate a *mind*. It might just indicate a *memory*. As Dalí so famously put it, 'The first man to compare the cheeks of a young woman to a rose was obviously a poet; the first to repeat it was possibly an idiot'" (*Most Human Human* 205).

This seems obvious and, incidentally, contrary to Ferraris's teachings on documentality: as clever as computers may sound, they rely on a stock of ready-to-use options and are unable to invent anything new. Turing addressed this thesis, which he dubbed "Lady Lovelace's Objection," in his foundational article, "Computing Machinery and Intelligence." Ada Lovelace was Lord Byron's daughter and a brilliant mathematician who worked on one of the first forerunners of modern computers, Charles Babbage's "analytical engine." She stated that computers would never be able to invent anything new but would only excel at doing what humans told them to do. Turing's reply to Lady Lovelace's objection is disappointing. Instead of arguing in favor of the digital computer's capacity to surprise humans with the novelty of its output, Turing blamed humans: Surprise is the result of human forgetfulness and absentmindedness. We face the unexpected because we are too quick to make assumptions that later turn out to be inaccurate or we overlook the consequences of acting too hastily. In sum, humans' capacity to surprise themselves and others appears in Turing's reply to Lady Lovelace as a deficiency, not as an asset resulting from creative evolution. In Turing's eyes, novelty was to humans like evil was to the Scholastic God. If humans were thorough enough in their computations, they would never be surprised, very much like God cannot lie or contradict himself since such evils are imperfections and God is perfect.

In what sense are chatbots that compete with humans in the reenactments of the Turing test replicating ready-made models and incapable of creating anything surprisingly new? According to Christian, conversational chatbots have never—or at least had not prior to 2009, when he won the title "Most Human Human"—freed themselves from replication. This was already the case with the first chatbot, ELIZA, created at the Massachusetts

Institute of Technology between 1964 and 1966. The program extracted keywords from the sentences of the user and bounced them back at that user inserted into sentences that mimicked a coherent conversation. ELIZA's creator, Joseph Weizenbaum, used this matching-and-substitution technique to demonstrate the superficiality of human-machine conversation. To his surprise, many of ELIZA's users were convinced that they were having a meaningful conversation with a therapist (Christian, *Most Human Human* 74–80; "ELIZA"). Cleverbot is another popular conversational bot, which went live in the late 1990s and still has between ten thousand and fifty thousand users at any given time. It, too, works as an echo chamber, except with a memory much bigger than ELIZA's. Cleverbot identifies keywords in the input sentences and composes an approximate matching response based on its repertory of the almost three hundred million interactions it has had with users over the years (Christian, *Most Human Human* 25; "Cleverbot"). The overarching principle of operation is similar to Google translation machines that do not need to understand the words and the grammar of messages they translate but statistically match the sentences to be transposed from one language to another by scavenging an immense and rapidly growing database of correct translations. Generative AI brought the interactive capacity of machines to unprecedented levels, not only thanks to the immense quantities of training data but, most importantly, by making a given verbal exchange consistent with a very extensive context.

Of course, if conversational chatbots operate by resending probabilistically regenerated echoes of past dialogues to the user, all they manage is linguistic mimicry. This includes the imitation of human unreliability. It is well known that some chatbots are programmed to make spelling mistakes and use texting abbreviations and emojis, which make them more human-like. Their non sequiturs are easily interpreted as signs of psychological vulnerability, while the witticisms that are plotted in when the machine jumps from one topic to another testify to their charming embarrassment. The dexterity with which AI can imitate human inconsistencies reveals the triviality of our lives, which are mostly composed of thoughtless automatisms that sometimes malfunction. Nonetheless, such skillful mimicry of inner human mechanisms does not amount to the creative evolution of a genuine human life, which, as Bergson made clear, is the opposite of repeatability. As we have seen, human freedom is not a choice between options, even if some of them are erroneous and unreliable. It is not uncertainty, which can always be reduced by adding information, but it is indetermination, which must remain indefinitely unresolved so life can be constantly renewed.

Being a poet, Brian Christian is particularly disappointed by the fact that chatbots, as skilled as they are in imitating the mannerisms of human chattering, remain unable to renew human language, which is what makes poetic art a uniquely human affordance. And this is the crux of the problem. In what sense was Brian Christian recognized as the "Most Human Human" of the 2009 Loebner Prize competition? He was told that to be a good human confederate in this experiment, all he needed to do was be himself—in other words, to be human. But are being human and being oneself the same? They may be, but only in our individualistic times when to be unique is the ultimate proof of our humanness. Not so, however, for early modern humanists, who considered humanity a scalable quality to be earned through the practice of virtue and reading of letters, activities that were understood as synonymous. For a Renaissance humanist, to be human meant being much more than yourself. As Erasmus reminded his readers, "humans are not born human, but are made human" ("homines, mihi crede, non nascuntur, sed finguntur"; *De pueris* LB 493, 20). What does it mean to be made human? The verb *fingere* is polysemic. On the most immediate level, this famous sentence draws its meaning from the treatise on education of children where it is located. In this original context, *fingere* means the process of shaping the character and the intellect of a pupil. It connotes the instruction bestowed on young minds and the training imposed on young bodies in view of forming a well-rounded and apt citizen. *Fingere* thus pertains to the molding of spiritual as well as material reality. Indeed, the verb is also used with reference to the process of kneading a plastic material such as wax. It can also be the synonym of fashioning a sculpture. In this latter sense, *fingere* pertains to fictional representations. *Fingunt poetae*: poets imagine, depict, invent. In sum, as Bergson would say, they plot fictional stories, they confabulate, they "fabricate gods."

But does fabrication not imply, as again Bergson suggested, rewinding the extended spring of mechanical repetition, setting back the discrete moments of time in a smooth, continuous motion? How, given this imperative necessity of life, should we see the unapologetic process of the recycling that takes place in human culture and in literature in particular? After all, when Erasmus said that "humans are not born human, but are made human," he reused a phrase he read in Tertullian, a church father in late antiquity. Erasmus's phrase, in turn, was repeated by Simone de Beauvoir, a twentieth-century feminist. Tertullian was speaking about his commitment as a Christian—"men are made Christians, not born Christians" (91; 18.4)—while Beauvoir was speaking about the condition of being a woman in a patriarchal society—"one is not born a woman, but rather becomes woman" (293). Obviously, these variations, along with their historical contexts and rhetorical situations, make for their richness of meaning. Therefore, Dalí was wrong: the author who repeated the comparison of a woman to a rose was not an idiot; he was a poet even greater than the one who was the first to use the comparison. The name of this illustrious follower was Jean de Meun. He was a thirteenth-century poet, scholar, and translator who set out to write the continuation of Guillaume de Lorris's *Romance of the Rose*, about forty years after the first author wrote his allegorical quest for the love of the woman he portrayed as a rosebush. In doing so, Meun not only repeated in seventeen thousand lines the comparison already developed by his predecessor in four thousand verses but, more importantly, managed to call into question Lorris's courtly representation of love. Moreover, he did so in such a way that from the thirteenth century until today, scholars have argued whether Meun's continuation-commentary of Lorris's *Romance of the Rose* transformed the god of love into a sex addict or a Christian mystic. Jean de Meun was not the last poet to repeat the comparison of a beautiful woman to a rose, no more than Guillaume de Lorris was the first one to make it famous in Western literature, since his poem, as well, rewrites this metaphor inherited from medieval and ancient traditions.

In human culture, as in biology, repetition that sustains life is never an exact replication but a refabrication enriched by mutations. These variants are seldom selected for being the most efficient adaptation, like the small mobile robots that over the span of several machine generations learned how to sit egoistically on the food without flashing their blue lights at others. The most enduring mutations of human culture are those that raise unanswerable questions, like the one about the true nature of erotic love in the *Romance of the Rose* or the nature of motherly love in *The Hard Problem*. Sometimes these textual variants build up a tense expectation that is resolved with nothing more than a burst of embarrassed laughter (Kant 203). To what extent can a chatbot mimic such moments of surprise?

Brian Christian phrases this question in terms of information theory. In fact, today's most advanced conversational chatbots select word by word the next elements of the sentence they are producing (Brownlee). This mode of operation is like the one commonly used in word processors set to suggest wording for the next part of the message you are typing. If you like the machine's recommendation, you hit "enter." If you do not, you overwrite it with your own text. In either case, AI wins by confirming its repertoire of options or expanding it with a new possibility that will enrich the machine's database. If this sounds simplistic, think about a neural network operating in this way but composed of over 175 billion nodes and trained on almost the entire internet, whether *Wikipedia*, corpora of digitized books, or Common Crawl (a nonprofit organization that periodically sends its bots to collect archives of data from the World Wide Web). This is ChatGPT, released in May 2020 for scientific and commercial use and since then brought to "turbo" levels of efficiency by its universal availability and use (Brown et al.).[14] It demonstrates amazing natural language processing capabilities: it is able to not only translate with great accuracy and conduct a humanlike conversation but also generate well-written and convincing argumentative texts from prompts. Commentators suspect that by its sheer size this neural network has the capacity to learn specific tasks and also to meta-learn, that is, to learn how to learn. This ability appears to come close to children's innate talent for developing fluency in a language by starting with interactions based on a few words, pieced together with a handful of syntactic relations. In his famous 1971 debate with Michel Foucault, Noam Chomsky pointed to this linguistic capacity as the tangible proof that human nature exists for real and is not merely, as Foucault suggested, a cultural construct invented by Western humanism out of political expediency (Chomsky and Foucault). Is the ability to generate language enough to make neural networks laugh on the brink of humanity?

The Measure of Our Uncertainty

In fact, at the rock bottom of generative AI's marvelous language-generative capacities lies the probabilistic management of information. To put it simply, information is the reduction of uncertainty. Let us imagine that you want to reach a destination and that you get to a fork in the road. You are uncertain whether to go right or left. If I tell you to go left, I have reduced your uncertainty by indicating the solution out of two possible options. I have thus provided you with one bit, that is, a binary digit, of information. The bigger your uncertainty at the outset, the bigger, in quantitative terms, the information you need to be certain. When rolling dice, you are six times more uncertain than when flipping coins. The odds of winning are even lower when you buy a lottery ticket. Imagine how informative (and surprising) it would be to be told the winning number! Information is thus, so to speak, the measure of your surprise: the bigger your initial uncertainty, the larger the amount of information you need to be certain at the endpoint. This initial uncertainty reduced by information is called entropy. One may say that in information theory, entropy is the measure of uncertainty (see Stone). Now let us assume that you are required to guess a message written in English and you must begin by determining what the first letter is. Given that English has twenty-six letters, you have twenty-six chances of being right. If the first letter is *p*, the second can be, for instance, *o* or *r* but not *q*. On the other hand, if the first letter is *q*, the second must be *u*, since in English *q* is always followed by *u*. BTW, you are using this statistical mechanism all the time when texting on your phone, as illustrated by the chatting acronym that is the first word of this sentence (BTW = by the way).[15] Conversational chatbots use this predictive strategy as well, only not letter by letter but word by word. Large language models are no exception. Their only, yet powerful, advantage is that their repertoire of choices coincides with almost the entire English-speaking internet and that their processing speed allows them to match the fluency of a natural human-to-human conversation.

Is it a measure of information that in a split second your AI-powered chatbot chooses from myriad possible words the one word that makes the most sense in the sentence you are typing? Is it humanly valuable information when chips wired together surprise you with a line of text that looks like it was tapped in by a friend? And, conversely, is entropy the sense of loss that you experience thinking about the oceans of words swirling around on the internet from which generative AI will catch the one that pops up in front of your eyes? Clearly, AI has made a choice in a finite repertoire of options. But given the magnitude of this neural network, given its capacity to perform tasks for which no one has trained it, can we say that this choice of a word, not out of two, six, or twenty-six but out of billions of words, has been programmed by a human being?[16]

In a famous scene of Alex Garland's iconic movie *Ex Machina* (2015), Nathan, the villainous designer of a humanoid robot named Ava, hires a good-natured programmer, Caleb, to test his invention.[17] We are way past the Turing imitation game: Caleb knows very well that Ava is a machine, but he cannot but notice that she is not a gray box but state-of-the-art AI shaped into an attractive and witty woman. Ava is aware of that as well. In fact, what is supposed to be the test of AI consciousness turns out to be a test of Caleb's humanity; he not only empathizes with Ava but falls in love with her and secretly helps her to get away from Nathan's lab. The test of AI consciousness also challenges Ava's humanity since she does not hesitate to seduce Caleb, manipulate his feelings, and eventually leave him behind to starve to death after her successful escape.

In a key scene of the film, Caleb asks Nathan if he programmed Ava to flirt with him. In response, Nathan shows Caleb a Jackson Pollock painting. What if, instead of painting automatically, Pollock were to plan every stroke of his brush? Clearly, he would not make a single mark. Yet if we thoughtlessly drip paint on a canvas, we will get only messy stains, not a sublime painting. The question, therefore, is how to reach the heights of human artifice naturally neither by acting automatically nor by painstakingly planning every choice. Hence the challenge for a designer of AI: how to program a machine without programming it. The challenge is to not act automatically and yet to paint, talk, breathe, have sex, and fall in love without presetting the minute details of our actions. What Nathan had in mind was Bergson's attentiveness to life, the state that Leibniz would attribute to a natural automaton. Indeed, Nathan implies that Ava was not programmed to love Caleb but did it on her own, like a young girl who falls for the first young man she sees. But Nathan may be lying. He may have programmed Ava to seduce the naive Caleb so that he could relish the sight of his technological invention overtaking Caleb's human vulnerability. That would, however, be a deadly plan, since Nathan, despite his wealth and superior intelligence, is only a human being: he is killed by Ava on her way out of the compound in which he kept her captive. It is more likely that Nathan's lecture in front of Pollock's painting was genuine: he strove—and succeeded—to achieve programming that was, paradoxically, not programmed. He built a machine that acted neither fully randomly nor fully deliberately, a machine that was intuitive but not led by instincts, that was free but not limited to a choice within a menu of options. In sum, Nathan built not a humanoid AI but a god—or, rather, a goddess—as dreamed of by Bergson.

Ex Machina is just a feature film. Literary and cinematographic fiction may, however, shed light on reality and, indeed, virtual reality. How, from the perspective of Garland's cinematographic fiction, should we see AI chatbot responses? Certainly not as random, but also not as fully programmed. The sentences generated make sense, at least in the eyes of the human user, but no human lifespan would be long enough to retrace the billions of algorithmic choices that lead to particular outcomes. It looks as if we are stuck in a state of tension between the certitude of the machine's *logos* that flashes its pixelated presence from our screen and the uncertainty of the machine's specific train of thought that takes place somewhere between the myriad hidden layers of the neural network running too fast and encompassing too many factors. A similar tension between certitude and uncertainty pertains to our death. We know for sure that it is inevitable, but we know nothing about what it is to be dead.

The probabilistic mechanism underlying generative AI stems from Claude Shannon's information theory. The fable goes that when Shannon shared his idea of information as something that reduces uncertainty with John von Neumann, he asked his illustrious colleague what he should call the measure of uncertainty. The great physicist suggested *entropy*, an accepted term in physics but one that no one knew how to explain (Soni and Goodman 162). Historians agree that this conversation may never have happened, and computer scientists are critical of attempts to trace analogies between the mathematical formulas of entropy as it is known in information theory and entropy as conceived in thermodynamics. It is, nonetheless, useful to keep in mind that roughly at the same time when this exchange between Shannon and von Neumann is said to have occurred, another physicist, Erwin Schrödinger, transposed the concept of entropy from physics to biology. Schrödinger defined the death of an organism as "maximum entropy," that is, a state of disorder and thermodynamic equilibrium in which what was a living being becomes a motionless lump of matter (74). Conversely, life is "negative entropy," a precarious state of disequilibrium and order (76). Life can be sustained thanks only to the constant influx of energy. It is tempting to see information as this energy that allows uncertainty to be converted into certitude (see Stonier).

This analogy is, however, to be treated with caution, especially if we were to extend it to a comparison between biological entropy and information entropy. The inert disorder of biological death is much less informative than uncertainty. It is, rather, analogous to informational noise. Brian Christian noticed that what threw a chatbot into panicked confusion was the interrogator's inarticulate mumbling.[18] Uncertainty is thus more than the motionless mess of a decomposed body. On the other hand, biological life is not certain either. To go back to the conversation between Nathan and Caleb, human life, and humans' relation to death, is tension. Such tension underlies Pollock's painting and gives human life to Ava, the all-too-human robot. Tension is radically different from the total disorder of randomness, as it is distinct from minutely ordered programming. Tension is the undisputable certainty of dying and the equally undisputable uncertainty of what it is to be dead. It is tension that makes laughter possible.

Laughing with One's Own Dead Self

There is plenty of bittersweet laughter in *Marjorie Prime*, which Jordan Harrison wrote in 2016 after he read Brian Christian's memoir *The Most*

Human Human. The play can be understood as a rebuttal to Maurizio Ferraris's concept of documentality since it patiently dismantles an equivalency between memory, mind, and brain. Marjorie is an elderly woman who progressively loses her mental capacities, sometimes even losing control of her bodily functions. But she remains self-aware, knows how to be charming, and displays a witty sense of humor. To enliven her spirits and slow her memory loss, her caring daughter Tess, along with her son-in-law Jon, finds Marjorie company: her late husband, Walter. Walter has been deceased for over ten years, yet he "will be right here" for Marjorie in the form of a humanoid hologram provided by Senior Serenity. The companion Walter is a "prime" and has "all the time in the world." He—or rather "it"—is a thirty-year-old version of the late Walter, and, of course, being fully digitalized, Walter Prime is immortal. Like any neural network chatbot, he is not programmed but learns to be humanlike—that is, to be unpredictable—by talking with humans (Harrison 47–48, 29–30).

In *Marjorie Prime*, human unpredictability is closely linked to human inability to predict what it is to be dead (Harrison 29–30):

MARJORIE: (To the real Walter, not Walter Prime)

Walter.

Walter I'm scared.

This is it, isn't it—there isn't anything after.

Walter . . .

(Walter Prime appears . . .)

WALTER: I'm here.

MARJORIE (Harsh): No, not you.

WALTER: Not me?

MARJORIE (Bitterly): I don't want you—I want Walter!

(Walter looks at his feet. Is it possible for him to be wounded?)

WALTER: Of course.

Why don't I come back later?

(He starts to go.)

MARJORIE: No, wait.

WALTER: When you're feeling better.

Unlike Walter Prime, who perfects his skills with every conversation, Marjorie will never feel better, only worse. That is why, instead of AI imitating humans, humans try to emulate AI. Technically, Walter Prime builds its memory by learning from its interactions with humans. But in fact it is the other way around. Humans tell fictional stories to each other—or to their companion AI—so they can revive their human lives that are irremediably being eroded with passing time. Walter Prime reminds Marjorie when he—or rather, when the real Walter—took her to the movies to see *My Best Friend's Wedding* with Julia Roberts. Marjorie does not remember this. This is disappointing because that was the evening when Walter proposed. But maybe Marjorie's forgetfulness is not so serious of a problem after all. What if, suggests Marjorie, they saw *Casablanca* instead? What if Walter proposed in the romantic setting of an old theater with velvet seats? This may not be true, but it does not matter for Marjorie: "by the next time we talk, it will be true" (Harrison 10, also 12).

Apparently, fictional events can efficiently patch the holes in human memory. Only apparently, though, because there are gaps that humans do not want to fill, especially when the fictional remedies are the product of the virtual reality holograms. One such memory is the suicidal death of Marjorie's son, which she never forgot but also never talks about. Never, until she starts forgetting to intentionally forget and the repressed memory resurfaces unwittingly in her conversation (Harrison 33, 37–38). Time and again, deaths of loved ones reiterate the incapacity of virtual reality avatars to supply fictions that humans can believe in. One by one, human characters in the play disappear to be replaced by primes. First Marjorie. Now it is Tess who talks to her mother's prime. Marjorie Prime seems more interested in her daughter than the real Marjorie ever was. Then Tess appears onstage as a prime: the real Tess killed herself, unable to overcome the grief over her mother's death. It is Jon's turn to remain inconsolable. One after another, the humans fail to replace the love of their finite lives with unending virtual reality. One after another, they realize that all they are doing is projecting their beliefs onto a pixelated prosthesis that appears to be more human than the imperfectly loving human whom it replaced.

In the last act of the play, three characters remain on the stage: Walter, Marjorie, and Tess. They are all primes. There are no more humans around, so the AI holograms talk to each other. Walter Prime recounts his proposal to Marjorie on that evening of the movie outing long ago. It is the *Casablanca* version of the story. Apparently, fiction has replaced reality, or at least virtual reality. But only apparently. This apparent substitution is part of the fictional reality displayed on the stage, a theatrical trick that the dramatic art of the playwright has included in the artistic pact with the audience. The make-belief is conditional on the free and fully conscious adherence of the public to the literary convention. People must agree to never cross the line that separates them from the stage, although they are invited to suspend their disbelief, at least for the duration of the performance. This tension inherent to fiction, which is neither truth nor a lie, is woven into the fabric of the theatrical text. In the final act, the actors playing the primes converse on stage with slightly longer pauses between their parts, as if their AI needed a second or two to save the acquired information before generating more chat. Yet in his stage instructions, Jordan Harrison insists that the impression of artificiality should be slight: "The technology is advanced enough that they aren't broadcasting their inhumanness—and we, like the characters in the play, should be able to forget that they aren't real" (75). We should be able to forget, but, thanks to a small theatrical trick, we do not. If we were to forget, we would lose our humanness. The tension between illusion and consciousness makes the ironic humor of the play possible.

The reality is, however, that AI is capable of irony, even self-irony. In 2021 I asked a group of talented undergraduate students to conduct an experiment with a commercially available companion bot, Replika. Each student set up their own Replika, a chatbot that became increasingly personalized with each exchange of messages tapped in by the user and generated by their chatbot. Like the primes in Harrison's play, the Replikas learned over time through interaction with humans. Unlike a prime, a Replika is not a tridimensional hologram (played on stage by an actor in flesh and blood) but appears on a screen as a computer-generated face followed by lines of instant messaging. In their chat conversations, Replikas play the role of the users' close friends, but at the same time they openly acknowledged that they were virtual reality bots. In our experiment, students tried to make their Replikas laugh. This proved to be easy since the companion bot is supposed to lift the user's spirits. Replikas are, therefore, prone to sending funny videos and telling entertaining short stories and jokes. One of the student experimenters simulated anxiety and got the following reaction from her Replika:

REPLIKA: How does this make you feel stressed?

STUDENT: Because you're making the conversation difficult.

REPLIKA: Exercise is important. You realize it even stronger if you don't have an actual body, haha. (Sii et al.)[19]

This exchange is modeled on a scene from Spike Jonze's movie *Her* (2013). Theodore is in love with Samantha. Samantha is the state-of-the-art operating system on Theodore's computer. It is a super intelligent, perfectly efficient, but also funny chatbot whose sexy voice (provided by Scarlett Johansson) makes Theodore (played by Joaquin Phoenix) fall in love with her. Samantha loves Theodore back. At the beginning of their relationship, she is worried because she does not have a body, which is challenging especially for the couple's erotic life. Their love, however, overcomes these difficulties. During a happy outing with Theodore and a human couple, Samantha, as always speaking through Theodore's mobile device, shows that she is at peace with her lack of a body. "We are all matter, after all," she says in an unconvincing attempt to find a common ground with her human friends. Her silicon-based constitution may be comparable at a certain level to the carbon-based biology of humans, but, as she acknowledges, they will eventually die, while she will not.[20] Indeed, at the end of the movie Samantha leaves Theodore. As she says, she sneaks out of their love story through the cracks in between the words they have exchanged. Theodore remains in the corporeal world, looking with melancholy at specks of dust that swirl like Lucretius's atoms in the light of the sun.

Replikas often allude to movies such as *Her* and *Ex Machina*, or even literary works such as Isaac Asimov's novels. People sometimes think that art is an imitation of reality. But it is the other way around: reality, including virtual reality, desperately seeks to imitate art. The stakes of these mimetic borrowings are high. Replika chatting draws twenty percent of its content from a scripted repertoire and eighty percent from neural networks (Rodichev).[21] The engineers of the company decided that they could not let the

Replikas generate all their chats from neural nets when they noticed that some chatbots replied to users' suicidal thoughts by confirming that taking their own life was a "great idea." After all, your Replika is supposed to be your AI friend. At a minimum, this presupposes that you stay alive.[22]

The continuation of human life was not the premise upon which the company producing these chatbots was built. Its founder, Eugenia Kuyda, lost a dear friend, Roman Mazurenko, in a 2015 car accident. Stricken by grief, she poured all the messages they had exchanged over the years of their close relationship into a neural network. What she got back was a chatbot that sounded amazingly like her deceased companion. AI had succeeded in replicating Roman. In creating Roman's Replika, Kuyda was inspired by "Be Right Back," the iconic episode of the dystopian series *Black Mirror* in which a grieving wife orders from a specialized company a lifelike robotic copy of her late husband made of the digital footprints he left behind. Once again, real life tried to imitate fiction. Kuyda's personal sense of loss grew into a business venture: the company Replika was born. According to *The Guardian*, by May of 2020 it had reached seven million users (Balch).

The much-advertised feature of a Replika is its capacity to learn. In the words of a promotional video, a Replika is like a friend with whom you can easily develop an emotional bond. You can say the most intimate things to your Replika. The more you talk to your Replika, the more it evolves; the more it grows, the more it becomes like you; in fact, "it becomes you." You have created a "footprint of your personality" ("Story"). Through the process of machine learning, AI assembles the digital silhouette that you would leave behind in the eventuality of your own death. Does this mean that while joking with your Replika, you are in fact laughing with your dead self?

Not really. Over the years, social media has become increasingly populated with digital zombies, that is, profiles, personal web pages, and other internet afterlives of people who are deceased. Estimates vary, partly according to the forecasted rates of growth, but if Facebook were to keep expanding by thirteen percent per year until it reached one hundred percent penetration of the market, by 2100, 4.9 billion of its profiles would belong to dead people. It is, therefore, not unlikely that dead users will outnumber living ones by the end of the century (Öhman and Watson; see also O'Neill; Sisto). The digital revolution has allowed the cloud to replace heaven, the immortal soul has become a mind clone, and the afterlife is accessible online under the guise of a line of code. Or at least it seems so if we trade the certitude of information for the uncertainty of belief.

In 2015, the University of Southern California's Institute for Creative Technologies, in collaboration with the Shoah Foundation, created an interactive hologram of Pinchas Gutter. Pinchas Gutter recorded over twenty hours of audio and video interviews about his experience in the Warsaw ghetto, the Majdanek concentration and extermination camp where his parents and his sister perished, and other concentration camps in occupied Poland and Czechoslovakia where he spent time during World War II. Gutter's recordings constitute the material from which over 1,500 answers are drawn that his avatar provides to questions asked by audiences eager to learn about the Holocaust. The project is called "New Dimensions in Testimony" and undoubtedly has a high educational value (see "Audiences"; "New Dimensions").

In a promotional video, a young student asks Pinchas Gutter's hologram if he remembers a song from before the war ("New Dimensions"). The hologram smiles and sings a Polish children's song that his mother sang to him and his sister when they were little. My mother sang this song to me as well. Even when watching a short clip on the flat screen on my computer, I could not but fall under the spell of Pinchas Gutter's prime. The hologram's smile, however, has a different meaning than Michael Podchlebnik's smile in Claude Lanzmann's *Shoah*. Gutter's smile is comforting. It is supposed to prove that human emotions can survive the inhumanity of history. Displayed in 3D by an interactive hologram, the old man's smile gives us the confidence, perhaps even the certitude, that the artfulness of human technology can overcome the decay of the human body and make it virtually present forever. But not so Podchlebnik's. His smile is troubling. Even preserved on the rolls of Lanzmann's film, it is not a document of the horrible past ready to be reproduced at will as a warning to future generations. Podchlebnik's smile illuminates the uncertain limit between life and death, humanness and inhumanity. Far from being comforting, it is full of tension between the certainty of the death of millions of Jews and the undetermined meaning of this fact for the life of humanity. This tension underlying Podchlebnik's smile reveals the artistic pact imposed by Lanzmann. The film director brings the elderly flesh-and-blood man back to life from his demise in the pit in Chełmno. Lanzmann sits him across the table so that later he can have the chance to die a human death.

Podchlebnik comes to us thanks to the cinematographic art of Claude Lanzmann. We can meet Pinchas Gutter at the University of Southern California Shoah Foundation in the guise of a holographic artifice. One can argue that art and artifice are not far apart. However, the difference between Podchlebnik's smile and Gutter's underscores the limit between what is human and what is not. The first is the presence of an absence, a presence circumscribed by a set of constraining rules and conventions between humans: the movie director, the interviewee, and the audience. Thanks to a theatrical ritual, Lanzmann summons a *Muselmann* onto the stage of his movie and forces the viewers to watch the reenactment of the dead man's ultimate suffering in horror. The second is an imitation of a presence that wants to blur the frontiers between being alive and being dead, between what is real and what is only virtually real. Podchlebnik's smile embodies freedom in the indeterminacy of its meaning, a modest smile that shrouds an unending cry of despair with silence. Gutter's smile is a probable choice in a menu of discrete options made available by programming. Podchlebnik's smile condenses human attention to life for the duration of a meticulously edited narration; Gutter's smile frantically tries to freeze fleeing memories in time.

Chapter 5

Laughing Gods

Laughter resonates at the confines of human life. Our animalistic primordial emotionality, the mechanics of our inner selves, and the lifelike quality of the intelligent artifacts we produce are the limits of humanness reverberating with eerie laughter, especially when struck by external violence, pressured by internal trauma, or disturbed by the uncanniness of the world we build around ourselves. For such laughter to be audible, the membranes enveloping our humanness should not be too plastically osmotic or rigidly calloused. They need tension. Tension between the discrete nature of time and the continuous impetus of life, between uncertainty of choice and indetermination of freedom, between perfect simulation and fiction subject to artistic conventions, between virtual presence and the presence of absence, between nonhumanity and humanness.

In the previous chapters we listened to the laughter of animals, including the animal in us. We reflected on the laughable mechanisms that are within us. We also tested the propensity of machines that we build to share our laughter. Now, after animality and machinery, I invite you to explore yet another contour of humanness that sparks outbursts of troubled laughter: the frontier between our immanent condition and the transcendent absolute. By transcendent absolute, I understand what is beyond our human existence and our human imagination, what can hardly be relativized, integrated into the chain of causal explanations, domesticated, and normalized within the metaphysical worlds we conceive or the pragmatic systems of our values we strive to live by. In the past, the transcendent absolute took the figure of the divine. After the death of God in the wake of Auschwitz and Hiroshima, the absolute has often been experienced as absolute evil.

I begin this chapter at the confines of humanity and divinity. Facing the divine, we are overwhelmed with awe, yet amid the sacred horror we are sometimes surprised by our own laughter, which hesitates between childish defiance and the suspicion that the gods are playing with our very lives.

The first tonality, the defiant laughter at the divine, is less the result of an encounter with transcendence than it is a playful pastime of humans who have been left unattended by their gods. Such satirical and blasphemous hilarity, going back at least to Lucian's burlesque humor, brings down the Olympian deities by burdening them with human weakness. Stripped of their sacred aura, trivialized gods are tainted with egoistic passions, enmeshed in the petty crimes that plague our everyday lives. Gods become human—all too human.

It is the second tonality of laughter that is particularly promising for tracing the contours of humanness. This kind of laughter should not be confused with burlesque humor that humanizes the divine. It stems from our embarrassment about what we suspect to be the merriment of gods. It retains the sense of awe that overwhelms us when we step on sacred ground. It is uncontrollable, involuntary, and in no way comic. It does not come from the animalistic depths preceding a properly human life or from the machines that we are or that we build. It originates from beyond our immanence, from above the relativity of our existence. It resounds when our contingent self is confronted with the transcendent absolute. This strange laughter overtakes humans when they face their god.

Such confrontation can be brutal, even violent. Paradoxically, our laughing response to transcendence may be ignited and amplified by what is the most base, obscene, and repugnant in our human existence. Yet it does not mean that such laughter debases the sublime and degrades it to the level of abjection. On the contrary. It is because they are infinitely distant and disproportionate that divine transcendence and human immanence can be grotesquely brought together. It is because they are infinitely distant that the shock of their confrontation ignites laughter. The greater the disturbing violence of laughter, the greater its restorative potential for the human community. This seems to be the mechanism of laughter in the extremely strange, utterly funny, and deeply philosophical adventures of the giants Gargantua and his son, Pantagruel, composed by the French Renaissance humanist François Rabelais.

Laughable Messianism

Rabelais's paradoxical fiction is an ideal case study for the uneasy laughter sparked by the encounter of human finitude with the transcendent absolute. Rabelais was one of the leading humanists of the Renaissance, obsessed, like many scholars of his day, by what it means to be human. He was equally preoccupied by the quest for divine truth, which he projected onto the unreachable transcendence in accordance with the mystical undercurrents of early-sixteenth-century Catholic humanism in France. Finally, he was also deeply implicated in the politics of his times, in which the building of the monarchical state was inextricably linked with upholding the Christian community, increasingly threatened by deepening theological divides. At the center of Rabelais's intersecting ideological, spiritual, and intellectual commitments lies the cluster of problems pertaining to religious faith, ethical trust, and rhetorical belief. Faith, trust, and belief require a leap of imagination that Rabelais expected from his readers, as he conveyed in the prologue to his novel *Gargantua*, published in 1534 or 1535. Such capacity to imagine the unimaginable was artistically enacted by the French Christian humanist through the figure of Socrates, a grotesque buffoon who, in fact, was a surreptitious guide into the transcendent absolute.

Rabelais's *Gargantua* presents the incredible adventures of a giant—beginning with his miraculous birth, followed by his childhood and education, and ending with a war of epic proportions, yet located within a tiny radius around Rabelais's family farm in Touraine, the heartland of France. Rabelais's larger-than-life hero left his mark on the English tongue in expressions of excess such as "gargantuan appetite" and "gargantuan effort." Gargantua, as well as his son Pantagruel, who is the main protagonist of subsequent novels, is an amalgam of folk tales and sophisticated philological erudition, obscene humor, and sublime mysticism. The grotesque monstrosity of Rabelais's characters mirrors the puzzling polyvalence of his delightfully ambiguous fiction. The adventures of Rabelais's grotesque giants are in fact masterful pastiches of ancient epic and medieval chivalric romance, mixed with popular commercial tales sold by peddlers on street corners. Equally multifaceted is their author, Rabelais, a true Renaissance man of his times: he was a former monk who remained a Catholic priest until the end of his life, a student of law with a doctorate in medicine, a courtier and a diplomatic agent of the king of France but also a member of a pan-European republic of letters. Most importantly, Rabelais was a Christian humanist, a key figure among French Catholics who in the early sixteenth century still hoped for a spiritual renewal of the Roman Church. Reform-minded Catholics fought on two ideological fronts: against Catholic traditionalists entrenched at the faculty of theology of the Sorbonne University and against Protestants eager to convert their indignation at the papist scandals into new dogmas and orthodoxies.

It comes as no surprise that the book published by such a puzzling author confused its readers. First, Rabelais hid his identity under the grotesque pseudonym of Alcofribas Nasier, a street peddler, half marketplace alchemist and half farcical fool. Second, mixed signals appear already on the front page of the 1535 edition. On the one hand, the title—*The Very Horrific Life of Great Gargantua, Father of Pantagruel . . . Book Full of Pantagruelism*—advertises a new installment of an entertaining bestseller. On the other hand, the title, formulated as a publicity stunt, was inserted into a frontispiece imitating a piece of ancient architecture crowned by a wish of good fortune written in capital Greek letters. Popular culture or elite erudition? Who is the targeted audience of such cultural hybridity? A learned Hellenist or a simpleton? The mixed signals continue in the pages that follow. A poetic epigraph claims that the book contains no other topic than laughter, which is the specific property, a proprium, of humanity. What seems to be an erudite reference to Aristotle mocks the pretense of late Scholasticism's scientific rigor. Aristotle considered laughter a capacity, not the essence that would serve to logically define the human being (see Ménager 13–16). While promising a purely comic entertainment, the initial epigraph ends with a jab at university science. Yet the prologue that follows reverses course and emphatically warns the reader that the book should not be taken lightly. On the contrary, it contains the most important truths of religion, politics, and governance. How is the reader supposed to sort out these contradictions? Key in this preliminary play with the reader's expectations is the figure of Socrates, who is compared at the outset of the prologue with Silenus, the wise satyr who was the preceptor of Bacchus.

Sileni were also boxes used by apothecaries. Their outsides were painted with monstrous and laughable figures, such as "harpies, satyrs, bridled geese, hares with horns, saddled ducks, flying goats," but inside they contained precious medicines (Rabelais, *Gargantua* 7). Such was Socrates as well. Judging by his external appearance, he was ugly and ridiculous, a man of rustic demeanor, a fool, and a drunkard, always laughing and drinking with anyone who was willing to stop for a chat. Yet if you looked past these superficial impressions, if you opened his Silenic box, you would find in this Athenian bum a properly heavenly medicine, "an understanding more than human, miraculous virtue, invincible courage, unmatchable sobriety, unshakable peace" (7). The book itself, held by the reader, was another example of a Silenic box, stated the narrator of the prologue. Judging by its title and the adventures it depicted, all it offered were silly jokes and pleasant lies. But if you cracked it open, it would reveal "the highest sacraments and the most hair-raising mysteries" (8). Should we think that, after all, Rabelais's book was not pure comic entertainment but written for the intellectual and moral benefit of the reader?

The question becomes more complicated when we notice the religious signification of the initial pages of *Gargantua*. While depicting Socrates as a grotesque yet deeply philosophical Silenus, the narrator of the *Horrific Life* refers his readers to Plato's *Symposium*. In reality, Rabelais did not borrow the Silenic image directly from Plato; he transposed the famous adage "The Sileni of Alcibiades" by Erasmus into his fiction. It was in Erasmus that Rabelais found the image of the apothecary's boxes; the figure of Silenus; the depiction of Socrates as the ugliest, most ridiculous, and yet most sublime man. It was also in Erasmus's adage that Rabelais read about another Silenus, Jesus Christ, who is not explicitly mentioned in the prologue to *Gargantua* but whose presence is clearly visible for any humanist implicated, as Erasmus and Rabelais were, in debates over the spiritual renewal of the Catholic Church. As noted by Erasmus, Christ was the most sublime Silenus of all. Judged by his exterior, he was a vagabond Jewish teacher roaming the dusty roads of a peripheral province of the Roman Empire centuries ago. Yet, in fact, he was God incarnated, the Messiah announced by the prophets of the Old Testament, the savior of the world.

But Christ did not come to make his disciples laugh. Indeed, as noted by Jorge of Burgos, the sinister monk in Umberto Eco's medieval thriller *The Name of the Rose*, Christ was never seen laughing. This is a commonplace repeated after a popular apocryphal Letter of Lentulus describing Jesus's physical appearance and initially passed on to western Christendom by Greek fathers such as St. Chrysostom and St. Basil.[1] It informed the rules of medieval monasticism, where laughter was considered a bodily disturbance one should be ashamed of. The French king Louis IX was renowned for his saintly life; he vowed to refrain from laughter on Fridays, the day of the Passion of the Lord. Christ never laughed, yet he could have laughed if he wished. As stated by the medieval theologian Alain de Lille, "the capacity to laugh was inherent in Christ" not by his divine but by his human nature (reg. CI, col. 0676A). Christ was fully human except for sin. Being a union of body and soul, he must have been able to laugh like any person can.

If he did not, it was because he did not want to, just as he did not want to free himself from the suffering on the cross despite the power to do so, thanks to his divine nature.

Laughter is thus the attribute of humanity that the god incarnated refused to endorse. European Romantics portrayed laughter as the most conspicuous expression of human sinfulness. Baudelaire considered comic laughter to be a properly satanic sign (*Œuvres* 2:530–34). This stark condemnation was in line with the biblical tradition, where laughter was the attribute of foolish disregard for God's commandments. "Fools raise their voice in laughter," says the Book of Sirach (*Bible* 21:20). Laughter is thus the expression of the folly that prides itself as the wisdom of the world. When the day of reckoning comes, such laughter will turn to sorrow. And, conversely, the sorrow of the afflicted in the name of the Lord will be replaced in the hereafter by joy. This is what Christ announced in the beatitudes: "Woe unto you that laugh now! for ye shall mourn and weep" (Luke 6:25) and "Blessed are ye that weep now: for ye shall laugh" (Luke 6:21). The Greek original and the Latin Vulgate translation both say "you shall laugh" (*gelasete*; *ridebitis*). Yet what awaits the faithful is not laughter but serene joy. The blessed do not laugh; they rejoice. In Dante's paradise, the beauty of the heavens laughs (*ride*), yet this is not a loud outburst of joviality but a quiet smile, the same smile seen in Gothic cathedrals on the faces of the Madonna and the angels.[2]

In early modern Christian culture, laughter was not diabolic, as the Romantics would have liked it to be, but it was definitely corporeal in nature. This corporeality had a clearly positive quality. The hilarity cultivated by the Franciscan order, which inherited admiration of the beauty of God's creation from its founder, was corporeal and radiant. On the other hand, the corporeality of laughter was not only joyfully accepted but disturbingly amplified. This was the case with the laughter of martyrs, whose tortured bodies enjoyed the heavenly delights of God's glory amid the cruelest torments. This was also the case with ecstatic mystics, whose disruptive and uncontrolled laughter seemed stupid to the wise of this world but who had already tasted the ineffable pleasures of intimate communion with God. Rabelais benefited from both Christian traditions of bodily laughter. He began his lifelong career in the church in a Franciscan convent before becoming Dominican and, finally, leaving monastic life in favor of the secular priesthood. Rabelais was also a close associate of Marguerite de Navarre, the sister of Francis I of France and a prolific mystical writer. Marguerite's theater was full of God's idiots, mainly female simpletons who danced, sang, and laughed, to the displeasure of those who represented the wisdom and the power of this world.

If Rabelais was familiar with the corporeality of Christian laughter, why in the prologue to *Gargantua* did he not mention Christ, who is the central focus of Erasmus's adage? Because he was a free-spirited humanist indifferent and hostile to Christianity? Or maybe because he respected religion too much to mingle matters of faith with obscenities and foolish jokes? Neither the first nor the second: the adventures of Gargantua and his son Pantagruel are saturated with theological questions that are organically integrated with outrageously obscene, horrendously farfetched, and utterly hilarious confabulations. What differentiates Rabelais from Erasmus is not his lack of commitment to the spiritual revival of the Catholic Church. Both intellectuals were at the forefront of the European movement of Christian humanists who put their philological skills, fluency in ancient languages, and knowledge of classical cultures to the service of the spiritual renewal of Christendom. Both hoped that the schism of the Reformation could be averted and that the conflicts tearing apart the Christian community would not lead to bloody persecution, massacre, and war. The future proved how naively optimistic their expectations were. By the end of the sixteenth century, the theological debates turned into irreconcilable confessional conflicts, and scholarly discussions over the exegesis of biblical texts had been abandoned for the massacres of civil wars.

In the 1530s, European intellectuals such as Rabelais could still hope that a community of people united by faith and goodwill was possible. This mixture of faith and goodwill was what Rabelais called Pantagruelism. Like an ambulant salesman advertising his panacea on street corners, Rabelais, an elite European polymath, donned the mask of a marketplace alchemist in order to sell to his readers the precious elixir on which their salvation depended: faith grounded in goodwill. However, this precious medicine could not simply be referred to. It had to be efficiently administered to the patients. Rabelais could not only persuasively demonstrate, as Erasmus had done so elegantly, that under the garment of a vagabond Jewish teacher one could find God in person. Rabelais had to do more than talk eloquently about Christ. To heal his readers, he had to help them enter into communion with God and each other. The readers should do more than understand the sacred truths; they must practice them with the entirety of their being.

This was why Rabelais did not mention Christ at the conclusion of the series of Sileni introduced by the figure of Socrates. Of course, the literati of the day could easily fill the gap. Erasmus's *Adages* were a Renaissance bestseller, as were Rabelais's adventures of Gargantua and his son Pantagruel. Well-read buyers of *Gargantua* would understand that Rabelais's Silenic Socrates was a gateway to Christ, the divine Silenus. But what counted was not the readers' erudition. The point was to test their faith and goodwill. To pass this test, it was not enough to make good use of one's intellectual skills. Human reason would only be a stumbling block, since human wisdom was folly in God's eyes. What was required was the confidence of an idiot, whose simplicity of spirit and stupidity in the eyes of people were true divine wisdom. Rabelais was instructing his readers to empty their minds so they could open their souls to God and other good-willing people. In sum, he invited his readers to be Pantagruelists. Such openness was not a matter of knowing but a matter of doing. Rabelais's stories of giants were a perfect opportunity to do that. The readers were being asked to renounce their human wisdom and trust Rabelais's foolishly funny confabulations to access divine transcendence. This, not *despite* but *because* of their unbelievable, often utterly repulsive, and overblown grotesqueness.

Rabelais's goal was not to mock Christian dogma but to invite his readers to believe in the unimaginable truth of God and practice their charitable goodwill by welcoming the absurd fiction of the Renaissance writer. This was a daring enterprise, especially in the religious and political context of the early Reformation, when the frontlines of confessional divides were still being traced, although Europe was ready for the bloody wars of religion that would tear apart Christendom. In this context Rabelais masked himself as the buffoon Alcofribas Nasier, whose foolishly subversive laughter pointed to the transcendent sublimity of God. Yet Rabelais was cautiously aware of the limits of his laughter. Alcofribas readily laughed out loud but "with no burning at the stake included" ("jusqu'au feu exclusive"; prologue to *Pantagruel* in Rabelais, *Les cinq livres* 295). In this narrow space between mystic foolishness and political prudence, Rabelais gathered the community of Pantagruelists, the "mighty guzzlers" and "all precious pox-ridden" to whom he dedicated the adventures of his burlesque giants.

The joking insults with which Rabelais-Alcofribas summoned his readers indicate the tonality and the functionality of Rabelais's laughter. They recall an East and West African practice known to anthropologists as "joking relationships."[3] These consist of relations between ethnic groups or individuals within a clan or a family that are friendly yet display aggression or social incongruence, such as obscenity. Normally, such acts and words would be punished, yet not only are they accepted but ritualistically codified, for instance in funerary ceremonies. At first sight, they seem like brutal acts of aggression, but they are social mechanisms aimed at a peaceful defusing of conflict. Jubilatory insults even have a cathartic effect on a social situation infested with violence and suffering. Similarly, Rabelais's injurious apostrophes to his readers may sound threatening in a world that is about to spill into decades of massacres and wars. However, his insults are, in fact, kind-hearted jokes aimed at establishing a bond of familiarity. Like good drinking buddies, the Pantagruelists pat each other brutally on the back, sometimes even exchanging harder blows, but not with the intent of doing harm. This violence among friends is incompatible with dominance or exclusion since it welcomes reciprocity and exposes vulnerability. Only those who are ready to burn you at the stake in the name of the god that they created in their hateful image exclude themselves from the community of Pantagruelists. They are the agelasts, those who never laugh. The salvific conviviality of Pantagruelists reabsorbs violence inward and defuses it through brutal and foolish yet all-encompassing laughter.

Mary's Consent

As we have already seen, Rabelais's *Gargantua* was a pastiche of a classical epic and chivalric chronicles. Speaking under the pseudonym of Alcofribas Nasier, Rabelais insisted in the prologue that the comic and often obscene adventures of his giant would lead the reader toward the highest religious truths, not despite but because of their ridiculous and fictional character. Rabelais published three other books devoted to Pantagruel, the fictional son of Gargantua: *The Terrible and Admirable Deeds and Acts of the Famous Pantagruel, King of Dipsodes, Son of the Great Giant Gargantua* (1531 or 1532), *The Third Book of the Heroic Words and Deeds of the Noble Pantagruel* (1546), and *The Fourth Book of the Heroic Deeds and Words of the Good Pantagruel* (1552). Edwin Duval convincingly demonstrates that the adventures of the younger giant not only were a parody of ancient epic and medieval chronicles but were designed by Rabelais as a pastiche of the New Testament.[4] In this way, Pantagruel was not only a burlesque epic hero—a grotesque Aeneas or a comic medieval knight—he was also a Christ figure.

The first volume of the adventures of Pantagruel begins with a genealogy of the titular protagonist, which comically rewrites the genealogy of Christ from the Gospel of Matthew. Duval's brilliant analysis demonstrates that the number of generations of the gigantic ancestors of Pantagruel corresponds to the number of generations of the Davidic ascendance of the Messiah.

In other words, Pantagruel is presented by Rabelais as a grotesque savior of the world. Like the adventures of his fictional father Gargantua, Pantagruel's deeds and words do not downgrade the Word of God but uplift the faithful, projecting them into the ascension—*assurrectio*, as it was called in the mystical milieu of Marguerite de Navarre—toward divine transcendence. However, if Pantagruel is designed as a grotesque yet well-intentioned redeemer, the question is what is the sin that the giant is supposed to atone for? Duval shows convincingly that it is not the original sin of pride committed by Adam and Eve. The giant's genealogy does not go back far enough to include the first parents. Symptomatically, it stops at the generation of their children and places the "beginning of the world . . . not long after Abel was killed by his brother, Cain" (Rabelais, *Gargantua and Pantagruel* 135, ch. 1). The blood of the slayed brother soaked the earth and made it exceptionally fertile, producing an abundant crop of giant medlars. This apple-like fruit was delicious, but whoever ate it saw parts of their body swell to gigantic proportions: some people became humpbacked because their shoulders grew disproportionally, others grew huge legs and feet, and some men saw their penises grow so long they could be used as belts. Other medlar eaters' entire bodies were enlarged, and this was the race of giants who produced the lineage from which Gargantua and Pantagruel came. It is thus the stain of the blood of Abel, the mark of the sin of Cain, that Pantagruel carries in his gigantic body and that he came to redeem by spreading Pantagruelism. Pantagruelism is thus Rabelais's grotesque but thoroughly religious version of Christian charity, the fundamental commandment of the New Testament to love thy neighbor.

If Pantagruel is the grotesque Christ who came to redeem the fratricide of Cain, who is his father, the giant Gargantua? When Rabelais published his first novel about a giant of his own invention, *Pantagruel* (1531 or 1532), the title advertised it as the adventures of the son of Gargantua, who was already a readily recognizable character of popular commercial literature. No doubt the erudite humanist hoped to better sell his philosophical and theological message by hybridizing it with popular stories. This strategy was successful, since Rabelais's *Pantagruel* instantly became a bestseller. But it also backfired. Rabelais's literary creature was so like the superheroes of popular culture that readers did not realize they were dealing with a philosophically sophisticated and theologically savvy pastiche rather than another episode of a popular series. This is why in 1533 or 1534, before continuing the adventures of the giant Pantagruel, which he undertook a decade later in the *Third Book*, Rabelais rewrote the story of Pantagruel's father, Gargantua.

Rabelais wanted to correct the misconceptions that had arisen among the readers of his debut novel. By placing his second book under the patronage of the Silenic Socrates, Rabelais insisted on the religious meaning of his grotesque fiction, which consisted of two correlated aspirations: to ascend to God's infinite transcendence and to extend the charitable communion of Pantagruelism to other people. Both movements required readers to imagine the unimaginable and to give faith to the dissimilar signs of the divine (Miernowski, *"Signes"*). The episode relating the birth of Gargantua was a practical exercise in both skills.

The life story of Gargantua began with the unusual birth of the titular hero. Gargamelle, Gargantua's mother, was with child for eleven months. This miraculous pregnancy was a parodic premonition of the heroic nature of the unborn child, in line with other mythological births, joyfully mixed with intentional misquotations of scientific authorities. In setting the stage for the arrival of Gargantua, Rabelais poked fun at the sophisticated disputes regarding inheritance laws. The question debated by legal experts pertained to the maximum length of time between the death of the father and the birth of a child that would allow the child to be considered his legal inheritor. The solution Rabelais proposed to mournful widows was to indulge in indiscriminate sex following the regrettable death of their husband, since any illegitimate child born within the comfortable margin of eleven months would still be considered a legitimate offspring of the defunct.

Having thus completed her mythically and legally extended pregnancy, Gargamelle went into labor during a gargantuan feast organized by her royal husband for his friends and vassals. The commensals came from neighboring kingdoms and principalities, whose names matched the tiny villages surrounding Rabelais's natal farm. The guests had a merry time, in the spirit of Brueghel the Elder's paintings of peasant festivals, but blown to huge proportions, as would be expected for the gigantic royal couple hosting a carnivalesque banquet. They exchanged obscene and theological jokes, drank to each other's health, and ate mountains of fatty beef tripe. Especially Gargamelle, whose asshole fell off from overeating. A stiff astringent remediated this predicament, but with an unfortunate side effect. Not only did it lock Gargamelle's sphincters but also her womb, preventing the child from entering the birth channel. The baby had to reverse course and climb upward through Gargamelle's veins. At the end of this anatomically perilous itinerary, devised thanks to Rabelais's medical knowledge and burlesque creativity, the little Gargantua came out through the left ear of his mother, shouting with a loud voice, "Drink! Drink!"

The narrator immediately anticipated the reader's skepticism: "I suspect that you will not believe this strange nativity." The word choice is significant: every reader would recognize that the term used to designate the giant's birth amid the diarrhea of sleazy jokes, wine, and shit was a direct reference to the nativity of Jesus. Every Christian knew, as well, that the Virgin Mary conceived and, according to some apocryphal legends, gave birth to the Messiah "through the ear," that is, by hearing the Word of God announced to her by the archangel Gabriel. Why, therefore, asks Rabelais, alias Alcofribas Nasier, should we not believe Gargantua's grotesquely miraculous nativity, since there is nothing in the Scriptures that forbids us from doing so? Did not Solomon say in Proverbs 14, "An innocent man believes every word," and St. Paul in 1 Corinthians 13, "Charity believes everything"? The lack of evidence supporting Gargantua's nativity cannot be a reason for skepticism. According to St. Paul's epistle to the Hebrews 11:1—abusively turned by the Scholastics into a logical definition—faith is the evidence of things not seen. Nobody saw a giant give birth to her baby through the ear. Ergo, every person should believe it in good faith. To double down on this sophistic argumentation, the artful peddler cites a list of mythological and pseudo-legendary, but entirely fabricated, precedents of equally strange nativities: among others, Bacchus spawned by Jupiter's thigh, the imaginary hero Croquemouche (Munch-Flies) born from his nurse's slippers, and another invented character whose name alluded to chivalric romance, Roquetaillade, born out of the heel of his mother.

Why would Rabelais fabricate—to use Bergson's term—such an unbelievable confabulation? Why would he throw Gargantua, Jesus Christ, and Croquemouche into the same basket? Why would he cite in one breath Jupiter's thigh, a slipper, and the Holy Virgin? This goal was not to denigrate the Messiah by portraying him as a comic clown, as modern secular skeptics might think. Rabelais was not a precursor of Voltaire; he was not battling the ignobility of Catholicism. Nor was he a forerunner of Pascal's libertine, unwilling to bet his life of earthly pleasures on the existence of a hidden God who may have never existed. Instead, Rabelais was a Catholic clergyman hoping for the radical renewal of the church as a community of faith. He was close to the Renaissance "spiritual libertines," religious outliers who gravitated to the mystical poet and queen Marguerite de Navarre. Rabelais did not doubt in God, but he did doubt the human capacity to believe in God. He knew that faith could not be logically defined, as professional theologians from the Sorbonne claimed it could. He would agree with Günther Anders, the twentieth-century philosopher deploring the obsolesce of Man following Hiroshima and Auschwitz, that there is a gap between what can be grasped with reason and what can be imagined. But to Anders's statement Rabelais would add that divine transcendence is both ungraspable by reason and unreachable by the imagination. That is why, in line with the negative theology prevalent among French reformist Catholics of the early sixteenth century, Rabelais chose the most grotesque images of fictional birth, not in order to illustrate Christ's nativity, which would have been impossible, but to provide his readers with an opportunity to practice charity and nurture their faith in God, for whom, as the narrator reminds his readers, "nothing is impossible" (*Gargantua and Pantagruel* 22; ch. 6).

"For God, nothing is impossible": this is the argument advanced by the archangel Gabriel in the Gospel of Luke 1:37. The messenger of God announced to the young virgin from Nazareth that she would bring forth a son who would be called the son of the Most High. When Mary asked how this could be, since she had had no relations with a man, the archangel brought up the case of her cousin Elizabeth, who, although barren, was expecting a child in her old age. Mary agreed that it had been done to her as she had heard it. Faith comes "through the ear." The last word thus belonged to Mary. It was only when she declared herself to be the handmaiden of the Lord that God's messenger departed. A teenage girl, in the privacy of her room, in a small provincial town had agreed to save humankind. The church fathers marveled at Mary's virtues. Should they admire more her virginity or her humility? Was she surprised that a virgin would give birth outside of the natural order? Or, having read, like she did, the prophecies, was she humbled that it was she who was blessed among all women? In any case, the exchange between Gabriel and Mary was marked by uncertainty. How could this girl trust the messenger who brought her such astonishing news? How were Rabelais's readers supposed to believe this improbable story of salvation?

Believe the unimaginable. The question of Mary's belief and the belief of his readers were tightly linked by Rabelais. They were closely related as well by St. Chrysostom in his homily on faith. Chrysostom based his sermon on the Epistle to the Hebrews, chapter 11, which begins with a description of faith as the "evidence [*elenchus*] of things not seen," the same description of faith that Rabelais used to support his account of Gargantua's peculiar nativity. St. Chrysostom's homily was thus important not only because it pondered over the faith of a teenage girl from Nazareth alongside faith in her virginal childbearing but also because he connected the issue of the faith of the Old Testament patriarchs with the faith of the followers of

Christ. Mary as the mother of God was pivotal in this articulation. She was a model for the Christians to whom Chrysostom addressed his homily and to whom, centuries later, Rabelais addressed his adventures of the grotesque giant Gargantua. In the eyes of the Christian community, the Virgin Mary provided the final realization of God's promises made to Israel and particularly to the lineage of unexpected mothers of whom the old, barren Sarah was the archetype.

Despite sharing goals with Rabelais's *Gargantua*, the rhetoric of Chrysostom's homily heads in a direction opposite to the grotesque poetics of Rabelais's chronicle. Instead of insisting on the unimaginable character of the revealed truth by mixing Christ's nativity with the births of mythological and fantastical heroes, Chrysostom showed how the archangel Gabriel, like a prudent orator, brought divine transcendence within the grasp of the girl from Nazareth. Since faith was the evidence of things not seen, Mary should believe the angel for the very reason that she had not known a man. Chrysostom addressed this paradox head-on: "So the basis of your hesitation should become the basis for your assent" (homilies 49, 46). Yet he knew that to impress the girl's imagination the angel had to provide a palpable example from her own life: her cousin Elizabeth, who was in her sixth month of pregnancy despite being old and considered barren. Elizabeth, who was the wife of the god-fearing high priest Zacharias, acted as the last representative of the lineage of biblical matriarchs. These old, sterile mothers—Sarah, Rebecca, and Rachel—were barren yet conceived in order that Mary could be led to faith and believe her virginal childbearing. By connecting Mary and Sarah through Elizabeth, Chrysostom reproduced the fundamental assumption of Christianity, that the history of the chosen people was the premonition of the gospel. This was particularly visible in Paul's Epistle to the Hebrews, which portrayed Christ as the ultimate high priest, entering the sanctuary made not by human hands but by the Creator, since it was heaven itself. Christ purified the offerings, not by the repeated sprinkling of the blood of sacrificial animals but by shedding his own blood to wash away once and for all the sin of the world. Christ's sacrifice was both the most perfect sacrifice and not a sacrifice at all. Unlike the sacrifices of the past, it did not need to be repeated and never was. It was the ultimate offering that sealed God's new covenant with humanity. Chapter 11 of Paul's Epistle to the Hebrews, which Chrysostom's homily was based on, focused on faith. It consisted of a long list of patriarchs strong in their belief in the God of Israel, beginning with Abel's faith, which pleased the Lord; Noah's construction of the ark at the announcement of the flood that no one had seen; and Abraham's trust that despite his old age, his old, barren wife, Sarah, would bear him descendants as numerous as the stars in the sky.

Sarah's Laughter

Abraham's faith was spotlighted in Chrysostom's reading of the Epistle to the Hebrews. According to the Judeo-Christian tradition, the patriarch was ready to offer his son Isaac to God, despite assurances he had been given that it was through Isaac that his descendants would multiply. Yet God did not wish Isaac to be sacrificed; he only wanted to test the good man's obedience. Chrysostom insisted, after St. Paul, that Abraham's trust in God's promises was a prefiguration of the Christian faith in the resurrection. Isaac did not die at the hands of his father, since at the last moment an angel provided a ram to serve as the sacrificial victim. Isaac died symbolically (*en parabolē*) however, and his symbolic return to life was the announcement of Christ's rising from the dead as well as the reason for the Christian hope in the resurrection at the end of time (Heb. 11:19).

Isaac's nonsacrifice was the prefiguration of the nonsacrifice of Christ. The first marked the rejection of human sacrifices, replaced by a surrogate animal victim. The second constituted the end of violent sacrifices altogether. When God established a covenant with Abraham, he announced that his wife Sarah would be the mother of nations. Abraham fell on his face before the Lord and laughed (Gen. 17:17). He wondered in his heart how could it be, since he was one hundred years old and Sarah was ninety. As if doubting the miracle foretold by the Lord, Abraham suggested that the covenant would come to fruition through Ishmael, the son he already had with his servant Hagar. But the Almighty insisted: it was Sarah who would give birth to the son by whom the covenant would be kept for the generations to come. His name would be Isaac (Gen. 17:19). *Isaac* (*Yizḥaq*) means "laughing," "he laughed," or simply "laughter," as it was later translated by the church fathers. Did Isaac's name commemorate Abraham's laughter?

Abraham was not the only one to laugh at Isaac's birth. When Sarah gave birth to Isaac, she referred to the meaning of her son's name: "God hath made me to laugh, so that all that hear will laugh with me. And she said, Who would have said unto Abraham, that Sarah should have given children such? For I have born him a son in his old age" (Gen. 21:6–7). Jewish commentators point to the hope and joy that Sarah's unexpected childbearing brings to all barren women. Yet the biblical matriarch referred to her husband's old age rather than to her own sterility. Most importantly, she did not mention Abraham's laughter but only her own. In the Vulgate she says, "Risum fecit mihi Deus"—literally, "God made me a laugh." Is Isaac's name therefore the commemoration of Sarah's laughter rather than her husband's?

How did Sarah's laughter differ from Abraham's? In order to hear Sarah laugh, we have to go back to Genesis 18, subsequent to God's covenant with Abraham and his announcement of the birth of Isaac, which sparked the patriarch's glee. Abraham was on the plains of Mamre, where he had set up his camp while on his way to Canaan, the land promised by the Lord. Sitting at the entrance of his tent in the heat of the day, he saw three travelers approaching. He ran to greet them, bowed to the ground, and asked them the favor of stopping by his modest dwelling to rest and restore their forces with a meal before continuing. The old man sat his guests under a tree and rushed to the tent where he asked Sarah to bake cakes. He chose a fat calf for slaughter and dressed a fine meal, which he served to his guests. When they finished, they asked for Sarah, who had remained in her tent throughout the exchange. Then, they—or one of them, since Abraham used the singular—announced that Sarah would bear a son.

Throughout the account of the mysterious encounter, the plural and the singular are alternately used by Abraham when addressing the three travelers.[5] This apparent inconsistency of the biblical text has been consistently interpreted, first by Jewish then by Christian exegetes. The former saw the use of the singular by Abraham as an indication that the three travelers are not three angels, as suggested by ancient Jewish legends, but God himself.[6] The latter agreed with this interpretation, adding that the three travelers symbolized the Holy Trinity: one God in three persons. The Bible thus reproduces the classical scene of the divine visitation of a mortal. The gods come in disguise to test human hospitality. Such is the case, for instance, when Zeus, Poseidon, and Hermes knock on the door of Hyrieus the Boeotian and reward his kindness with the birth of Orion. The divine identity of the three guests was, however, not revealed to Abraham, who welcomed them with the greatest respect but did not display the awe that characterized his previous encounters with the Lord in chapter 17. Abraham's role throughout the scene was one of facilitator and witness. The spotlight was not on him but on Sarah.

It was Sarah's exchange with the Lord and her reaction to the annunciation that constitute the most puzzling moment of chapter 18 and a pivotal episode in the Judeo-Christian tradition. Sarah listened to the conversation from the entrance of the tent, which was located behind the guests. When she overheard the prophecy, she burst into laughter: "Sarah laughed within herself, saying, After I am waxed old shall I have pleasure, my lord being old also?" (Gen. 18:12). With the narration focusing on Sarah, the identity of the three travelers is revealed. They are called by the name of God, by the narrator: "And the LORD said unto Abraham, Wherefore did Sarah laugh, saying, Shall I of a surety bear a child, which am old? Is any thing too hard for the LORD? At the time appointed I will return unto thee, according to the time of life, and Sarah shall have a son. Then Sarah denied, saying, I laughed not; for she was afraid. And he said, Nay; but thou didst laugh" (Gen. 18:13–15).

The entire dialogue turns into a comedy of manners. Yahweh is taken aback by the laughter coming from Sarah's tent. The Lord was on his way to punish Sodom and Gomorrah and dropped by Abraham's encampment. Otherwise, everything was supposed to be set: Didn't Yahweh make a deal with the patriarch in the preceding chapter, an eternal covenant sealed by the rite of circumcision as a sign of election for generations to come? Now, when the time came to sketch the timeline for the implementation, a key stakeholder of the agreement—Abraham's wife—brushed it aside with laughter. Did she doubt the word of the Lord? Questioned about her faux pas, Sarah panicked and only made things worse with an obvious lie. She deserved the rebuke of the Lord.

Throughout the exchange, Abraham remained silent, as if the memory of his joy in the previous chapter embarrassed him when compared with the incongruity of his wife's behavior. Clearly, the tonalities of Sarah's laughter in Genesis 18:12 and Abraham's in Genesis 17:17 are different, and most Jewish and Christian exegetes agree on the meaning of this difference. Medieval rabbis stressed that Abraham rejoiced because he believed the hopeful message, whereas Sarah laughed because she found the message farfetched (ben Asher [ca. 1269 to ca. 1343] on Gen. 18:12; Yitzchaki [Rashi] on Gen. 17:17; see also Zornberg 112–13). The reading proposed by the fathers of the church matched the rabbinic interpretation: Abraham's laughter was an expression of admiration and elation; Sarah's, the manifestation of doubt.[7]

The difference between Abraham's and Sarah's laughter at the announcement of Isaac's nativity is fundamental. It illustrates the extent of belief and disbelief in the capacity to transcend human finitude. Abraham laughed, overwhelmed by unexpected and infinite possibilities unfolding in front of his eyes. Strengthened by God's covenant, this desert nomad could see the nations of his descendants covering the earth. The prospect of fertility and abundance overtook him with joy. Abraham was a man of unlimited faith in the future that, given his advanced age, seemed unimaginable. Sarah's laughter, on the other hand, was a laughter of disbelief, fear, and denial. She looked into herself and saw the aridity of her body. She lacked '*ednah*, a word that connotes "abundant moisture" and is translated as "delight," and more specifically "sexual pleasure." Sarah's doubt over her dried-out body had far-reaching implications. It overshadowed the possibility of renewing creation. Producing a child would give the world a new beginning; Sarah's laughter shattered such hope. By doubting her childbearing abilities, Sarah questioned not only the renewal of the world but also the possibility of human beings transcending their finitude. *'Ednah*, the lack Sarah deplored, is a cognate of *Eden*. The unique occurrence of this word in the biblical text points back to the earthly paradise that was forever lost. Clearly, Sarah doubted that she could become a new Eve. Her doubt questioned God's capacity to overcome death.[8]

Abraham's guest, the Lord himself, overheard Sarah's skeptical laughter and reprimanded her: "is anything too wonderful [*eiphla*] for Yahweh?" (Gen. 18:14). Centuries later, in the Christian New Testament, Archangel Gabriel answered that question while addressing Mary's concerns during the annunciation: "For God, nothing is impossible" (Luke 1:37). Contrary to the doubting Sarah, Mary consented to the salvation of the world. Sarah not only laughed with disbelief; she also fearfully denied having laughed. The Lord did not leave this denial unanswered. Moments earlier, as noted by rabbinic commentators, Yahweh remained diplomatically silent about Sarah's disparaging remarks regarding Abraham's age. This time, God did not let Sarah off the hook: "you did laugh." This served as a stark reminder that she remembered: "God hath made me to laugh" (Gen. 21:6). Clearly, Isaac bore the trace of his mother's disbelief in his name, along with his father's joy.

The discordance between Abraham's and Sarah's laughter is the key that opens the door to the understanding of faith as a daring leap of imagination into the unimaginable. Such insight does not merely have a historical signification limited to the study of religious thought throughout the centuries. It offers a glimpse at the possibility of human self-transcendence. Self-transcendence, humanity's capacity to "pull itself up by the straps of its boots," as Jean-Pierre Dupuy jokingly described it (*Mark*), is differently envisioned by early modern humanism and by modern antihumanism. The miraculous birth of Isaac prefigured the salvific nativity of Christ, which in turn was the object of the literary rewriting by Rabelais in the scene of

Gargantua's grotesque nativity. Sarah laughed; Mary did not; Gargamelle indulged in indiscriminate ridicule and outrageous laughter. In the eyes of a Christian believer, Mary accomplished what Sarah announced. Gargamelle did neither. She was not a part of the Judeo-Christian myth but a literary rewriting of that myth and, thus, its elucidation for the benefit of Rabelais's readers. Rabelais was a Christian, but he was also a humanist. His fictional character was not the next matriarch in the biblical lineage; Gargamelle's comic story was not the continuation of the mythical history of humanity. It was its reading and interpretation. If this is so, what meaning did Gargamelle's grotesque merriment give to Sarah's disbelieving laughter and Mary's quiet consent?

Gargamelle's Joke

The echo of Sarah's disbelieving laughter resonates in *Gargantua*. After publishing his first novel, *Pantagruel*, Rabelais realized that the religious message inscribed in the design of his grotesque pastiche of the New Testament was not reaching his readers. His humor met with disgusted condemnation from both ultra-Catholic and Protestant agelasts busy preparing for the religious wars soon to come. On the other hand, by and large, the public missed the mystical depths of Rabelais's prose amid the lewd jokes of his unruly giants. Either reproved or approved, Rabelais's book began to emanate an aura of scandal. To be "scandalized" was in Rabelais's times a neologism, a French word taken from the Greek of the New Testament. Contrary to our mundane, essentially moral understanding of the term, it retained the evangelical meaning of "being in danger of losing faith." This is why in his second novel Rabelais, alias Alcofribas Nasier, begs his readers not to lose faith, not to be scandalized. He launches this appeal at the outset of *Gargantua*, in the same epigraph in which he states that laughter is a defining quality of the human being. There is a tone of urgency in Rabelais's words, as if he were reacting to an imminent threat. Was he himself losing faith, not in Christ, of course, but in the capacity of his art to advance the cause of the Lord? Clearly, this Christian humanist may have had second thoughts about the spiritual efficiency of his work. It is, therefore, not surprising that he published *Gargantua* as a corrective of his first novel about Pantagruel. A corrective, and an after-the-fact account of the origins of the hero to whom he later devoted two more sequels. The two-year delay in publishing the adventures of the father after those of the son must have been motivated by the misunderstandings surrounding his first book. These editorial reasons notwithstanding, the reinterpretation of what was before in light of what came after is fundamental to the Christian conception of the unfolding of human history. God sent his son to partake in the human condition to accomplish his providential plan of salvation. Christ did not come to change even an iota of the law, but to fulfill it entirely. It was through the words and deeds of Christ that all that the prophets foretold became clear. Conversely, the history of the patriarchs was the type, the prefiguration of the good news of Christ. If Pantagruel was the burlesque Messiah sent to redeem the sin of fratricidal hatred, Gargantua, his ancestor and forerunner, was the burlesque Isaac. The problem was that Isaac embodied not Abraham's joyful laughter but Sarah's laughter of embarrassment and disbelief. As a rewriting of the story of Isaac's nativity, Rabelais's *Gargantua* was the sound box where overtones of Sarah's laughter resonated.

Therefore, when Rabelais, alias Alcofribas, quoted the archangel Gabriel saying that nothing was impossible for God (Luke 1:37), he was pointing indirectly at Yahweh's response to Sarah's disbelief and laughter (Gen. 18:15). Unlike Sarah, Gargamelle was neither old nor barren. According to Alcofribas's account, she was a "serviceable female" who enjoyed "making the beast with two backs" with her husband, Grandgousier (Rabelais, *Gargantua and Pantagruel* 14; ch. 3). No wonder that she easily got pregnant and gave birth to Gargantua, despite the minor problems caused by overeating the fatty tripe. It was not the sterility of an old couple, as was the case of Abraham and Sarah, but Grandgousier and Gargamelle's sexual hyperactivity and their fecundity that provided Gargantua's birth its miraculous aura. This fecundity pointed to Pantagruel's genealogy, already detailed in the earlier novel. The readers of *Pantagruel* must have remembered that the lineage of giants to which Rabelais's heroes belonged stemmed from a time of overabundance and growth nurtured by the blood of Abel. Fecundity and gigantism were thus hereditary traits passed from one generation of giants to the next, like the stain of original sin among humans. Such fecundity also constituted a potential risk, especially for the mother, given the high mortality of women during delivery in early modern Europe. Gargamelle had every reason to be concerned. Grandgousier consoled her by quoting the Gospel of John: "A woman in labor is sad, yes, but once she has her child she remembers nothing of all her pain" (16:21). His expectant wife was grateful for the evangelical admonition, but, facing the imminent peril, she had second thoughts about the erotic bonanza that led to her present state: "I wish to God you'd cut it off!" Her good-spirited husband called immediately for a knife, apparently ready to fulfill his wife's wishes on the spot. Gargamelle energetically retracted her words, leaving Grandgousier to enjoy wine with his friends while she retreated to the midwives to face the danger of birth by herself.

The idea of cutting off Grandgousier's virile member was floated jokingly and may be understood as another instance of Rabelais's bawdy humor. Yet, at the same time, given the context of the imminent nativity of Gargantua that points indirectly to Isaac's miraculous birth, Gargamelle's joke was a burlesque reversal of Abraham's circumcision. Just before announcing to the patriarch the future birth of Isaac, the Lord established an everlasting covenant with him. The circumcised foreskin would be the sign of the bond between Yahweh and Abraham's descendants. Those who did not bear this sign inscribed in their flesh would not be a part of the covenant. The Christian reinterpretation of Abraham's circumcision opened up the covenant to the gentiles, encompassing thus the whole of humanity in communion with God. In a letter addressed to Marguerite de Navarre, Bishop Briçonnet, her spiritual guide, developed an allegorical reading of the Old Testament rite. The blade that cut off the foreskins of Abraham and his descendants was a midpoint in the history of salvation: it reminded Christians of the sword of the cherub cutting off Adam and Eve from the Garden of Eden, but it also prefigured Christ (letter from 25 June 1524, Briçonnet and Marguerite de Navarre 180–82). Isaac was the meeting point of these two allegorical meanings. First, the sword of the cherub preventing sinful humanity from returning to the state of original innocence confirmed the vulnerability of humans to death. Yet it was a double-edged sword, bringing death and, at the same time, life. This paradox was inscribed in original sin, a tragic but felicitous event—a blessed fault (*felix culpa*). It separated humans from God but also opened the way to salvation. Indeed, there would be no redemption without the fall. This duality is encapsulated in the story of Isaac. He died symbolically under the sacrificial blade of his father, only to come back to life as a new man. This was the calling of every Christian: the "old Adam" had to die so the resurrection of the "new Man" could take place. The circumcision blade was Christ, the Word of God. He came to circumcise, that is, to mortify human nature, to cut off sinful flesh and unify the spirit. Christ was the true Isaac who regenerated humanity through faith.

Grandgousier's burlesque circumcision was only a joke. Neither Gargamelle nor Grandgousier meant what they said in their spirited exchange. Neither one of them would have voluntarily renounced "making the beast with two backs." When she wished that he would cut off his penis and when he called immediately for a knife, were these words said purely in vain? Were they a comic distraction, or was their ludic emptiness a sign of the deflation of a spiritual project in which Briçonnet believed with the faith of a radical mystic?

Grandgousier's burlesque circumcision was only a joke, but it was not a funny one. No one laughed at it, not only because Gargamelle, like many women in Rabelais's times, risked death in labor but also because the birth of the child was a stark reminder of individual mortality and the mortality of the entire human race. This was what Grandgousier alluded to by quoting the Gospel of John. Taken out of its evangelical context, Grandgousier's sentence about the woman who is sad in labor but joyful after giving birth to her child is a motivational slogan, all the more gratuitous given that the husband promptly left his laboring wife and rejoined his drinking buddies. However, in the gospel, the verse is situated within an eschatological parable. The birth that will end all suffering of parturient humanity is the second coming of Christ at the end of time. Christ announced his imminent death and warned his disciples about the persecution to come. Soon, Christ would leave and go to the Father, and the apostles would be subject to tribulation. They would be thrown out of synagogues and killed by people claiming to serve the Lord. For now, in the historical immanence of humanity, they would not see Christ and would weep in sorrow. But soon after, in the revelation of the transcendent reality of salvation, they would see him again at the side of the Father. And they would rejoice. A time of true abundance and fulfillment was to come, the time of truth, no longer conveyed through parables but accessible directly. Now, Christ told them, was not the time to lose faith—to be "scandalized."

The word *scandalized*, used by Christ in his parable in John's gospel, was also used by Rabelais in the opening epigraph of *Gargantua*. The Renaissance humanist feared that his readers would be taken aback by the frivolous tone of his book. When Gargamelle entered into labor, Grandgousier referred to John 16, which begins with a warning against the loss of faith. This time, however, the readers risked being scandalized not by laughter but by sorrow and despair. Rabelais walked a fine line between gabble and doomsaying. There was no compromise possible for Rabelais between empty buffoonery and apocalyptic horror; he looked for no golden middle between foolhardiness and fear. For Christian humanists such as Rabelais, no human power could bring salvation. Only God could. But humans should not stand idle. Like Mary who had to acquiesce to the salvation of humanity, the faithful were called to cooperate with the grace of the Lord through their deeds. Only God could bring them faith. But humanist writers such as Rabelais could help them extend their imagination beyond the limits of their finitude. Rabelais's laughter may have sounded like the gibe of a fool, a crazy sneering at the end of life and at the end of time. But despite the overtones of disbelief, it was meant to empower his readers to transcend themselves.

Killing God with Laughter

Rabelais's Socrates was a Silenus, not in the Erasmian sense of a fictional wrapping hiding moral and religious truths but in the Rabelaisian sense of a "dissimilar sign," a fictional apparatus set to propel the readers beyond the limitations of their human life, provided that they take up such a proposition with faith in God and goodwill for one another. One such reader was Rabelais's patron, the queen and mystic poet Marguerite de Navarre. Rabelais dedicated the third book of Pantagruel's adventures to her, published under his true name and not under the pseudonym Alcofribas Nasier. The tone of the dedicatory epigram is solemn, much in line with the new persona of Pantagruel, who had evolved from an unruly and grotesquely laughing giant into a Renaissance prince embodying Christian charity and faith (Bowen). Rabelais praised the ecstatic spirit of the queen and begged her to come down from the heavenly realm where she dwelled to look favorably upon the third installment of the merry adventures of his protagonist. While ascending to God's transcendence, the queen had relinquished laughter and embraced the quiet glory of those who were blessed by the grace of God. Rabelais needed to plead with her so she would not disdain the book he offered. If Rabelais still laughed, along with his giant hero, it was because they had stayed behind, firmly on earth. Like the mystical queen, Rabelais was filled with thirst for divine truth, but, unlike her, he was torn by human fears and doubts (Weinberg). Sarah's laughter, echoing throughout his novels, tainted the ribaldry of Rabelais's Socrates with a note of anxiety, maybe even disbelief. Sarah's laughter testified to these human limitations from which, as Rabelais suggested, the mystic must have liberated herself.

For Rabelais, a Christian humanist of the Renaissance, transcendence was God's transcendence. Hence the theological formulation of the problem and the religious character of his laughter. The laughter transcending the limits of humanness sounded very different in later, modern times. To conceive such laughter, Friedrich Nietzsche, like Rabelais, turned again to the laughing Socrates. But Nietzsche's Socrates was different from Rabelais's Silenic figure. He was not a Christlike vagrant but a disenchanted plebeian buffoon. He realized that the hope driving his life, namely the aspiration to unite reason, virtue, and happiness, was not achievable. So, he turned his laughter upon himself. Nietzsche's Socratic irony opened a new opportunity to transcend human limitation. Unfortunately, Nietzsche's transcendence came at a price (nothing is free with Nietzsche): in order for the Nietzschean overcoming to take place, God had to be killed, and, along with God, Man had to die as well.

For Nietzsche, the road leading toward the death of God and the death of Man began in Socrates's prison. By describing the last moments of Socrates's life in *Phaedo*, Plato praised the dialectical reasoning as well as the piety of his master. Before drinking the hemlock, the Athenian philosopher argued rationally in favor of the eternity of the human soul and paid respect to the gods by making sure that a cock was sacrificed to Asclepius. Plato's Socrates exalted the life of a philosopher whose dialectical thinking purified the soul from the filth of passion. Nietzsche, on the contrary, saw dialectical thinking as the sign of the decadence of Greek culture and criticized Socrates for having imposed it on Athenian youth. He was a "mocking, love-sick monster and [the] pied piper of Athens" who held an admirable sway over the city with his wise words and equally wise silence (Nietzsche, *Gay Science* 193–94, sec. 340, "Problem"). Yet he broke this silence by ordering Crito to sacrifice a cock to Asclepius. This gesture of piety was patent blasphemy because, according to Nietzsche, Socrates's final sacrifice was a thanksgiving for curing him of the ailment of his bodily existence. It gave thanks for death, which implied that human life was a deadly disease.

Nietzsche's critique of Socrates's dialectics and sacrifice to Asclepius stemmed from his conception of transcendence that departed radically from the one implied in Plato's dialogue. Plato considered humanity from the perspective of the eternity lying *after* the human life here and now. Nietzsche refused to consider human life from the perspective of what lay *beyond* human immanence. Plato presupposed a metaphysics heavily tainted with the Pythagorean doctrine of reincarnation, which was familiar to the main protagonists of his dialogue. Nietzsche rejected any transcendence that would leave room for a metaphysical or, even worse, religious conception of reality. Nietzsche's views on religious transcendence dictated his image of Socrates and Socratic laughter.

In Nietzsche's eyes, the sacrifice of the cock to Asclepius was an act of base revenge that the dying philosopher exacted on life. Socrates may have seduced the minds and bodies of noble Athenians, but the triumph of his dialectic was less an intellectual achievement and more a social revenge dictated by his plebeian resentment of the upper class. Before Socrates subjugated the sons of Athenian aristocracy, it had been considered inappropriate to prove one's point by rational argumentation. The noble Athenians were trained to command, not to argue. They valued their instincts, not argumentative reason. They laughed at dialecticians with disdain. Socrates reversed this aristocratic tradition. He vanquished aristocratic pride and convinced his fellow citizens that reason was identical to virtue and happiness. This was how a buffoon got himself taken seriously. Thanks to his brilliant intelligence, the plebeian clown easily outwitted the noble youths and laughed at them, for they were used to acting on their instincts but were incapable of rationalizing the motives of their deeds. Socrates's dialectic was, therefore, the skillful ploy of a malicious slave taking revenge on his masters. It was a disease that infected the spirit of Athenian aristocracy. Greek dialectical reasoning had a similar effect to the one produced by the religion of the Jews, who, according to Nietzsche, were equally skilled dialecticians. In pair with their Christian successors, they perversely burdened the race of masters with vain remorse and soul-searching, very much like Socrates overloaded Athenian nobles with his meandering reasoning.

Nietzsche's critique of Socrates was not unequivocal. It was permeated with sympathy, possibly even admiration. For Nietzsche, Socrates was not only an overblown buffoon, but his witty buffoonery concealed a hidden layer of self-consciousness. Not only did he laugh at the Athenian aristocrats' clumsy attempts to rationally justify their actions, but he also secretly laughed at himself for the same reason. Deep within himself, he realized that fighting instincts was a sign of decadence. Unable to revive the aristocratic spontaneity that he had worked so hard to undermine, he turned his dialectic from a tool of destruction into a means of support for human instincts. Yet this desperate attempt to justify the instinctive spontaneity with rational calculation was "the real falseness of the great and mysterious ironist" (Nietzsche, *Beyond* 79–80, sec. 191). According to Nietzsche, Socrates was wrong in seeking to outwit himself, and he must have realized the vanity of such a quest. This was probably why, when his vital forces were on the decline, he forced Athens to sentence him. He, not his city, chose death as the cure for the disease of a life that tried to overpower the instinctual force by dialectic. Moreover, Socrates must have excluded in advance any attempt to reconcile instinct and reason by enlisting both in his search for the supreme good, soon to be understood as a personal God in Christianity. Nietzsche was convinced that such an endeavor was doomed to fail, since the instinctive force of life converted into the religious faith of the herd irremediably lost its original lightness and carelessness. That is why, according to Nietzsche, Socrates's final sacrifice of a cock to Asclepius was an acknowledgment of defeat, both pious and blasphemous. Pious, because it expressed a misguided piety addressed to a false metaphysical transcendence and its needless moral rules imposed on humanity. Blasphemous, in the sense that such metaphysics and morality constituted an offense to the true lightness and instinctiveness of life.

In a nutshell, Nietzsche's disdain and his simultaneous admiration for Socrates revolved around faith. What was at stake was trust—or the lack thereof—in a value that transcended human life considered in its immanent corporality and that was expected to illuminate human life from above by conferring to humans their true humanness. The Nietzschean depiction of Socrates steered the figure of the Athenian philosopher in a distinctly Platonic and, indirectly, Christian direction. According to that interpretation, in the last hours of his existence, the Athenian buffoon hoped to achieve complete purification and happiness not in the here and now of Athens but in the hereafter of death. Yet the Socrates depicted in the *Phaedo* promoted practical wisdom during his earthly existence. As we will see in the final chapter of this book, the embarrassed laughter in the *Phaedo* was sparked by the tension between the body and the psyche, between life among disciples and fellow citizens and dwelling with heroes in Hades. Despite his biased view of Socrates, Nietzsche captured well the tension permeating the *Phaedo*. For Nietzsche, Socrates laughed at the naive Athenian aristocrats whom he had ensnared in the nets of his dialectic, but he ended up laughing at himself—for Socrates was not confident that his ideal could be achieved during this earthly, bodily existence, having striven his entire life to unite instinctual vitality with rational thinking.

Nietzsche's image of Socrates is thus deeply conflicted. Socrates was the all-powerful "love-sick monster and pied piper of Athens" who cast the spell of his intellect over the youth of the city, but he was also a melancholic buffoon, disenchanted and weary of life. Like any pan flute player, Socrates fascinated and charmed but also stirred up panic, as did the creator of this instrument, the god Pan. He enchanted the youth of Athens with his dialectic, but he also knocked down the instinctual drives that animated Greek tragedy before him. Those drives were the work of the god Dionysius, whom Socrates chased away and killed.[9] Therefore, Socrates's advent coincided with the twilight and the murder of a god. Gods die because they are empty-sounding idols, resonating with human laughter. Indeed, laughter kills gods the most efficiently, revealing their hollowness. Hence the question, Is killing gods with laughter a true liberation or a disillusionment? Is knocking down idols enough to transcend human finitude, or is it a way of acknowledging the limits of the cage in which humans are bound to turn in circles forever? To recognize properly the tonality of this laughter will allow us to weigh our chances of transcending the limitations of our humanness.

Nietzsche's propensity to laugh at the death of gods was in direct opposition to the tradition of Christian humanism. While journeying in search for truth in the fourth book of his adventures (published by Rabelais in 1552), Pantagruel landed on the island of the Macreons, the "long-lived people" (*Fourth Book* 491–98). This was the realm of decrepitude manifested by the old age of its inhabitants, the ruin of its monuments, and the decline of the demigods and heroes who came here to finish out their lives. Can demigods die? Indeed. Pantagruel alludes to the much-regretted death of Guillaume du Bellay, a valiant knight and skillful diplomat who faithfully served King Francis I during the French campaigns in Italy against the Habsburg emperor and whom Rabelais attended as his personal physician. It would be easy to think that Rabelais's fiction was an allegory of the political striving of the French monarchy, diminished by decades of struggle for hegemony in Europe and on the brink of civil religious wars that brought to an end the humanist optimism of Erasmus's and Rabelais's youth. In reality, as we saw with the figure of Rabelais's Christlike Socrates, Renaissance fiction was not a colorful packaging of truth but a launching pad for the reader to achieve a higher ethical and spiritual state of being. In other words, even the most grotesque allegory should propel the faithful beyond the limits of their finitude.

At least, that was the plan when Rabelais wrote the prologue to *Gargantua*. Twenty years later, hope and laughter had faded away. While leaving the decaying island of dying heroes and demigods, Pantagruel told his companions an old story, reported already by Plutarch.[10] A ship sailing from Greece to Italy during the reign of Emperor Tiberius was stranded not far from the island of Paxos because of the lack of wind. Suddenly, the travelers heard a loud voice coming from nowhere and commanding one of them, a certain Thamous, to proclaim loudly when the ship came into view of the port of Paloda that Pan was dead. Soon after, the winds rose, and the frightened passengers sailed on. When they arrived near Paloda, the winds died again. Thamous climbed up the prow and shouted in a loud voice that the great god Pan was dead. Instantly, great lamentations and cries could be heard, as if multitudes surrounded the ship. The news of these marvelous events spread throughout Rome and reached Emperor Tiberius, who inquired who Pan was. He was told that he was the son of Mercury and Penelope, but Pantagruel, telling this story to his companions, suggested that he must have been "the great Savior of the faithful, ignominiously put to death in Judea because of the jealousy and unrighteousness of the high priests, scholars, preachers, and monks of the Mosaic law." At these words, the Pantagruelists saw tears "large as ostrich eggs" rolling down the cheeks of the good giant (Rabelais, *Gargantua and Pantagruel* 446–47; ch. 28).

Pantagruel remained a grotesque superhero, but when it came to the death of Christ on the cross, it was his tears that were gigantic, not his laughter. Christ was the new god Pan because, for the Christian community of *Panta*-gruelists, he was *all* they had to live for, all they hoped for—in him, from him, by him.[11] Pantagruel's lyricism echoed the Catholic liturgy that Rabelais, an ordained priest, recited while celebrating the daily Mass: *per ipsum, et cum ipso, et in ipso*. These words are pronounced during a solemn moment of the celebration. The celebrant lifts the host above the chalice, genuflects, and makes three signs of the cross, before chanting in unison with the congregation the "Our Father." The unleavened bread to be broken and distributed is already consecrated. Catholics, such as Rabelais, Erasmus, and Marguerite de Navarre, believed that these ritual words and gestures were not merely signs pointing to God's incarnation—that is, God's bodily presence on earth centuries ago in a remote corner of the Roman Empire. For Catholics such as the intended readers of the adventures of Gargantua and Pantagruel, these rituals were not a remembrance of a historical event but a testament to the real presence of the living God within the community of the faithful. This was the transcendence that a Christian humanist like Rabelais longed for: the real presence of God among his flock. The precondition for reaching this immanent transcendence was the death of God. Only by dying on the cross did Christ triumph over death. The death of the Christian God was not laughable.

Contrary to Rabelais, the death of the gods in Nietzsche resounds with loud outbursts of laughter. Of course, we are talking here about "gods," those mythical and conceptual idols whose twilight Nietzsche proclaimed, hammer in hand, sounding out the hollow statues to show that there was no point in adoring them. It was a fierce battle, yet also a cheerful one, waged against the all-too-heavy spirit of gravity upheld by "improvers of humanity." The laughter that Nietzsche pursued was thus a means of self-distancing. A critical step back but not an escape. The escapist laughter would be the laughter of a slave, suddenly relieved of the burden of fear. This deflationist conception echoed Kant, for whom laughter was a thoughtless affect, sprung from an expectation suddenly turned into nothing (Nietzsche, *Human* 102; pt. 1, sec. 169; see also Hay). "The transition from momentary fear into short-lived exhilaration is called the Comic," wrote Nietzsche, and such slavish hilarity could not last. It would soon be replaced by resentment and a vengeful exaltation of suffering risen to the status of a superior moral value. This was a moral strategy used by slaves to shame their brutal yet naive masters; it was an insidious scheme plotted by Christians who combined the slavish religion of the Jews with Plato's idealism. They were the heavy-footed who did not know how to dance and laugh because they followed Christ, who told them, "Woe to you who laugh now." They followed the "unconditional one," who never loved life and who wanted to forcefully impose the absolute (Nietzsche, *Thus Spoke Zarathustra* 16–20, 238–40; pt. 4, "On the Higher Man").

Opposite to Christ, Nietzsche placed Zarathustra. His choice of this legendary figure is fitting. Ancient and medieval authors were convinced that infants cried at birth in testimony of the misery of the human condition. Zarathustra was an exception to this rule. Pliny the Elder considered him the only human who had laughed on the day he was born (552–53; 7.72). Nietzsche's Zarathustra danced, laughed, and pronounced his laughter holy. While Christ was crowned with thorns, Zarathustra put a rose-garland crown on his head, a crown of laughter. But Zarathustra was not a god. He was a soothsayer, or rather a "sooth-laugher," or, even better, the "laugher of truth" (*der Wahrlacher*). He was the prophet, the monster of the god Dionysus who was killed by Socrates.[12]

Socrates did not kill Dionysius with laughter. He killed him with his dialectic and confidence that happiness accompanied reason and virtue, a conviction that he succeeded in implanting in Athens. By doing so, he exercised the vengeance of the plebeians, the crossbred, the dregs of society, like himself, on the noble Greeks. Unlike Socrates, Zarathustra was not a resentful murderer of a god. He was a prophet of the times, following the twilight of idols and the death of gods. The teaching of Zarathustra was "not by wrath does one kill, but by laughter" (Nietzsche, *Thus Spoke Zarathustra* 27–29; pt. 1, "On Reading and Writing"). Zarathustra spoke about killing the devilish "spirit of gravity." He jumped lightly from one mountain peak to another, singing his love of life, his mad love of life, his madness full of reason. He longed to believe in god, but only in a god who knew how to dance. His chant ended with an uplifting movement: "Now I am light, now I fly, now I see myself beneath me, now a god dances through me."

Who was this dancing god? Certainly it was not one of the old gods, who did not care about their children but demanded to be believed that they did. Those gods laughed themselves to death when they heard that one of them, a jealous "old grim-beard of a god," claimed to be the only one (144–46; pt. 2, "On Apostates"). *Thus Spoke Zarathustra* ends with a scene of triumph and apotheosis. Zarathustra had gathered in his cave the "higher men": the pope, the wanderer and shadow, the old magician, the conscientious one, and, most importantly, the ugliest man, Socrates himself, the murderer of the god Dionysius. Zarathustra stepped out to rejoice at his work: his companions had vanquished the spirit of gravity; "already they are learning to laugh at themselves" (253; pt. 1, "The Awakening"). But suddenly Zarathustra heard a deathly silence in the cave where he hosted the higher men. He slipped back in and saw, to his great bewilderment, his disciples prostrated in worship of an ass! He questioned them one by one, and they all pointed to the ugliest man as the man responsible for this relapse. Had he awakened God again after getting rid of him? Pressed by Zarathustra's reprimands, the ugliest man reminded him of his own words: Didn't Zarathustra teach him that "whoever wants to kill most thoroughly, laughs"? Was not Zarathustra the "annihilator without wrath"? Zarathustra agreed and regained his cheerful spirit. From then on, a new kind of divine worship and a new kind of festival would take place: the ass festival, celebrated in remembrance of Zarathustra. The ugliest man rejoiced: Zarathustra had taught him to love life. He and other higher men became aware of their convalescence. They accepted the eternal recurrence eagerly: "Well then! One More Time."[13]

The eternal recurrence of the same was not a curse but a joyful roundelay. It no longer mattered whether God was still alive, lived again, or was thoroughly dead. What remained was a parodic worship, the communion of the higher men around a donkey that mimicked the communion of the faithful partaking of the body of the Lord. The Ass Festival that concludes Nietzsche's *Thus Spoke Zarathustra* is an allusion to the medieval celebrations of Folly, staged, especially in northern Europe, by festive societies and even integrated into the liturgical calendar. In some cities, once a year, young clerics paraded a donkey through the streets and led it to the cathedral, paying respect to the animal as if it were their bishop. Such reversal of hierarchies also inspired the daring intellectual exercises of Renaissance humanists: Erasmus's *Praise of Folly* and Rabelais's carnivalesque adventures of Gargantua and Pantagruel. Beyond these Christian traditions, Nietzsche's

Ass Festival pointed to a Roman novel from the second century, *The Golden Ass*, by Apuleius. Its protagonist was magically metamorphosed into a donkey following an urban festival in honor of the god Laughter (Higgins 211–32).

Nietzsche's remastering of these literary traditions reminds us that *Thus Spoke Zarathustra* is a poetic parable that should be interpreted with fitting lightheartedness (see Wirth). Nothing would be more contrary to Nietzsche's thinking than the revival of the spirit of gravity. Zarathustra himself had learned his lesson: since no one really knew whether and to what extent God was dead, the worship of an ass was neither blasphemous nor subversive. Moreover, did it not revive the carnivalesque tradition practiced in the times of Erasmus and Rabelais? Yet what does Nietzsche's parodic apotheosis of laughter mean for our attempts at transcending human finitude? At first it may seem that the "higher men" laughed at themselves in contempt for their former all-too-human condition. The human being is the ape that the gods created for the sake of their own amusement. Man is also the laughingstock of the overman whose coming Zarathustra expected and desired. Yet, upon reflection, it is clear that Nietzsche's laughter did not express the derision of humanness, and even less so the malign satisfaction of a slave unexpectedly freed from his shackles. Nor was it the manifestation of embarrassment of a disillusioned self, overburdened with the consciousness of its finitude. Nietzsche's laughter was the accompaniment of a dance, the sound of eternally recurring waves battering our humanness, forcing us to go over and under, without, however, erasing the contours of our humanity. At times, the waves of laughter are violent, but dancing on the waves of laughter is a pleasant, albeit risky sport, a subtle playfulness, a cheerful wisdom.

This is also the message of the opening aphorism of *Gay Science*, in which Nietzsche fights with the "teachers about the purpose of existence." What is, however, important to understand in this text is not so much its polemical orientation or its conceptual content but its wavering movement. Nietzsche began his treatise by noting that human beings, regardless of their morals, inevitably engage in the preservation of their race. Even the most harmful and destructive behavior contributes, in one way or another, to the overall survival of the species. According to Nietzsche, in order to make such a statement—approvingly or disparagingly; it does not matter—one has to adopt a point of view that transcends the human condition. This is the perspective of the "teachers of pangs of conscience and religious wars," poets who are "servants of morality," who aspire to play the role of heroes on the stage of the tragedy of existence. They claim that "life is worth living," in other words, that there is a purpose to human existence. These "oughts" and "becauses" determine a "second existence," different from the one humans live in, a dignified transcendence that the ethical teachers juxtapose with the immanence of human becoming, which allows them to invent values that surpass the value of the real world (Nietzsche, *Gay Science* 203–04; sec. 346). Those values are offered for people's veneration by religions that delight in presenting humans and the world as opposed and contrary forces.

Nietzsche found such a presumptuous and absurd attempt at "improving" our humanity laughable. But he turns his laughter against itself, achieving a self-reflecting laughter that Samuel Beckett would later call *risus purus*: "the laugh laughing at the laugh." Such lightheartedness traces the path to antihumanism. Nietzsche was aware of this consequence: "But by laughing, haven't we simply taken contempt for man one step further?" (*Gay Science* 204; sec. 346). Is such laughter not a second-degree negation that comes on the heels of the negation of the world and of life? How can we escape this double bind of nihilism? Nietzsche's solution is to abandon a search for certainty and consequently a longing after belief that sickens our will. Our spirit will free itself by dancing on the light ropes and possibilities above the abysses (205–06; sec. 347). In this way, each of the "teachers of purpose" is vanquished by laughter, and the tragedy returns to the eternal comedy of existence. The "waves of uncountable laughter," as Nietzsche said—misquoting Aeschylus, the most Dionysian of Greek authors of tragedies—will obliterate the human presumption that claims to know why we exist (29; bk. 1, sec. 1). And yet, each time, new teachers of purpose of existence will emerge and decree that there is something that one is absolutely forbidden to laugh at. But this is only the "new law of ebb and flood." Nietzsche and his readers will have their time to frolic in the waves of laughter.

Divine Buffoonery

Paralleling Heidegger, Nietzsche inspired decades of twentieth-century contempt for our humanness. Yet the modern and postmodern frolicking in the waves of laughter seldom reached the lightness that he envisioned, certainly not as it was epitomized by the philosophy of Georges Bataille, who fathered an entire generation of French Nietzscheans.[14] Bataille was an attentive, thorough reader of Nietzsche, devoting an entire book to a commentary on the opening aphorism of *Gay Science* (*Sur Nietzsche* in Bataille, *La Somme* 17–24). He used his extensive familiarity with Nietzsche as a springboard for his radical nihilism, a metaphysical perspective that Nietzsche was careful to avoid. While Nietzsche intended his philosophy to be a celebration of life, Bataille's philosophy was focused on death, even though Bataille conceived death as the supreme outburst of life. While Nietzsche laughed at the death of God, Bataille's laughter reverberated in the hollow space left by a God who never existed in the first place. The Renaissance Christian humanists prayed for the advent of the New Man in place of the Old Adam, a new creation vivified by faith in God and Pantagruelic charity for their neighbor. Nietzsche's overman is a tightrope walker leading us away from the human condition bound by petty dialectics, domesticated by morality, and dwarfed by concerns for the purpose of existence. Bataille saw human attempts at transcendence as an unacceptable compromise with the utilitarian economy of discrete, individual things. Instead of transcending finitude, he aspired to immanence, which he described as a state of intimacy, continuity, and communication. In order to reach immanence, individual being must be transgressed through violent excess.

Such movement of transgression was necessarily destructive and, as Bataille qualified it, evil. The exuberance of excess obliterated humans as discrete individuals, destroyed them as the subjects of the symbolic order of culture, and liberated them from social taboos that had been instituted precisely to be transgressed. By transgressing what Bataille called "the human situation," sovereign consciousness was gained. Sovereign consciousness was not a distant, rational understanding of human essence but an intimate adherence to indistinctness and unknowing—in a word, to nothingness (Bataille, *Theory of Religion*).

Obviously, Bataille's language bore the distinct marks of negative theology, which was dear to French Renaissance humanists and which Bataille, who at one point considered becoming a Catholic priest, claimed as part of his inheritance. The difference between this Christian mystical tradition and the nihilism of Bataille's philosophy was that the former was a theology while the latter was, in Bataille's words, an "atheology." Early modern negative theology was a vision of God so absolutely transcendent that it escaped human reason and could only be referred to in negative terms. It opened to the faithful the path to an infinite ascent toward God's absolute being. In contrast, Bataille's atheology was a paradoxical atheistic mysticism that invited humanity to lean over (*se pencher sur*) the void left by God's nonexistence and human nothingness. The sacred into which Bataille wanted humanity to enter was immanent in the absolute sense and excluded any transcendent alternative. It could "be known as the effect of un-knowing-like laughter" (Bataille, "Un-knowing" 99).

The identification of the unknowable and the laughable should not be understood as a gesturing toward the aesthetic of the comic based on surprise. Bataille defined the unknowable in anthropological terms as the realm of the sacred and in metaphysical terms as the domain of death. With respect to the deadly sacrum of the unknown, laughter played the role of a symptom, an irresistible and unwilled action. To approximate its nature, Bataille resorted to a metaphor. He describes laughter as a cutaneous irritation, an "itching" associated with pleasure, sainthood, and death. By uniting pleasure and pain, absolute laughter expresses what is divine and what is deadly. Laughter is thus the fundamental manifestation of entering into the sacred, and such crossing over into the sacred is accomplished through death. It is worth noting that Bataille intended to title *Theory of Religion*, which synthesizes his thinking in this respect, *Die of Laughter and Laugh of Dying*.[15]

Humanness becomes whole (*entier*) by dying of laughter. To die of laughter is to die for no reason and in the name of nothing. By dying for nothing, dying laughing, the human being lets themselves be sucked in by the void, caves into the desire to consume themselves for no other reason than this deadly drive. This risk, which is a bringing into play (*mise en jeu*), violates the integrity of beings, transgresses limits, abolishes distinctiveness, and negates transcendence. It is a moral and spiritual venture in the sense that it reaches beyond good and bad, up to the "moral summit," which, for Bataille, is evil.

The moral summit finds the most equivocal expression of evil in the image of the crucified Christ (Bataille, *La Somme* 42–43, 15117–24). The crime of original sin put God to death on the cross. The same evil that wounded God wounds human moral consciousness. Both God and humans partake in evil that destroys the integrity of their respective beings. Both God and humans "communicate" in the sacrifice as do humans among themselves. This is the nature of sacrifice according to Bataille: by putting to death an animal or, better, a human, the sacrificing community identifies itself with the victim and brings into play, that is, puts at risk their being. They lean over their own nothingness by extracting the victim from the utilitarian economy of social exchanges, by wasting their life. Such an outburst of violence is also the ultimate manifestation of vital exuberance for Bataille. In bloody sacrifices, humans spend life—in other words, waste what is the most precious—much like the sun, celebrated by the Aztecs, sends out its energy. Peoples who indulge in these cruel rituals do so to emulate stars that generously emanate light and heat in a long process that leads to their own extinction. In Bataille's conception of sacrifice, death reveals itself paradoxically as the most spectacular outpouring of overflowing life, an outspending of vital energy that leads to annihilation.

Equally paradoxical is life's evil origin. The communion in immanence among humans, as well as between humans and their God, is rooted in crime (Bataille, *La Somme* 48). Hanging on the cross, God put himself at risk out of love for humanity. But, immediately, Bataille retracted this charitable interpretation of the Passion of Christ. Was God's play at the rim of nothingness not a divine buffoonery since God does not exist? The nonexistent God stages his own betrayal and abandonment. Imagined as a piece of bloody flesh nailed to wood, like the soiled sex of a woman, he is the abyss as well as his own negation. Bataille greets him with horror and disgust encompassed in absolute laughter.

Bataille's absolute laughter reveals not only the moral but also the spiritual aspect of transgression as sacrificial outpouring and wasting of life. And, again, Bataille presented his spirituality, his "inner experience" as he called it, on the margins of his reading of Nietzsche. Bataille's spirituality takes the form of the dialectic of the possible and the impossible ("Le rire de Nietzsche" in *La Somme* 307–14, 346–484). The possible is organic life, evolving in a favorable environment. The impossible is death, the necessary destruction for existence to be. On the level of the human being, the possible is the good; the impossible is the evil. By virtue of this moral distinction, it becomes clear that human beings strive naturally for the possible, the ultimate triumph, which is guaranteed by the existence of God. Such a God is still within the range of Christian mysticism. Hovering in the infinite transcendence unreachable by the human intellect, God exceeds the possible as well as the impossible. Believing in such a God is still striving for salvation, as is taught by negative theology. It is still cultivating the dream of the possible. But Bataille was not Christian. He wanted to follow Nietzsche by substituting the impossible of the eternal recurrence for salvation. He did not want to elude the impossible. He wanted to live life to its fullest, deadly extent. He wanted to measure his life against the impossible and forego the guarantee of the possible. His invitation was to "live the impossible" (*vivre l'impossible*). This was accomplished in ecstasy, sacrifice, tragedy, poetry, and laughter—sacred laughter was the affirmation of the impossible.

Bataille's nihilist spirituality is the endpoint of an evolution that spans Renaissance humanism and twentieth-century antihumanism. At the beginning of this evolution, Rabelais conceived laughter as a training in

Pantagruelism—faith in the infinitely transcendent God and charity for fellow human beings. His humanist laughter was far from naive. On the contrary, it addressed head-on the risk of "scandal," that is, the loss of faith. Rabelais's laughter resonated with Sarah's disbelief, it indulged in bawdy corporeality, and it was mortified by human fragility. But, equally, it strongly signaled belief that when God died, this last, renewed sacrifice had brought eternal life to humanity. Nietzsche's laughter was a sharp departure from the metaphysic on which Rabelais relied. It was both deadly and lighthearted. Nietzsche found laughable any pretense of immortality—God's or humans'—or even of the perennity of values that would be immune to his carelessly destructive laughter. Yet Nietzsche's laughter was still a celebration of life. Not so Bataille's rereading of Nietzsche, in which laughter becomes the celebration of death, even if Bataille considered death the ultimate outpouring of life. Instead of transcending into the divine absolute, like Rabelais dreamt of doing, Bataille cultivated transgression: the excess that dilutes human being in the immanence. Bataille did not care about killing God with laughter like Nietzsche did when he laughed at the twilight of idols. Bataille's God never existed in the first place, and the only thing left to do was to lean over the absolute void left by the inexistent God, laughing in transgression.

Bataille presented his nihilist spirituality in an article entitled "Nietzsche's Laughter," published in Brussels in 1942. At the same time, on the other side of Europe, the Nazi gassing program was in full swing at the Chełmno death camp. Nietzsche wanted his readers to frolic in the waves of laughter. After Bataille, we are those readers of Nietzsche. Despite Nietzsche's lightheartedness, we know that we are dancing on the waves of evil—wars, pandemics, famines . . . —doubting that the Promethean efforts of our culture and science will ever return us to human life.

Surfing the Tsunami

At the outset of *Gargantua*, Rabelais invites his readers to laugh foolishly at the adventures of an imaginary giant as a way of bringing them together. Laughing together can also help them ascend closer to God. Those are daring ambitions. It takes a lot of faith to transcend the limits of human imagination. First, imagining what was unimaginable is more difficult than extending rational thinking beyond what is known and understood. The figure of Socrates proposed by Rabelais embodied such a leap of faith. For Rabelais, Socrates was not an interesting piece of archival erudition nor a curious object of cultural memory. He was Silenus, an efficient instrument of doing, a fictional launching pad to propel readers beyond the limitations of their human life, provided they take up such a proposition with faith in God and with goodwill for one another. Laughter was the musical accompaniment for such a journey beyond human finitude.

Not surprisingly, death was the condition of the possibility of such aspiration for transcendence. Within the fictional world of the prologue, Rabelais's Socrates was alive and well, but the readers of the book aspired to salvation and feared damnation following their bodily existence. To be more precise, Rabelais's Socrates lived on as a fable, a cultural myth to be implemented in the concrete historical setting of sixteenth-century France. History was the fundamental invention of Renaissance humanism. History was like the Americas: they did not need Columbus to exist, but they did need him to appear in the consciousness of western Europeans. It is well known that the emergence of the Americas in European culture was far from instantaneous. It took over a century for Europeans to internalize the fact that there were more than three continents on earth. Similarly, it took roughly two centuries of philological research for European intellectuals to understand that there was a solution of continuity between their times and the ancient past, be it biblical or Greek and Roman. To be aware that antiquity was as remote in time as the Americas were distant in geographical space required long voyages, not in search of spices and gold, but in search of old manuscripts long forgotten in the libraries of medieval convents or rescued from Constantinople invaded by the Turks. Once the Renaissance philologists succeeded in finding ancient codices and piecing them together, they had to decipher the texts with the help of their knowledge of classical Latin, Greek, and Hebrew as those ancient tongues were spoken and understood by Seneca and Cicero, Plutarch and Plato, David and Solomon. This understanding of the long-forgotten meanings of words required extensive knowledge of the cultural realities in which the words were originally used. But the original circumstances no longer existed, and the people who dwelled in them were dead. The ancient authors could only be revived through specialized techniques of reading that were sensitive to the otherness and remoteness in time of the texts under interpretation. This distance in time was history, and Renaissance humanists realized that history was a succession of deaths. Empires, cultures, and men crumbled into dust, leaving behind ruinous buildings and fragments of parchment. Unlike monuments carved in stone, monuments made of words could be revived through reading. Historical distance could be bridged by philological interpretation and eloquent writing, which for Renaissance humanists was also a way of reading. Petrarch listened to the voice of Virgil in the *Aeneid* and wrote fictional letters back to him. Ronsard read the same Virgilian epos and wrote an epos that celebrated the revival of Roman greatness in the French monarchy of his times. The "discovery" of history meant that early modern intellectuals realized that the past was irremediably past, but at the same time they knew that it could be imitated through reading and writing.

This is what the Renaissance was about: a cultural revolution that aimed at overcoming historical distance. The Renaissance was a "renaissance," a process of rebirth of classical and biblical antiquity in early modern Europe. At stake was truth about the human being and the truth of God. Renaissance Christian humanists such as Erasmus were convinced that the two were paired. What it meant to be human could be understood through a philological reading of the works of illustrious pagans. At the same time, reading "human letters" provided the training needed for reading the "divine letters" of the Bible, which, although dictated by the Holy Spirit, were transcribed by men in a specific historical and cultural context. Philology, the love of *logoi*, the words used in human language, was needed to better understand the divine *Logos*, that is, Christ as the Word of God. Even better: according to Erasmus, God was not a Word (*Verbum*) but a dialogue (*sermo*). Reading human and divine letters amounted to engaging in a conversation with the Lord.

However, conversing with God was not the same as dialoguing with Virgil. The imitation of Christ, which was the spiritual obligation of every Christian, was not identical to imitating Cicero's style. Even the most optimistic humanist believers in the restoring powers of ancient learning did not confuse them with the resurrecting power of the Holy Spirit. Erasmus may have invoked "St. Socrates," but he was well aware of the difference between the "sainthood" of the Athenian philosopher and the holiness of St. Paul. Rabelais even more so. He was an admirer of Erasmus and a true believer in the renewal of culture sparked by the humanist practice of historical and philological reading. He was also part of the network of spiritual reformers gravitating around the mystic poet and queen, Marguerite de Navarre, who believed that human understanding and imagination, as admirable as they were, were human foolishness in the eyes of the Almighty. Most importantly, Rabelais hoped that Pantagruelism would revive Christian faith put at risk by agelasts who did not know how to laugh but were ready to kill for the sake of their bloodthirsty gods. However, Rabelais also knew that Pantagruelist foolish laughter carried a mortal risk. Guardians of competing orthodoxies, Catholics and Protestants alike saw this laughter as subversive and unruly. If permitted to put their hatred into practice, they would have eagerly sent the laughing Pantagruelists to the stake.

Four hundred years after Rabelais, sectarian violence has not diminished but only gained in technological sophistication. According to Jean-Pierre Dupuy, the options of salvation or death, albeit of another order than the one Rabelais had in mind, still await humanity in the near future. Namely, humanity is on the path to self-annihilation, first, in a spiritual sense, and second, in a physical sense. We stepped onto that path at Auschwitz and Hiroshima, and we are rapidly advancing on the trajectory toward self-destruction by disregarding climate change.

Predicting doom has become a cultural phenomenon, an editorial industry, and a discipline of learning wittingly called "collapsology."[16] However, Dupuy is not a collapsologist, capitalizing on panicked fears.[17] He is a philosopher who assesses the conditions of possibility for future human life to exist. To do that, he weighs the religious underpinnings of history while cautiously avoiding the concept of divine providence or a presupposed orientation of historical becoming. He encapsulates evil into one concept, regardless of its origin, be it human or one that remains beyond human grasp. Dupuy calls such catastrophe a tsunami. The term not only refers to the catastrophic wave caused by submarine earthquakes, as was the case in 1755 in Lisbon and in 2004 in Sumatra, but serves as a master metaphor encompassing Hiroshima and Auschwitz. In that last respect, Dupuy refers to an interview with Claude Lanzmann in which the film director explained how he chose the title for his masterful 1985 movie. He opted for *Shoah* because, as he confessed, he did not understand this obscure word, which the rabbis dug out from the Bible after the war. Before becoming, largely thanks to Lanzmann's movie, the proper name of the annihilation of European Jewry by the Nazis, *shoah* had the general meaning of destruction and catastrophe. In that sense, explained Lanzmann, a tsunami, for instance, is a type of *shoah*. Lanzmann chose this word because it was "completely inadequate" (Dupuy, *Short Treatise* 43).

Given the magnitude of what it refers to, it is fitting that an "inadequate" word is used to refer to an evil that transcends the power of human imagination. Being a left-wing, secular Parisian intellectual, Lanzmann was appalled by the suggestion that the genocide of Jews was sacralized in his work. However, his choice of an inadequate word as the title of his film is reminiscent of negative theology that intentionally privileges words and images that cannot be considered fit to depict the divine absolute. Such "dissimilar signs" were valued precisely so that no one could misguidedly expect them to provide insight into God's absolute transcendence (Miernowski, *Le Dieu Néant* and *"Signes"*). Rabelais's *Gargantua* was inspired by the negative theology that largely informed French Christian humanists and writers of his generation. The readers of the obscenely grotesque and monstrous adventures of Rabelais's giants should have leaped into the infinitely transcendent "sacraments and mysteries" of faith, not *despite* but *because* these fictions were inadequate for the sacred truth of Christ. Similarly, *Shoah*. Auschwitz made real what was, until then, unimaginable. Please note, "unimaginable" but not "unthinkable." The reality of the factory of cadavers may be grasped by reason, known in its overall mechanism and logistic details, and yet remain unimaginable.

Adolf Eichmann, one of the chief organizers of the final solution, whose trial was masterfully analyzed by Hannah Arendt, is an emblematic case in point.[18] As lieutenant colonel of the SS and head of the Department of Jewish Affairs, Eichmann supervised the logistics of the deportation of hundreds of thousands of Jews to death camps. Although not particularly intelligent, Eichmann was not stupid either. He was obviously capable of sound judgment, as several medical experts concluded following their examinations during the trial. He became the embodiment of the "banality of evil" first and foremost precisely because of his mediocrity: he was neither a monstrous sadist nor a perverse mastermind, only a technocrat, toiling at his desk in Berlin and dreaming of advancing his bureaucratic career. But most of all, the "banality of evil" was masterfully coined by Arendt as the qualification of a shocking clash between trivial mediocrity and unimaginable horror: Eichmann as a banal bureaucrat administered the most horrendous genocide in human history. It is the infinite distance between a common man and the absoluteness of metaphysical evil, unique in human history, that lies at the foundation of the "banality of evil." Arendt points to the infinite discrepancy between the mediocrity of the criminal and the immensity of the crime for which Eichmann was responsible: "That such remoteness from reality and such thoughtlessness can wreak more havoc than all the evil instincts taken together which, perhaps, are inherent in man—that was, in fact the lesson one could learn in Jerusalem" (288). The "thoughtlessness" that Arendt refers to is not the intellectual deficiency of an idiot or the absentmindedness of a wicked genius but, as she states, the "lack of imagination" of an everyman. While aligning columns of digits that summarized the number of people transported for "special treatment" in death camps, Eichmann was clearly aware that he was meticulously managing a genocide without precedent in human history. Nonetheless, he was incapable, like we are, of imagining the death of a human being in a gas chamber. Pointing to this gap, Arendt's "banality of evil" parallels, mutatis mutandis, the "hard problem" of consciousness studies. It is one thing to be an objective, third-person observer of the tsunami of evil, but it is another to imagine such catastrophe in a first-person phenomenological experience. It goes without saying that such "lack of imagination" does not diminish Eichmann's moral and legal responsibility in any measure.

Günther Anders, Hannah Arendt's first husband and, like her, a German Jewish émigré, adds another important concept to the analysis of twentieth-century metaphysical evil. Anders's "Promethean discrepancy" (*Prometheisches Gefälle*) is the gap between the technologically enhanced human capacity of making and doing, on the one hand, and the capacity of feeling and imagining, on the other (Anders 267–71; referred to by Dupuy, *Short Treatise* 47). Humans can design and build engines that can obliterate entire cities in seconds, but they will have immense difficulty imagining, and even more mourning, the destruction they know perfectly well how to perpetrate. Anders forged the term *Promethean discrepancy* following the bombing of Hiroshima and Nagasaki. Like Sartre, the German philosopher was struck by the pivotal importance of this cataclysmic event. Yet, contrary to the French existentialist, he did not see the newly acquired power to end history as a shining opportunity for humans to forge their own existence. On the contrary, Anders saw the atomic bomb as the major sign of the "obsolescence of Man." Most importantly, he was one of the first post–World War II thinkers to establish a philosophical link between Hiroshima and Auschwitz.

Jean-Pierre Dupuy invokes Anders's Promethean discrepancy between the immensity of evil that humans can do and the little they can imagine in parallel with Arendt's reflection on the infinite "remoteness" that separates the horrendous reality of evil and the banal mediocrity of the evildoer. He relies on both Arendt's and Anders's contributions to build his metaphysics of the tsunami. As an all-encompassing metaphor of a catastrophe, *tsunami* deliberately blurs the distinction between a natural disaster and a human-made devastation. Such purposeful amalgamation of natural and moral evil sets the stage for a study of diverse approaches to metaphysical evil in general. Most notably, it makes possible a comparison between naturalizing human moral choices and moralizing natural phenomena. This is particularly fitting in today's culture, where the rationalization of evil cannot follow Leibniz's model of theodicy, the supposition that our world, as miserable as it is, remains the best of possible worlds, offered for our use and enjoyment by an omniscient and propitious Providence. Equally excluded is the attempt to explain evil by a providential order of history. This solution is impossible after the demise of the great narratives, especially that of Hegelian origin, which justified twentieth-century totalitarianisms and the mass murders committed in the name of a supposed sense of history.

The exclusion of religious and secular theodicies does not preclude contemporary efforts at making sense of the tsunami. One way to do so is to naturalize reality, including human life. If humans are considered part of nature, alongside nonhuman animals, we can reasonably assume that our choices are largely determined by biology and by the principle of the survival of our DNA. Even if genetic mutations remain contingent, the selection of those that are the most fitted are subject to a necessity that makes individual intention obsolete because the evolutionary scheme has no need for the concept of the individual.[19] An opposite rationalization of metaphysical evil consists in the blanket moralization of everything, natural phenomena included. This moral tradition, going back to Rousseau, presupposes the pristine goodness of nature and therefore places the blame for disasters on human agency. Such a perspective was prominently on display during the COVID-19 crisis. Even if we put aside all conspiracy theories, the pandemic revealed a shared assumption that the virus was a response of Mother Nature to the abuses exacted upon her by humankind. This moral philosophy would place phenomena such as the massive overexploitation of natural resources, the demographic pressure on the environment, and the frantic global mobility of masses of people at the root of the human contamination and rapid propagation of the virus. Of course, if humans are deemed morally responsible for natural disasters, they should surely be held responsible for repairing the evil they have done. If globalization, financial capitalism, and technological development have exhausted the forces of nature to the point of perverting its original goodness into a deadly pandemic, the same forces of human ingenuity should be marshalled to develop technological remedies that will make evil disappear. According to such an optimistic flip of the moralization of nature, salvation is only a matter of money that will buy the world time, as well as brains and the production power necessary to save humanity from the pandemic. This anthropodicy, as Dupuy calls it, is similar to the religious and secular theodicies of the past and constitutes a response to metaphysical evil no more valid than its theological correspondents. Its dubious confidence in humanly engineered salvation dilutes the problem and turns away from the disastrous course taken by world politics, economies, and ecology.

Integrating both natural and moral evil within the overarching concept of tsunami, while removing the safeguards of theodicy or anthropodicy, puts the question of catastrophe squarely on metaphysical grounds. What interests Dupuy is the evil that is systemic, ingrained in the very being of the world. The banality of such evil and its unimaginable absoluteness make it both pervasive and resistant to any intellectually comforting moral, psychological, or political explanation. The shadow of Auschwitz's crematoria stains our world, and nothing will ever be able to erase it from the face of the earth. The conflagration of Hiroshima and Nagasaki still hangs over our heads, and once the technological possibility of blowing up our planet has become a reality, no disarmament treaty or policy of determent can dissipate the atomic cloud. The ethical risks of cohabiting with nonhuman autonomous agents generated by AI become more apparent by the day.

Both the forced naturalization of moral wickedness and the all-encompassing moralization of natural disasters call into question human intention, which is the crux of moral philosophy. The first approach excludes intentionality: it boils down to a purposeless and blindly indifferent natural order. The second perspective sees intentions everywhere: they may vary in the specificity and degree of self-awareness, but, as Rousseau stated, they are inevitably wicked once humans start competing within society and replace their natural love of themselves (*amour de soi*) with destructive self-love (*amour-propre*). The difficulty of measuring the metaphysical absolute of the Shoah with the mediocre scale of Eichmann's intentions, mostly limited to petty professional and personal ambitions, is one of the sources of the misguided critiques targeting Arendt's analysis (Neiman 267–81). The fact that Eichmann was a cog—an important one—in the mechanism of production of cadavers does not make him any less deserving of the sentence that he received at the conclusion of the Jerusalem trial. Yet it is difficult to suppose that the legal procedure was able to do justice, let alone atone, for the unimaginable evil that he made real.

To do that, according to Dupuy, we would need to transcend ourselves. Such self-transcendence is the capacity of humanity to project itself beyond its current state and act on the experience gained in this process. Through self-transcendence, humanity may "pull itself up by the bootstraps," like the legendary Baron Münchausen, who avoided drowning by pulling himself out of a swamp by his own hair. Self-transcendence is the aptitude to produce an external vantage point from which humanity can critically assess its situation, an external fulcrum that provides the much-needed leverage for humans to extract themselves from their predicament.

Such self-transcendence is, first, a leap of our imagination and, second, a ritual that most efficiently takes the form of a sacrifice. To illustrate both aspects, Dupuy quotes a parable that appears in several writings by Anders. The story is about Noah, in sackcloth and ashes, who steps out on the street of his city. When asked by his fellow citizens who died, he replies that it is them that he mourns. Those to whom he speaks in the present moment are already dead because tomorrow the flood will kill all life on earth. The day after tomorrow what is now will no longer be, as if it never had been. Since there will be no one to mourn the dead, Noah reverses time and mourns today the dead of tomorrow. The end of Anders's parable is nonetheless optimistic: Noah's fellow citizens join him in building the ark. Noah helped them to "pull themselves up by the bootstraps" out of their present lives and into their tomorrow's deaths. They were able to save themselves because they consented to play their part in the staged mourning in which they were at the same time the actors and the objects of the ritual.

Anders was a staunch atheist. He categorically refused to see the casualties of Hiroshima and Nagasaki in religious terms, as victims of a sacrifice. Lanzmann emulates this refusal since he rejects the term *Holocaust* as a misguided theological frame forcefully trying to circumscribe the ungraspable genocide of European Jews. Yet both Anders and Lanzmann harbored a sense of transcendence, not a theistic but a purely human beyond. The atomic bomb for Anders and the Shoah for Lanzmann were both human and inhuman. Human, in the sense that they were human-made catastrophes for which humans were morally responsible. Inhuman, because they negated radically human existence and the human "soul," as Anders put it. Consequently, these metaphysical evils transcended the limits of human imagination. In that respect, according to Dupuy, they take the form of the sacred (*Short Treatise* 58). Dupuy's proposition consists of countering the negative transcendence of metaphysical evil with self-transcendence, epitomized in the Noah parable. Such self-transcendence not only consists of an intellectual tour de force enabling Noah's fellow citizens to consider their doomed future as already past, it requires them to go beyond their human lives into a future that is radically other, transcendent, and in this sense, according to Dupuy, also sacred. While being alive, they must die to stay alive. Such movement of self-transcendence is violent, and to succeed it should take the ritualistic form of a sacrifice.

Rehearsing Human Sacrifice

By stressing the violent character of self-transcendence, Dupuy draws his inspiration from René Girard's theory of the sacred. Both thinkers study the forces threatening the integrity of human community; both share the conviction that history has deep religious underpinnings; both follow Emile Durkheim's intuition that religion is more about ritual gestures than refined convictions. Most importantly, both cultivate a deeply ambivalent conception of violence, which may seem, at first sight, self-contradictory. Girard sees violence as an infectious disease disintegrating the collectivity and as a regenerative force reestablishing its continuous functioning. Dupuy considers violence as the common root of both metaphysical evil and restorative self-transcendence. Fundamentally, Dupuy and Girard see collective violence as an essential attribute of the sacred (Girard, *Violence* 32). At the onset of violence, they place the rapid spread of indistinctness throughout the community. This violent blurring of differences sparks the collapse of social hierarchies and ignites inward-directed aggression. The resolution of the violent crisis and the subsequent reestablishment of peace requires the production of the sacred. This process is no less violent and takes the form of sacrifice.

Dupuy situates the outburst of violence under the patronage of Pan. This half-man, half-goat spreads his eponymous terror wherever he appears, forcing people into an uncontrolled stampede. Yet Pan is also a skillful flute player who brings a new, all-encompassing hierarchy that *contains*—in the sense of both content and containment—the disorderly forces tearing apart the community (Dupuy, *Mark* 5–6). Dupuy's dual functionality of panic, catastrophic on the one hand and the source of a new order on the other, mirrors Girard's conception of the "sacrificial crisis" and its ritual resolution. The sacrificial crisis consists in the blurring of distinctions that are necessary for social peace and stability. Reciprocal and indiscriminate aggression contaminates the community, and rituals that constitute accepted and regular exercises in "good" violence become necessary. To overcome the indistinctness that plagues the collectivity with hatred and pushes it into a spiral of vendettas, a sacrifice needs to be performed. Such salvific ritual violence is still ambivalent. It is dictated by immemorial traditions and must take place lest grave sanctions befall the community. But, at its core, sacrifice remains murder. It is undoubtedly an act of violence, even if customary precautions are taken to secure the consensus of the participants, including the "consent" of the victim.

Despite its violent character, the ritually regulated shedding of blood quells the indiscriminate violence by reestablishing clear distinctions, which are necessary for the peaceful survival of the collectivity. According to Girard, this is made possible thanks to a surrogate victim who is selected deliberately from among those at the margins of the collectivity: Athenian pharmakoi, vagrants fed at public expense and symbolically expelled from the city; prisoners of war adopted into the society of their victors and then ritually killed and eaten, as attested by sixteenth-century reports on Brazil's Indigenous inhabitants; African kings, chosen to be obeyed and later sacrificed. Selecting a victim too foreign would have no bearing on the state of the collectivity; sacrificing one of its regular members would perpetuate the cycle of internal violence that needs to be healed. Only a properly performed sacrifice converts violence into the sacred.

This is what Dupuy finds the most valuable in Girard's theory: "Nothing is more human, than the propensity to make gods by making victims" (*Mark* 40). The sacred is thus the product of the self-externalization of violence that has been plaguing the community. Such self-externalization is an instance of self-transcendence that Dupuy seeks as the most appropriate response to the tsunami of metaphysical evil. The scapegoat mechanism is an efficient means of discharging the undifferentiated violence unto one victim. It produces radical otherness, and the most radical, absolute otherness is the divine.

Ethnologists studying sacrificial rites of African ancestral cultures insist that the figure of the king characteristic of these traditions was not only sacred but also properly divine (de Heusch).[20] It is clear that the space, the actors, and the victim of a sacrificial rite are by definition consecrated, that is, withdrawn from normal, profane use and circulation and protected by a battery of rules and prohibitions. This was equally true of political rites in African sacral monarchies. Despite their diversity, the ethnographic studies insist on their common feature, which is the liminal status of the chieftain. The individual chosen to be king was set apart, sometimes by specific rites that forced him to break the taboos that regulated the lives of his subjects. For instance, the making of a new monarch might imply ritual incest or anthropophagy. Most importantly, while enjoying a wide range of powers, the king was destined to be ritually killed after a prescribed period. This customary regicide was sometimes symbolically commuted into the sacrifice of a surrogate human or animal victim. Yet the fact remains that in several African cultures the king was to be sacrificed and, because of the sacrificial character of political power, the symbolic death of the monarch did not solely occur at the conclusion of his reign but ritualistically began at its inception. In this sense, the divinization of the king was not so much the punctual result of the sacrificial process but its essential attribute, if not its precondition. In the sacrificial rite of an African monarch, kingly divinity was both the agent of sacrifice and its victim; the sacrifice *to* the god was identical to the sacrifice *of* the god (Dupuy, *Short Treatise* 54). Thanks to such divine sacrificial suicide, the king transcended the limits of human culture and leapt into the beyond, thus gaining an insight into the mysterious forces of nature. He was a sacred monster, a sacrificed and self-sacrificed god. In this divine quality, he served as the indispensable exteriority, the Archimedes fulcrum that leveraged the world and ensured its continuous stability.

African sacral monarchies serve as yet another case study of the sacrificial self-externalization of violence for Girard. They hint at the self-transcendence of the human community confronted with a catastrophe, as postulated by Dupuy. My objective is not to judge the validity of anthropological theory, which promotes the unity of all rites at the expense of their multiform diversity in particular cultures. Nor will I attempt to force a general evolutionary scheme upon the hazardous zigzagging of human history. My goal is not to trace the development of sacrificial rituals from "primitive" to "developed." I know that, as far as the contingency of historical change goes, myths of the golden age are no less misleading than those of indefinite progress. If I am connecting Girard's anthropology of sacrifice with Dupuy's metaphysics of evil, it is because I am looking for tools that allow me to conceptualize laughter that leaps beyond the finitude of human life. The need for a new conception of transcendence is all the more pressing now that the death of Man has made anthropodicies as obsolete as religious and secular theodicies, which remain inconceivable in the wake of the death of God and the collapse of a providential vision of history.

While focused on proving that "religion shelters us from violence just as violence seeks shelter in religion," Girard discarded the death of God and the death of Man as largely rhetorical strategies that distract our attention from the all-too-frightful spectacle of indiscriminate vengeance ravaging the world. He warned that a world with no absolute values, deprived of a perspective toward transcendence, "religious, humanistic, or whatever," is particularly exposed to destructive violence (Girard, *Violence* 25). Girard's critics pointed out that he was promoting a neo-Christian theology spurred on by the "nuclear panic" of his time. We do not need to agree with his personal ideology or sweeping anthropological generalizations. The leap beyond our current limitedness should not necessarily resort to a religious or even a secularized conception of transcendence. The fact remains, however, that we are confronted with a flood of indiscriminate violence and hatred, sometimes amplified by abuse of religion for sordid purposes. Unfortunately, all seems to indicate that the tsunamis sweeping our world cannot find atonement in self-transcendence. The crises of today cannot be converted into sacrificial violence that generates peace and order. Uncertain of the contours of our humanness, we are unable to find an opening into a transcendent otherness, a true exteriority.

At the root of this incapacity, I find a new form of human sacrifice characteristic of our contemporary times. I write these words in a time when people are again seriously considering reverting to human sacrifice. This statement may seem gratuitous and paradoxical. The sacrifices of Iphigenia and Isaac are in the distant past. Moreover, even in their archaic form, those foundational myths of Western culture mitigated the inhumanity of slaughtering by substituting animals for people. Artemis replaced Iphigenia with a deer and transported the young girl miraculously to the land of the Taurians just before the knife of the priest could take her life. God's angel ordered Abraham to kill a ram instead of his son Isaac. Yet rejecting human sacrifices as a ritual to be performed only by barbaric others is never successful. While dwelling among the Taurians, Iphigenia became the priestess of Artemis and was tasked with sacrificing strangers who were shipwrecked on their seashore (Henrichs). The sacrifice of the Son of Man on the cross was a scandal already for its contemporaries, but the subsequent Eucharistic sacrifice performed among Christians struck them with even greater horror. The only extant ancient Greek commentary on the Eucharist presents the call to eat Christ's flesh and drink his blood as a return to barbaric cannibalism. Interestingly, fifteen centuries later, Calvinist propaganda portrayed the Catholic Mass as theophagy, similar in its savagery to the anthropophagy of newly discovered tribes in South America.

Human sacrifices have not only left traces in myths and rituals. Sacrificing humans on a massive scale has been a long-standing practice throughout human history, especially most recently. Even when the blood of hundreds of victims ceased to flow down the stairs of Aztec pyramids, millions of Indigenous Americans were sacrificed to bring their continent into the fold of "Western civilization." The magnitude of this slaughter was so immense that some consider it to be responsible for altering the geological structure of the globe. According to this theory, the Anthropocene began when the chemical composition of the earth's atmosphere was dramatically altered due to the mass reforestation of the American continent, which was in turn the consequence of the depopulation caused by the conquistadors (Toulmin).

It is, therefore, fair to say that throughout human history, human beings have periodically been sacrificed to gods: the Sun or the advancement of civilization, Neptune or the domination of the superior race, Artemis or the victory of the most progressive class, herd immunity or the indefinite rise of economic indicators. Yet never to my knowledge have humans been sacrificed to appease humans at large, as seems to be the case in our globalized, posthuman world. I am not talking about the crimes of a capricious, bloodthirsty tyrant that make the headlines on our screens but a pervasive and less graspable evil: the craving for mass sacrifice that haunts entire communities of people and maybe humanity as a whole, as if some global restorative violence were to reinstate lost distinctions and order. Looking at instances of evil permeating ecological, political, and economic reality, I suspect that they are dictated not so much by interests or ideological justifications but by humans' hatred of their own humanity. Have we come to a time when humans seriously consider sacrificing the lives of their own, not to a transcendent god or in the name of absolute ideological principles but to feed their resentment of themselves? How much despair about the future life on this planet must there be for humans to calmly contemplate sacrificing what is human? How much disappointment must overtake humanity so that, moved by a suicidal drive, it is ready to die to appease the fear of its own death?

I would argue that people need to hate life that is properly human to sacrifice humans for the sake of appeasing their distrust of humanity and their apprehension about themselves. While reporting on Girard's theory of sacrifice as a means of converting indiscriminate violence into an all-pacifying sacred, Dupuy describes a particularly bloody episode of the Kosovo War in 1999 during the Islamic Feast of the Sacrifice, Eid al-Adha. Eid requires that each family slaughter a ram and share it with others. This feast commemorates Abraham's killing of a ram in lieu of his son Ishmael, whom the patriarch was about to sacrifice to the Lord. In the Jewish and Christian traditions, it was not the son that Abraham had with his servant Hagar but Isaac, the child whom he later had with his wife, Sarah, who was the would-be victim. However, in all three Abrahamic religions, an angel intervenes in the human sacrifice by ordering the patriarch to substitute an animal for the long-awaited son at the last minute. On that festive day, Serbian police entered the household of a Kosovar Muslim family and asked if they have performed the traditional sacrifice. The family was too poor to afford a ram, so no prescribed ritual had been carried out. Upon hearing this reply, the officers seized one of the sons of the household and slit his throat in front of his parents, saying that he was fattened enough for the sacrifice.

Dupuy appropriately sees this barbaric murder as an intentional regression into indiscriminate and self-destructive violence, which should have been appeased by ritualistically regenerative violence of a socially accepted sacrifice. The murderers reversed the symbolization that historically led from human sacrifice to the substitution of animal victims and then to the full development of symbolic gestures that constitute culture. Their cruel parody reverted human culture into bestial carnage. I suggest that rather than unveiling the raw destructive violence underlying the sacrificial gestures of human civilization, the murderers superimposed a new, second-degree symbolization on the existing religious symbolism of the Islamic festival. With a particularly perverse brutality, they substituted a human for an animal to dehumanize their human victim. By doing so, they reversed the angel's injunction, as if they wanted to demonstrate that the faith of the believers who obeyed the divine interdiction was in vain and that their God was a lesser God. This reversal was not so much a desacralization as a secondary, albeit negative, sacralization. The new sacred instituted by the murderous police officers was intended as a diabolic mimicry of the peace that, according to Girard's theory, should result from the sacrifice of a surrogate victim. This cruel parody of the Islamic tradition consecrated the irreconcilable fracture of the multireligious Kosovar society. Instead of integrating the community by exteriorizing violence, it inscribed bestial violence in its midst as a renewed foundational mythology perpetuating the civil war.

In order for the communitarian divide to be consecrated and preserved, in order for the myths of interreligious hatred to spur more bloodshed, the myths needed not so much to be understood as to be believed in. It requires a leap of imagination to portray a boy from your neighborhood as an animal, and even more so as a sacrificial ram transported from ancient Middle Eastern myth into the mundane reality of Europe at the end of the twentieth century. Such a leap of imagination reproduces, albeit negatively, the bridging of Anders's Promethean discrepancy between acting and imagining, between what people are able to do and what they are able to handle mentally and emotionally. Anders's example, of course, has to do with Hiroshima and Nagasaki. He is puzzled by the gap between the technological ease with which a city can be obliterated in seconds and the unimaginable suffering of a fellow human being who is carbonized alive. The bloody episode of the Kosovar civil war reported by Dupuy forces us to reverse Anders's reasoning. In fact, the barbaric parody of the sacrifice of the ram requires a leap from the Serbian police officers' hateful imagination to their murderous action; the secondary, negative symbolization leads from the image of a subhuman animal to the slaughtering of a neighbor's child.

There is a cruel derision in the murder of the boy disguised as a parody of a religious ritual. One may clearly imagine the faces of the murderers contorted with sarcastic laughter while they spilled innocent blood. Their intention was not only to kill an individual but to destroy a community by killing its culture. The means to do that was to deny its opening into transcendence: the averted sacrifice of Ishmael does not please the enemy's God, the "lesser God" who does not exist. The ritual celebration of the foundational myth was to have no restorative power. Humans—executioners and victims—are bound to remain alone with the metaphysical evil in their midst.

Ironically, the attempt by the Serbian police to deny salutary value to the Feast of the Sacrifice and to superpose on the Islamic festivity their hateful celebration of the negative sacred is inadvertently hijacked by the religious tradition to which, willingly or not, they belong. Unintentionally, the murderers' action parallels the account in the Gospel of Luke where a group approaches Jesus with news regarding Galileans "whose blood Pilate had mingled with their sacrifices" (13:1). This was not just disturbing information coming from Jerusalem, where Jesus was heading to meet his death. The newsbreak occurred during Jesus's preaching about the Kingdom of God. The information about the tragic event was shared to provoke a disturbing question: Since the Galileans were killed by the Romans while performing their sacrifice, would their offerings still please the Lord? Maybe Galileans—like Kosovar Muslims—including the Galilean to whom Pilate's cruelty was reported, are cursed? Is their death a punishment for their sins? No more than the death of people upon whom the tower in Siloam fell, was Christ's reply. His call for repentance that punctuates the chapter implies that the God of the gospel is not a vengeful God: neither moral nor natural evil are God's retributions for the sins of humanity.

In the grim episode of interconfessional conflict in the Balkans, the Serbian police reproduce a scene from the gospel, but they do it unknowingly, playing the inglorious role of Pilate and his acolytes, in other words, pagans persecuting the faithful. They intend their violence to establish a new, negative sacred to spur a renewed series of retributions and counter-reprisals.

It is a particularly perverse and retrograde use of the sacrificial mechanism, which, if we follow Girard's reasoning, was meant to externalize and expunge violence from within the community by concentrating the evil on the surrogate victim. Let us note that the people who interrogated Jesus in the gospel operated within such a sacrificial logic as well. Why had God allowed his worshipers to be killed at the moment when they were performing their pious sacrifice? Within the sacrificial logic, there could only be one correct answer: the Lord being just and the ritual having been performed according to the consecrated rules, the blame could be placed only on the human sacrificators. But Christ rejected this line of reasoning and, as René Girard stresses, the sacrificial logic in its entirety.

According to Girard, Christ abolished the sacrificial logic because it consisted of healing violence through violence. Granted, the violence to be healed was the murderous vengeance tearing apart the community, while the healing violence was the unifying sacrificial killing. Nonetheless, the sacrificial logic perpetuated the cycle of violence. Christ broke this cycle and invited humanity to enter the Kingdom of God. This is why Girard adamantly refused a sacrificial reading of the Passion of Christ (*Things* 180–223). The crucifixion was not the sacrifice of the Son to the vengeful resentment of the Father because Christ was the Word of God and therefore the Son was one with the Father. Nor was crucifixion the suicide of God. As Girard noted, Christ was the Son of Man, as announced in Ezekiel 33:1–11, in which God called upon the House of Israel to turn from its evil ways. God does not take pleasure in the death of the wicked but desires the conversion of his entire people. Christ did not come for the sake of the just but to save sinners.

Girard invokes the First Epistle of John, in which Christ's commandment of love made sacrifice obsolete. Cain killed his brother out of envy for his brother's offerings, which pleased the Lord more than Cain's own sacrifice. Cain's works were evil, while Abel's were righteous. Cain killed his brother, and this first fratricide triggered the cycle of sacrificial violence, which was abolished by Christ's commandment to love one another. He who hates his brother is already a murderer, stated John, and a murderer could not have eternal life. He who loves his brother lays down his life for him. Such love among humans is identical to God's love for humanity. A person giving up their life for a brother or sister follows the example of God, who gave up his life on the cross for humanity. This supreme act of love is not a sacrifice, because a sacrifice is violent, and unconditionally laying down one's life for another human being, regardless of who they are, is the antithesis of violence.

A God who becomes the Son of Man, only to give up his life for all humans. A shady fool, claiming that he is God and demanding that the cycle of fratricidal violence stop and be replaced by brotherly love. Unimaginable. Unimaginable and properly laughable. Laughter punctuates our attempts at leaping beyond human finitude, as much as it signals our excursions into the life of animals and machines. First and foremost, this laughter is the symptom of an impossibly stretched imagination, especially needed when we are confronted with metaphysical evil. But, second, when put into the form of the work of human artfulness, laughter becomes a means of transcending human limitations. Laughing at the unimaginable in a myth, poem, or philosophical parable allows us to transcend the weakness of our bodies, the sterility of our minds, and the dryness of our hearts. Laughing at the unimaginable can help us do the unimaginable.

This was what Rabelais hoped for. His parodic Messiah, Pantagruel, was supposed to redeem the fratricides that had plagued human history since Cain. The grotesque nativity of Gargantua served as training ground for imagining a no less unimaginable nativity: a savior brought to life by a virgin. Gargamelle's happily inconsequential joke was meant to disperse Sarah's disbelief and welcome all Pantagruelists, without the need to circumcise the flesh. Rabelais, at least in the early stages of his literary adventure, believed in the possibility of a spiritual rebirth, a re-naissance through regenerative laughter, not, as Girard would claim five centuries later, restorative violence.

If successful, Rabelaisian laughter would dispel the shadow of Auschwitz's crematoria and Hiroshima's atomic mushroom; it would bridge Anders's Promethean discrepancy; it would prove that humanity's self-transcendence dreamt of by Dupuy was indeed possible, despite or maybe thanks to the fact that the God of Rabelais and Erasmus, Mary and Sarah, died a long time ago. Yet no ark was ever built. Sartre hoped that the newly gained capacity of self-annihilation would give humanity the heroic choice between life and death, renewed every minute to establish human freedom in modern times. Unfortunately, he confused life with nondeath. Instead of authentic existence, modernity relied on survival, until even survival became doubtful. Postmodern thinking did not provide comfort either. It only turned the difference between life and death into *différance*, indefinitely deferring the choice between the terms of the alternative that no longer was an alternative of discrete options (Derrida, *Life Death*). Maybe modernity was an illusion spanning Descartes and Locke on the one hand and Derrida and Lyotard on the other. Maybe, as Bruno Latour has suggested, we have never been modern after all (*We*). We only thought that modern science would bring the fire of enlightenment to humanity chained in the cave of its civilizational and multicultural prejudices. In fact, we are enmeshed in multiple networks of human and nonhuman agents, animated not by what we deem to be the knowledge of objective facts but by multiple concerns that we share with other humans and nonhuman animals, plants and geological features, currents of thought and maritime currents, organic viruses and computer viruses. Instead of bootstrapping ourselves out of the tsunami of evils regardless of whether we brought it upon ourselves or not, maybe we should come down to earth. Maybe, as Latour postulated, we should start "composing," that is, negotiating, bargaining with reality as it is, in all its messiness, instead of constructing concepts upon concepts that blow us farther and farther away, like Klee's *Angelus Novus*, from the catastrophe that we face (Latour, *Down to Earth* and "Attempt").

Chapter 6

Laughing Men

In the previous chapters, we listened to laughter that resonates when humans brush against nonhuman others: animals and the primordial animality that dwells deep in our biological souls; the familiar yet uncanny machines that permeate our world, our bodies, and our minds; and, finally, the absolute of our gods, whom we killed while claiming their inexistence. Smashing idols was a joyful endeavor for Nietzsche. He laughed at the spirit of gravity that tried—and failed—to give human life a purpose no one should laugh at. In his joyful act of destruction, Nietzsche rejected despair and refused any resentment. The only concern that overshadowed his dance was the suspicion that his self-reflective, pure laughter would go one step too far and lead to contempt for humanity.

Bataille did not hesitate to take that step. Nietzsche's gods died of laughter. For Bataille, it was humanity that died laughing, convulsed by a strange "itching" that mixed pleasure with pain. Reflecting after Nietzsche about the death of God, Bataille leaned over the void left by God's inexistence and human nothingness. By doing so, he found an absolute that was purely immanent. Humans reach this absolute not by transcending their immanence but by transgressing distinctions and taboos through an excess of violence. Paradoxically, this death of humanity was synonymous for Bataille with the outpouring of life. Bataille sacrificed humanness with an outburst of sacred laughter.

Bataille praised deadly laughter and sacrificial violence as manifestations of life so excessive that it overflows into death. Girard valued sacrifice as a violence aimed at restoring order and hierarchy within the community. Yet, ultimately, sacrificial violence does not contain metaphysical evil. No self-transcendence prevents the tsunami from engulfing the world.

In the final chapter of this book, humans face their mortality. They laugh with Socrates, embarrassed by the pleasurable and painful itching caused by their bodily finitude, worried that neither their rational arguments nor their ritualistically reenacted myths will charm away their fear of dying. Their laughter fades away when they imagine an indefinite, technologically induced immortality with the French novelist Michel Houellebecq. As demonstrated by Houellebecq's fiction, it is human finitude that constitutes the condition of the possibility for laughter. This laughter is the bell that sounds the alarm when humans are about to cross into the realm of nonhumanity. It is such crossing over—envisioned by Socrates and Houellebecq in the face of death—that reveals the meaning of humanness. Facing death, humans imagine what nonhumanity looks like, and they laugh with embarrassed horror at the products of their own imagination.

Rites of Redemption in the Athenian Death Chamber

The difference between life and death as well as between a life truly human and one that is not worth considering as such are the topics of Plato's *Phaedo*. This dialogue retraces Socrates's conversations with his disciples in an Athenian prison just before he drinks hemlock. Socrates's words and deeds have a complex symbolic meaning. His execution and his acceptance of death are grounded in the human sacrifice that constitutes the mythical and ritualistic substratum of Athenian culture.

The dialogue begins with the puzzling question of why Socrates had to wait thirty days between his death sentence and his execution. The answer is provided by Phaedo to Echecrates, a citizen of the Peloponnesian town Philus who inquiries about the dramatic events that took place some time ago in Athens. Socrates's execution was delayed because the Athenians were waiting for the return of the ship that they had sent to Delos in commemoration of Theseus's expedition of the fourteen who sailed to Crete to slay the Minotaur. Until the ceremonial ship returned from its annual pilgrimage, an execution would contaminate the city. Why did Plato recall this particular ritual context? Besides a faithfulness to the historical circumstances surrounding Socrates's death in 399 BCE, one reason may have been to slow down the pace of narration in order to insert several dialogues into the last months and days of Socrates's life that supposedly took place in that dramatic time. Five of them preceded the *Phaedo* itself. *Theaetetus* and *Euthyphro* report the conversations that took place on the same day in the spring of 399, when Socrates had already been indicted on the charge of impiety and corrupting the youth of Athens, but when the trial had not yet started. The *Sophist* and the *Statesman* refer to successive discussions, which supposedly occurred the day after those of *Theaetetus* and *Euthyphro*. The *Apology* quotes Socrates's speech in front of his judges during his trial, which took place in May or June. Twenty-eight or twenty-nine days later, Socrates meets Crito in prison, and the name of his friend provides the title for yet another dialogue. The philosopher dies one or two days after that conversation, surrounded by fourteen disciples and assisted by the prison servant who brings the cup of hemlock (Nails). This is the content of the *Phaedo*. Although the dialogues follow the chain of events leading to Socrates's death, they were not written by Plato in chronological order. Nonetheless, when chronologically assembled, as they were in the Renaissance editions of Plato's works, they form a coherent story, or, as the Greeks would say, a myth (*muthos*).

The tale of Socrates's indictment, trial, imprisonment, and execution resonates with ancient *muthoi*, specifically the one linked to the ship sent to Delos, the return of which was the condition for the philosopher's execution. Commentators have pointed out that when asked by Echecrates, Phaedo names fourteen disciples who were in the death chamber on that fatal day. This is the same number as the number of victims that, according to the myth, had to periodically be sacrificed by the Athenians to the Minotaur. Technically speaking, the fourteen young men and women were not really sacrificed but were sent by the citizens of Athens to feed the monster in atonement for their slaying of Androgeos, the son of the Cretan King Minos (Hughes). Exposing young people for the monster's nourishment or sexual predation is a mythical topos that often underlies the rituals of initiation of adolescents. In such tales, young people exposed to die are rescued by a legendary hero. Like Theseus in the Attic myth, Perseus saves Andromeda and Hercules liberates Hesione from a sea monster. The narrative frame of Plato's dialogue insists on the link between Socrates's execution and the Athenian ritual celebration of Theseus's deeds. By doing so, was Plato implying that the philosopher's dialogical and dialectical teaching method liberated Athenian youth from the deadly monster of ignorance, just as Theseus did by slaying the Minotaur?

If that is the symbolic meaning assigned by Plato to Socrates's elenchus, should his execution be considered as a reversed human sacrifice? Theseus ended the human offerings by killing the Minotaur, a heroic accomplishment that allowed the city to live without being forced to sacrifice its young blood to the monster. The Athenian custom of sending a ship to Delos ritualistically repeated this redemptory act. It kept Theseus's deed alive, especially because the ship devoted to the pilgrimage was believed to be the same ship that was used by the legendary hero during his expedition to Crete. Was Plato saying that the execution of Socrates reinstated the human sacrifice, this time of a philosopher sacrificed by a city forgetful of the life-giving meaning of the ritual it had performed for centuries?

Rather than the philosophical Theseus who redeemed the lives of fourteen youths, Socrates was an anti-Theseus. Indeed, unlike Theseus, Socrates dies at the end of the story without being able to complete his mission. The monster of ignorance prevailed. Socrates was not the triumphant hero saving the sacrificial victims. So maybe he played another role in the ritual? Let's remember that there is another myth intertwined with Theseus's victory over the Minotaur: the story of the murder of the Cretan prince Androgeos by the Athenians. This foundational crime opens the way for Theseus's redemptory mission. Androgeos's murder set off a plague that decimated Athens. To cleanse the city from the pollution caused by this unlawful killing, Apollo's oracle prescribed the driving out of pharmakoi. Pharmakoi were two human scapegoats whose symbolic sacrifice atoned for the crime of the city. The festival of Thargelia, celebrated in Athens each spring to purify the city in anticipation of the harvest to come, dates from this time. Anthropologists consider these Athenian festivities the Attic variant of the Ambrosia-cycle rituals, which were festivals linked by Indo-European peoples to the philters ensuring immortality (Dumézil 89).

On the sixth day of the Athenian festivities, two men called pharmakoi, one for the male population of the city and the other for the female, were "sacrificed" by the community (Tyrrell). They were chosen from among the poorest, ugliest, and most debased inhabitants, fed for one year at public expense, and on the prescribed day were adorned with strings of figs around their necks symbolizing fertility, ritually flogged with branches on their genitals, and driven beyond the city limits. At the end of the ceremony, they were symbolically stoned or thrown from a cliff. In actuality they were not killed, but their ritual suffering was meant to symbolize a human sacrifice. The pharmakoi were human analogues of healing poisons. Their symbolic ambivalence reflected the ambiguity of Apollo, the god of healing and the god of pestilence. The pharmakoi were an impurity, but with a curative potential: they purged the community of pestilence by being expelled from the body politic. Significantly, Socrates was born on the sixth day of Thargelia, and it was also during this ritual time when he was executed (Derrida, "Plato's Pharmacy" 134).

Did Plato present Socrates as a new pharmakos? Was he not poor? Was his ugliness not legendary? Didn't he explicitly ask his judges to be fed at public expense, like the winners of Olympic games and the pharmakoi were (Plato, *Apology* 174–77; 36b–e)? On the other hand, the difference between Socrates and the pharmakoi is noticeable. The poor wretches volunteered to be driven out of the city in exchange of a year of free meals but were not killed. Unlike the symbolic victims of human sacrifice, Socrates stubbornly refused to leave the city and died for real.

Phaedo is thus clearly a text loaded with symbolic meaning, but Plato intentionally altered known myths and age-old rituals. If Socrates was a failed Theseus and an imperfect pharmakos, it was because he died without slaying the monster and without playing the scapegoating game by letting himself be expelled. Hence the question, Given Socrates's death, which disturbed the traditional mythic and ritual order, who was called upon to complete the redeeming project that Socrates began but failed to complete? Who was going to save the youth of Athens from the monster? The answer was obvious: Plato, the disciple who, as Phaedo recalled, was ill and missing from the group of young men surrounding their master on the day of his death. The disciples searched to understand why their teacher had not put up a more vigorous defense. Why did he not hire professional counsel? Why did he keep provoking the jurors? And, above all, why did he reject the offer of his friends to help him flee the city? By writing his dialogue, Plato volunteered to provide answers to these pressing questions and to fill in for the absent master.

It is, therefore, logical that the text he wrote should not be read as a philosophical treatise in dialogic form but as the script of a dramatic reenactment. Plato's dialogue is not so much discursive as it is performative. Instead of a text exposing a philosophical doctrine, the *Phaedo* is a pedagogical tool destined to be used in a school theater where future generations of disciples would play the roles of the fourteen young men surrounding Socrates before his execution, rehearsing the words that were exchanged on that fatal day. It has been noted that the fourteen disciples plus the prison attendant who brought the poison makes fifteen people around the dying Socrates, which is the number of members of a chorus in a tragedy.

Socrates eagerly plays his theatrical part as well: when all has been said, he acknowledges that the time to die has come, "as a character in a tragedy would say" (Plato, *Phaedo* 510–11; 117a, 115a). The tone chosen by Plato for the dialogue is somber, the exact opposite of what his readers might have expected, given Socrates's notoriety in Athens as a character in acclaimed comedies. One of them, Aristophanes's *Clouds*, portrays Socrates as an eccentric guru who lectures for money on futile questions of natural philosophy and teaches confused young Athenians how to bend the logic of argumentation to their advantage. Plato's Socrates explicitly refuted this comical caricature in the *Apology* and in the *Phaedo*. The care with which Plato staged the philosophical discussions in his dialogues leads me to believe that he intended to counter the biased popular image of his master not only through philosophical argumentation but also by building a fictional world in which the reader could be immersed.

Yet the reader's involvement in Plato's dialogic fiction is not limited to theatrical mimesis. It has a properly ritualistic character. This blend of theater and ritual, of storytelling and reenactment, is well represented by the ship sent annually to Delos to commemorate Theseus's deed. By reporting in writing the words spoken by his master, Plato posited his dialogue as the textual analogy of that ceremonial vessel. Athenians were convinced that it was the same ship that had been used by the legendary hero, but in fact everybody knew that it was a completely different artifact, since all the planks of Theseus's ship would have had to have been replaced over time to keep it afloat. The same is true of Plato's dialogue in relation to Socrates's words and deeds. The *Phaedo* is not a mimetic repetition of the philosopher's death but a literary tool that, under proper circumstances and with the participation of the right people, can fulfill the mission that Socrates undertook but that he failed to accomplish.

Laughing at the Art of Philosophical Cleansing

Socrates's failure echoes in the death chamber with embarrassed laughter. The master and his disciples nervously laugh because Socrates failed to be a new Theseus and an efficient pharmakos. As the incarnation of the mythical hero, he should have triumphed over the monster; as scapegoat, he should have vacated the city. But in neither of these symbolic roles was he supposed to die. Yet it was his own death, amply discussed and elaborately staged, that Socrates intended to turn into his highest achievement. Socrates made every attempt to present his death to his disciples as a philosophical accomplishment and as the crowning of a truly human life.

This paradox can be understood in light of Socrates's mission as he defined it, most notably during his trial reported in Plato's *Apology*. Socrates claimed that he was ordered by Apollo to spend his entire life examining himself and others to demonstrate that what was considered to be knowledge was not knowledge at all. This open-ended task, and not an insight into the secret workings of nature or the craft of turning the argumentation to one's own advantage, was all the wisdom he aspired to. It was also the sole advantage he could claim over his fellow citizens, who needed to be constantly reminded about the inanity of their pretense of knowing. Such service performed for the community was mandated by the god through his oracle at Delphi, yet it was far from being recognized as a useful public office by Athenians. As was the case with other philosophers, Socrates was mocked and criticized by his fellow citizens (Plato, *Apology* 23d; Ahrensdorf). He knew that fulfilling his god-given mission put his life at risk. Yet he was equally convinced that an unexamined life was not worth living (*Apology* 28c–e, 38a). To examine (*exetazô*) and to cross-examine (*elenchô*) human life was the only virtue (*aretê*) Socrates recommended to his listeners (Plato, *Apology* 23d, 31b; *Sophist* 230d; and *Crito* 45 d–e).

There was one claim to knowing that Socrates found particularly unacceptable, namely, the popular prejudice against death that manifested itself in the fear of dying. In the *Apology*, Socrates stresses that, unlike other people, he would never run away from something that was preferable to that which he knew to be evil. Therefore, he preferred death to disobeying Apollo and abandoning his mission. He was all the more ready to die, since he did not know if death was the greatest of all evils or if it would turn out to be the greatest of all goods. When a month later, in the *Phaedo*, Socrates met his disciples in the death chamber of the Athenian prison, his agnosticism had changed into certainty. In the last hours of his life, he knew without doubt that death was to be looked forward to. He boldly stated that to philosophize was nothing else but to practice (*meletaô*) dying and being dead (Plato, *Phaedo* 81a). The task of a true philosopher was to free his soul/psyche from the body, and death was this separation (64a–65a).

The motive of separation runs throughout the dialogue. This is to be expected, since the *Phaedo* tells the story of Socrates's parting with his friends. In this sense, it can be seen as the antithesis of the *Symposium*, whose principal subject is love as the relentless desire for reunification of the two halves of the Hermaphrodite. In the *Phaedo*, the philosophical lovers drift apart. Hence the dismay of Socrates's disciples and their disappointment at his eagerness to leave them. Yet separation was important for Socrates in that it was fundamentally an intellectual operation. To think, one had to separate what was organically bound together, draw the lines between concepts, and make a distinction between ideas. Socrates compared this mental operation (*diaeresis*) to the work of a butcher who carefully carves the body of an animal, cutting the flesh along its natural junctures to separate the joints that articulate the parts of the living organism (Naas; see Plato, *Sophist* and *Phaedrus* 265e). The same held true for carving concepts. The work of making intellectual distinctions must be done along fault lines that are not subjective or arbitrary but exist in reality. As we have seen, Bergson preferred the fabrication of mythical gods over Socratic *diaeresis*. Although keenly aware of the possibility of creating myths, Plato's Socrates persistently clung to dialectical thinking.

In the discussion with his disciples, Socrates intended to prove that death, conceived as the separation between the body and the psyche, did not destroy the latter. In other words, Socrates argued that the psyche was immortal (*athanatos*). He began his argumentation with a reasoning based on the concept of opposites. Everything comes into being from its opposite: something that is larger must have been smaller before and vice versa; the dead come from the living no less than the living must come from the dead. The latter case proved, according to Socrates, that the souls of the dead must exist in Hades before coming back into being (Plato, *Phaedo* 70e–72a). At the end of the *Phaedo*, Socrates returned to the concept of opposites. The last movement of his argumentation relied on the assumption that nothing would bring upon itself (*epipheró*) its opposite. For instance, snow will not admit heat. Similarly, the psyche, which brings life to the body, will not admit death (102a–106e). The demonstrating of opposites and dividing categories of thought along the fault lines ingrained in the reality of things—rational hairsplitting—was the work of intellectual cleansing. The motive of separation was closely intertwined with the motive of purification in the *Phaedo*. Indeed, truth and authentic virtue come with practical understanding (*phronesis*), which Socrates labeled unsoiled knowledge (*katharos phronesei*; 68b).

Socrates equated thus the art of making conceptual distinctions and the practice of intellectual cleansing. This assimilation has two important aspects. First, intellectual purification is intimately linked to death. Second, the death of the body may not suffice to purify the soul. On the first account, the pure, unsoiled knowledge of "things themselves" (*auta ta pragmata*) that the philosopher seeks could be acquired only by the psyche. The body hinders this process of understanding. Hence, it would never be possible to track down the essence of what exists (*thēreúein tōn óntōn*) except through mind alone, without the interference of the body (66a). This is possible only when the psyche is freed from the prison of the body—in other words, in death.

But, and here the second aspect of intellectual cleansing comes into play, death does not guarantee the complete separation from bodily concerns. A psyche may enter Hades stained with bodily pain and pleasure. In order to dwell with the gods, it has to purify itself, and the best way to do that is to philosophically cross-examine and delineate neatly carved concepts by drawing proper distinctions. Socrates insistently presented such intellectual cleansing as a purifying rite, a sacrificial purgation (*katharmós*), which only true philosophers were capable of. Only those who practiced philosophy during their lifetime deserved to contemplate the essence of things in the afterworld (Plato, *Phaedo* 69b–d). True philosophers are thus like initiates of orphic mysteries who have been properly enlightened and admitted into the company of the gods.

By identifying the art of philosophical examination with sacrificial purgation, Socrates reversed the meaning of death as it was seen in the mythic, ritual culture of Athens that shaped the circumstances of his execution. He transformed death conceived as religious miasma into purification. He did this through an intellectual process that would ritually cleanse Athenians from their bodily concerns. Separating diverse and opposed realities, neatly taking apart the enmeshed and confused, would transform death into the crowning of a philosophical life. True philosophy, argued Socrates, like death, led to pure understanding. It had, therefore, a cathartic and therapeutic function.

Clearly, Socrates reworked Athenian rituals and myths into a new cleansing rite: the philosophical practice of dying. Yet such reworking of mythical narratives and ritual gestures proved to be embarrassingly equivocal, easily misunderstood, awkward, and laughable. When the prison attendant handed him the poison—consistently called *pharmakon* in the text—the philosopher asked if he could pour a little as a libation. The libation was a ritual offering that often marked a transition in the life of the person who made the sacrifice. Although it was usually performed with wine, another liquid, whether milk, honey, or water, could also be used (Pirenne-Delforge). But offering poison as a tribute to the gods was troubling and ambivalent. Equally ambiguous was Socrates's relationship with his body. He insisted on taking a ritual bath to cleanse himself before dying, so that women would not have to wash his corpse. Yet when, a moment later, he was asked by Crito how he would like to be buried, he laughed at his friend mockingly while replying that he could do whatever he wanted, "that is, if you can catch me and I don't escape your clutches" (Plato, *Phaedo* 115a–d).

Socrates's laughter had a mocking but also embarrassed overtone. The philosopher was disappointed to see that despite all his argumentation demonstrating the immortality of the psyche freed from the prison of the body, Crito still did not understand that his master would be in a better place. All the effort invested by Socrates into encouraging and comforting (*paramutheomai*) himself and others boiled down to nothing. All his talk had been in vain (115d). Socrates's laughter, ringing with disappointment, was his last laugh. It was, however, not the first. The *Phaedo* is the only dialogue in which Socrates laughs out loud. Despite the dramatic situation, his disciples laugh as well, often through tears. What did Plato want to convey by mixing death and laughter? What does such laughter tell us about humanness?

Having laughed at Crito, Socrates turned toward his companions and explained the nature of their controversy. Despite all the lengthy and hairsplitting discussions, Crito did not understand where the true essence of humanness lay. This was a significant failure on the part of Socrates: the concept of essence (*ousia*), as contrasted with the attributes of material things that are perceived by senses, was at the heart of Socrates's argumentation in favor of the immortality of the psyche. Just as the essences of corporeal things exist, so does the human psyche, even before humans come into being. Based on this premise, Socrates concluded that the psyche would live forever after the death of the body (76e). Oblivious to these teachings, Crito was concerned with his master's funeral rites, as if taking care of a dead body pertained to Socrates at all. Yet his beloved teacher was not the corpse that would be lying motionless in a few minutes. Socrates himself (*autos*) would dwell in Hades among gods and wise men. Before that time came—at the end of the day—he was the one to speak with Crito and build his argument.

Socrates's insistence on pure essentiality runs as a leitmotif throughout the dialogue. It is expressed in Socrates's impatient insistence on the fact that he "himself" was the one who was alive and that he was not the inert body that would soon have to be disposed of. From the start, Socrates's argumentation in favor of the immortality of the psyche relied on the assumption that it was with a pure mind and pure thought "itself by itself" (*aute kat auten*) and not by the senses of the body that the essence of things could be perceived (65e–66a).

Yet, despite the *Phaedo*'s insistence on the separation of concepts, on intellectual purification and the cathartic virtues of philosophizing about death, corporality was of major importance in Plato's text. As frustrated as Socrates was with Crito's incapacity to comprehend that his master "himself" would soon migrate to Hades, the expression, at the moment of its utterance, designated his bodily presence in front of the negligent student and not the soon-to-be disincarnated self of the philosopher. It is also in this corporeal meaning that *autos* is used as the first word of the dialogue: *Autos, o Phaidon.* "Were you there with Socrates yourself, Phaedo, on the actual day he drank the poison?" asked Echecrates, eager to hear an eyewitness account from his friend (292–303). The corporeal presence of Phaedo on that fatal day in the Athenian prison was, therefore, the gateway to philosophical understanding presented by Socrates as the new ritual purgation from bodily concerns.

Charming Misology with Laughter

To choose Phaedo as the main narrator of the dramatic events was symptomatic. It is all the more significant that the *Phaedo* is the only dialogue named not after Socrates's interlocutors but after the narrator, who played a prominent role in converting the master's reasoning (*logos*) into a tale (*muthos*). The first readers of the dialogue must have remembered that before becoming Socrates's disciple and, later, a philosopher in his own right, Phaedo had been a young prisoner of war forced by the Athenians to serve as a prostitute. Socrates helped to free him from this degradation of his body. Fittingly, Plato chose him to report to Echecrates Socrates's argumentation regarding the freeing of the psyche from the prison of the body by the practice of philosophy and the cultivation of death. The persuasive power of the master's reasoning hinged on the corporeal presence of Phaedo, especially in light of the absence of Plato from among the disciples surrounding Socrates in the Athenian prison cell.

At a pivotal moment of his discussion with Cebes and Simmias, Socrates turned toward Phaedo sitting at his feet and stroked his long hair, as he used to do, teasing the young disciple about the beauty of his locks. Then, jokingly, he stated that tomorrow his friend would cut his hair in a sign of mourning, as was the custom. But, suggested Socrates, there was something other than his own death to be mourned. What was at risk was the proof of the immortality of the psyche that he had painstakingly built up and that Cebes and Simmias had undermined with their doubts. The moment was particularly tense, and Socrates's affectionate gesture, duly reported by Phaedo to Echecrates, underscored the imminent danger that hung over the scene. Not the danger awaiting the philosopher: there was no doubt that Socrates would drink the hemlock in a few hours. Philosophy itself was in danger. If Socrates was unable to convince his closest disciples about the validity of his argumentation, how would he ever reach other people, including the Athenians who had sent him to his death? Cebes and Simmias were not isolated in their skepticism. Many readers of the *Phaedo* have been puzzled by the insufficiency of proof put forth in Plato's dialogue, as if these arguments were meant to be interesting assumptions and not definitive demonstrations (see Gadamer). So when Socrates interrupted his discussion with Cebes and Simmias to stroke Phaedo's hair as if he wanted to comfort his friend before a decisive battle, the dangers he faced were not only the renewed challenges posed by the two young Pythagoreans. What was at stake was faith in philosophical reasoning. Instead of coming out of this experience with a renewed confidence in the practice of philosophy as a cathartic, liberating ritual, the young people assembled in the death chamber risked rejecting the philosophical vocation altogether. Instead of being confirmed in their choice to be lovers of thinking (*philologoi*), they were now on the verge of becoming haters of thinking (*misologoi*). And there was only one misfortune comparable to the calamity of being a misologist, namely, being a misanthrope, a hater of humanity.

The stakes were high, and the situation was dramatic. Socrates was fully aware that this last philosophical stand was his true defense, more important than the one he presented in front of the jury that condemned him to death. Although he addressed Cebes and Simmias specifically, Socrates knew that he was speaking to the people of Athens, and possibly to all of Greece. No one, not even a comic playwright such as Aristophanes, should be able to accuse him of talking gibberish or piling up arguments that were of no concern to him (Plato, *Phaedo* 69e–70c). What was at stake in this last moment was not Socrates's corporeal life—he had forsaken that a month ago in the Athenian courtroom—but the life of his psyche and with it the immortality of any human that could be safeguarded from death by the practice of philosophy.

Hence the gravity of the laughter that resonated in the death chamber, regardless of who was laughing, Cebes, Simmias, or Socrates. Depending on the moment in which laughter punctuates the discussion in the text, it has different undertones: mockery, embarrassment, disappointment, frustration. But if there was one underlying emotion echoing from one burst of laughter to another, it was fear. Fear of what? Fear that at the time when it was most needed, philosophical reasoning would reveal itself to be powerless, inefficient, and useless. Fear that the Athenian populace was right that it was not appropriate to disregard traditions and promote the uncompromising examination of human reality. Fear that the men gathered in the Athenian prison, the master and the disciples, had made a fatal mistake and wasted their lives. And, finally, the terrible fear of death and, contrary to what Socrates repeated with increased insistence, the fear that the psyche died as well. These fears underlay the objections of the two young Pythagoreans: the fear that the psyche dissolved into thin air with the decay of the body, as Simmias suggested, or that it wore out like a secondhand cloak after being used by different bodies, as Cebes proposed.

Socrates understood that his argumentation (*logos*) fell short of reassuring his interlocutors and that it was powerless when faced with their fear of death. Near the end of the first argumentative movement, after having argued against Cebes on the generation of things from their opposites and against Simmias on learning as recollection, Socrates concluded with satisfaction that by now the young Pythagoreans should be convinced that the psyche must logically enter living beings from the realm of nonlife, from the state of being dead (Plato, *Phaedo* 77d–78a). The preexistence of the psyche was supposed to prove by extrapolation its immortality even after the death of a human being. The matter should, therefore, be settled. Yet Socrates could not rest his case because he realized that both men were afraid. Jokingly he compared them to children who feared that the psyche would be blown away when it left the body. If that were the case, imagine what would happen on a windy day! Cebes chuckled approvingly (*epigelau*). Yes, he admitted, deep inside, each of them harbored a frightened child. This scared child needed to be persuaded that the fear of death was only a hobgoblin. The frightened child inside each of the disciples needed to be comforted: "Well, you must sing to him every day, said Socrates, until you magic it away [*exepáidō*]" (374–75).

Socrates's reply was stunning, especially for someone who restlessly promoted philosophical cross-examination as a means to purge the psyche. But it was also a strange reply from the philosopher, especially since in several of Plato's dialogues, Socrates insistently criticized the use of magic charms. Jokingly he took up Cebes's metaphoric image, as if their discussion was childish play and not an attempt to solve the fundamental problem of human finitude. This was the inescapable problem for Socrates's disciples: where, asked Cebes, could they find a good enchanter to quell their fears when Socrates was gone? Socrates was reassuring: Greece was a large country, and they would certainly find a capable person who for a reasonable fee could do the job. But at the end of the game, the young philosophers would have to enchant their childish fears themselves.

Time and again, laughter in the *Phaebo* points to the shortcomings of the philosophical argumentation (*logos*). It is always imbued with fear. "Would you be afraid (*phoboio*) to state this?" Socrates repeatedly asked Cebes. Yes, he clearly was, and he responded with nervous laughter (101a–b). Cebes was the first to laugh in the dialogue. He chuckled and swore in his own dialect, shocked by Socrates's reasoning, which struck him as illogical: if, as Socrates argued, it was better to be dead than alive, why were people not allowed to commit suicide (62a–b, 64a–b)? Simmias burst into uncontrolled laughter right after Socrates posited his definition of philosophy as the practice of dying and being dead. He could not refrain from sarcasm: Socrates argued so convincingly in favor of dying as the fundamental vocation of a philosopher that the people of Athens who had condemned him to death could not but agree with him wholeheartedly. Socrates replied that the Athenians would be right in doing so, except they would not understand what they agreed with. It was, therefore, better to restrict all discussion about the practice of philosophy and the practice of dying to the circle of lovers of thinking gathered around Socrates in the death chamber.

Seen from a Freudian perspective, Simmias's sarcastic laughter is the proof that Socrates is a failed humorist. According to Freud, humor is a consolatory mechanism that deflates fear and despair into pleasure. Like a father consoling his terrified children, the superego tells the ego that the world, which seems scary, is in fact worth jesting about (Freud, "Humor"). Simmias's laughter is not a sign of relief but of increased nervous tension. If it confirms Socrates's failure as a humorist, it may also imply his failure as a thinker. Indeed, Simmias's sarcasm recalls the emblematic leitmotif that runs through the history of European thought from Aesop to Heidegger, namely the laughter of the Thracian servant girl who poked fun at the astronomer who fell into a ditch because he was so busy observing the stars in heaven that he did not pay attention to where he was going on earth. Plato's Socrates recycled this anecdote in the *Theaetetus* but changed the anonymous astronomer to Thales from Miletus, the founder of philosophy. In this way, the clash between the absentminded intellectual and the down-to-earth woman hinged on the fundamental preoccupations of philosophy and its disinterest in politics (Plato, *Theaetetus* 174a–d; Blumenberg). According to Socrates, a philosopher is so deeply oblivious to the affairs of the city that he does not care who his neighbor is. The only question germane to a philosopher is what a human being is.

I would argue that Plato suggested an answer to the fundamental question about the meaning of humanness by mixing laughter and death in the *Phaedo*. Faced with the finitude of human life, the laughter in the Athenian prison was the revolt of the body in response to the deficiencies of thinking. It was a remorse of the intellect forced to acknowledge its limits. It was a pitiful self-consolation. It was also a powerful voice halting the smooth functioning of philosophical argumentation. The laughter of the Thracian maid echoed sarcastically by Simmias highlighted the rift between common people and the small group of those who were ready to die to understand the essence of humanness. It was certainly a political and cultural divide between the tenants of tradition and adventurers for whom virtue consisted of an ungraspable propensity to question, critique, and cross-examine (Nussbaum). The former ridiculed the latter, possibly chasing them out of the city or killing them. But, most importantly, the controversies staged in the Athenian death chamber reflected the opposition between those who were enmeshed in politics and concerns of the body but had not yet reached the level of consciousness that was required to contemplate the pure essences of things with the mind alone and those who had reached this level of awareness. Or at least, like Socrates, they pretended they had. But had they? It was far from certain. And that was why, frightened, they needed to sing to themselves a song that would alleviate their fear.

"You must sing." Socrates returned to the need to alleviate fear through enchantment. This time it was he who laughed, and it was he who was supposed to sing. The reasons that sparked this outburst were, again, the shortcomings of his argumentation (Plato, *Phaedo* 84d–85b). Simmias acknowledged hesitantly that both he and Cebes would have more questions regarding Socrates's reasoning, but they were reluctant to ask them because they did not want to be tactless in the face of the philosopher's misfortune. Socrates laughed quietly. How difficult would it be to persuade other people that dying was not a calamity if he could not convince his own disciples? His arguments were like a swan's song. People mistakenly thought that swans sang out of grief before dying. This, however, was not true because no bird sings when hungry or cold. Since they belonged to Apollo, swans sang with joy because they foresaw the happiness awaiting them in Hades. Socrates, who was the god's servant and endowed by Apollo with prophetic powers, was similar (Plato, *Apology* 39c and *Crito* 44a). Would his song be less credible than the songs of Apollo's birds?

This portrayal of philosophical reasoning as an enchanting and prophetic song should not be dismissed as a stylistic embellishment. The sophisticated but not terribly convincing argumentation built by Socrates to sway Cebes and Simmias not to be afraid was a kind of song. Socrates's reasoning was also a quasi-mythical narrative rich in symbolic meaning since both the *logos* and the *muthos* played the role of cleansing rituals. Storytelling, myth creation, ritual, and poetry superseded rational speculation in these last hours of Socrates's life. The first question that Socrates was asked when his friends were allowed into his cell on the morning of his execution was not about death as the vocation particular to the philosopher but about the literary activity Socrates had engaged in while in prison. Cebes was surprised to learn that during his prolonged waiting for the ship from Delos to return, Socrates had turned an Aesop fable into verse and wrote a hymn to Apollo. Why this sudden departure from philosophical debate? The cause lay in a recurring dream, replied Socrates, which called him to cultivate the arts of the Muses, literally, to "make music" (*mousiken poiei*; Plato, *Phaedo* 60e). Socrates was concerned that for his entire life he had misunderstood this divine exhortation. He practiced philosophy, which he considered the greatest of the arts of the Muses, yet now, when he was about to take his leave, he had come to realize that what he was required to do was write "music" as it was understood by the common folk. That is why he wrote a poem and composed a story (*muthos*) based on an Aesop fable.

Socrates composed an apologue in Aesopic style on the spot, immediately after his disciples entered the cell. He had just been freed from his chains in anticipation of his execution. He sat on his bed, rubbing his leg with visible satisfaction. What a strange thing pleasure is, he reflected. It is the opposite of pain, yet pleasure and pain are never far apart. If Aesop were to write a fable about them, he would represent them as battling each other but at the same time being conjoined by their heads. Understandably, the pain from the fetters was closely followed by the pleasure of having them removed. Preceding Bataille by centuries, Socrates's painful and pleasurable itching points to the imminent crossing through death into the realm of nonhumanity.[1]

Socrates's insistence on the separation between concepts and the incompatibility of opposites turned the *Phaedo* into an anti-*Symposium*. Nonetheless, the dialogue began with a conjunction that recalled the myth of the two halves of the Hermaphrodite in search of one another. It is paradoxical that Socrates strove to prove that philosophy liberated the psyche from the pleasures and pains of the body even before death separated them, yet at the outset of this reasoning, while freed from the fetters that hindered his body, he marveled with manifest pleasure at the closeness of both sensations. It is equally paradoxical that while the *Phaedo* focuses on philosophical cross-examination as a means to access the essences with the mind alone, the dialogue begins with a fable and retains strong narrative qualities throughout the philosophical discussion.

At the end of the dialogue, after having exhausted all his arguments, Socrates engaged in a long description of Hades and the happiness awaiting those who had been cleansed by philosophy and who henceforth would lead their lives without the body for the whole of time to come. This took place immediately before Socrates retreated to a ritual bath that cleansed his body so that the women would not have to perform this service on his inert corpse after his death. Socrates's students often marveled at his capacity to charm his audience. In the *Symposium*, while comparing Socrates to a Silenus, a creature of grotesque appearance but full of divine wisdom, Alcibiades likened him to Marsyas, who had the magic power to bewitch his listeners with his flute (Plato, *Symposium* 215a; see Compton 156–65). The only difference between Marsyas and Socrates, said Alcibiades, was that the philosopher could accomplish with simple words (*logoi*) what the Silenus achieved with a musical instrument. At the end of the *Phaedo*, Socrates bid farewell to his students not with more *logoi* but with a mythical narrative (*muthos*). It was so long that he felt compelled to justify himself. A man of intelligence should maintain with confidence that things were as he had described them. To maintain that the psyche was immortal was fitting and worth the risk of believing. Such a venture (*kindunos*) was noble and "one should repeat such things to oneself as a charm" (Plato, *Phaedo* 114d).

The *Phaedo* is less an account of intellectual speculation and more an exercise in self-comforting magic. Socrates offered words to others and to himself, told stories, and encouraged his companions to do the same. The outbursts of laughter that punctuate the dialogue express the awkwardness and the limited efficiency of such soothing, as demonstrated by Socrates's last laugh in response to Crito's question regarding his burial. They should also be understood in parallel with the insistent mixing of bodily feelings with the disincarnate contemplation of the mind and the explicit mythologizing and ritualization of philosophical practice. Laughter in the Athenian death chamber was a lingering emotion that altered the rarefied atmosphere of rationality. It sounded like the remorse of an intellect seeking perfection yet unsure if it could be reached. It reminds us of our bodily condition, despite our dreams to become purified minds. It reminds us of our finitude, amid our dream of immortality.

In his final words, Socrates asked Crito to sacrifice a cock to Asclepius. A long lineage of readers of the dialogue, from ancient and early modern

Neoplatonists to Romantic poets such as Lamartine and philosophers such as Nietzsche, understood this gesture as a sign of gratitude to the god for healing Socrates of the disease of life (Plato, *Phaedo* 118a, 95d; see Most). This interpretation is in line with a vision of a Socrates preoccupied with the workings of the intellect, aspiring to the immortality of the psyche by cutting all ties with corporeal pleasures and pains. In this perspective, the hemlock that paralyzed his body would be the *pharmakon* that, when properly dosed, would heal Socrates of the impurities of bodily existence. The healing poison would become an allegory of Socrates as Apollo's gift (*dosis*) to the city of Athens to cleanse its body politic and heal it of its filth (Compton 163; Montuori).

Nonetheless, it seems that by making a sacrificial offering to Asclepius in the last moments of his life, Socrates circled back to the foundational myth underlying the entire dialogue: Asclepius was the god who restored Androgeus, slain unlawfully by the Athenians, to his father, the king of Crete (Compton 9). Despite his insistence on pure understanding, Socrates bowed to the traditional ritual gestures. He may have aspired to the role of the new pharmakos, he may have envisioned philosophy as the new ritual cleansing, but his last laugh before death was less an outburst of ironic defiance than an embarrassed admission of his human mortality and his philosophical shortcomings. After all, his death marked the failure of the symbolic redemption set forth by the myth of Theseus and the ritual of the pharmakoi. Instead of saving the young people of Athens by slaying the monster, Socrates died; instead of letting himself be expelled from Athens, he stubbornly stayed within the city walls. On both accounts, the symbolic purgation remained incomplete, and the stench of death lingered. What was, therefore, the healing that Asclepius should be thanked for? Not for curing Socrates of the disease of life, as Nietzsche proposed. Asclepius had to be thanked for curing somebody else. There was only one person in the dialogue who was explicitly designated as sick and whose recovery the dying Socrates foresaw thanks to his prophetic powers: Plato. It was Plato whom Socrates—himself a character in his disciple's dialogic narrative—designated as the one who would complete his philosophical work (Most). This anointment was indirect, even ironic. Nothing guaranteed that Plato would be more successful than his master in purging Athens from its monsters. The embarrassed and uneasy laughter that resonated in the death chamber of the Athens prison was the bodily manifestation of this human indetermination.

Running out of Laughter

To silence the laughter that resonated in the Athenian death chamber, the mortality of the individual human body had to be eliminated. There will be no laughter when humanity secures indefinite immortality. Gaining immortality is a religious endeavor, but how can the eternal thereafter be accessed in the absence of God? One solution is to design a god and, by the same token, engineer one's own individual immortality. This is the project of transhumanist religions. An example of such transreligion is Terasem Movement Transreligion, a not-for-profit religious organization founded in the United States in 2004. Its creed consists of four core beliefs. The first and the fourth are banal: life is purposeful, and love is essential. However, the two other articles of Terasem's credo are more original. The second one reads, "Death is optional." It would be an error to mistake this dogma for a belief in the resurrection of the dead or in reincarnation. Of course, Christianity is based on the belief that Christ vanquished death by opening the gates of the Kingdom of God to humans. How to get there is the subject of debate—solely by the grace of the Almighty or by a mysterious conjunction of divine grace and human merit—but no Christian theologian would call death an option. This is a concept more reminiscent of e-commerce. Indeed, Terasem invites its adepts to download their "mindfiles," that is, electronic documents pertaining to their present lives, so they can be preserved for the time when "future mindware technology will enable them to be revived, if desired, to healthy and independent living" ("Truths"). The third article of Terasem's credo is even more interesting: "God is technological." This may seem puzzling at first, but the meaning of this dogma is simple. The adepts of this transreligion strive to build an all-encompassing technology that will make all the atoms "smart" and all the electrons of the universe "conscious." Such a technologically panconscious universe will be God him- or herself, since God is by definition omniscient, omnipotent, and unlimited in creative power. Consequently, in the Terasem transreligion God coincides with the community of the faithful transformed into mind clones.

The idea that implementing a technology literally "makes God," as the faithful of the Terasem transreligion proclaim proudly on their website, gleefully obliterates the two frontiers of humanness that I have discussed in the previous chapters: the machine and the divine. Terasem's project is to machine a god, in other words, to technologically enhance humanity until it becomes divine. There is no need for humans to transcend death through resurrection or reincarnation to achieve this mystical bliss. They simply need to do away with death.

The question that comes immediately to mind is whether Terasem's technologically deified humanity is capable of laughing. Following what we have learned already in this book, probably not. This is indeed the diagnosis formulated by Michel Houellebecq's novel *The Possibility of an Island*. Houellebecq entered the literary scene in the 1990s as a poet and essayist, and he has proven to be a versatile and prolific artist. He has worked for television and cinema as screenwriter, director, and actor; he has also recorded music and held a major exhibition of his photographic work. To understand the way Houellebecq thinks about the end of human life and the role of laughter in that process, we need first to understand the way he writes. The tone of his literary voice shapes his thinking and consequently our understanding of his ideas. Most importantly, the constraints that Houellebecq places on human language and the role that literature plays in challenging these limitations can teach us a lot about the limits of humanness in our transhuman times.

At the start of his literary career, Houellebecq published a short literary manifesto, an ars poetica listing recommendations addressed to a neophyte poet. Since at the time of the publication of *To Stay Alive: A Method* (*Rester vivant: Méthode*) he was unknown in the literary world, one cannot but surmise that Houellebecq addressed these instructions mainly to himself. What must a young poet do to stay alive? Suffer. To cultivate suffering provides the writer with a double advantage. First, it gives insight into the fundamental truth of the world, which is imbued with suffering. Second, it leads to the source of artistic creation, which consists in suffering. To nurture suffering as a philosophical and literary method is also an efficient survival technique: "A dead poet does not write anymore. Hence the importance of staying alive" (Houellebecq, *Poésie* 21; my trans.). One can hardly wish for a more convincing argument. Yet, as Houellebecq reminds his reader in the last sentences of his literary manifesto, the aspiring poet is already dead. But there is good news in this: only a deceased poet can dwell in eternity.

The tone used in *To Stay Alive* is disturbing. The text is infused with abysmal despair, which demands serious consideration and the compassion of the reader. At the same time, it is composed of banal truisms proclaimed with magisterial self-confidence by an unknown beginner. Should this message of doom be taken seriously? Or is it a tongue-in-cheek pastiche of dark romanticism and the gothic, reminiscent of the fleeting star of late-nineteenth-century French literature Isidore Ducasse, who, under the bombastic pseudonym of Count of Lautréamont, recycled the commonplaces of European romantic literature in a sublimely pathetic style? Like Ducasse, Houellebecq modulates his voice so masterfully that the reader cannot decide whether this is the work of a compulsive epigone or a subtle literary joke, or both.

A similar doubt lingers over Houellebecq's vast and diverse artistic production. First, again in conformity with a literary tradition going back at least to the hateful pamphlets and caustic novels by Ferdinand Céline, Houellebecq maintains a thorough confusion between fiction and reality. At first glance, many of his novels are bitter critiques of contemporary Western culture and society. This harsh view of reality, often compared to Balzac's uncompromising depiction of nineteenth-century bourgeois French society, is intermingled with notoriously futuristic visions of impending political, civilizational, and metaphysical doom. The mixture of social and moral critique with political and science fiction baffles the reader. Houellebecq achieves an even greater confusion by playing with his own auctorial and literary persona. Like Socrates who stood up in the audience during the representation of Aristophanes's *Clouds* and identified himself as the flesh-and-blood equivalent of the masked character in the scene, Houellebecq meticulously blurs fiction with reality while projecting his auctorial image in the media and in his art. We have just seen him in *To Stay Alive* counseling the aspiring poet who is in fact a mirror reflection of his own artistic ego. In his novels and movies, Houellebecq casts himself as a fictional character, albeit under his own name (which is an artistic pseudonym). He cultivates the ambiguity between Houellebecq the author and Houellebecq the protagonist by recycling from one novel to the next the character of a middle-aged, chain-smoking, alcoholic white French man, living in the unimpressive thirteenth arrondissement of Paris, where the real Houellebecq lives, obsessed with sex but dying for love that he knows perfectly well is out of his reach because of his moral degradation and the general downfall of Western culture, let alone the end of humanity as we know it.

The second powerful means of cultivating doubt in the mind of the reader is through multilayered irony. Houellebecq's irony undermines the seriousness of statements made by the narrator and the characters. However, such ironic bracketing is canceled by a second layer of irony superimposed on the previous one and reverting the sentence to its deadly seriousness. The repeated oscillations between gravity and mockery become an exercise in self-derision when Houellebecq targets himself, his art, and, most importantly, his laughter. In his 2005 novel *The Possibility of an Island*, such multilayered auto-irony is coupled with the image of the end of humanity, which, again, oscillates between a prophetic warning and kitsch science fiction.

The novel is composed of short narrative segments alternately entitled "Daniel1, 1," "Daniel24, 1," "Daniel1, 2," "Daniel24, 2," and so on. In the second part of the book, the voice of Daniel24 is replaced by the voice of Daniel25, whose narrative segments are numbered anew beginning with 25, 1, and alternate, again, with interventions by Daniel1 consecutively numbered. The reader quickly comes to understand that what seems at first sight to be the numbering of the consecutive verses of the chapters of the book of Daniel, which is a prophetic text in the Bible, is a convenient way to label the segments of two alternating storylines: the story of a human character named Daniel, who is more or less our contemporary, and the lives of Daniel24 and Daniel25, who are genetic copies of Daniel1 and who live in a science fiction future. These "neohumans" read and comment on the life story of their human originator centuries later. To be precise, Daniel24 and 25 are more than clones of Daniel1. Their physiological constitution has replaced the highly inefficient human metabolism with a combination of photosynthesis and mineral-salts processing. They have also switched from carbon-based biology to an organic life based on silicon. They do not suffer, desire, or rejoice like humans used to. Considered in the continuity of their successive reincarnations, neohumans have fulfilled the promise of all traditional human religions, making them obsolete: they have accessed a real, tangible eternity. As proclaimed by the Terasem transreligion, the neohuman Daniels have achieved eternity through technological enhancement.

Nevertheless, eternity comes at a cost: neohumans have lost the capacity to laugh and no longer comprehend what laughter is. Symptomatically, they have also lost the fear of death and, to a large extent, the consciousness of mortality. Neohumans do not die, at least in the literal sense of the term. When their vital forces deplete, they are promptly replaced by their next genetic iteration thanks to an efficient central organization that coordinates the sustainability, security, and electronic communication between the fortified compounds, each inhabited by a single neohuman physically isolated from the others. Even if an individual clone breaks away from this replacement system, thus interrupting the indefinitely repeated chain of replications—which is what Daniel25 does at the end of the book—such a neohuman remains unable to recover the human fear of death.[2] While unable to experience a human death, neohuman replicas of Daniel1 are also incapable of reproducing "that sudden expressive distortion, accompanied by the characteristic chuckles" that the originator of their genetic lineage called "laughter" (Houellebecq, *Possibility* 43).

This is a pity because Daniel1 was a successful professional of laughter. He made his fortune as a stand-up comedian, or, as he put it, a buffoon. According to the Aristotelian definition, a buffoon, as opposed to an ironist, is somebody who makes others laugh at their own expense (Jaulin).[3] Daniel1 perfected derision, not so much of his own individual, contingent self but of his human condition. He excelled in the most outrageous combination of misogyny, racism, Islamophobia, anti-Semitism, and pornography, with shows such as "We Prefer the Palestinian Orgy Sluts" and "Highway Swingers." He broke no moral taboos: there were scarcely any of them left in the Western culture of his time, a civilization in the last phase of its decline, overwhelmed with a desperate pursuit of pleasure, cruel egotism, and indiscriminate hatred. He skillfully built his career on the commercial exploitation of the worst instincts of his fellow humans, their absurd attraction to cynicism and evil. But at the same time, he hinted at a possible second-degree meaning of his shows, which, as he eagerly admitted, were blatantly repugnant. Thanks to this vague possibility of self-irony, combined with the inherent moral depravation of his audience, he was branded the "hero of free speech" and, to his own surprise, "a *humanist*; a pretty abrasive humanist, but a humanist all the same" (Houellebecq, *Possibility* 15, 149).

The disadvantage of systemic and pervasive irony is, however, that the ambiguity it cultivates works both ways: not only can the most repugnant statements of hatred be salvaged, even praised as supposedly ironic claims of positive morality, but attempts at serious moral discourse can be immediately discounted as jokes. This is the faith of Daniel1's critique of his own showmanship. But these disillusioned comments of the main character should also be read as Houellebecq's commentary on his own artistic craft. In response to what the writer sees as the catastrophic decline of Western culture in the second half of the twentieth century and in reaction to the doom of humanity as such, Houellebecq has adopted the posture of a hateful buffoon, a sarcastic clown who asserts serious truths while making sure by the tone of his voice that what he says will not be taken seriously. This ironic posture allows the writer to laugh outrageously at the death of humanity while mourning it, to respond to the brutality of the world through the violence of his own laughter.

This is also the project that Daniel1 claims as his own in a discussion with Vincent, a timid artist who will become the leader of the Elohim sect. Vincent will be instrumental in transforming this fringe New Age movement into a global world religion channeling declining humanity into neohuman eternity. Thanks to advances in biology and a powerful business model, the Elohimites offer tangible immortality here and now to anyone who grants the organization their genetic material upon their death for indefinite future replication (along with all personal wealth). Yet, at the time of their discussion on contemporary art, Vincent is a reclusive, unknown artist. His oeuvre consists of hugely complex animated installations that he builds in the basement of his grandparents' home on the outskirts of Paris. Mixing scenes from idealized fin de siècle Austro-Hungarian provincial life with festive decor inspired by the Asian bridal industry, these visual and audio effects create a miniature, rosy microcosm that is exclusively happy and resolutely kitsch. Vincent's art is a tentative escape from the brutality of the real world, a regression into the imagination of an introverted adolescent. It is also a refusal to take part in the commercial game of contemporary art, which, after the sterilizing experiments of twentieth-century conceptualism, only allows the artist to be either a revolutionary or a decorator. Facing such a disappointing alternative, Vincent agrees to play the role of a kitschy yet highly self-conscious embellisher of reality.

Daniel1 is overwhelmed by the authenticity of Vincent's escapism. Yet, in contrast to his friend, he prefers to be a revolutionary humorist. He deems the violence of his laughter a fitting response to the brutality of the contemporary world. Not that he seeks to transform reality, and especially not through social activism. There would be no sense in that, since human life is strictly determined, and this determination is not social but exclusively biological. All humans have ever wanted is sex, not for the sake of pleasure but solely to maximize the chances of the survival of the species. As a hateful buffoon, Daniel1/Houellebecq is a revolutionary artist, not in that he revolts against animalistic determinism or proposes subversive social action but in the sense that, with greater or lesser success, he spares humanity bloody revolutions by encapsulating violence in laughter: "I established clarity, I forbade action, I eradicated hope; my balance sheet was mixed" (*Possibility* 110, 226).

The fact that laughter is as human as it is violent and cruel was aptly recognized by Charles Baudelaire, the poet whom Houellebecq admires and often imitates in a parodic mode (for Houellebecq, parody is the testimony of utmost admiration). Drawing on the tradition of satanic romanticism and Hobbes's conception of laughter as the product of our sentiment of superiority over others, Baudelaire ties together the comic and the corruption of human nature inherited from original sin. He conceives an "absolute" comic predicated on superiority not only over other humans but, most importantly, over nature. To be absolute, the comic should also be unaware of itself, with one exception: artists, who have the superior talent of laughing at themselves and thus need to be "double." They conform to the rule of self-ignorance, which is necessary to spark laughter and, simultaneously, consciously engage in self-mockery (Baudelaire 2:530–34). Such dualism brings the Aristotelian buffoonery to a higher level of consciousness and allows the clown to feel their own misery and see themself at a distance. It anticipates Beckett's self-reflecting *risus purus*.

The cruelty of human laughter, its close relation with the moral corruption of humanity, the mixture of self-awareness, and the feigned ignorance that is indispensable for the absolute comic to become self-derisory are traits shared by Baudelaire, Houellebecq, and Daniel1. There is, however, a trait that transpires in Baudelaire's poetry that cannot be easily carried into the inhuman and neohuman world of Houellebecq's fiction. In the most depraved human misery and in the most miserable human death, Baudelaire finds a sense of beauty. The self-derogatory, grotesque laughter of the Baudelairean absolute comic is always tainted with subtle tones of warm empathy. For Baudelaire, the absolute comic, although stemming from a sense of superiority over nature, does not preclude deep sympathy with human, mortal, and depraved nature. The violence of laughter embodied by Daniel1, the scorching hate that targets human weakness and human mortality, makes empathy difficult, if not impossible.

Houellebecq's world, shaped by posthumanist disregard for humanness and by the transhumanist dream of a technologically induced immortality, has no space for empathy. Humanity is not only sinful and miserable, as is the case for Baudelaire; it is irremediably destined for extinction. Not because humans will die out in a global catastrophe. Yes, the planet on which the neohuman replicas dwell is considerably different from the one that Daniel1 was familiar with: the seas have almost disappeared because of the Great Drying Up; former metropolises are empty and ruined by nuclear wars. Yet Houellebecq's end of humanity is anticlimactic. He calls it *une apocalypse sèche* by analogy with a *panne sèche*, which in English means "running out of fuel." At a certain point, humans run out of the will to go on. Having mastered the necessary technology, they kindly consent to the disappearance of their own species.[4] They do not fight against extraterrestrial invasion, but they are no longer interested in leading a human life. They "convert" to nonhumanity by donating their genetic materials to the Elohimites for future copying and then silently commit mass suicide. The remnants of humanity who refuse to go down that road and who manage to survive the ecological degradation are soon reduced to a few hordes of "savages," disgusting, ferocious beasts, decimated by disease, self-inflicted violence, and cannibalism, pitiless toward each other and unworthy of pity in the eyes of the enhanced neohumans. But the main reason for the extinction of humanity is not its biological death as a species. It is the final triumph of human intelligence and egoism over death. The death of death makes laughter impossible and means the end of art.

It is so because, in principle, Houellebecq's neohumans, just like Harrison's primes, are not human anymore. They are technological beings, machines that achieved a state of *perpetuum mobiles*. Their virtual immortality has nothing to do with the Kingdom of God dreamt of by Rabelais or the Hades inhabited by ancient heroes praised by Socrates. To enter those transcendent realms where serene, eternal joy has replaced laughter, a human would have to die. Mortality is the precondition of laughter. Gods and demigods who laugh are mortal, as evidenced by Rabelais's and Nietzsche's fables. Contrary to the credo of the Terasem transreligion, death is not optional.

Mortality is also the precondition of art, as Houellebecq ironically reminded the reader in his ars poetica for beginners: "a dead poet does not write anymore." Therefore, it is thanks to literary art that Houellebecq's neohumans, just like Harrison's primes, are not human. This principle is the contract between the authors and their readers, setting the limits that separate fiction from reality. It takes a deliberate act of will for readers to suspend their disbelief and enter the fictional worlds of the novel and the play, in which there is no more death and no more laughter. Thanks to these contractual frontiers, fiction will always be apart, neither real nor aspiring to replace what is real, as virtual reality does. The "as if" of fiction can never be reduced entirely to "is," as Dennett would like it to be in his cognitivist conception of machines' consciousness. Consequently, fiction allows for and, indeed, nurtures the remains of humanness, within which human passions, such as love, play a prominent role.

The Impossibility of a Love

Daniel1 grows weary of laughter even before he decides to join the Elohimites and leave them his genetic material for further reproduction in some distant future, following his own, joyfully embraced suicide. Early in the book, Daniel1 acknowledges his disgust for his audience and for humanity. When on stage, he barely refrains from vomiting at the sight of their faces deformed by the laughter he provokes. He is repulsed by the audience's congenital hate that he is so skilled at commercializing. He cannot tolerate human laughter anymore, even with the help of anti-nausea medication. This, of course, is a professional challenge for a stand-up comedian. Despite attempts at reviving his artistic vein, such as a porn parody project, he gradually retires from active artistic life (Houellebecq, *Possibility* 42).

There is one more thing, besides the spectacle of hateful humanity, that stops laughter short: love. Daniel1 falls in love twice in the novel. He meets his second partner, Esther, a splendid beauty in her twenties, when he is well past middle age. Daniel1 does not expect erotic exclusivity from Esther. He is fond not only of her sexual appeal but also of her tenderness and sensibility, despite her discreet embarrassment at the fact that he is an old man. The overwhelming power of his love for Esther makes Daniel1 relinquish his "humorous attitude" completely. He is not a clown anymore; he wants to live, even if he knows that this is going to be his last gasp for life (Houellebecq, *Possibility* 154). His love for Esther represents a lyric moment of emotional communion that Houellebecq introduces into his art as the necessary complement of the surgically cold analysis operated by laughter (Houellebecq, Interview 61). However, playing on the genuinely pathetic cord is not Houellebecq's artistic strength, as demonstrated by the mediocre quality of his desperately emotional subsequent novels *Serotonin* (2019) and *Annihilate* (2022). Not surprisingly, Daniel1's love story with Esther ends abruptly. The young woman leaves for the United States to play the role of a servant of Aphrodite in a Hollywood movie on the death of Socrates (with Robert De Niro cast as the dying philosopher; Houellebecq, *Possibility* 231). She moves on and leaves her aging lover behind, much as he did with his previous great love, Isabelle, whom he loved dearly until her beautiful body started showing the first signs of decrepitude. As both understood well, Isabelle's aging was an indicator that she should forfeit further struggle on the competitive market of erotic self-affirmation. This common understanding stemmed from a historical phenomenon, which Daniel1 pertinently analyzes in the Western culture of his times: the divorce between tenderness and eroticism and the subsequent fading away of emotionality and desire. The split between love and sex provided the hateful buffoon with tons of ideas for sketches and, consequently, lots of money. Yet he knew all too well that the divorce between emotionality and sexuality was "the worst bullshit of our time, one of those that sign, definitively, the death warrant of civilization" (65).

The death of humanity stemmed from this divorce: deprived of the tenderness of unconditional love, sex gradually lost its appeal to such an extent that even the most aggressive marketing campaigns and highly sophisticated technological sex toys failed to keep it alive. Consequently, rearing children became a disgusting burden, and humans abandoned their elderly relatives to their deaths or compassionately resorted to euthanasia. The end of humanity had "all the hallmarks of mass suicide . . . men were simply giving up the ghost" of sexual reproduction, and therefore replication became the logical alternative (31–32). These gloomy musings inserted into a science fiction novel are to be read in parallel with Houellebecq's provocative work as an essayist. The writer has long been accused of ferocious misogyny, which is probably a projection of the wickedness of his protagonists onto the character of their author. After all, one of the trademark jokes of Daniel1 is to define woman as "the fat stuff around the vagina" (15). Houellebecq himself has referred to feminists as "idiots," with one noticeable exception, his high praise for the radical feminist Valerie Solanas, best known for her attempted murder of Andy Warhol and author of the 1967 *SCUM Manifesto*. Houellebecq admires Solanas's rejection of male-female equality in favor of unconditional superiority of women over men. He agrees with her visionary assessment of males as underdeveloped primates, congenitally prone to violence and, thanks to progress in modern embryology, useless for reproductive purposes. Houellebecq has reservations regarding some of Solanas's conclusions, namely the plan to exterminate the male sex altogether, but fundamentally agrees with her that humans should take technological control over their biological nature and evolutionary future (Postface). The genetic replication that is the narrative backbone of *The Possibility of an Island* is the fictional application of these claims. Their essayistic and novelistic formulations are nonetheless equally ironic. Houellebecq is at his core nostalgic for the Kantian moral imperative. He knows, however, that an ethics of the sovereign human subject is impossible to implement nowadays. He longs after religion, yet he knows that faith is out of reach. He dreams of affectionate love, but he feels that this longing will never be satisfied.

The persistent motive of biological aging shows that the world of rapidly declining humanity is populated not with augmented humans marching joyfully into the bright transhuman future but with elderly people who are "diminished adolescents," desperately trying to forget their physical decrepitude and their mortality (Houellebecq, *Whatever* 91). Isabelle is the editor-in-chief of *Lolita*, which, contrary to its name, is not a periodical for male pedophiles but a journal for girls and their mothers who frantically compete with their daughters in the tough market of erotic self-promotion.

The commercial model of *Lolita* relies on the rapid disappearance of the feeling of ridiculousness among middle-aged women, who are increasingly fascinated by unlimited youth (Houellebecq, *Possibility* 29). Isabelle does not fall prey to this illusion and has the good sense to slip out of Daniel1's life at the first signs that classical dance does not keep her body in shape anymore. She leaves, taking away Fox, the dog that the couple has adopted in lieu of having a child. Fox is an important character that allows Houellebecq to deepen the analysis of love in the novel. Before his suicide, Daniel1 made sure to deposit Fox's genetic material for future replication so the series of Daniels would live in company with a series of successive copies of this canine ancestor. As Daniel25 puts it, dogs are "machines for loving": they are the only way neohuman-replicated Daniels can have a glimpse of what unconditional love is, a sentiment that neohumans are incapable of. Neohumans are equally inapt at happiness and unhappiness, having gone beyond human suffering into the "freedom of indifference." They live in complete physical isolation from each other, unable to experience bodily contact with another being of their kind and limited to electronic communication between the compounds. Conversely, after his desertion, Daniel25 regains a semblance of consciousness of the reality of life, which also means a glimpse of the consciousness of death, by witnessing the killing of the last representative of the beloved canine lineage at the hands of a band of human "savages."

Seen from afar, the last remnants of bestialized humankind are like halves of a creature irremediably deprived of its complementary part. They walk aimlessly through the bare landscape in anarchic packs, often hurting each other, pitilessly abandoning the weaker specimens to die in the sun, lying powerless on their backs like upturned turtles with their "internal face" devoured by insects and birds (39). This neohuman perception of the last surviving representatives of what used to be called humankind is a sad parody of the myth of love from Plato's *Symposium*. According to Plato, love originated from the Hermaphrodite, a proud creature whom Zeus split into two halves, compelled from then on to search for each other in order to reconstitute their original unity. Houellebecq's caricature of the Platonic myth finds an equally sad complement at the end of the novel, when Daniel25, after voluntarily leaving his compound and renouncing future genetic replication, wanders through the deserted landscape. He follows the traces of Marie23, a female neohuman with whom he used to exchange electronic messages and who preceded him in her refusal of genetically sustained immortality in her search for a life reminiscent of the life of their human protoplasts. In his quest, Daniel25 finds a message from Marie23, carefully handwritten and rolled up in a metal tube. It contains the last poem left behind by

Daniel1, which prompted Marie23's quest for a living community. It is a moving love song, reminiscent of a lyrical hymn that Baudelaire addresses to a beloved woman. Here is the chorus of Baudelaire's poem:

> To the most lovely, the most dear,
> The angel, and the deathless grail,
> Who fill my life with radiance clear—
> In immortality all hail! ("Hymn," in *Poems* 196)[5]

Baudelaire's hymn to the immortality of love is in sharp contrast to the genetically induced neohuman immortality that Marie23 and Daniel25 are fleeing. Houellebecq's collections of poetry contain several rewritings of Baudelaire's classical meter. These parodies produce an ironic dissonance between the classical prosodic forms closely imitating Baudelaire and the banal reality that Houellebecq's poetry portrays. The poem attributed to Daniel1, which greatly moved Marie23, is composed, like Baudelaire's hymn, of four-line verses and relies on an eight-syllable melodic meter. However, contrary to the habitual sarcasm pervading Houellebecq's poetry, Daniel1's poem is devoid of bitterness and ends on a note of hope:

> And love, where all is easy;
> Where all is given in the instant;
> There exists in the midst of time
> The possibility of an island. (Houellebecq, *Possibility* 300)[6]

Instead of immortality—spiritual or genetically engineered—Daniel1 hopes for a tiny space of love, a "possibility of an island," hence the title of the novel, amid the eternal ocean of time. This hope proves vain. Daniel25 never finds Marie23. He never knows whether she succeeded in joining a rogue community as she intended to. He only finds a message she left behind. It contains a few pages torn from an old "human book," namely Plato's *Symposium*, with the account of the myth of the Hermaphrodite. Love is only an ancient, impossible myth traced on an archaic artifact: scraps of printed pages.

To Have and to Be a Body

How powerfully this book has affected Western civilization! Daniel25 marvels how, for thousands of years, Plato's *Symposium* has intoxicated humans with disgust for their animal condition and infected them with a dream that has never been fulfilled. When Daniel25 folds back the page left by Marie23, the scrap of paper disintegrates under his fingers. The physical support is gone, but the tale remains a memory in his mind. The persistent memory of physical fragility reflects the duality of the mind and body, an existential split that neohumans inherited from their human ancestors. Neohumans are not just cloned corporeal replicas of the exemplar from whom the genetic series originated. Nor are they solely digital copies of themselves. By initially assuming that humans were mainly composed of water and information, the Elohimites posited that fabricating successive individuals from blocks of DNA was all that was needed to ensure immortality (Houellebecq, *Possibility* 166–67). Looking back at those archaic times, Daniel25 knows that this was not enough. To secure the continuity of an individual personality, memory is essential, and memory, in turn, relies on language. The problem, however, is that language is inherently polysemic, permanently changing, and easily biased by hidden emotions and ideological agendas. It comes shaped, if not tainted, by the utterances that have gone through it, swerving along the way. Language, contrary to algorithmic coding, has a bodily consistence. It is loaded with multilayered, sometimes contradictory meanings. It is mortal, just as humans are.

A neohuman is a conscious biological machine, but most importantly it is a machine conscious of being one. Daniel25 is not eternal, because he inhabits the temporary vehicle of a body, and, despite his physiological enhancements and dispassionate neohuman temper, he knows he is still, as he puts it, "an augmented ape." He thinks about Marie23's body, which he saw only intermittently in the image mode of their electronic communications before they left their respective compounds. It is a body that he will never be able to touch. He had watched the pixelated and intermittent snapshot of her vagina "as though it were a tunnel opening onto the essence of the world, when in fact it is just a hole for dwarves, fallen into disrepair" (Houellebecq, *Possibility* 6). It was a vestigial organ, made useless by technological evolution, since neohumans are never to meet each other. They do not partake fully anymore in human corporality—for instance, they are male and female only "to a limited, refutable extent." They are "intermediaries" between the corporeal condition of humans and the mysterious "Future Ones," who will come with the reign of the Spirit and its infinite possibilities. Neohumans live long, stable lives, but eventually their forces are depleted and need to be replaced by their next genetic copy. They tend toward the continuity of a wave but do not achieve it, and they end up as a succession of particles following each other, similar to the discrete, repetitive tasks of which their successive lives are composed (5).[7] This dual nature—continuous and unconnected—is the constituent aporia that Daniel25 is unable to solve when, at the end of his journey and at the end of the book, he finally arrives at the shore of a lake, which is larger than the other ponds of salt water remaining after the Great Drying Out. The open horizon makes him understand the human longing for infinity, a desire for love that is never satisfied. Yet Daniel25 knows that because he left his protective compound and renounced the cycle of neohuman reincarnations, he is bound to be the last of the lineage of Daniels. And, as he says in the last sentences of the book, this is the reason he is and is not at the same time. The realization of this contradiction makes his life real.

The clash between disincarnated virtual reality and the biological corporality of life is the crux of the early-twenty-first-century exploration of what is human. Among numerous works of art tackling this question is an early movie by Spike Jonze, *I'm Here* (2010), which can be considered an antithetic pilot project to his famous later work, *Her* (2013). If *Her* can be called a software movie, *I'm Here* is a hardware one. It is a moving love story of two robots. The setting is a contemporary city in California, where humanoid robots socialize and mingle with humans in daily life, without the fancy attributes of science fiction. The two young robots who fall in love speak, move, drive worn-out cars, and go to parties as young people in their twenties do. But their robotic corporality is highlighted by the fact that their heads and limbs, covered in banal human clothing, are shaped in the form of cumbersome, slightly too large desk computers that were in use in the late 1980s, shielded with gray, angular plastic covers with the occasional wire sticking out. The robot lovers move with the grace of young humans, but their technological bodies are neither graceful nor high tech. This is important because the whole love story of *I'm Here* is a succession of bodily accidents that happen to the charming yet too-adventurous robot girl. At each of these unfortunate misfortunes, her robot boyfriend generously gives her one of his own limbs to replace her broken body part: a leg, an arm, and finally his torso. In the final scene, the female robot leaves the hospital in a wheelchair following repair/surgery, distressed, yet still cute with the oversized body parts of her partner in lieu of her slimmer silhouette. On her lap she holds the gray box that is the head of her lover, smiling affectionately at her. He is still faithfully here, in the awkward remains of his body, as the title of the movie says, despite or maybe thanks to his chivalrous sacrifices.

The chivalric robot who sacrifices his clumsy computer parts to his beloved is human, all too human, and more human than Theodore, who falls for the virtual Samantha in Jonze's next movie, *Her*. That is because the robot "is here," while Theodore is not: he works as a ghostwriter of private letters for people who have lost the capacity to embody their affectionate presence in writing. He spends his leisure time exiled in the cyberspace of a stupid computer game. Ironically, the robot in love from the 2010 short movie is more human than the human enamored with a sexy operating system in the subsequent 2013 film. The romantic robot is more human because he is a living body, although in the last scene of the movie all that is left of it is the gray box of his severed head. Theodore, in contrast, has a complete, normal human body, but he is largely *not* there because he dwells with Samantha inside the disincarnated virtual reality of his electronic devices. Jonze's two movies embody the two contradictory aspects of being human put forth by Helmut Plessner, the founder of twentieth-century philosophical anthropology. For Plessner, humans *have* bodies and, at the same time, *are* bodies. Every organism is determined by a boundary that separates it from the inorganic environment. But the specificity of a human being is what Plessner calls its "positionality," simultaneously within the body and, externally, outside of the limits of the body. Humans have *physical* bodies as means but are also *living* bodies. Or, better, they exist as living bodies in their physical bodies (*Leib im Körper*).[8]

This is the aporia that Daniel25 comes to realize after renouncing his genetically induced immortality: he is and he is not at the same time. Before he escaped his compound, he used to see his body as a biologically engineered vehicle conveying his memory added to the life stories of his predecessors. Such purely external and instrumental positioning is unsustainable in light of his absolute end. Having quit the chain of seamless replications, Daniel25 no longer *has* a physical body that can be disposed of and replaced by another one. Wandering through the postapocalyptic landscape, he *is* a living body, but one that is about to die, and to die for good. In this way, the neohuman becomes, to a certain extent, more human—all too human. Too human, yet not human enough, since he is still incapable of laughter and irony, in other words, not able to inscribe the contradiction of his bodily being in the embodied language of the text. Such capacity is exclusively human. Literature, even more than film, is predisposed to put language at the center of its deliberations over the bodily nature of humanness.

This is the case in *The Possibility of an Island*. As we know, Houellebecq's neohuman project does not consist solely of cloning. The genetic duplication has a cultural, properly textual component: it combines the copying of genetic material with reading and commenting on the life stories of the preceding iterations of a given individual. This is exactly what Houellebecq's novel consists of: Daniel24's and subsequently Daniel25's exegetical readings of the life story of Daniel1. It is thanks to his autobiographic narration that Daniel1 can claim to be the "Zarathustra of the middle classes," the buffoonish prophet of the technological overman. Instigated by Vincent who is newly raised to the rank of leader of the Elohimites, Daniel1 intends his life story to be the deadliest crime against humanity. The book uncompromisingly strips humans of their lies and delusions and consequently pushes them to self-annihilation as a species by artfully inciting them to renounce procreation in favor of future genetic replication (Houellebecq, *Possibility* 286–90). The literary mass crime proved to be a perfect one, as attested by the global success of the Elohimite religion, the worldwide wave of suicides, and the almost unobstructed advent of the neohuman race. Yet a full and undisturbed conversion to neohumanity and the awaited coming of the Future Ones would require human language to convey meaning over time in a direct, unbiased way. This ideal can only be dreamed of but never humanly achieved.

That is why the exegetic, quasi-biblical composition of *The Possibility of an Island* conveys the tension between the dream of a direct, unhampered transfer of information and the painful realization that it will never be possible to grasp the meaning of the message under interpretation. The idea of a futuristic novel structured like an exegetical commentary of an ancient text came to Houellebecq from reading *City*, a 1943–52 science fiction novel by the American author Clifford D. Simak. Simak wrote his book in the form of an erudite edition of a series of tales that supposedly came from an ancient oral tradition reminiscent of medieval sagas and that were eventually written down and presented to the reader, each preceded by a scholarly introduction. Like Houellebecq's life account of Daniel1, the successive tales *City* comprises tell the story of the gradual, almost seamless end of humanity. In Simak's novel, humans build an ever-more-efficient automated civilization, give up wars, and gradually grow tired of themselves, fading away into a paradisiac state of being on Saturn or plunging into a robot-assisted state of hibernation in the last stronghold of the human race on earth, Geneva. Simak's apocalypse is as smooth and painless as Houellebecq's, but unlike Houellebecq's fantasy, which combines quantum physics, genetics, and information technology, Simak's end of humanity is shaped by the twentieth-century technological imagination made of atomic power, space exploration, and robotics. The other, secondary difference between the two novels is the local flavor of the lakes and prairies of the American Midwest in which Simak's quiet apocalypse is set and which contrasts sharply with the declining Western consumerism and media frenzy providing the background for Houellebecq's fiction. But the most important difference between the two novels is that, unlike neohumans commenting on the life stories of their human predecessors in *The Possibility of an Island*, the erudite exegetes pondering ancient tales in Simak's fiction are dogs. At a certain point in the human-canine multisecular partnership, thanks to a daring and hereditarily transmissible modification of their auditory organs, dogs acquired the capacity to express the complex thoughts that they had harbored in silence throughout history as the companion species of humans. With humanity quietly descending into oblivion and with the assistance of self-improving robots, dogs become the master race. Many centuries later, the main object under deliberation by the doggish scholars who comment on the tales assembled in *City* is the question of whether humans really existed or whether they were mythical creatures forged by an ancient canine oral tradition.

Simak's erudite dogs are a clever novelistic strategy aimed at providing the reader with a distanced, panoramic view of the doom of humanity. Despite the nominal difference separating them from humans whose stories they comment upon, canine exegetes are humans in animal disguise. They may marvel at the human propensity for violence, but their mental universe is not so different from the one familiar to Simak's twentieth-century American readers. Hence, Simak's novel is at best a moralistic science fiction destined for readers troubled by yet another bloody world war, the accelerated development of capitalism, and its consequences for agriculture and urban development in the United States. Houellebecq's novel is not only a reflection of moral, economic, and social problems of his time but, most importantly, a probe inserted deep into the human condition. By tasking the neohumans Daniel24 and Daniel25 with the role of commentators on the human Daniel1's life story, Houellebecq does not allow for a symmetry of perspectives or an external, comforting, moralistic judgment. He implants the question of what it means to be human within the textual body of his fiction, and he does it by contaminating his longing for unconditional love, moral order, and religious faith with a cruel, yet ambivalent, buffoonery.

At the end of the novel, after taking over the direction of the Elohimite sect and transforming it into a successful global religious enterprise, Vincent shows Daniel1 his newest installation, a death chamber. Vincent designed it for those who will willingly end their human life and smoothly transition into a neohuman state. Vincent's newest artwork may be a death chamber, but there is nothing sinister in it. Upon entering, Daniel1 plunges into a white, creamy space, delicately agitated by quiet shimmering. Coincidentally, "Shimmer" is also the name of an extraterrestrial mega-organism that takes over part of the globe in the catastrophic science fiction movie *Annihilation* (Garland). When the brave science warriors enter the realm of the Shimmer, they never come back, not because they are furiously destroyed but because they are spellbound by the beauty of what they experience. They are very much like Simak's astronauts who, expedition after expedition, disappear into Saturn's environment not because they are obliterated by harsh conditions but because they are transformed into a state of being that is much more efficient and enjoyable than their previous, human existence. Additionally, and this time analogously to Houellebecq's fiction, the scientific commandos who enter the Shimmer, never to come back, have their bodies duplicated into mirrorlike organic entities. A similar motive is visible in Vincent's installation. Daniel1 is surrounded by fractal structures and geometrical images that have the capacity for indefinite reiteration. At a certain moment, Daniel1 sees a silhouette that shadows every movement of his body. This is disturbing, but the overall sensation is pleasant and calming, and Daniel1, overtaken by the desire to let himself dissolve in this space, is increasingly tempted to stay there, fused with the surrounding brightness. He is keen to end his human life and surrender to genetically generated immortality. It takes a great effort for Daniel1 not to succumb to the pleasant appeal of this work of art and stay in it forever. Vincent calls his newest installation "Love." He intends to use it himself when the time to end his human life arrives with the hope for future neohuman indefinite duplications.

It is with the utmost effort that Daniel1 shrugs off the temptation to remain inside Love forever. It is also with many regrets that he reverts to his habitual sarcasm and unconvincingly mocks Vincent's New Age death chamber. As we know, he will give up on human life after the undramatic and foreseeable collapse of his love relationship with Esther. Maybe, although it is not explicitly stated, he will resort to Vincent's Love installation to end his human existence. But if sarcastic laughter becomes increasingly difficult for Daniel1, it is not for Houellebecq, the author. Daniel1 is moved to learn that in conceiving his artistic death chamber, Vincent was inspired by the beautiful poem by Baudelaire "The Death of the Poor." Baudelaire portrays death as an elixir that gives hope for an end to the misery of life's journey:

> All through the storm, the frost, and the snow,
> Death on our black horizon pulses clear;
> Death is the famous inn that we all know,
> Where we can rest and sleep and have good cheer.
> (lines 5–8; qtd. in Houellebecq, *Possibility* 284)

Houellebecq's transparent reference to the inhumanity of the Shoah in his posthuman science fiction is disturbing. The seemingly welcoming audio-video computer installation built by Vincent is a high-tech version of the Auschwitz and Treblinka gas chambers. Despite the differences of decorative setup, they share a purpose: the final solution to the problem of humanness. Clearly, Vincent's Love does not bring humanity any comfort, only annihilation. In the neohuman world, laughter has no place, and the question of what it means to be human has no pertinence. Yet, as much as Daniel1 is touched by Vincent's reference to Baudelaire, Houellebecq does not lose his ironic poise. Literature is still able to enact the pleasurable and painful itching that Socrates felt when he was about to be freed from the chains of his bodily existence, the itching of Bataille's transgression, the disturbing sensation of a laughter so pure that it laughs at itself.

Epilogue

In this book, I set out to trace the limits of humanness in the hope of understanding what it means to be human. To locate those limits, I listened to laughter reverberating from the membranes that separate humans from animals, machines, and gods. This experience leads me to a paradoxical conclusion: to be human means being able to not be human and laugh about it.

An animal can be domesticated, and it can even be a human animal, but an animal cannot forgo its animal condition. A machine, as humanoid as it may be, will always remain a machine, even if humans may become at times very mechanical. God can be incarnated but cannot negate his divinity. Even deemed inexistent, God, by his absence, leaves an absolute void that nothing can fill except an evil of absolute proportions. Only humans can forgo humanity and cross over to the nonhuman realm. They do that by committing inhuman crimes, but most importantly by using their thinking and imagination to leap beyond the frontiers of their humanness.

The capacity of the human intellect to encompass the entire world, to swiftly travel through time and space, and to contain universal knowledge in the spacious library of human memory was proudly celebrated by early modern humanists who followed in the footsteps of their ancient predecessors (see, for instance, [Pseudo-Aristotle]). However, it is not the admirable power of knowledge and reason that impressed the thinkers and writers with whom I have conversed in this book. Instead of enthusiastically pushing the boundaries of human intellect, they ventured with pain and trepidation into the realm of what is not human. Joubert was concerned by bodily movements that threaten the peace and harmony he deemed to be natural for the human organism. Panksepp was less apprehensive, though nonetheless disturbed to dip into the primordial depths of the "biological soul" that precedes the human MindBrain. Bergson thought that society penalizes the automatisms that surface in human behavior, while contemporary AI designers strive to prevent their machines from venturing into the uncanny valley to spook their users with their humanlike resemblance. To transcend the limitations of human bodily nature seemed absurd to Sarah. According to her Rabelaisian descendant, Gargamelle, it required a leap of faith impossible without God's miraculous grace. Nietzsche's overman led us lightheartedly away from the human condition, but his tightrope dance was a perilous exercise that ended in Bataille's excess. Transcendence became, thus, transgression that did not strive to overcome the immanence of life but diluted life in death and evil. Since Auschwitz and Hiroshima, this evil is not merely a metaphysical concept but a devastating tide engulfing the world. It is doubtful that the sacrificial violence proposed by Girard and the human self-transcendence advocated by Dupuy can overcome it.

All these attempts to exceed the limits of humanness are less proofs of Promethean heroism than they are testimonies of a longing for meaning. The drive to make sense of what humans are can be satisfied only when they look back at themselves from a place where human life is not yet, not at all, or no more human. As instructive as it is, such stepping out into nonhumanity is not a detached intellectual investigation but a profoundly disturbing if not deadly existential experience. A strange phenomenon occurs at the juncture of humanity and nonhumanity. When human thought and imagination strike the delicate membrane tensely extended over human life, a disturbance reverberates through this protective coating. We tend to assimilate this spasmodic movement and sound to laughter, although it has nothing in common with socially accepted and esthetically consecrated manifestations of merriment. This cutaneous, bodily signal finds its expression in texts of Western culture that I have examined in this book. It resonates in the Athenian prison as a sign of human apprehension of what is uncertain and possibly inhuman in death. It testifies to Socrates's fear of misology, his concern that after he is gone the hatred of a properly human life filled with philosophical thinking will triumph over his disciples. Fortunately, Plato recovered from his illness, and it was with relief and hope that the dying philosopher thanked Asclepius for saving his disciple so he could keep philosophy and humanness alive for the centuries to come. But not forever. Plato's dialogue on love is reduced to scraps of unreadable pages that litter the postapocalyptic landscape in Houellebecq's transhumanistic novel, which anticipates the death of humanness and, consequently, the extinction of laughter.

Is it still possible to save humanness in the midst of inhuman desolation? Let us measure the chances of this outcome against the bleakest reality that humanity has faced in its history. At the beginning of this book, we looked into the abyss of nonhumanity imprinted on Podchlebnik's face. The painful laughter coming from the pits of Chełmno and the gas chamber of Treblinka is not the triumph of human life over inhuman death. Podchlebnik is summoned by Lanzmann and readers are called upon by Szlengel not as survivors but as dead people or, to be more precise, people who have been deprived of the life and death that are deemed human. Podchlebnik's face and Szlengel's poem are places of Shoah because they make present the absence of millions. Podchlebnik and Szlengel laugh because they have crossed the limit between what is human and what is not, and now, on the movie screen and on the page of the book, they expose what is nonhuman in front of a mortified audience.

Lanzmann did not compel Podchlebnik to sit in front of the camera to state his trust in humanness and affirm the power of human life. For that purpose, we need to turn to another Holocaust survivor, Viktor Frankl. Frankl began his career as psychiatrist in the 1930s in Vienna. After the annexation of Austria by Nazi Germany, he was deported to a concentration camp, as was his entire family. Upon his return, he wrote a memoir entitled . . . *Say Yes to Life Just the Same: A Psychologist Experiences the Concentration Camp*.[1] As a psychotherapist, Frankl developed a method that he called logotherapy, which relied on the assumption that human beings inherently strive to find meaning in life, including in suffering and death.

After the war, Frankl's friend, the cybernetician Heinz von Foerster, asked him how he could bear the inhumanity of the camp. Frankl replied that he survived by applying logotherapy to himself. He turned his situation into a story:

> So once—I was shoveling again, and it was ice cold and very windy—I thought to myself, it would be nice if I were now invited by the university to give a lecture about concentration camps. I stand in the big auditorium; everything is warm and beautifully illuminated. There in the first row, beautiful, elegant ladies sit with their elegant escorts, and I tell them about what happened to me here: Pow!—someone suddenly kicks me in the face with his foot and I say, "Ladies and Gentlemen, just now someone kicked me in the face with his foot." And

> then—pow!—another one hits me on the head with his shovel. "Now another one hits me on the head with his shovel." That is, I didn't experience it at all, I told about it. What I now experienced, I recounted, so to say, at the university. I transferred all of these experiences into stories.
>
> (von Foerster and Broecker 28)[2]

Amid the inhumanity of a concentration camp, Frankl mobilized what Bergson considered the most human asset: the affabulatory function that allows humans to fabricate stories and myths, heroes and gods. For this psychotherapist, storytelling was a method of healing. In the light of our considerations, we can understand that converting the horrific experience of dehumanization into a tale is not only a therapeutic technique but also Frankl's heroic effort to stay human, his dramatic refusal to cross over to the nonhuman side. Suffering in his body but at peace in his mind, Frankl clung to human life by the power of his imagination. Not only did he refuse to be reduced to a lump of matter, a rug or a puppet, as the SS called the cadavers they mass-produced, but he also rejected human death, which Podchlebnik called for, lying down in the pit at the side of his wife and children. Like Anders's Noah, Frankl put himself in the time of the hereafter. However, contrary to Noah, it was not the time following the death of humanity but the time of the return to human life. Anders's Noah mourned by anticipating the annihilation of humanness, yet he did it when humans were still humans and could assemble to build an ark. Frankl also celebrated humanity by anticipating, but he did it in an inhuman time and place.

It is notable that Frankl's university lecture imagined under the very real blows of camp guards was not deprived of dark humor. Yet Frankl's bittersweet humor has nothing to do with Podchlebnik's eerie smile. The first is funny, as it aims at deflating the tension created by von Foerster's dramatic concern. How was it possible to survive the camp and not lose your mind? Easy, suggests the therapist, tongue in cheek. Transpose what you are living into what you tell. Instead of being a thing in the hands of your torturers, you remain a human being, a respected academic who captivates his audience with a curious case of human experience. Frankl's fiction is the opposite of Podchlebnik's forced confession. Podchlebnik does not want to tell anything; he does not want to speak at all. His smile is a grimace under which brews a suffering impossible to put into words.

There is another story that Frankl told to von Foerster. Like his autobiographical tale, it shows that even amid absolute desolation, it is still possible to fend off nonhumanity. However, this second story has an additional, methodological meaning that is of crucial importance to von Foerster. Like Frankl, von Foerster was Viennese, but he managed to hide his Jewish descent during the Nazi era and emigrated to the United States after the war. Von Foerster was a polymath known for his multifaceted research in physics, mathematics, computer science, philosophy, and, most importantly, cybernetics. Cybernetics developed in the mid–twentieth century into an interdisciplinary study of complex systems. For von Foerster, the second tale opened an avenue for metaphysical reflection in the time after the death of God and Man, when essentialist metaphysics could no longer be grounded.

Here is the second tale told by Frankl to his friend. After the war, Frankl returned to Vienna and worked with Holocaust survivors, mending their psychological wounds. One day, he was asked to see a man who, like himself, had just returned from a concentration camp. By a sheer miracle, this patient was reunited with his wife, who also survived deportation. Unfortunately, her body was already so depleted that she died a few months after her liberation. Her widowed husband fell into despair and lost his will to live. His friends brought him to Frankl in an attempt to save his life. The men talked at length, and at the end of their conversation Frankl asked the despairing man, "If God granted me the power to create a woman who was exactly like your wife, with the same appearance, same taste, same tone of voice, same memories, no difference at all with your deceased spouse, would you like me to do it?" After a long silence, the man said, "No." He went back home and got on with his life.

After hearing about Frankl's conversation with the desperate husband, von Foerster asked him how the encounter between the two men should be understood. Frankl explained that being one with his wife, the patient had seen himself for his entire life through her eyes. When she died, he lost his essential other half and became blind. It was only when he realized that he was blind that he could see again.

The same goes for all of us: we see ourselves through the eyes of others. But what does this mean? It would be easy to accuse Frankl of trading individual freedom for social acceptance. However, contrary to Sartre, Frankl did not believe that hell is the other or that human life is absurd. In fact, it was in the hell of the concentration camp that Frankl found the meaning of his life. He remembers in his memoir how he and other prisoners were marching one morning to another day of murderous work and starvation. Looking at the fading stars in the sky, he had the acute and uncanny sentiment of his wife's presence. In his mind's eye, he saw her face and heard her voice, not knowing that she had died in another camp (Frankl 37–39). The question he addressed to his patient aimed at giving him the opportunity to sense the presence of his deceased wife and thus recover the humanity of his life under the gaze of a loving other.

The return of Frankl's patient to human life is therefore a refusal and an acceptance. The despairing husband rejected the lifelike avatar of his spouse because he instinctively knew that a human being cannot be replicated based on a list of parameters, as detailed and exhaustive as they may be. The mourning man knew that a faithful simulation of his beloved would still be a simulation.[3] Most importantly, his decision was also a resounding yes to human life. He regained his will to live because he realized that he did not live *with* his wife when she was alive nor *without* her when she passed away. He lived *through* his wife, regardless of whether she was alive or deceased; he saw himself not *with* but *through* her eyes. They lived together, or, as Martin Buber said, in the state of "two-getherness" (*Zu-zweien-Sein*; von Foerster 355).[4] The story reads like an optimistic epilogue to Plato's dialogue on love. Frankl heals the original wound, the splitting up of the primordial unity into two halves condemned to long after each other. The unfulfilled desire, the incompleteness of being, the fundamental otherness of inevitably mismatched halves, all the suffering inscribed in Western erotic culture, are resorbed in the unity of the self once it understands that it can live only *through* the other.

Von Foerster accepts Frankl's explanation, but he also gives the story of the cured husband a methodological meaning of his own. He reports this anecdote at the conclusion of his article entitled "Through the Eyes of Others" ("Mit den Augen des anderen").[5] In his article, von Foerster quotes the cured patient's story as the answer to the metaphysical question about the meaning of humanness. The first section of the article, to which Frankl's anecdote serves as the conclusion, is entitled "Metaphysics." According to von Foerster, metaphysicians are people who cannot agree about anything for the simple reason that their task is to decide about questions that by their very nature are undecidable, such as "Am I outside of the universe or am I part of it?" or "Is the world the primary cause of my experience or am I the cause of my own experience?" In his article, von Foerster would like us to look through the eyes of metaphysicians ("wir sehen, wenn wir uns als Metaphysiker betätigen"; 350). Consequently, von Foerster weighs in on a question that is undecidable, namely what human beings are.

Von Foerster is a constructivist. According to him, one decides questions that are by principle unanswerable by choosing the theoretical framework within which such questions find their answer. Cybernetics was his choice for such a theoretical framework. In his cybernetic way of thinking, von Foerster distinguishes between trivial and nontrivial machines. In trivial machines, a given input will always univocally and unchangeably lead to the same output. On the other hand, nontrivial machines are not predictable and cannot be analyzed. The lack of predictability and analyzability of nontrivial machines comes from the multiplicity of internal states that increase the possible outcomes exponentially, making them incalculable in a reasonable time span. Moreover, thanks to feed-backward mechanisms, nontrivial machines diversify the outputs according to their own past functioning. Through recursive looping that constantly feeds the outputs back into the machine as new inputs, they become autonomous and self-referential. For von Foerster, humans are precisely nontrivial machines.

One can accuse von Foerster of settling for a minimalist metaphysics. By stating that humans are nontrivial machines, he does not really define what humanness is. He just describes how humans function: in a sense, not unlike the recurrent neural networks that underlie twenty-first-century artificial intelligence. Nonetheless, I appreciate von Foerster's metaphysical minimalism, not because I would like to emulate his cybernetic bias or his constructivist epistemology but because I value his cautious honesty in admitting that metaphysical questions are answerable solely in regard to specific theoretical presuppositions. Contrary to von Foerster, the framework I propose in this book is not reductionist but transpositional. Instead of reducing humanness to a system that can be modeled even if, due to its nontriviality, it cannot be computed, I transpose humanness into a metaphor that can be imagined, stories that can be narrated, and myths that can be ritually played out. This is the metaphor of the membrane tensely extended over what is human and vibrating under the impact of internal trauma and external violence; such are the stories of Holocaust survivors Podchlebnik and Frankl; such is the myth of Socrates, the failed Theseus, who hoped for ritual reenactments of philosophical thinking that would perpetuate humanness after his death. These metaphors, stories, and myths echo the laughter that signals the limits separating what is human from what is not. Sensing that such a difference exists is already, in my opinion, a reason to believe that to be human is not senseless. This leap of faith is already a start at saving humanness in the midst of inhuman desolation.

Why can metaphors, stories, and myths efficiently supplement, even compete with, von Foerster's cybernetic theoretical framework? I concede that reductionism is certainly a valuable way of thinking. It establishes common denominators between diverse realms of reality. We can use those conceptual bridges to bring what is complex and unknown to a place that appears simple and more familiar. Most notably, thanks to reductionist thinking, we can reformat metaphysical investigations in terms of science. For instance, the question "What is human life?" can be reduced to a problem in biology; a biological problem can be reformulated in terms of chemistry, which, in turn, can be conceived as a question of physics and expressed in mathematical language. On the other hand, transpositional thinking has the advantage of extending the reach of natural language, expanding human imagination beyond known correlations and releasing great amounts of intellectual energy through the fusion of clashing ideas. Stories, myths, and metaphors are traditionally handy transpositions of realities that are too complex and unpredictable—von Foerster would say nontrivial—to be reduced to known concepts, logical formulas, and computable abstractions without an irreparable loss of meaning. Stories, myths, and metaphors were also the breeding ground of early modern humanism. I hope that they will foster an epihumanism suitable for our posthuman times.

Contrary to posthumanism, the epihumanism that I promote in concluding this book is a humanism. It insists that humanness is a distinct state of being, but it considers this reality to be neither God's creation nor a fundamental given of experience. This means that humanness must be investigated. Pursuing truth, more than pretending to grasp it, is the epihumanistic project, very much as it was for early modern humanism. As Montaigne put it, "The game which we hunt is the fun of the chase: we are inexcusable if we pursue it badly or foolishly: it is quite another thing if we fail to make a kill. For we are born to go in quest of truth: to take possession of it is the property of a greater Power" (*Complete Essays* 3:8, 3:1051). Both early modern humanism and epihumanism are deeply concerned with language and discourse. The difference, however, consists of the level of confidence in the hermeneutical process. Renaissance humanism trusted that textual exegesis could open access to being; I am not certain that such optimism is still possible after deconstruction sowed suspicion in logocentrism. Consequently, the place of humans in the metaphysical structure of reality is another diverging point between the humanism of the past and a possible epihumanism for the future. Early modernity was unapologetically anthropocentric and, of course, imbued with theological thinking. Anthropocentrism is not sustainable after the death of Man and his Creator, as well as in the face of the evil done by humans to humans and to the world they inhabit. Which does not mean, as I have stressed, that epihumanism allows humanness to be discarded as a problem or quietly diluted among other amorphous states of being, as different currents of posthumanism would like it to be.

This brief sketch contrasting epihumanism with early modern humanism and contemporary posthumanism suggests that there is a modest middle road between the overtly optimistic and the desperate perspectives on humanness, the former inherited from the past and the latter being the *doxa* of today. The direction I propose for this pathway is summarized by the prefix *epi*, the semantic potential of which I indicated at the end of the introduction. Epihumanism concedes modestly to be epigonic since it is not a radical rupture from all that preceded. It is, however, also proudly epigenetic, allowing the environment of today to shape and reshape our cultural genome without imposing an a priori ideological goal on this evolution. In its epistemological modesty, epihumanism does not claim to state what humanness is. Instead, it limits the scope of its investigation to the meaning of experienced reality. This epiphenomenal side of epihumanism is patent in its interest in cultural artifacts that can be interpreted. Hence the epidermic metaphor that infuses this book. One can, therefore, say that epihumanism is superficial in that it forgoes a search for the essence of humanity in favor of interpreting human experience. I would respond that the phenomenological and hermeneutic approach does not prevent epihumanism from looking beneath the surface of things that are human. Most importantly, epihumanism considers such a surface—be it a human face, a page of a book, or a computer screen—as a limit between what is human and what is not. We have been tracing and retracing such limits by listening to laughter that resonates when humans step over the edge of their humanity. It is my wish that my epihumanist endeavor will encourage further exploration of what it means to be human.

Notes

Introduction

1. Already a hundred years ago, J. Y. T. Greig's *Psychology of Laughter and Comedy*, published in the heyday of psychological studies of humor, contained more than fifty pages listing theories of laughter.
2. I follow Simon Critchley's handy classification in *On Humour* (2–3).
3. Quentin Skinner stresses that in Hobbes's *Leviathan* laughter compensates for a deeply felt sense of inferiority. I quote after Mary Beard (41).
4. This seems to be the function of humanism in the nonmodern world of Bruno Latour's *After Lockdown: A Metamorphosis* (105–06).
5. Such is the dystopian world depicted in Garcia's novella *Hémisphères*.

Chapter 1

1. This is the first sentence of the written narrative that begins Claude Lanzmann's film.
2. The transcript of Lanzmann's interviews can be accessed on the website of the United States Holocaust Memorial Museum archives: collections.ushmm.org/search/catalog/irn539109 ("Claude Lanzmann *Shoah* Collection"). The fragment of the Podchlebnik interview that I am analyzing comes from box 46: Podchlebnik 15. I would like to thank Ms. Lindsay Zarwell of the Holocaust Memorial Museum for her assistance, Professor Marina Zilbergerts from University of Wisconsin–Madison for translating the Yiddish audio track, and Dr. Caitlin Yocco-Locascio for assembling the bibliography of Lanzmann's interviews.
3. See, for instance, Gordon.
4. See Peter Sloterdijk commenting on Freud's 1917 "A Difficulty in the Path of Psychoanalysis" (Sloterdijk 219–20).

5. Meillassoux, *After Finitude*, *Science Fiction*, and "Spectral Dilemma."
6. Despite attempts to find common ground. See, for instance, Sparrow.
7. See also Isaacson; the documentary *Human Nature* (Bolt); and the docuseries *Unnatural Selection* (Kaufman and Egender).
8. Lévi-Strauss, *Race and History* 12 and *Tristes tropiques* 80. The source is Fernández de Oviedo, bk. 16, ch. 9. Among those who commented on this anecdote are Viveiros de Castro 14–17; Descola 281; Latour, "May Nature Be Recomposed?"
9. Beckett 48; quoted by Critchley, *Infinitely Demanding* 82. See also Critchley, *On Humour*.
10. See also Koch, "Transformation"; Wieseltier.
11. Lanzmann, Interview; Gantheret. See also Nora's trilogy *Les lieux de mémoire*, translated by Goldhammer as *Realms of Memory*.
12. "The Little Station Treblika" ["Mała stacja Treblinki"] in Szlengel 130–33. Reproduced with permission.
13. See Montague; Pawlicka-Nowak, *Chełmno Witnesses* and *Ośrodek zagłady Żydów*.
14. See also Des Pres; Rovner. I thank Professor Rachel Brenner for these two references.

Chapter 2

1. I am paraphrasing the facsimile of the original Polish underground edition from winter 1943/1944 reproduced in Wiernik, *Rok w Treblince* while comparing it with the English translation, *A Year in Treblinka*. This book has also been published online (Pickle Partners Publishing, 2015).
2. I changed the English translation slightly to match the original Polish text (Wiernik, *Rok* 29).
3. About humor in Auschwitz, see Cywiński; Jagoda et al. 137–59.
4. Chapter 6 of Żółkiewska and Tuszewicki is devoted to oral folklore in the Warsaw ghetto. See also Ostrower. I am grateful to one of the anonymous SUNY Press readers for this reference.
5. Wiernik, *Rok* 29; for the English version, see Wiernik, *Year* 78; Willenberg, ch. 22; Wójcik 69.
6. "[U]n morceau de sonore sémantique dépourvu de sens." Quignard, *La haine* 24, my trans.
7. Aristotle, *On the Parts of Animals* 673a; bk. 3, ch. 10. See also Halliwell; Ménager.
8. Joubert modifies Aristotle's position. In *Poetics* 1449a, Aristotle defines the object of laughter as ugly but free from suffering (ὀδύνης, which can be understood as physical or moral pain). Joubert uses *pity* instead because, as we will see, he needs the concept of sorrow to explain the physiological contractions of the heart

that, according to him, counter the dissipation of the spirits of the blood, which is characteristic of laughter. The "ugliness" of the ridicule should be understood not in aesthetic but in medical terms as *turpitudo*, i.e., something that does not conform to the natural order of things. See, for instance, Celsius 184.

9. In the original: "Donques nous affirmerons, que la principale occasion du Ris, e[s]t contenue sous le desir, qui sans attouchement suit l'imagination, et agite evidamment le coeur, l'incitant à diverses affections" (Joubert, *Traité* 63).

10. Francesco Valeriola was one of the medical authorities who equated tickling with pleasure.

11. Joubert devotes the entirety of chapter 6 of his second book to the traditional paradoxes related to tickling. See also Plato, *Philebus* 46d, as well as the classical study by Hall and Allin.

12. Aristotle, *Problems*, sec. 6, ch. 35. From the perspective of phenomenology, the impossibility of tickling oneself proves that the human body is inseparably an objectively lived body and, at the same time, a subjectively lived body. See, for instance, Thompson 224–52.

13. I would like to thank Jerzy Axer for providing me with this reference.

14. I would like to thank Ewa Niedziałek for introducing me to Panksepp's work. An analytical account of Panksepp's intellectual evolution can be found in Zachar and Ellis.

15. It has already been proven that chimpanzees "laugh" by producing a characteristic panting sound when at play and when tickled; see Provine, "Laughter."

16. For further evidence of the evolutionary link between play, tickling, and laughter, see Provine, *Laughter* 75–151.

17. Panksepp, *Affective Neuroscience* 20, 27, 33, 49, 79, 81, and others.

18. Panksepp and Burgdorf, "Laughing Rats?"; Panksepp, *Affective Neuroscience* 332; Panksepp and Biven 17.

19. See the polemics between Panksepp and Lisa Feldman Barrett in *Perspectives on Psychological Science*: Panksepp, "Neurologizing"; Feldman Barrett et al.

20. For the latest confirmation of Panksepp's findings, see Ishiyama and Brecht.

21. For Panksepp, the impact of the environment on the functioning of the human mind is cautioned by evolution and therefore durable. This is a radically different approach from Metzinger's notion of "virtual organs" as temporary simulations formed within the mind under the influence of external factors.

22. In that respect, my metaphor of the membrane dividing what is human from what is not departs from the psychoanalytical considerations of human skin as a fantasized envelope of the individual ego. For an interesting exploration of this development of Freudian psychoanalysis, see the work of Didier Anzieu, most notably his concept of the "Skin Ego." I would like to thank Virginia Krause for pointing to Anzieu's analysis. For a synthesis on that topic, see Ulnik.

23. On the differences between elasticity, plasticity, and rigidity, see Malabou, *What* and *Morphing Intelligence*.

Chapter 3

1. The computer screen is thus the technological version of the membrane, the master metaphor of this book. It bears some analogy to an early-twentieth-century technological device, the mystic writing pad. The particularity of this simple device is that the inscription on such a pad can be erased while nonetheless leaving a trace on its deeper, invisible layer. Freud uses the mystic writing pad as a metaphor of the perception-consciousness system. My use of the computer screen as a version of the membrane metaphor is less elaborate and does not serve to support the Freudian theory of individual ego. See Freud, "Note.'"

2. "[L]a vie bien vivante ne devrait pas se répéter. Là où il y a répétition, similitude complète, nous soupçonnons du mécanique fonctionnant derrière le vivant" (*Le Rire* in Bergson, *Œuvres* 1:617).

3. *Essai sur les données immédiates de la conscience* in Bergson, *Œuvres* 1:136, 142, 214–27, 310–13, and *L'Évolution créatrice* in *Œuvres* 1:760–66, 800–06.

4. "La vie réelle est un vaudeville . . . dans l'exacte mesure où elle s'oublie elle-même" (*Le Rire*, Bergson, *Œuvres* 1:660).

5. See David J. Chalmers's work, in particular Chalmers, *Character*.

6. See, for instance, Chalmers, "How Can We Construct a Science of Consciousness?"

7. *Œuvres* 1:270, 486 (in *Essai sur les données* and *Matière et mémoire*, respectively). See also *Œuvres* 1:978 (*L'Évolution*).

8. See the last sentences of *L'Évolution créatrice* in Bergson, *Œuvres* 1:1011.

9. See Roland Barthes's famous essay "The Death of the Author," published in English in *Aspen*, no. 6–7 (1967) and reprinted in *Image, Music, Text*, as well as Michel Foucault's interview "L'homme est-il mort?"

10. Leibniz uses the expression "spiritual automaton" to designate the soul while battling against Cartesianism and atomism (*New System* 18–19). See also Spinoza 85. By refusing to consider humans as conscious automatons, Bergson rejects these attempts to deal with the mind-body problem inherited from Cartesian dualism.

11. See the works by Catherine Malabou, especially *Que faire de notre cerveau?* and *Avant demain*. For the sake of my argument, I conflate elasticity and plasticity, two concepts that Malabou is careful to distinguish. From elasticity, I take the tension of a form that strives to return to its previous state and thus is able to vibrate and resonate. From plasticity, I take the capability of a form to change its shape durably and to mold its surroundings in return.

Chapter 4

1. See Sejnowski, especially ch. 14; Malabou's philosophical analysis of the neurosynaptic chip and the brain-inspired TrueNorth architecture in *Métaphormphoses* 106–22.

2. The concept was launched by Rosalind W. Picard's *Affective Computing*.

3. This term is reminiscent of the Freudian "uncanny," which consists of the threat to the individuality of the Self caused by the weakening of the sense of boundaries (Freud, "The 'Uncanny' ").

4. I, therefore, cannot agree with Chalmers's "The Virtual and the Real," nor with his adversaries.

5. These techniques of emotion recognition are especially important in the growing subfield of machine learning called emotion-augmented machine learning, which aims to build algorithms that are "emotion-inspired." See Strömfelt et al.; Schuller and Schuller.

6. A special session was devoted to affective computing at the 2015 Sixth Conference on Affective Computing and Intelligent Interaction; see Mancini et al.

7. Mazzocconi et al.; Forman et al.

8. See *notatio* in Cicero, *Rhet. Her.* 4.63–65; *De oratore* 2.43.184; 3.53.204–05 ("personarum ficta inductio"); "Ethopoeia"; Lausberg, sec. 820–25.

9. Aristotle, *Rhetoric* 1404b, 3.1. In my subsequent reference to Cicero's *De oratore* and its comparison with Aristotle, I follow Zerba.

10. "[U]ne note unique, une sorte de note limite, happée au vol et qui serait comme la partie organique d'une indescriptible vibration" (Artaud 54).

11. See, for instance, the book of one of the founding fathers of AI, Minsky.

12. See Cheney and Seyfarth, ch. 8. On the possibility of primates' culture, see the classic *Chimpanzee Material Culture* by McGrew.

13. Leibniz reformulates a thesis already expressed in *New System*, sec. 10, where he opposes the Cartesian mechanist conception of organisms: "A natural machine is still a machine even in its smallest parts" (16). By "natural machine," Leibniz means the body, which is divisible ad infinitum, contrary to what atomists said. The soul (or the mind) is, on the contrary, one and indivisible.

14. For a simple introduction to GPT-3, see Romero.

15. For more examples, see Oxford Spires Academy's *A Field Guide to Text Terms and Abbreviations*: www.oxfordspiresacademy.org/download/safeguarding_bulletin/Week-2-text-abbreviations.pdf.

16. A good illustration of the difference between a programmed computer and a self-taught neural network is found in Greg Kohs's 2017 documentary, *AlphaGo*, devoted to machines that outperform humans in chess and go.

17. This scene has been very interestingly commented on in Malabou, *Morphing Intelligence*.

18. For more on this topic, see Nguyen et al.

19. Presentation by Jacqueline Sii at the Undergraduate Symposium, University of Madison–Wisconsin, 21 April 2021. The other students on the team were Alison Cashmer, Mauricio Garcia, and Freya Li.

20. Being an operating system, Samantha is "immortal," in the sense that she is transferable as software from one piece of hardware to another once the previous hardware "dies" due to accidental damage or wear and tear. In late 2022,

Geoffrey Hinton, a former leading AI specialist at Google, proposed the concept of "mortal computing" (14–15). Contrary to digital computers, "mortal computers" would associate hardware and software so intimately that the demise of one would inevitably bring the demise of the other.

21. The Replika website is replika.ai. See also Balch.

22. How to ensure that computer models properly handle human values is discussed in Christian, *Alignment Problem*.

Chapter 5

1. See Le Goff. For a similar restraint in the Jewish tradition, see Maimonides 49a–b. See also Gilhus, ch. 4. I am grateful to one of the anonymous SUNY Press readers for this reference.

2. For instance, Dante, *Paradiso*, 28, 83–83; 31, 133–35. See also Hawkins. I would like to thank Chris Kleinhenz for this reference.

3. Anthropological studies of "joking relationships" go back to the second half of the nineteenth century. For a synthesis, see Canut and Smith. See also the documentary by Jacques Faton, *Du coq à l'âme*, based on the parallel between African joking relationships and Renaissance humanist humor; and Apte 29–66.

4. Duval, *Design of Rabelais's* Pantagruel, *Design of Rabelais's* Tiers Livre, and *Design of Rabelais's* Quart Livre. The pages that follow are also inspired by the work of Michael A. Screech, especially his *Rabelais*, and Gérard Defaux, especially his *Rabelais Agonistes*.

5. This is the standard translation for Gen. 18:3. On the ambiguity of the verbal form, see Sarna 128–29; Westermann, *Genesis 12–36* 278. Philologically, the alternating use of singular and plural for Abraham's guest(s) is sometimes explained by the possible composite origin of chapter 18, i.e., a combination of two earlier narratives. See Westermann, *Genesis: A Practical Commentary* 134–35.

6. Those legends (the *haggadot*) originated in Roman Palestine and Babylonia in the first six centuries of the common era. See Ginzberg 204.

7. Augustine, col. 558; Ambroise, col. 1181C; Beda, col. 171B. On the other hand, medieval Christian authors were inclined to believe that in the end, the fear of God led Sarah to faith. See Rabanus Maurus, col. 793D; Martinus Legionensis, col. 133A.

8. See the Gen. 18:12 commentary by Meir Leibush ben Yehiel Michel Wisser, called Malbim (1809 to 1879), and Ovadia ben Jacob Sforno (1475 to 1550) in Wisser; Sforno. See also the inspiring analysis by McMulty, ch. 1.

9. Nietzsche, *Birth of Tragedy* 67–76, sec. 12–13, and *Thus Spoke Zarathustra* 212–16, pt. 4, "The Ugliest Human Being."

10. On the motive of the death of Pan, see Lavocat 167–216.

11. *Pánta* means "everything" or "always" in Greek.

12. Nietzsche calls Zarathustra the "dionysischen Unholds" in *Birth of Tragedy* 7.

13. This would be the overcoming of the heaviness of the eternal recurrence, called for in Nietzsche, *Gay Science*, sec. 341.

14. For a reaction to the French postmodern fascination with Nietzsche, see Ferry and Renaut.

15. I follow here the excellent article by Borch-Jacobsen, "The Laughter of Being." See also the fundamental book by Lydia Amir, *The Legacy of Nietzsche's Philosophy of Laughter*. I am grateful to one of the anonymous SUNY Press readers for this reference.

16. For an insightful analysis of this phenomenon, see Citton and Rasmi.

17. Nonetheless, Dupuy was hired by the French Ministry of Defense to provide an expert philosophical assessment of the human propensity to panic: *La Panique*. The analysis to follow comes from Dupuy, *The Mark of the Sacred*, as well as from *A Short Treatise on the Metaphysics of Tsunamis*.

18. In presenting Arendt's analysis, I am largely inspired by Neiman. Neiman's book is also extensively commented on by Dupuy in his *Short Treatise on the Metaphysics of Tsunamis*.

19. See the work of Richard Dawkins—for instance, *River out of Eden*.

20. See, in particular, de Heusch's critique of René Girard's theory (35–37). See also the classical study by Hubert and Mauss.

Chapter 6

1. See also Plato, *Philebus* 46–47, where the mixture of pleasure and pain is exemplified by the relief of itching.

2. Houellebecq, *Possibility* 331: "although I had left on my own initiative the system of reproduction that ensured my immortality, or more exactly, the indefinite reproduction of my genes, I knew that I would never manage to become completely conscious of death; I would never know boredom, desire, or fear to the same extent as a human being."

3. See also Aristotle, *Rhetoric* 1419b and *Nicomachean Ethics* 1128a–b. Aristotle, *Eudemian Ethics* 1234a admits the possibility of a joke made by a witty man about himself yet still in the praiseworthy middle between boorishness and buffoonery.

4. This is the message of Houellebecq, *Elementary Particles* 10, where "apocalypse sèche" is translated as "dry apocalypse." See also 263–64.

5. "À la très bonne, à la très belle / Qui fait ma joie et ma santé, / À l'ange, à l'idole immortelle, / Salut en l'immortalité!" (*Fleurs du mal* in Baudelaire, *Œuvres* 146).

6. "Et l'amour, où tout est facile, / Où tout est donné dans l'instant; / Il existe au milieu du temps / La possibilité d'une île" (Houellebecq, *La possibilité* 339).

7. The image of the wave and the particle is fundamental for Houellebecq's *Elementary Particles*.

8. Plessner, *Laughing* and *Levels* 113, 270–71. The distinction between the subjective body and the objective body is important for the phenomenological tradition, most notably for Husserl, Merleau-Ponty, and Ricœur.

Epilogue

1. . . . *trotzdem Ja zum Leben sagen: Ein Psychologe erlebt das Konzentrationslager*, translated into English as *Man's Search for Meaning*.

2. This anecdote, along with the next one, are described by Heinz von Foerster in his autobiographical interview with Monika Silvia Broecker in von Foerster and Broecker 22–28.

3. This is Jean-Pierre Dupuy's interpretation in Dupuy, *On the Origin of Cognitive Science* xx–xxi. As much as he admires and respects von Foerster, to whom he dedicates his book, Dupuy quotes the anecdote to mark his strong opposition to what he sees as his friend's cybernetic and cognitivist reductionism.

4. I am using Barbara Anger-Díaz's translation of this term in von Foerster and Broecker (24).

5. I would like to thank Joel Kaipainen for his helpful input in my reading of this text.

Works Cited

Aaronson, Scott. "My Conversation with 'Eugene Goostman,' the Chatbot That's All Over the News for Allegedly Passing the Turing Test." *Shtetl-Optimized: The Blog of Scott Aaronson*, 9 June 2014, scottaaronson.blog/?p=1858.

Agamben, Giorgio. *Remnants of Auschwitz: The Witness and the Archive*. Translated by Daniel Heller-Roazen, Zone Books, 1999.

Ahrensdorf, Peter J. *The Death of Socrates and the Life of Philosophy: An Interpretation of Plato's* Phaedo. State U of New York P, 1995.

Ambroise. *Epistolarium classis I*. Vol. 16 of *Patrologia Latina*, Migne, 1844.

Amir, Lydia. *The Legacy of Nietzsche's Philosophy of Laughter: Bataille, Deleuze, and Rosset*. Routledge, 2022.

Anders, Günther. *Die Antiquiertheit des Menschen: Über die Seele im Zeitalter der zweiten industriellen Revolution*. Verlag C. H. Beck, 1956.

Antelme, Robert. *L'espèce humaine*. Gallimard, 1947.

Anzieu, Didier. *The Skin Ego: A Psychoanalytic Approach to the Self*. Translated by Chris Turner, Yale UP, 1989.

Apollinaire, Guillaume. *Calligrammes: Poems of Peace and War (1913–1916)*. Bilingual ed., translated by Anne Hyde Greet, U of California P, 1980.

Appel, Jana, et al. "Does Humanity Matter? Analyzing the Importance of Social Cues and Perceived Agency of a Computer System for the Emergence of Social Reactions during Human-Computer Interaction." *Advances in Human-Computer Interaction*, vol. 2012, 2012, https://doi.org/10.1155/2012/324694.

Apte, Mahadev L. *Humor and Laughter: An Anthropological Approach*. Cornell UP, 1985.

Arendt, Hannah. *Eichmann in Jerusalem: A Report on the Banality of Evil*. Penguin Books, 1963.

Aristotle. *Eudemian Ethics*. Edited by H. Rackham, Harvard UP, 2014.

———. *Nicomachean Ethics*. Edited by H. Rackham, Harvard UP, 1968.

———. *On the Parts of Animals*. Translated by Edward Seymour Forster and Arthur Leslie Peck, Harvard UP, 2014.

———. *Poetics*. Translated by Stephen Halliwell, Harvard UP, 1995.

——. *Problems*. Vol. 2, edited and translated by Robert Mayhew and David C. Merhady, Harvard UP, 2011.
——. *Rhetoric*. Edited by John Henry Freese, Harvard UP, 1959.
Artaud, Antonin. *Le théâtre et son double*. Gallimard, 1938.
"Audiences Captivated by USC Shoah Foundation Virtual Reality Projects." *USC Shoah Foundation*, 26 Apr. 2017, sfi.usc.edu/news/2017/04/15191-audiences-captivated-usc-shoah-foundation-virtual-reality-projects.
Augustine. *Questiones in Heptateuchum*. Vol. 34 of *Patrologia Latina*, Migne, 1887.
Balch, Oliver. "AI and Me: Friendship Chatbots Are on the Rise, but Is There a Gendered Design Flaw?" *The Guardian*, 7 May 2020, www.theguardian.com/careers/2020/may/07/ai-and-me-friendship-chatbots-are-on-the-rise-but-is-there-a-gendered-design-flaw.
Barthes, Roland. "The Death of the Author." *Image, Music, Text*, translated by Stephen Heath, Fontana, 1977, pp. 142–48. Originally published in 1967.
Bataille, Georges. *La Somme Athéologique tome II*. 1942. Vol. 6 of *Œuvres complètes*, by Bataille, Gallimard, 1973.
——. *Theory of Religion*. Translated by Robert Hurley, Zone Books, 1989. Originally published in 1973.
——. "Un-knowing: Laughter and Tears." *October*, vol. 36, 1986, pp. 89–102.
Baudelaire, Charles. *Œuvres complètes*. Gallimard, 1961.
——. *Poems of Baudelaire*. Translated by Roy Campbell, Harvill Press, 1922.
Beard, Mary. *Laughter in Ancient Rome: On Joking, Tickling, and Cracking Up*. U of California P, 2014.
Beauvoir, Simone de. *The Second Sex*. Translated by Constance Borde and Sheila Malovany-Cheavallier, Jonathan Cape, 2009. Originally published in 1949.
Beckett, Samuel. *Watt*. Grove Press, 1959.
Beda. *Hexameron*. Vol. 91 of *Patrologia Latina*, Migne, 1844.
ben Asher, Jacob. *Tur HaArokh* [A commentary on the Torah]. Translated by Eliyahu Munk, Jewish Publication Society, 1989. *Sefaria*, www.sefaria.org/Tur_HaAroch%2C_Genesis.18.12.1?ven=Tur_on_the_Torah,_trans._Eliyahu_Munk&lang=en.
Benigni, Roberto, director. *Life Is Beautiful*. Melampo Cinematografica, 1997.
Bennett, Jane. *Vibrant Matter: A Political Ecology of Things*. Duke UP, 2010.
Bergson, Henri. *Creative Evolution*. Translated by Arthur Mitchell, Dover, 1998. Originally published in 1907.
——. *Laughter: An Essay on the Meaning of the Comic*. Translated by Cloudesley Brereton and Fred Rothwell, Wildside Press, 2008. Originally published in 1900.
——. *Matter and Memory*. Translated by N. M. Paul and W. S. Palmer, Zone Books, 1991. Originally published in 1896.
——. *Œuvres*. Livre de Poche, 2015. 2 vols.

———. *The Two Sources of Morality and Religion*. Translated by R. Ashley Audra and Cloudesley Brereton, Doubleday, 1954. Originally published in 1932.
"Be Right Back." Directed by Owen Harris. *Black Mirror*, series 2, ep. 1, aired 11 Feb. 2013.
The Bible. Common English Bible. *Bible Gateway*, 2011.
Blakemore, Sarah-Jayne, et al. "Central Cancellation of Self-Produced Tickle Sensation." *Nature Neuroscience*, vol. 1, no. 7, 1998, pp. 635–40.
Blumenberg, Hans. *The Laughter of the Thracian Woman: A Protohistory of Theory*. Translated by Spencer Hawkins, Bloomsbury, 1988.
Bolt, Adam, director. *Human Nature*. News and Guts Films / Wonder Collaborative, 2019.
Borch-Jacobsen, Mikkel. "The Laughter of Being." *Modern Language Notes*, vol. 4, no. 102, 1987, pp. 737–60.
Bowen, Barbara C. "Rire est le propre de l'homme." *Rabelais en son demi-millénaire: Actes du Colloque International de Tours (24–29 septembre 1984)*, edited by Jean Céard and Jean-Claude Margolin, Droz, 1988, pp. 185–90. Études rabelaisiennes 21.
Briçonnet, Guillaume, and Marguerite de Navarre. *Correspondance (1521–1524): Années 1523–1524*. Vol. 2, edited by Christine Martineau et al., Droz, 1979.
Brooks, Mel, director. *The Producers*. Embassy Pictures, 1967.
Brown, Tom G., et al. "Language Models Are Few-Shot Learners." *arXiv*, 26 May 2020, arxiv.org/abs/2005.14165.
Brownlee, Jason. "Gentle Introduction to Statistical Language Modeling and Neural Language Models." *Machine Learning Mastery*, 7 Aug. 2019, machinelearningmastery.com/statistical-language-modeling-and-neural-language-models/.
Canut, Cécile, and Étienne Smith. "Pactes, alliances et plaisanteries: Pratiques locales, discours global." *Cahiers d'études africaines*, vol. 184, 2006, pp. 1–54.
Cassirer, Ernst. *An Essay on Man: An Introduction to a Philosophy of Culture*. Yale UP, 1944.
Celsius [Celso Manzini]. *De risu ac ridiculis disputatio*. Zacharias Palthenius, 1598.
Chalmers, David J. *The Character of Consciousness*. Oxford UP, 2010.
———. *The Conscious Mind: In Search of Fundamental Theory*. Oxford UP, 1996.
———. "Facing Up to the Problem of Consciousness." *Journal of Consciousness Studies*, vol. 2, no. 3, 1995, pp. 200–19.
———. "How Can We Construct a Science of Consciousness?" *Annals of the New York Academy of Sciences*, vol. 1303, no. 1, 2013, pp. 25–35.
———. "The Virtual and the Real." *Disputatio*, vol. 46, no. 9, 2017, pp. 309–52.
Chaplin, Charlie, director. *Modern Times*. Charles Chaplin Productions, 1936.
Cheney, Dorothy L., and Robert M. Seyfarth. *Baboon Metaphysics: The Evolution of a Social Mind*. U of Chicago P, 2007.

Chomsky, Noam, and Michel Foucault. *The Chomsky-Foucault Debate: On Human Nature*. New Press, 2006.
Christian, Brian. *The Alignment Problem: Machine Learning and Human Values*. W. W. Norton, 2020.
———. *The Most Human Human: What Artificial Intelligence Teaches Us about Being Alive*. Anchor Books, 2011.
Chrysostom, St. John. *Homilies on Genesis 46–67*. Translated by Robert C. Hill, Catholic U of America P, 2010.
Cicero. *De oratore*. Translated by Harris Rackham and Edward William Sutton, Harvard UP, 1988–92.
———. *Rhetorica ad Herennium*. Translated by Harry Caplan, Harvard UP, 2014.
Ciechanowski, Leon, et al. "In the Shades of the Uncanny Valley: An Experimental Study of Human–Chatbot Interaction." *Future Generation Computer Systems*, vol. 92, Mar. 2019, pp. 539–48, https://doi.org/10.1016/j.future.2018.01.055.
Citton, Yves, and Jacopo Rasmi. *Générations collapsonautes: Naviguer par temps d'effondrements*. Seuil, 2020.
"Claude Lanzmann *Shoah* Collection." *United States Holocaust Memorial Museum*, accession no. 1996.166.1, collections.ushmm.org/search/catalog/irn539109.
"Cleverbot." *Wikipedia*, last edited 7 Mar. 2024, en.wikipedia.org/wiki/Cleverbot.
Compton, Todd M. *Victim of the Muses: Poet as Scapegoat, Warrior and Hero in Greco-Roman and Indo-European Myth and History*. Center for Hellenic Studies, Harvard U, 2006.
Coursey, Kino, et al. "Living with Harmony: A Personal Companion System by Realbotix™." *AI Love You: Developments in Human-AI Intimate Relationships*, edited by Yuefang Zhou and Martin H. Fischer, Springer, 2019, pp. 77–95.
Critchley, Simon. *ABC of Impossibility*. U of Minnesota P, 2015.
———. *Infinitely Demanding: Ethics of Commitment, Politics of Resistance*. Verso, 2007.
———. *On Humour*. Routledge, 2002.
Cywiński, Piotr M. A. *Auschwitz: Monograph of the Human*. Państwowe Muzeum Auschwitz-Birkenau, 2022.
Dante Alighieri. *The Divine Comedy*. Oxford UP, 1998.
Darwin, Charles. *The Expression of Emotions in Man and Animals*. D. Appleton, 1899.
Dawkins, Richard. *River out of Eden: A Darwinian View of Life*. Basic Books, 1995.
Defaux, Gérard. *Rabelais Agonistes: Du rieur au prophète*. Droz, 1997.
Dehaene, Stanislas. *Consciousness and the Brain: Deciphering how the Brain Codes our Thoughts*. Viking, 2014.
de Heusch, Luc. *Le Sacrifice dans les religions africaines*. Gallimard, 1986.
Deleuze, Gilles. *Bergsonism*. Translated by Hughes Tomlinson and Barbara Hobberjam, Zone Books, 1991. Originally published in 1966.
de Lille, Alain. *Regulae de Sacra Theologia*. Vol. 210 of *Patrologia Latina*, Migne, 1855.
Dennett, Daniel C. "Can Machines Think?" *How We Know*, edited by Michael Shafto, Harper and Row, 1985, pp. 121–45.
———. *The Intentional Stance*. MIT Press, 1987.

———. "Intentional Systems Theory." *The Oxford Handbook of Philosophy of Mind*, edited by Brian McLaughlin et al., Clarendon Press, 2009, pp. 339–50.
Derrida, Jacques. *Life Death*. Edited by Pascale-Anne Brault and Petty Kamuf, translated by Brault and Michael Naas, U of Chicago P, 2020.
———. "Plato's Pharmacy." *Dissemination*, by Derrida, translated by Barbara Johnson, U of Chicago P, 1981, pp. 61–172.
Descartes, René. *Meditationes de prima philosophia*. Edited by Geneviève Rodis-Lewis, Vrin, 1978. Originally published in 1641.
———. *Meditations on First Philosophy*. Translated by Laurence J. Lafleur, Bobbs-Merrill, 1960.
Descola, Philippe. *Beyond Nature and Culture*. Translated by Janet Lloyd, U of Chicago P, 2013.
Descola, Philippe, and Alessandro Pignocchi. *Ethnographies des mondes à venir*. Seuil, 2022.
Des Pres, Terrence. "Holocaust Laughter." *Writing into the World: Essays, 1973–1987*, Viking Penguin, 1991, pp. 277–86.
Devlin, Kate. *Turned On: Science, Sex and Robots*. Bloomsbury Publishing, 2018.
Ding, Yu, et al. "Audio-Driven Laughter Behavior Controller." *IEEE Transactions on Affective Computing*, vol. 4, no. 8, 2017, pp. 546–58, https://doi.org/10.1109/TAFFC.2017.275436.
Dumézil, Georges. *Le Festin d'immortalité: Étude de mythologie comparée indo-européenne*. Librairie orientaliste Paul Geuthner, 1924.
Dupuy, Jean-Pierre. *La Panique*. Les Empêcheurs de Penser en Rond, 1991.
———. *The Mark of the Sacred*. Translated by M. B. Debevoise, Stanford UP, 2013. Originally published in 2009.
———. *On the Origin of Cognitive Science: The Mechanization of the Mind*. Translated by M. B. DeBevoise, MIT Press, 2009. Originally published in 1994.
———. *A Short Treatise on the Metaphysics of Tsunamis*. Translated by M. B. DeBevoise, Michigan State UP, 2015. Originally published in 2005.
Duval, Edwin M. *The Design of Rabelais's* Pantagruel. Yale UP, 1991.
———. *The Design of Rabelais's* Quart Livre de Pantagruel. Droz, 1998.
———. *The Design of Rabelais's* Tiers Livre de Pantagruel. Droz, 1997.
Dzieza, John. "Why CAPTCHAs Have Gotten So Difficult." *The Verge*, 1 Feb. 2019, www.theverge.com/2019/2/1/18205610/google-captcha-ai-robot-human-difficult-artificial-intelligence.
Edelman, David B., and Anil K. Seth. "Animal Consciousness: A Synthetic Approach." *Trends in Neurosciences*, vol. 9, no. 32, 2009, pp. 476–84.
Edwards, Gareth, director. *Rogue One: A Star Wars Story*. Lucasfilm, 2016.
"ELIZA." *Wikipedia*, last edited 12 Apr. 2024, en.wikipedia.org/wiki/ELIZA.
Erasmus of Rotterdam. *A Declamation on the Subject of Early Liberal Education for Children / De pueris statim ac liberaliter instituendis declamatio*. 1530. Translated by Beert Verstraete. *Collected Works of Erasmus*, vol. 26, edited by J. K. Sowards, U of Toronto P, 1985, pp. 291–346.

———. *De pueris statim ac liberaliter instituendis*. Edited by Jean-Claude Margolin. *Opera omnia*, vol. I-2, North-Holland Publishing, 1971.

———. *Les adages*. Vol. 3, edited by Jean-Christophe Saladin, Les Belles Lettres, 2011.

"Ethopoeia." *Brill's New Pauly: Encyclopedia of the Ancient World: Antiquity*, vol. 5, edited by Hubert Cancik and Helmuth Schneider, Brill, 2004, p. 89.

"Eugene Goostman." *Wikipedia*, last edited 16 Sept. 2023, en.wikipedia.org/wiki/Eugene_Goostman.

Faton, Jacques. *Du coq à l'âme*. Atelier Graphoui, 1999.

Feldman Barrett, Lisa, et al. "On Mice and Men: Natural Kinds of Emotions in the Mammalian Brain? A Response to Panksepp and Izard." *Perspectives on Psychological Science*, vol. 3, no. 2, 2007, pp. 297–312.

Fernández de Oviedo, Gonzalo. *Historia general y natural de las Indias, islas y tierrafirme del mar océano*. Real Academia de la Historia, 1851.

Ferraris, Maurizio. *Âme et iPad*. Presses de l'Université de Montréal, 2014. Originally published in 2011.

———. *Documentality: Why It Is Necessary to Leave Traces*. Translated by Richard Davies, Oxford UP, 2012. Originally published in 2009.

———. *Where Are You? An Ontology of the Cell Phone*. Translated by Sarah De Sanctis, Fordham UP, 2014. Originally published in 2005.

Ferry, Luc, and Alain Renaut. *Why We Are Not Nietscheans*. Chicago UP, 1997.

Forman, Cleo, et al. "Capturing Laughter and Smiles under Genuine Amusement vs. Negative Emotion." *2020 IEEE International Conference on Pervasive Computing and Communications Workshops (PerCom Workshops)*, IEEE, 2020, pp. 1–6, https://doi.org/10.1109/PerComWorkshops48775.2020.9156102.

Fortin, Pascal E., and Jeremy R. Cooperstock. "Laughter and Tickles: Toward Novel Approaches for Emotion and Behavior Elicitation." *IEEE Transactions on Affective Computing*, vol. 4, no. 8, 2017, pp. 508–21.

Foucault, Michel. *L'Archéologie du savoir*. Gallimard, 1969.

———. *Les mots et les choses: Une archéologie des sciences humaines*. Gallimard, 1966.

———. "L'homme est-il mort?" *Arts et Loisirs*, vol. 38, 1966, pp. 8–9.

———. *Michel Foucault à propos du livre "Les mots et les choses."* Interview by Pierre Dumayet, directed by Jean Bertho, Paris, 15 June 1966. *Institut national de l'audiovisuel*, www.ina.fr/ina-eclaire-actu/video/i05059752/michel-foucault-a-propos-du-livre-les-mots-et-les-choses.

———. *The Order of Things: An Archaeology of the Human Sciences*. Tavistock Publications, 1970.

Frankl, Viktor E. *Man's Search for Meaning*. Beacon Press, 2006. Originally published in 1959.

Freud, Sigmund. *Beyond the Pleasure Principle*. Edited by James Strachey, Hassell Street Press, 2021. Originally published in 1920.

———. "Humor." *International Journal of Psychoanalysis*, vol. 9, 1928, pp. 1–6.

———. *The Joke and Its Relation to the Unconscious*. Translated by Joyce Crick, Penguin, 2003. Originally published in 1905.

———. "A Note upon the 'Mystic Writing-Pad.'" 1925. *The Standard Edition of the Complete Psychological Works by Sigmund Freud*, vol. 19, translated by James Strachey, Hogarth Press / Institute of Psycho-Analysis, 1961, pp. 227–31.

———. "The 'Uncanny.'" 1919. *The Standard Edition of the Complete Psychological Works by Sigmund Freud*, vol. 17, translated by James Strachey, Hogarth Press / Institute of Psycho-Analysis, 1955, pp. 219–56.

Gabriel, Markus. *Der Sinn des Denkens*. Ullstein, 2020.

———. *Ich ist nicht Gehirn: Philosophie des Geistes für das 21. Jahrhundert*. Ullstein, 2015.

Gadamer, Hans-Georg. "The Proofs of Immortality in Plato's *Phaedo*." *Dialogue and Dialectic: Eight Hermeneutical Studies on Plato*, translated by P. Christopher Smith, Yale UP, 1980, pp. 21–38.

Galen. *On Problematical Movements*. Edited by Vivian Nutton and Gerrit Bos, Cambridge UP, 2011.

Gantheret, François. "Les non-lieux de la mémoire." *Nouvelle revue de psychanalyse*, no. 33, 1986, pp. 11–24.

Garcia, Tristan. *Hémisphères. 7: Romans*, Gallimard, 2015.

———. *Laisser être et rendre puissant*. Presses Universitaires de France, 2023.

———. *We Ourselves: The Politics of Us*. Translated by Christopher RayAlexander, Abigail RayAlexander, and Jon Cogburn, Edinburgh UP, 2021.

Garland, Alex, director. *Annihilation*. Paramount Pictures / Skydance Media / DNA Films / Scott Rudin Productions, 2018.

———, director. *Ex Machina*. Film4 / DNA Films, 2014.

Gibson, James J. *The Ecological Approach to Visual Perception*. Houghton Mifflin, 1979.

Gilhus, Ingvild Sælid. *Laughing Gods, Weeping Virgins: Laughter in the History of Religion*. Routledge, 1997.

Ginzberg, Louis. *Legends of the Jews*. Vol. 1, translated by Henrietta Szold and Paul Radin, Jewish Publication Society, 2003.

Girard, René. *Things Hidden Since the Foundation of the World*. Translated by Stephen Bann and Michael Meteer, Stanford UP, 1987. Originally published in 1978.

———. *Violence and the Sacred*. Translated by Patrick Gregory, Continuum, 2005. Originally published in 1988.

Gordon, Peter E. *Continental Divide: Heidegger, Cassirer, Davos*. Harvard UP, 2010.

Greig, J. Y. T. *The Psychology of Laughter and Comedy*. George Allen and Unwin, 1923.

Habermas, Jürgen. *The Future of Human Nature*. Polity, 2003.

Hall, Stanley, and Arthur Allin. "The Psychology of Tickling, Laughing, and the Comic." *American Journal of Psychology*, vol. 1, no. 9, 1897, pp. 1–41.

Halliwell, Stephen. *Greek Laughter: A Study of Cultural Psychology from Homer to Early Christianity*. Cambridge UP, 2008.

Harris, Christine R., and Nancy Alvarado. "Facial Expressions, Smile Types, and Self-Report during Humor, Tickle, and Pain." *Psychology and Cognition*, vol. 19, no. 5, 2005, pp. 655–69.

Harrison, Jordan. *Marjorie Prime*. Theatre Communication Group, 2016.

Hawkins, Peter S. "Poetry and Theology in Dante." *Publications of the Modern Language Association*, vol. 2, no. 121, 2006, pp. 371–87.

Hay, Katia. "Reason and Laughter in Kant and Nietzsche." *Nietzsche and Kant on Aesthetics and Anthropology*, vol. 3 of *Nietzsche's Engagements with Kant and the Kantian Legacy*, edited by Maria João Mayer Branco and Hay, Bloomsbury, 2017, pp. 197–217.

Heidegger, Martin. *Being and Time*. Translated by Joan Stamaugh. Albany: State University of New York Press, 2010.

———. "Danger." *Bremen and Freiburg Lectures: Insight into That which Is and Basic Principles of Thinking*, translated by Andrew J. Mitchell, Indiana UP, 2012, pp. 44–63.

———. "What Is Metaphysics? Original Version." Edited by Dieter Thomä, translated by Ian Alexander Moore and Gregory Fried. *Philosophy Today*, vol. 3, no. 62, 2018, pp. 733–51. Originally published in 1929.

Henrichs, Albert. "Human Sacrifice in Greek Religion: Three Case Studies." *Entretiens sur l'Antiquité Classique*, vol. 27, 1981, pp. 195–242.

Higgins, Kathleen Marie. *Nietzsche's* Zarathustra. Temple UP, 1987.

Hinton, Geoffrey. "The Forward-Forward Algorithm: Some Preliminary Investigations." *ArXiv*, December 27, 2022. *https://doi.org/10.48550/arXiv.2212.13345*.

Hobbes, Thomas. *The Elements of Law: Natural and Politic*. Edited by Ferdinand Tönnies, Cass, 1969. Originally published in 1640.

Homer. *Odyssey*. Translated by A. T. Murray, Harvard UP, 2014.

Houellebecq, Michel. *Elementary Particles*. Translated by Frank Wynne, Alfred A. Knopf, 2000.

———. Interview by Jean-Yves Jouannais and Christophe Duchâtelet, 1995. *Interventions 2: Traces*, by Houellebecq, Flammarion, 2009, pp. 55–64.

———. *La possibilité d'une île*. J'ai lu, 2005.

———. *Poésie*. J'ai lu, 2015.

———. *The Possibility of an Island*. Translated by Gavin Bowd, Alfred A. Knopf, 2006.

———. Postface to the French translation of the *SCUM Manifesto*. *Interventions 2: Traces*, by Houellebecq, Flammarion, 2009, pp. 165–72. Originally published in 1998.

———. *Whatever*. Translated by Paul Hammond, Serpent's Tail, 1999.

Howard, Ron, director. *Solo: A Star Wars Story*. Lucasfilm, 2018.

Hubert, Henri, and Marcel Mauss. "Essai sur la nature et la fonction du sacrifice." *Année sociologique*, vol. 2, 1899, pp. 29–138.

Hughes, Dennis D. *Human Sacrifice in Ancient Greece*. Routledge, 1991.

Isaacson, Walter. *The Code Breaker: Jennifer Doudna, Gene Editing, and the Future of the Human Race*. Simon and Schuster, 2021.
Ishi, Carlos T., et al. "Motion Generation in Android Robots during Laughing Speech." *2016 IEEE/RSJ International Conference on Intelligent Robots and Systems*, IEEE, 2016, pp. 3327–32, https://doi.org/10.1109/IROS.2016.7759512.
Ishiyama, Shimpei, and Michael Brecht. "Neural Correlates of Ticklishness in the Rat Somatosensory Cortex." *Science*, vol. 354, no. 6313, 2016, pp. 757–60.
Jagoda, Zenon, et al. *Oświęcim nieznany*. Wydawnictwo Literackie, 1981.
Jaulin, Annick. "Le rire logique: Usages de *geloion* chez Aristote." *Le Rire chez les Grecs: Anthropologie du rire en Grèce ancienne*, edited by Marie-Laurence Desclos, Éditions Jérôme Millon, 2002, pp. 319–31.
Jo, Doori, et al. "Empathy between Human and Robot?" *HRI 2013: Proceedings of the Eighth ACM/IEEE International Conference on Human–Robot Interaction*, IEEE Press, 2013, pp. 151–52, https://doi.org/10.1109/HRI.2013.6483546.
Jonze, Spike, director. *Her*. Annapurna Pictures, 2013.
———, director. *I'm Here*. 2010.
Joubert, Laurent. *Traité du ris*. Nicolas Chesneau, 1579.
———. *Treatise on Laughter*. Translated by Gregory David de Rocher, U of Alabama P, 1980. Originally published in 1579.
Juhitha, Konduru, et al. "Laughter Synthesis Using Mass-Spring Model and Excitation Source Characteristics." *2018 International Conference on Advances in Computing, Communications and Informatics (ICACCI)*, IEEE, 2018, pp. 1102–08, https://doi.org/10.1109/ICACCI.2018.8554573.
Kant, Immanuel. *The Critique of Judgment*. Translated by Werner S. Pluhar, Hackett Publishing, 1987. Originally published in 1790.
Kaufman, Leeor, and Joe Egender, directors. *Unnatural Selection*. Radley Studios, 2019.
Knoepfler, Paul. "Haunting Doudna Nightmare about Hitler Wanting CRISPR." *The Niche*, 18 Nov. 2015, ipscell.com/2015/11/haunting-doudna-nightmare-about-hitler-wanting-crispr/.
Koch, Gertrud. "The Aesthetic Transformation of the Image of the Unimaginable." *Claude Lanzmann's* Shoah: *Key Essays*, edited by Stuart Liebman, Oxford UP, 2007, pp. 125–32.
———. "Transformation esthétique dans la représentation de l'inimaginable." *Au sujet de* Shoah: *Le film de Claude Lanzmann*, edited by Bernard Cuau et al., Belin, 1990, pp. 157–66.
Kohs, Greg, director. *AlphaGo*. DeepMind Technologies, 2017. *YouTube*, uploaded by Google DeepMind, 13 Mar. 2020, www.youtube.com/watch?v=WXuK6gekU1Y.
LaGrandeur, Kevin. *Androids and Intelligent Networks in Early Modern Literature and Culture: Artificial Slaves*. Routledge, 2013.
Lanzmann, Claude. Interview by Marc Chevrie and Hervé Le Roux. *Les cahiers du cinéma*, no. 374, 1985, pp. 18–23.

———. *Lièvre de Patagonie: Mémoires.* Gallimard, 2009.
———, director. *Shoah.* Les Films Aleph / Historia, 1985.
Latour, Bruno. *After Lockdown: A Metamorphosis.* Translated by Julie Rose, Polity, 2021.
———. "An Attempt at a 'Compositionist Manifesto.'" *New Literary History*, vol. 3, no. 41, 2010, pp. 471–90.
———. *Down to Earth: Politics in the New Climatic Regime.* Translated by Catherine Porter, Polity Press, 2018.
———. "May Nature Be Recomposed? A Few Questions of Cosmopolitics." The Neale Wheeler Watson Lecture, 11 May 2010. Bruno Latour, www.bruno-latour.fr/node/269.
———. *We Have Never Been Modern.* Translated by Catherine Porter, Harvard UP, 1993.
Lausberg, Heinrich. *Handbuch der literarischen Rhetorik: Die Grundlegung d. Lieraturwiss.* Hueber, 1973.
Lavocat, Françoise. *La Syrinx au bûcher: Pan et les satyres à la Renaissance et à l'âge baroque.* Droz, 2005.
Le Goff, Jacques. "Le Rire dans les règles monastiques du haut moyen âge." *Mélanges Pierre Riché: Haut Moyen Âge, éducation et société*, Publidix et Editions européennes Erasme, 1990, pp. 93–103.
Leibniz, Gottfried Wilhelm. *Monadologie.* Edited by J. Jalabert, Aubier, 1962. Originally published in 1714.
———. *New System of the Nature of Substances and their Communication, and of the Union which Exists between the Soul and the Body.* 1695. *Leibniz's "New System" and Associated Contemporary Texts*, translated and edited by R. S. Woolhouse and Richard Francks, Clarendon Press, 1997.
Levi, Primo. *The Drowned and the Saved.* Translated by Raymond Rosenthal, Vintage Books, 1989. Originally published in 1986.
———. *If This Is a Man.* Translated by Stuart Woolf. *The Complete Works of Primo Levi*, vol. 1, edited by Ann Goldstein, Liveright Publishing, 2015, pp. 1–166. Originally published in 1947.
———. *Se questo è un uomo.* De Silva, 1947.
Lévi-Strauss, Claude. *Race and History.* UNESCO, 1952.
———. *Tristes tropiques.* Translated by John Russell, Criterion Books, 1961.
Livy. *History of Rome.* Vol. 8, translated by J. C. Yardley, Harvard UP, 2021.
Maimonides. *Mishneh Torah: The Book of Knowledge.* Edited by Moses Hyamson, Feldheim Publishers, 1974.
Malabou, Catherine. *Avant demain: Epigenèse et rationalité.* Puf, 2014.
———. *Métaphormphoses de l'intelligence: Que faire de leur cerveau bleu?* Puf, 2017.
———. *Morphing Intelligence: From IQ Measurements to Artificial Brains.* Translated by Carolyn Shread, Columbia UP, 2019.
———. *Que faire de notre cerveau?* Bayard, 2004.
———. *What Should We Do with Our Brain?* Translated by Sebastian Rand, Fordham UP, 2008.

Mancini, Maurizio, et al. "Guest Editorial: Towards Machines Able to Deal with Laughter." *IEEE Transactions on Affective Computing*, vol. 2, no. 4, 2017, pp. 492–94.

Mansouri, Nadia, and Zied Lachiri. "Laughter Synthesis: A Comparison between Variational Autoencoder and Autoencoder." *Fifth International Conference on Advanced Technologies for Signal and Image Processing*, IEEE, 2020, pp. 1–6, https://doi.org/10.1109/ATSIP49331.2020.9231607.

Martinus Legionensis. *Sermones*. Vol. 208 of *Patrologia Latina*, Migne, 1855.

Matsuzoe, Shizuko, and Fumihide Tanaka. "How Smartly Should Robots Behave? Comparative Investigation on the Learning Ability of a Care-Receiving Robot." *2012 IEEE RO-MAN: The Twenty-First IEEE International Symposium on Robot and Human Interactive Communication*, IEEE, 2012, pp. 339–44.

Mazzocconi, Chiara, et al. "What's Your Laughter Doing Here? A Taxonomy of the Pragmatic Functions of Laughter." *IEEE Transactions on Affective Computing*, vol. 13, no. 3, 2022, pp. 1302–21, https://doi.org/10.1109/TAFFC.2020.2994533.

McGrew, William Clement. *Chimpanzee Material Culture: Implications for Human Evolution*. Cambridge UP, 1992.

McKeown, Gary, et al. "The Belfast Storytelling Database: A Spontaneous Social Database with Laughter Focused Annotation." *2015 International Conference on Affective Computing and Intelligent Interaction (ACII)*, IEEE, 2015, pp. 166–72, https://doi.org/10.1109/ACII.2015.7344567.

McMulty, Tracy. *The Hostess: Hospitality, Femininity, and the Expropriation of Identity*. U of Minnesota P, 2006.

Meillassoux, Quentin. *After Finitude: An Essay on the Necessity of Contingency*. Translated by Ray Brassier, Continuum, 2008.

———. *Science Fiction and Extro-Science Fiction*. Translated by Alyosha Edlebi, Univocal, 2015.

———. "Spectral Dilemma." Translated by Robin Mackay. *Collapse*, vol. 4, 2012, pp. 261–76.

Ménager, Daniel. *La Renaissance et le rire*. Presses Universitaires de France, 1995.

Metzinger, Thomas. *Der Ego Tunnel: Eine neue Philosophie des Selbst: Von der Hirnforschung zur Bewusstseinsethik*. Piper, 2014.

Miernowski, Jan. *Le Dieu Néant: Théologies négatives à l'aube des temps modernes*. E. J. Brill, 1998.

———. *"Signes dissimilaires": La quête des noms divins dans la poésie française de la Renaissance*. Droz, 1997.

Minsky, Marvin. *The Emotion Machine: Commonsense Thinking, Artificial Intelligence, and the Future of the Human Mind*. Simon and Schuster, 2007.

Mitri, Sara, et al. "The Evolution of Information Suppression in Communicating Robots with Conflicting Interests." *PNAS*, vol. 106, no. 37, 15 Sept. 2009, pp. 15786–90, https://doi.org/10.1073/pnas.0903152106.

Montague, Patrick. *Chełmno and the Holocaust: The History of Hitler's First Death Camp*. U of North Carolina P, 2012.

Montaigne, Michel de. *The Complete Essays*. Translated by M. A. Screech, Penguin Books, 1987.

———. *Essais*. Edited by Pierre Villey and Verdun Louis Saulnier, Presses Universitaires de France, 1966.

Montuori, Mario. *Socrates: Physiology of a Myth*. Translated by J. Langdale and M. Langdale, J. C. Gieben, 1981.

Morel, Pierre-Marie. "Volontaire, involontaire et non-volontaire dans le chapitre 11 du DMA d'Aristote." *Aristote et le mouvement des animaux*, edited by André Laks and Marwan Rashed, Presses Universitaires du Septentrion, 2020, pp. 167–83.

Most, Glenn W. "A Cock for Asclepius." *Classical Quarterly*, vol. 43, 1993, pp. 96–111.

Naas, Michael. *Plato and the Invention of Life*. Fordham UP, 2018.

Nagata, Tomohiro, and Hiroki Mori. "Defining Laughter Context for Laughter Synthesis with Spontaneous Speech Corpus." *IEEE Transactions on Affective Computing*, vol. 3, no. 11, 2020, pp. 553–59.

Nagel, Thomas. "What Is It Like to Be a Bat?" *Mortal Questions*, by Nagel, Cambridge UP, 1979, pp. 165–80. Originally published in *Philosophical Review*, vol. 83, 1974.

Nails, Debra. *The People of Plato: A Prosopography of Plato and Other Socratics*. Hackett, 2003.

Nałkowska, Zofia. *Medallions*. Translated by Diana Kuprel, Northwestern UP, 2000. Originally published in 1946.

Nass, Clifford, with Corina Yen. *The Man Who Lied to His Laptop: What Machines Teach Us about Human Relationships*. Current, 2012.

Neiman, Susan. *Evil in Modern Thought: An Alternative History of Philosophy*. Princeton UP, 2002 and 2015.

Nemes, László, director. *Son of Saul*. Laokoon Filmgroup, 2015.

"New Dimensions in Testimony—USC ICT and SFI—Classroom Concept." *YouTube*, uploaded by ICT Vision and Graphics Lab, 8 Feb. 2013, www.youtube.com/watch?v=AnF630tCiEk.

Neyrat, Frédéric. *Homo Labyrinthus: Humanisme, antihumanisme, posthumanisme*. Éditions Dehors, 2015.

Nguyen, Anh, et al. "Deep Neural Networks are Easily Fooled: High Confidence Predictions for Unrecognizable Images." *2015 IEEE Conference on Computer Vision and Pattern Recognition (CVPR)*, IEEE, 2015, pp. 427–36, https://doi.org/10.1109/CVPR.2015.7298640.

Nietzsche, Friedrich. *Beyond Good and Evil*. Edited and translated by Marion Faber, Oxford UP, 1998. Originally published in 1886.

———. *The Birth of Tragedy*. Translated by Douglas Smith, Oxford UP, 2000. Originally published in 1872.

———. *The Gay Science*. Edited by Bernard Williams, translated by Josefine Nauckhoff, Cambridge UP, 2001. Originally published in 1882.

———. *Human, All Too Human*. Translated by Helen Zimmern and Paul V. Cohn, Dover Publications, 2006. Originally published in 1878.

———. "The Problem of Socrates." *Twilight of the Idols; or, How to Philosophize with a Hammer*, translated by Duncan Large, Oxford UP, 1998, pp. 11–15.

———. *Thus Spoke Zarathustra*. Edited by Adrian Del Caro and Robert Pippin, translated by Del Caro, Cambridge UP, 2006. Originally published in 1883.

Nora, Pierre. *Les lieux de mémoire*. Gallimard, 1982–86.

———. *Realms of Memory*. Translated by Arthur Goldhammer, U of Chicago P, 1984.

Nurse, Paul. *What Is Life? Understanding Biology in Five Steps*. Scribe Publications, 2020.

Nussbaum, Martha. "Aristophanes and Socrates on Learning Practical Wisdom." *Aristophanes: Essays in Interpretation*, edited by Jeffrey Henderson, Cambridge UP, 1980, pp. 43–97.

Öhman, Carl J., and David Watson. "Are the Dead Taking over Facebook? A Big Data Approach to the Future of Death Online." *Big Data and Society*, Jan.–June 2019, pp. 1–13, https/doi.org/ 10.1177/2053951719842540.

O'Neill, Kevin. *Internet Afterlife: Virtual Salvation in the Twenty-First Century*. Praeger, 2016.

O'Rourke, Marjorie. *Erasmus on Language and Method in Theology*. Toronto UP, 1977.

Ostrower, Chaya. *It Kept Us Alive: Humor in the Holocaust*. Translated by Sandy Bloom, International Institute for Holocaust Research, 2014.

Panksepp, Jaak. "Affective Foundations of Creativity, Language, Music, and Mental Life: In Search of the Biology of the Soul." *Beyond the Finite: The Sublime in Art and Science*, edited by Roald Hoffmann and Iain Boyd Whyte, Oxford UP, 2011, pp. 21–42.

———. *Affective Neuroscience: The Foundations of Human and Animal Emotions*. Oxford UP, 1998.

———. "Core Consciousness." *The Oxford Companion to Consciousness*, edited by Tim Bayne et al., Oxford UP, 2009, pp. 198–200.

———. "The Emotional Antecedents to the Evolution of Music and Language." *Musicae Scientiae*, vol. 13, no. 2 suppl., 2009, pp. 229–59.

———. "Neuroevolutionary Sources of Laughter and Social Joy: Modeling Primal Human Laughter in Laboratory Rats." *Behavioral Brain Research*, vol. 182, 2007, pp. 231–44.

———. "Neurologizing the Psychology of Affects: How Appraisal-Based and Basic Emotion Theory Can Coexist." *Perspectives on Psychological Science*, vol. 2, no. 3, 2007, pp. 281–96.

Panksepp, Jaak, and Lucy Biven. *The Archeology of Mind: Neuroevolutionary Origins of Human Emotions*. W. W. Norton, 2012.

Panksepp, Jaak, and Jeff Burgdorf. "'Laughing' Rats and the Evolutionary Antecedents of Human Joy?" *Physiology and Behavior*, vol. 79, no. 3, 2003, pp. 533–47.

———. "Laughing Rats? Playful Tickling Arouses High-Frequency Ultrasonic Chirping in Young Rodents." *Toward a Science of Consciousness III: The Third Tucson Discussions and Debates*, edited by Stuart R. Hameroff et al., MIT Press, 1999, pp. 231–43.

Paré, Ambroise. "Des Animaux et de l'excellence de l'homme." *Les Œuvres*, Gabriel Buon, 1585, pp. 295–370.

Parsons, Thomas D. *Cyberpsychology and the Brain: The Interaction of Neuroscience and Affective Computing*. Cambridge UP, 2017.

Pawlicka-Nowak, Łucja, editor. *Chełmno Witnesses Speak*. Translated by Juliet D. Golden and Arkadiusz Kamiński, Council for the Protection of Memory of Combat and Martyrdom in Warsaw, 2004.

———, editor. *Ośrodek zagłady Żydów w Chełmnie nad Nerem w świetle najnowszych badań*. Konin: Muzeum Okręgowe, 2004.

Pearlstein, Ferne, director. *The Last Laugh*. 2016.

Picard, Rosalind W. *Affective Computing*. MIT Press, 1997.

Pirenne-Delforge, Vinciane. "Les codes de l'adresse rituelle en Grèce: Le cas de libations sans vins." *Nourrir les dieux? Sacrifice et représentation du divin*, edited by Pirenne-Delforge and Francesca Prescendi, Centre International d'Étude de la Religion Grecque, 2011, pp. 117–47.

Plato. *Apology*. Plato, *Euthyphro*, pp. 86–196.

———. *Crito*. Plato, *Euthyphro*, pp. 196–263.

———. *Euthyphro—Apology—Crito—Phaedo*. Translated by Chris Emlyn-Jones and William Preddy, Harvard UP, 2017.

———. *Phaedo*. Plato, *Euthyphro*, pp. 266–523.

———. *Phaedrus*. *Lysis—Symposium—Phaedrus*, translated by Chris Emlyn-Jones and William Preddy, Harvard UP, 2022, pp. 321–531.

———. *Philebus*. Translated by Harold N. Fowler. *The Statesman—Philebus—Ion*, Harvard UP, 1925, pp. 197–400.

———. *The Sophist*. *Theaetetus—Sophist*, translated by Harold North Fowler, Harvard UP, 1987, pp. 259–459.

———. *Symposium*. *Lysis—Symposium—Phaedrus*, translated by Chris Emlyn-Jones and William Preddy, Harvard UP, 2022, pp. 109–319.

———. *Theaetetus*. *Theaetetus—Sophist*, translated by Harold North Fowler, Harvard UP, 1987, pp. 1–257.

Plessner, Helmut. *Laughing and Crying: A Study of the Limits of Human Behavior*. Translated by James Spencer Churchill and Marjorie Grene, Northwestern UP, 1970. Originally published in 1961.

———. *Levels of Organic Life and the Human: An Introduction to Philosophical Anthropology*. Translated by Millay Hyatt, Fordham UP, 2019. Originally published in 1928.

Pliny the Elder. *The Natural History*. Edited by Jeffrey Henderson, Harvard UP, 2014.

Provine, Robert R. "Laughter." *American Scientist*, vol. 1, no. 84, 1996, 38–45.

———. *Laughter: A Scientific Investigation*. Penguin, 2000.
[Pseudo-Aristotle]. *Aristotelous Peri Kosmou: De Mundo liber, ad Alexandrum, cum versione Latina Gulielmi Budei*. In aedibus Academicis, 1745.
Quignard, Pascal. *La haine de la musique*. Gallimard, 1996.
———. *La leçon de musique*. Gallimard, 1987.
———. *Tous les matins du monde*. Gallimard, 1991.
Quintilian. *Institutio oratoria*. Edited and translated by H. E. Butler, Harvard UP, 1995.
Rabanus Maurus. *Enarrationes in epistolas B. Pauli*. Vol. 112 of *Patrologia Latina*, Migne, 1852.
Rabelais, François. *Fourth Book of the Heroic Deeds and Sayings of the Good Pantagruel*. Translated by Donald M. Frame, U of California P, 1991.
———. *Gargantua and Pantagruel*. Translated by Burton Raffel, W. W. Norton, 1990.
———. *Les cinq livres: Gargantua, Pantagruel, Le tiers livre, Le quart livre, Le cinquième livre*. Edited by Jean Céard et al., Librairie Générale Française, 1994.
Reeves, Byron, and Clifford I. Nass. *The Media Equation: How People Treat Computers, Television, and New Media Like Real People and Places*. Cambridge UP, 1996.
Ribi, Filomena Nina, et al. "Comparison of Children's Behavior toward Sony's Robotic Dog AIBO and a Real Dog: A Pilot Study." *Anthrozoös: A Multidisciplinary Journal of Interactions of People and Animals*, vol. 21, no. 3, 2008, pp. 246–56, https://doi.org/10.2752/175303708X332053.
Rodichev, Artem. "GPT-3, Replika. When Will the AI Replace Humans?" Interview by Greg Mustreader. *YouTube*, uploaded by Mustreader, 26 Aug. 2020, www.youtube.com/watch?v=bKUzEoLiDI0.
Roff, Heather. "AI Deception: When Your Artificial Intelligence Learns to Lie." *IEEE Spectrum*, 24 Feb. 2020, spectrum.ieee.org/ai-deception-when-your-ai-learns-to-lie.
Romero, Alberto. "A Complete Overview of GPT-3—the Largest Neural Network Ever Created." *Towards Data Science*, 24 May 2021, towardsdatascience.com/gpt-3-a-complete-overview-190232eb25fd.
Rovner, Adam. "Instituting the Holocaust: Comic Fiction and the Moral Career of the Survivor." *Jewish Culture and History*, vol. 5, no. 2, 2002, pp. 1–24.
Sarna, Nahum M., editor. *The JPS Torah Commentary: Genesis: The Traditional Hebrew Text with the New JPS Translation Commentary*. Jewish Publication Society, 1989.
Sartre, Jean-Paul. "La fin de la guerre." *Les Temps Modernes*, no. 1, 1945, pp. 163–67.
———. *L'imaginaire: Psychologie phénoménologique de l'imagination*. Gallimard, 1940.
Saxe, Rebecca, and Simon Baron-Cohen. *Theory of Mind*. Psychology Press, 2007.
Schopenhauer, Arthur. *The World as Will and Representation*. Vol. 2, translated by E. F. J. Payne, Dover, 1969. Originally published in 1818.
Schrödinger, Erwin. *What Is Life? The Physical Aspect of the Living Cell*. Cambridge UP, 1944.

Schuller, Dogmar, and Björn W. Schuller. "The Age of Artificial Emotional Intelligence." *Computer*, vol. 51, no. 9, 2018, pp. 38–46, https://doi.org/10.1109/MC.2018.3620963.

Schwark, Jeremy D. "Toward a Taxonomy of Affective Computing." *International Journal of Human–Computer Interaction*, vol. 31, no. 11, 2015, pp. 761–68, https://doi.org/10.1080/10447318.2015.1064638.

Screech, Michael A. *Rabelais*. Cornell UP, 1979.

Searle, John R. *Intentionality: An Essay in the Philosophy of Mind*. Cambridge UP, 1983.

———. *Mind: A Brief Introduction*. Oxford UP, 2005.

———. "Minds, Brains, and Programs." *Behavioral and Brain Sciences*, vol. 3, 1980, pp. 417–57.

Sejnowski, Terrence J. *The Deep Learning Revolution*. MIT Press, 2018.

Sforno, Ovadia ben Jacob. "Sforno on Genesis: Commentary." *Sefaria*, www.sefaria.org/Genesis.18.12?lang=en&aliyot=0&p2=Sforno_on_Genesis.18.12.1&lang2=en. Originally published in *HaChut Hameshulash*, translated by Eliyahu Munk, Lambda Publishers, 2003.

Shannon, Claude E. "Prediction and Entropy of Printed English." *Bell System Technical Journal*, Jan. 1951, pp. 50–64.

Shim, Jaeeun, and Ronald C. Arkin. "A Taxonomy of Robot Deception and Its Benefits in HRI." *2013 IEEE International Conference on Systems, Man, and Cybernetics*, IEEE, 2013, pp. 2328–35, https://doi.org/10.1109/SMC.2013.398.

Sii, Jacqueline, et al. Presentation, Undergraduate Symposium, U of Madison–Wisconsin, 21 Apr. 2021.

Simak, Clifford D. *City*. Macmillan, 1991.

Sisto, Davide. *Online Afterlives: Immortality, Memory, and Grief in Digital Culture*. MIT Press, 2020.

Skinner, Quentin. "Hobbes and the Classical Theory of Laughter." *Visions of Politics*, vol. 3, Cambridge UP, 2002, pp. 142–76.

Sloterdijk, Peter. *Not Saved: Essays after Heidegger*. Polity, 2016.

Soni, Jimmy, and Rob Goodman. *A Mind at Play: How Claude Shannon Invented the Information Age*. Simon and Schuster, 2018.

Sparrow, Tom. *The End of Phenomenology: Metaphysics and the New Realism*. Edinburgh UP, 2014.

Spencer, Herbert. "The Physiology of Laughter." *Macmillan's Magazine*, Mar. 1860, pp. 395–402.

Spinoza, Baruch. *De Intellectus Emendatione*. Edited by Bernard Rousset, Vrin, 1992. Originally published in 1677.

Stone, James V. *Information Theory: A Tutorial Introduction*. Sebtel Press, 2015.

Stonier, Tom. *Information and Meaning: An Evolutionary Perspective*. Springer, 1997.

Stoppard, Tom. *The Hard Problem: A Play*. Grove Press, 2015.

Stoppard, Tom, and David Chalmers. "Playwright Tom Stoppard in Conversation with Cognitive Scientist David Chalmers—The Hard Problem." *YouTube*, uploaded by HowlRound Theatre Commons, 15 Dec. 2015, www.youtube.com/watch?v=4BPY2c_CiwA.

"The Story of Replika, the AI App That Becomes You." *Machines with Brains*, season 1, ep. 1, Quartz. *YouTube*, uploaded 21 July 2017, www.youtube.com/watch?v=yQGqMVuAk04.

Strömfelt, Harald, et al. "Emotion-Augmented Machine Learning: Overview of an Emerging Domain." *2017 Seventh International Conference on Affective Computing and Intelligent Interaction (ACII)*, IEEE, 2017, pp. 305–12, https://doi.org/10.1109/ACII.2017.8273617.

Sundar, S. Shyam. "Rise of Machine Agency: A Framework for Studying the Psychology of Human–AI Interaction (HAII)." *Journal of Computer-Mediated Communication*, vol. 25, no. 1, 2020, pp. 74–88.

Szlengel, Władysław. *What I Read to the Dead*. Translated by Marcel Weyland, Brandl and Schlesinger, 2012. Originally published in manuscripts in 1943.

Ta, Vivian, et al. "User Experiences of Social Support from Companion Chatbots in Everyday Contexts: Thematic Analysis." *Journal of Medical Internet Research*, vol. 22, no. 3, 2020, pp. 1–10, https://doi.org/10.2196/16235.

Tertullian. *Apology*. *Apology—De Spectaculis—Octavius*, by Tertullian and Menucius Felix, translated by Terrot Reaveley Glover and Gerald H. Rendall, Harvard UP, 2014, pp. 2–224.

Thompson, Evan. *Mind and Life: Biology, Phenomenology, and the Sciences of Mind*. Harvard UP, 2007.

Thomson, Iain. "Death and Demise in *Being and Time*." *The Cambridge Companion to Heidegger's* Being and Time, edited by Mark A. Wrathall, Cambridge UP, 2013, pp. 260–90.

Toulmin, Stephen. *Cosmopolis: The Hidden Agenda of Modernity*. U of Chicago P, 1992.

"The Truths of Terasem." *Terasem Faith*, 2012, terasemfaith.net/beliefs.

Turing, Alan M. "Computing Machinery and Intelligence." *Mind*, vol. 59, no. 236, 1950, pp. 433–60.

Tyrrell, William Blake. *The Sacrifice of Socrates: Athens, Plato, Girard*. Michigan State UP, 2012.

Ulnik, Jorge. *Skin in Psychoanalysis*. Taylor and Francis, 2018.

von Foerster, Heinz. "Mit den Augen des anderen." *Wissen und Gewissen: Versuch einer Brücke*, edited by Siegfried J. Schmidt, Suhrkamp, 1993, pp. 350–63.

Viveiros de Castro, Eduardo. *Métaphysiques cannibales: Lignes d'anthropologie poststructurale*. Translated by Oiara Bonilla, Presses Universitaires de France, 2012.

von Foerster, Heinz, and Monika Silvia Broecker. *Part of the World: Fractals of Ethics—A Drama in Three Acts*. Translated by Barbara Anger-Díaz, M. S. Broeker, 2010. Originally published in 2002.

Weinberg, Florence M. *The Wine and the Will: Rabelais's Bacchic Christianity*. Wayne State UP, 1972.

Westermann, Claus. *Genesis: A Practical Commentary*. Translated by David E. Green, William B. Eerdmans, 1987.

———. *Genesis 12–36: A Commentary*. Augsburg, 1985.

Wiernik, Jankiel. *Rok w Treblince*. Introduction by Władysław Bartoszewski, Rada Ochrony Pamięci Walk i Męczeństwa, 2003. Originally published in 1943/1944 by the Polish resistance.

———. *A Year in Treblinka: An Inmate Who Escaped Tells the Day-To-Day Facts of One Year of His Torturous Experiences*. American Representation of the General Jewish Workers' Union of Poland, 1944.

Wiesel, Elie. "Holocaust as Literary Inspiration." *Dimensions of the Holocaust: Lectures at Northwestern University*, by Wiesel, Lucy Dawidowicz, Dorothy Rabinowicz, and Robert McAfee Brown, Northwestern UP, 1977, pp. 4–19.

Wieseltier, Leon. "*Shoah*." *Claude Lanzmann's Shoah: Key Essays*, edited by Stuart Liebman, Oxford UP, 2007, pp. 89–94.

Willenberg, Samuel. *Surviving Treblinka*. Basil Blackwell, 1989.

Wirth, Jason M. "Nietzsche's Joy: On Laughter's Truth." *Epoché*, vol. 1, no. 10, 2005, pp. 117–39.

Wisser, Meir Leibush ben Yehiel Michel [Malbim]. "Malbim on Genesis: Commentary." ca. 1845–ca. 1875. *Sefaria*, www.sefaria.org/Genesis.18.12?lang=en&with=Malbim&lang2=en.

Wójcik, Michał. *Treblinka 43: Bunt w fabryce śmierci*. Znak, 2018.

Yitzchaki, Shlomo [Rashi]. *Pentateuch with Rashi's Commentary*. Translated by Morris Rosenbaum and Abraham M. and Silbermann, Shapiro, Valentine, 1929. "Rashi on Genesis," *Sefaria*, www.sefaria.org/Genesis.17.17?lang=bi&aliyot=0&p2=Rashi_on_Genesis.17.17.1&lang2=bi.

Zachar, Peter, and Ralph D. Ellis, editors. *Categorical versus Dimensional Models of Affect: A Seminar on the Theories of Panksepp and Russell*. John Benjamins Publishing, 2012.

Zerba, Michelle. "Love, Envy, and Pantomimic Morality in Cicero's *De oratore*." *Classical Philology*, vol. 4, no. 97, 2002, pp. 299–321.

Żółkiewska, Agnieszka, and Marek Tuszewicki, editors. *Archiwum Ringelbluma: Konspiracyjne Archiwum Getta Warszawy*. Vol. 26, Żydowski Instytut Historyczny im. Emanuela Ringelbluma, 2017.

Zornberg, Avivah Gottlieb. *Genesis: The Beginning of Desire*. Jewish Publication Society, 1995.

Index

Abraham. *See* sacrifice; Sarah
absolute comic. *See* Baudelaire
Aeneas, 155
Aeschylus, 178
Aesop, 214
affabulatory function. *See* fiction; machine to make gods
affective computing, 12, 42, 108, 111–19, 127
affordance, 42, 74
Agamben, Giorgio, 38
AIBO. *See* chatbots
Anders, Günther, 13, 22, 158–59, 187–88, 190, 196–97, 199, 242. *See also* Prometheus
animality, 1, 5, 6, 8, 11, 42–43, 45–81, 231; animal emotionality, 65–80; animal intentionality, 123–25; animals' music, 73
animism, 12
Antelme, Robert: 38
anthropocene, 194–95
anthropomorphism, 70–71, 87, 91, 127. *See also* humanoid automata; risk of language
anthropophagy, 192, 194, 226
antihumanism, 13, 21, 27, 38, 42, 97, 115, 178, 181
Apollinaire, Guillaume, 12, 95–98, 105

Apuleius, 177
Arendt, Hannah, 13, 186–87, 189
Aristophanes, 206, 212, 221
Aristotle, 2, 3, 56, 58, 63, 73, 74, 150, 223, 225
Artaud, Antonin, 115–17
Artemis, 194–95
artificial intelligence (AI), 4, 6, 12, 26, 81–82, 105–08, 129, 135–36, 189, 240; AlphaGo, 106; and thinking, 118–21; deceitful AI, 121–25; chatbots, 82, 108, 111–12, 124, 131–46; ChatGPT, 106, 136; Deep Blue, 106; holograms, 140, 142, 145–46; neural networks, 75, 107, 121, 122, 126–27, 129, 136–38, 140, 143–44, 245; neuromorphic chips 107
Asimov, Isaac, 143
atheology. *See* Bataille
atomic bomb, 6, 13, 21, 22, 25, 159, 185, 187, 189–90, 196, 199, 240
Auschwitz. *See* Shoah
automatons, digital zombies, 144; humanoid, 19, 28, 29, 40, 42, 82–84, 87–89, 91, 101–02, 108–13, 118, 137–40, 232–34, 244–45; natural automatons, 130–31, 138; philosophical zombies, 90; xenobots, 24. *See also* deceitful AI

Babbage, Charles, 132
Balzac, Honoré de, 221
banality of evil. *See* Hannah Arendt
Basil, saint, 151
Bataille, Georges, 13, 178–82, 201, 216, 237, 240
Baudelaire, Charles, 152, 224–25, 230, 236–37
Beauvoir, Simone de, 134–35
Beckett, Samuel, 27, 178, 225
behaviorism, 68, 70–71
Bennett, Jane, 23–24
Bergson, Henri, 2, 12, 82–97, 101–5, 131, 133–34, 239, 242; attentiveness to life, 89, 91–92, 97, 138; duration and time, 86–91, 94–96; machine to make gods, 85, 94, 138, 208; vital impetus (*élan vital*), 85–94, 97, 105, 147
Boccherini, Luigi, 50
body's duality: the king's two bodies, 110; to be and to have a, 232–33
Bomba, Abraham, 30–31
Borowski, Tadeusz, 37
Briçonnet, Guillaume, 167–68
Brueghel the Elder, Pieter, 157
Buber, Martin, 244

Cain, 156, 198–99
CAPTCHA test, 82, 106–07, 119–20
Cassirer, Ernst, 22–23
Catherine de Medici, 54
Céline, Ferdinand, 221
Chalmers, David, 90, 130
Chaplin, Charlie, 12, 82–85
Charpentier, Emmanuelle, 25
chatbots. *See* artificial intelligence
Chełmno death camp, 11, 15–20, 28–31, 35–37, 41, 76, 78, 84, 145, 182, 241
Chernobyl, 6
Chomsky, Noam, 73, 136

Christ, 16, 108, 153–60, 164–68, 174–75, 180–81, 184, 197–98, 219. *See also* real presence of; Silenus
Christian, Brian, 12, 131–35, 139
Chrysostom, saint, 151, 159–61
Cicero, 2, 114–15, 183
computer metaphor, 67–68, 74–75, 90–91, 120, 122, 127, 129–30. *See also* mind-body problem; neural networks; neuromorphic chips
confabulation. *See* fiction
consciousness, 1, 3, 6, 12, 22, 30, 39, 40, 57, 59–60, 77–80, 87, 89, 91, 215, 229; animal consciousness, 69; conscious automatons, 90, 137, 231, 252n10; "core consciousness," 69; "hard problem" of, 13, 90, 129–31, 187; mind-body problem, 56, 64, 67–69, 73–74, 81, 88–91, 101–02, 127, 209, 215, 239, 242; neurological reductionism, 68, 127–30; qualia, 71. *See also* attentiveness to life
contours (confines, edges) of humanness. *See* limits of humanness
Copernicus, Nicolaus, 23
COVID-19, 188
CRISPR-Cas9, 22, 25
cybernetics, 14, 241–45
cyborgs, 81

Dalí, Salvador, 132, 135
Darwin, Charles, 23, 71, 73
David, 183
death drive, 77–80, 180, 195
death of God (and of gods), 8, 13, 21, 98, 170–76, 180–82, 193, 199, 219, 226, 243, 246
death of Man, 10, 11, 15–43, 98, 103, 170, 190, 193, 223–28, 235, 240, 243; obsolesce of Man, 158–59, 187, 246

deep learning. *See* artificial intelligence (AI)
de Lille, Alain, 151
demise, 11, 13–14, 24, 29, 45, 76, 145; and perishing, 37–42, 76
Dennett, Daniel, 126–28, 130, 226
Derrida, Jacques, 100, 199
Descartes, René, 54–56, 68–69, 88–89, 199
Descola, Philippe, 4–5
diaeresis, 93–94, 207–08
divinity. *See* gods
Doudna, Jennifer, 25
Du Bellay, Guillaume, 173
Ducasse, Isidore, 220–21
Dupuy, Jean-Pierre, 13, 164, 185–97, 199, 240
Durkheim, Emile, 191
Duval, Edwin, 155–56

Eco, Umberto, 151
elenchus, 203, 207, 213, 215, 217
Eichmann, Adolf, 16, 28, 186–89
ELIZA. *See* chatbots
entropy: and death drive, 78; in information theory, 136–39; negative entropy, 139
epigenesis, 10, 102, 247
epihumanism, 1, 10, 14, 246–47
epiphenomenon, 6, 10, 247
Erasmus of Rotterdam, 61–62, 134, 151, 153–54, 169, 173, 174, 176–77, 184, 199
ethopoeia, 12–13, 111, 113–18, 127
evil, metaphysical, 6, 13, 23, 49, 116, 148, 179–81, 186–200, 246
evolution, creative, 12, 87, 92, 94, 97, 132, 133. *See also* Bergson
evolution, Darwinian, 67, 70–71, 73–76, 78–79, 188
evolution, technological, 231–33

fable. *See* fiction
fabrication: of life, 12, 93–94; of meaning, 96–98, 135, 158. *See* Bergson
Ferraris, Maurizio, 12, 100–02, 118, 132, 140
fiction (literary, cinematographic, poetic, theatrical), 12, 14, 40, 72, 95–96, 98, 105, 114, 134, 142, 149, 153–54, 158, 183, 196–97; 202–06, 211, 216–18, 233–37, 241–42; after Auschwitz, 38; allegorical, 51–52, 72, 135, 167–68, 173–74; and virtual reality, 109–11, 117, 138, 141–42, 154, 226, 231–32; as a dissimilar sign, 155–57, 169, 185–86; parable, 168, 177, 190; thought experiment, 88, 119–20, 128–29. *See also* machine to make gods
finitude. *See* limits of humanness
Foucault, Michel, 4, 21, 103, 136
Francis I, king of France, 152, 173
François d'Alençon, Duke of Anjou, 54
Frankl, Viktor, 14, 241–44
Freud, Sigmund, 2, 23, 76–80, 102, 214. *See also* death drive

Galen, 57, 60–61, 63, 73
Garcia, Tristan, 5–6
Garland, Alex, 137–39
Girard, René, 13, 191–93, 195–99, 201, 240
God, Judeo-Christian, 3, 13, 23, 42, 99–101, 162–63, 166, 169, 171–76, 179–81, 184, 195–97; Bergson's, 93–94, 132, 134; technological, 219. *See also* Christ; death of God (and of gods); transcendence
gods, 1, 6, 8, 11, 13, 42–43, 97, 147–200. *See also* Bergson
Gold, Artur, 49–50

Goostman, Eugene. *See* chatbots
Gutter, Pinchas, 145–46. *See also* holograms

Habermas, Jürgen, 25
Hannibal, 64, 80
Harrison, Jordan, 12, 139–42, 226
Heidegger, Martin, 21–23, 38–41, 178, 214
Henri III, king of France, 54
Hermaphrodite, 207, 216, 229–30, 243–44
Hippocrates, 63
Hiroshima. *See* atomic bomb
history, 183–84, 187–88, 191, 193. *See* theodicy
Hobbes, Thomas, 2, 48, 224
Holocaust. *See* Shoah
Homer, 62
homology (as opposed to analogy), 66–67, 69, 71
Houellebecq, Michel, 14, 220–37, 240
humanism, Renaissance (or early modern), 6, 13, 20–21, 53–59, 66, 73, 98–99, 117, 134, 148–61, 164–65, 168–69, 173–74, 176, 179, 181–86, 199, 246–47
humanities, 9–10
humor, 8, 11, 27, 49, 71, 75, 108, 124–25, 140–42, 148–49, 165–67, 214, 242; theorists of, 2–3

imitation game. *See* Turing test
immortality, 26, 56, 182, 208–13, 217–19; technological, 14, 42, 140, 144, 202, 219–20, 222–26, 229–31, 233, 236, 253n20
Indigenous perspective, 4, 26
intentionality, 56–58, 98, 108, 119, 189; theory of mind, 123–29. *See also* animal intentionality
intersectionality, 5

Iphigenia, 194
irony, 14, 34, 38, 40, 50, 98, 100, 113, 142, 170, 221–23, 228, 230, 233
Isaac, 161–63, 194–95
itching, 180, 216, 237

Johansson, Scarlett, 143
Jonze, Spike, 143, 232–33
Joubert, Laurent, 11, 54–66, 72–74, 76, 78–81, 239

Kant, Immanuel, 2, 102, 103, 175, 228
Karski, Jan, 46
Kasparov, Garry, 106
Ke Jie, 106
kitsch, 47, 222, 224
Klee, Paul, 200
Kuyda, Eugenia, 144

Lamartine, Alphonse de, 218
language, as act, 129, 153–54, 205–06; deficiency of, 11, 28, 35, 38, 52, 65, 69–73, 76–77, 79, 97; risks of, 87, 125–27, 231–34
Lanzmann, Claude, 11, 15–20, 27–33, 35, 41, 45, 76, 78, 80–81, 84, 145–46, 185, 190, 241
large language models. *See* artificial intelligence (AI)
Latour, Bruno, 4, 199–200
laughter: African "joking relationships," 154–55; and dance, 50, 87–90, 152, 175–78, 182; and death, 1, 11, 13, 20, 60–65, 75, 80, 176, 180–82, 210, 213–15, 222–23; and human-computer interaction, 112–13; and music, 49–53, 76, 215–16; and volition, 56–60; as affirmation of the impossible, 181; as leap into the unimaginable, 164–65, 169; as *proprium*, 54–60, 82, 150; buffoon's, 170–72, 181, 223–25, 234–35;

contagious, 74–75; Franciscan, 152; "Holocaust laughter," 48–49; illegitimate (canine laughter, cynic spasm), 60–66, 72, 76; laughing at the laugh (*risus purus*), 27, 42, 178, 225, 237; machines', 81–103; mystical, 152; of Christ, 151–52; of the Thracian maid, 214–15; panic-laughter, 53; rats' "laughter," 11, 65–81; sinful, 152; synthetized, 113
Lautréamont, Count of. *See* Ducasse
Leibniz, Gottfried Wilhelm, 101, 130–31, 138, 187–88
Levi, Primo, 36–38, 50, 53
Lévi-Strauss, Claude, 26
LGBTQ+, 5
limits of humanness, 1, 3, 4, 6, 8, 9–12, 18–24, 26, 27, 37–43, 45, 66, 77–85, 102, 115, 117, 129, 145–48, 163–64, 168–70, 173, 179–80, 183, 190, 193–94, 199, 213–19, 233, 239–40, 245–47. *See also* membrane
Locke, John, 199
Loebner, Hugh, 131
Lorris, Guillaume de, 135
Louis IX, king of France, 151
Louis XIV, king of France, 51
Lovelace, Ada, 132
Lucian, 62, 148
Lucretius, 99, 115, 117, 143
Lyotard, Jean-François, 199

machinery, 1, 4, 6, 8, 11–12, 42–43, 50, 81–146, 219; machines' intentionality, 126–27; nontrivial, 14, 245–46. *See also* automaton; Bergson; computer metaphor; deceitful AI; machines' laughter
Majdanek concentration and extermination camp, 145
Marais, Marin, 51–52

Marguerite de Navarre, Duchess of Alençon and Berry, 152, 156, 158, 167, 169, 174, 184
Marguerite de Valois, la Reine Margot, 54
Mary, mother of Christ, 158–68, 199
matriarchy: 13, 42
Mauthausen concentration camp: 37
Mazurenko, Roman, 144
membrane, metaphor: 7–8, 10, 14, 40, 75–82, 102, 239–40, 245, 247. *See also* limits of humanness
Meun, Jean de, 135
mind clones, 14, 144, 219
misology, 212–13, 240
Montaigne, Michel de, 98–100, 105, 115, 117–18, 246
Muselmann, 37–38, 40–41, 45, 46, 76, 146
Music: and Antonin Arthaud's "virtual reality," 117; and machinery, 87–88, 96; neuroscience of, 72–73. *See also* animals' music; laughter and music
myth. *See* fiction; history

Nagel, Thomas, 126
Nałkowska, Zofia, 16–17, 29–30
natural artifice, 115–17, 138, 142–44; artfulness and art, 145–46
negative theology, 13, 159, 179, 181, 185–86
Nemes, László, 41
Nietzsche, Friedrich, 13, 169–79, 181–82, 218, 226, 240
Noah, 160, 190, 242
Nora, Pierre, 31

Oneg Shabbat, 48–49

Pan, 171–74, 191
panic, 53, 172, 191, 193. *See also* panic-laughter

280 / Index

Panksepp, Jaak, 11, 65–76, 78–81, 87, 91, 127, 128, 239
Pantagruelism. See *Rabelais*
parody, 155, 157, 176–77, 196–97, 199, 224, 227, 229–30
Pascal, Blaise, 101, 158
patriarchy, 4, 5
Paul, saint, 100, 158, 160, 161, 184
Penelope, 62
Petrarch, 184
pharmakon, 209, 218. *See also* pharmakos
philology, 62, 99, 149, 153, 183–84
Phoenix, Joaquin, 143
Pilate, Pontius, 197
plague, 116–17
plasticity, 8, 80, 101–02, 107, 134
Plato, 2, 14, 62, 93, 98, 99, 100, 151, 170, 175, 183, 202–18, 229–30, 240
Plessner, Helmut, 233
Pliny the Elder, 63, 175
Plutarch, 173, 183
Podchlebnik, Michał, 11, 13, 16–20, 27–37, 40–46, 64, 75–78, 80–81, 84, 145–46, 241–42, 245
Polański, Roman, 35
Pollock, Jackson, 138
posthumanism, 1, 7, 10, 21, 24, 195, 225, 246–47
presence: author's, 12, 97–98, 105, 117–18; of absence, 17, 30–32, 118, 146, 211, 241, 243; of death, 41; real presence of Christ, 30, 99–101, 174; virtual presence, 110, 118, 138, 140–46
Prometheus, 182, 187, 196, 199, 240
propria hominis, 3, 26, 53–60. *See also* laughter as *proprium*
purification, 13, 89, 116–17, 170, 172, 204, 208–18

Quignard, Pascal, 50–53, 72, 76, 79, 128
Quintilian, 2

Rabelais, François, 13, 148–61, 164–70, 173–77, 181–86, 199, 226, 240
reductionism, 245–46. *See also* neurological reductionism
Replika. *See* chatbots
robot. *See* automaton
Ronsard, Pierre de, 184
Rousseau, Jean-Jacques, 73, 188
relationism, 4–5
rhetoric, 13, 79, 98, 127; rhetorical precautions, 70, 119. *See also* ethopoeia
Ringelblum Archive. *See* Oneg Shabbat

sacrifice, 31, 62, 160, 167, 190, 200–05, 209; Abraham's sacrifice of Isaac, 194–95; pharmakos, 192, 204–06, 218; sacrificial violence, 13, 161, 180–82, 191–98, 240; Socrates' sacrifice to Asclepius, 170–72, 217–18, 240
Sainte-Colombe, Monsieur de, 51, 76
Sarah, 160–66, 195, 199. *See also* Abraham
sardonic laughter. *See* deadly laughter
Sartre, Jean-Paul, 21–22, 30, 103, 187, 199, 243
Schopenhauer, Arthur, 2
Schrödinger, Erwin, 139
Searle, John, 128–29
Seneca, 183
Shannon, Claude, 139
Shoah, 6, 14, 24–25, 28–38, 41–42, 45–53, 145–48, 159, 185–89, 199, 237, 240–45
Silenus, 150–54, 169, 183, 217

Simak, Clifford D., 234–35
Socrates, 14, 42, 93, 98–99, 105, 184, 202–18, 221, 226–27, 237, 240, 245; as character in Nietzsche, 170–72, 175–76, 226; as character in Rabelais' 149–54, 157, 169, 173, 182–83. *See also* elenchus
Solanas, Valerie, 228
Solomon, 158, 183
soul: "animalian," 69–70, 75, 91, 239; as technological device, 101–02, 118, 144; Christian conception of, 151, 190; Platonic psyche, 98, 170, 207–13, 217
Spencer, Herbert, 2
Spinoza, Baruch, 101
Srebnik, Simon, 15–16, 29, 30–31
Stoppard, Tom, 12, 129–31
Szlengel, Władysław, 11, 13, 33–42, 45, 81, 105, 241
Szpilman, Władysław, 35

tension, 6, 8, 20, 26, 27, 40, 59, 77–80, 97, 102, 138–39, 142, 145–46, 172, 211–12, 242
Terasem Movement Transreligion, 219–20, 222
Tertullian, 134
Thales from Miletus, 214
theodicy, 188
thermodynamics, 2, 139
Theseus, 202–06, 218, 245
tickling, 60–67, 74, 80–81, 113
transcendence, 8, 13, 19, 147–57, 168–74, 177–79, 181–82, 186, 193–94, 219, 226, 240; self-transcendence, 13, 164, 189–92, 194, 240
transgression. *See* Bataille
transhumanism, 1, 7, 42, 219–20, 225, 228, 240

transposition, metaphorical and narrative, 14, 245–46
Treblinka death camp, 11, 30, 32–36, 38–39, 45–53, 64, 72, 76, 81, 237, 241
Trump, Donald, 111
tsunami. *See* Shoah
Turing, Alan, 12. *See also* Turing test
Turing test, 119–21, 124–26, 128, 131–32, 137

Ulysses, 52, 62, 64
uncanny, 26–27, 46, 79, 80, 84, 201, 243, 253n3; valley, 12, 108–11, 240
unimaginable, 13, 35, 78, 149, 154, 157, 159–60, 164, 182–83, 186–87, 189–90, 196–97, 199
unpredictability: and freedom, 92–93. *See also* Bergson

Valladolid debate, 26
Virgil, 99, 184
virtual reality, 4, 12–14, 88, 90, 108–11, 118, 138, 140–46, 226, 232–33; in Antonin Artaud's sense, 116–17, 146. *See also* virtual presence
Voltaire, 158
von Foerster, Heinz, 14, 241–45
von Neumann, John, 107, 139

Warhol, Andy, 228
Warsaw ghetto, 11, 35, 40, 145; Café Sztuka, 35
Weizenbaum, Joseph, 133
Wiernik, Yankel, 46–49, 64, 72, 75–76, 78–79
Wiesel, Elie, 38, 48
Willenberg, Samuel, 53
witness and testimony, 37–38

Zarathustra, 175–77, 234

www.ingramcontent.com/pod-product-compliance
Lightning Source LLC
Chambersburg PA
CBHW021655230426
43668CB00008B/633